Toward Pro-Poor Policies

Annual World Bank Conference on
Development Economics—Europe
2003

Toward Pro-Poor Policies

Aid, Institutions, and Globalization

Edited by
**Bertil Tungodden,
Nicholas Stern, and Ivar Kolstad**

A copublication of the World Bank and Oxford University Press

Edited by Bertil Tungodden, Nicholas Stern, and Ivar Kolstad

ISBN 0-8213-5388-8

Contents

Part III. Globalization

Acknowledgments

These proceedings are the result of a joint effort by the World Bank and the Chr. Michelsen Institute. The editors extend their thanks first and foremost to the authors and referees of this volume. We also thank François Bourguignon, Ingrid Johansen, F. Desmond McCarthy, Deena Philage, and Boris Pleskovic at the World Bank; Antonio Spilimbergo at the International Monetary Fund; and Alf Morten Jerve, Arve Ofstad, and Arne Wiig at the Chr. Michelsen Institute. Finally, we thank the editorial staff, in particular Alice Faintich and Kim Kelley, for their work on this volume.

Toward Pro-Poor Policies:
An Overview

BERTIL TUNGODDEN, IVAR KOLSTAD, AND NICHOLAS STERN

The fourth Annual Bank Conference on Development Economics in Europe took place in Oslo in June 2002, with more than 350 researchers from some 50 countries gathering for three days of discussion and debate on how best to combat poverty and promote development. In plenary sessions and workshops, the conference covered a range of important topics that varied from general questions on the causal links between poverty, inequality, and growth to specific debates about the value of the recent Heavily Indebted Poor Countries (HIPC) Initiative for debt relief.

Given the strength of the papers presented at the conference, selecting papers for this volume required making hard choices. We based our editorial decisions on two main criteria. First, we wanted to give the selected authors the room and opportunity to develop their arguments further. Second, we wanted a coherent book that would cover important topics in greater detail. In the end we chose papers that would illuminate three themes—aid, institutions, and globalization—that are central to the development debate.

On the subject of aid, during the past decade a wealth of research has shed new light on the debate about the role and effectiveness of development assistance to poor countries. That debate has been fueled by some well-publicized failures and by shared frustration with the huge poverty challenges that remain. These setbacks are undeniable. They stem in part from political factors; in part from ignorance; and in part from the simple fact that aid must involve risk taking, and hence some failures are inevitable. The research recognizes that rather than relying on anecdotes, we should look at both

Bertil Tungodden is a professor at the Norwegian School of Economics and Business Administration, Bergen, Norway. Ivar Kolstad is a senior researcher at the Chr. Michelsen Institute, Bergen, Norway. At the time of the conference, Nicholas Stern was senior vice president Development Economics and chief economist at the World Bank. He is currently head of the Government Economic Service and second permanent secretary to the U.K. Treasury.

Annual World Bank Conference on Development Economics—Europe 2003
© 2004 The International Bank for Reconstruction and Development/The World Bank

the trend of aid contributions and the potential for improvement. Has aid worked better in recent years? What can we learn from past mistakes and successes? The contributions to this book do exactly this, and we believe they provide a fresh guide to the future of aid policies.

Whatever we learn from the aid debate, we already know that aid alone will not solve the poverty problem. The quality of the recipient country's own institutions is a fundamental driver of development, a lesson that the development community has relearned in recent years. The recent work on institutions goes far beyond the issue of the state versus the market, which in many cases is not a fruitful question for discussion, because the two have complementary roles. It has moved on to the more rewarding pursuit of understanding how particular economic and political institutions (such as property rights, governance and accountability structures, and tax systems) measure up from the perspective of efficiency and distribution and their effect on values. Recent years have seen an increased focus on understanding the political processes driving the development of institutions, which is essential for those striving to improve institutional structures. We believe that the papers presented in this book add important insights to this debate.

Finally, discussing development policies without taking globalization into account is impossible under current circumstances. Integration is increasing steadily, for good and ill, as we are reminded not only by increasing international trade, capital, and technology flows, but also by the September 11 terrorist attacks on the United States and the severe acute respiratory syndrome (SARS) epidemic. Accelerating development requires setting policies and establishing institutions, in donor and recipient countries alike, that will allow poor countries to reap more of the gains of globalization. We also need careful analyses of how to cope with the risks involved in the process of international integration. The contributions in this volume examine these questions, focusing on how increased international labor and capital mobility present both opportunities and challenges for poor countries.

We recognize that the three themes are closely interrelated. For example, it is difficult to imagine a thorough discussion of aid that does not touch on the nature of national institutions and the effects of globalization on development. Nevertheless, we believe that the thematic structure provides a useful framework for presenting these papers. The following sections offer short summaries of the papers in each section.

Beyond the themes presented here—aid, institutions, and globalization—the Oslo conference included workshops on socially inclusive development, new approaches to public management, education, labor standards, innovation and entrepreneurship, and the ethics of development. We invite readers to study these contributions as well, and provide a complete program in the appendix.

Aid

The recent debate on aid and development has been strongly influenced by cross-country econometric studies showing that aid is effective in spurring growth and poverty reduction in countries with good policies, though not in those with poor policies (see, for example, Burnside and Dollar 2000). This has raised a number of important questions. How robust is this conclusion? How should we measure the efficiency of aid? Do these results imply that greater targeting of aid is necessary? Can aid be used to improve policies? Each paper in this section contributes to this debate.

Nicholas Stern outlines the main development challenges, as summarized by the Millennium Development Goals, and explains the need for "scaling up" the international community's efforts to combat poverty. By scaling up he means not only increasing the quantity of assistance, but also—and equally important—changing it qualitatively from past modes of promoting development. Yet in Stern's view, our understanding of development and poverty has progressed, as has our ability to apply that understanding, which is cause for optimism about the future of development. In particular, he argues that experience and analysis have shown that development rests on two pillars: improving the investment climate and empowering poor people. Stern applauds the recent move toward greater targeting of aid on countries that can use it effectively, but underlines the need for alternative approaches in those countries that lack the policies, institutions, and governance necessary to use aid well. He discusses how the World Bank has already reoriented itself in this regard, while calling for further development of our ways of measuring and evaluating the effectiveness of these new directions.

David Roland-Holst and Finn Tarp survey the evolution of thinking about development assistance over the past five decades, and conclude that the debate on the effectiveness of aid has focused largely on macro institutions and outcomes. They argue that donors should take care in applying what they characterize as simplistic, macroeconomic rules of thumb to the allocation of aid. Because aid and lending relationships are essentially microeconomic in nature, they believe that the international community should make use of conceptual innovations in modern microeconomic theory to improve the effectiveness of aid. In particular, they emphasize the idea of contractual ownership with concomitant real entitlements and responsibilities, which in their view is something quite different from the popular ideas of stakeholding and community participation. In addition, because the role of aid has changed with the rapid growth of trade and private capital markets, they argue that donors should become more aware of the interactions between public and private investments in poor countries and the need for more communication between the public and private sectors on development priorities.

Pro-poor growth has become a central concept in much of the development literature, but what does it mean? Should any growth process that contributes to a reduction in poverty count as pro-poor, or should we restrict the use of that term to growth processes that represent a significant move forward for the poor as well? In the first part of his paper, Stephan Klasen provides an insightful discussion of this question, arguing for a specific measure of pro-poor growth and pointing out basic links between inequality, poverty, and pro-poor growth. In his view, inequality-reducing policies—particularly those that focus on inequalities in the distribution of assets and on gender inequality—are extremely important for attaining pro-poor growth. In the second part of his chapter, Klasen presents an overview of the sectoral, regional, and functional distribution of pro-poor growth. Based on this he argues that in the short run, pro-poor growth should be labor intensive and focus mainly on growth in deeply poor agricultural areas. In the longer term, however, he sees potential for a broader set of pro-poor growth strategies, but argues that the value of these approaches will often depend critically on effective redistributive processes.

Lisa Chauvet and Patrick Guillaumont question the conceptual framework of the highly influential Burnside-Dollar model on aid effectiveness. The model assumes that aid has no effect on policy and that external shocks do not affect aid effectiveness, but Chauvet and Guillaumont question both these assumptions. In addition, they argue for including political stability and absorptive capacity in analyses of aid and growth. On the basis of this discussion, they offer an augmented econometric model of aid effectiveness. Testing the extended framework empirically, they find that aid actually improves policies in poor countries, economic vulnerability enhances aid effectiveness, political instability lowers aid effectiveness, and absorptive capacity matters.

In the final paper in the section on aid, Jean-Pierre Cling, Mireille Razafindrakoto, and François Roubaud present a somewhat critical perspective on the recent HIPC debt-reduction initiative and the poverty reduction strategy papers (PRSPs) that have helped implement it. These authors welcome the Bretton Woods institutions' greater emphasis on poverty reduction as their primary goal and their adoption of a partici-patory process for defining and monitoring poverty reduction, but they see a number of difficulties and contradictions in the new initiative. First, they question whether the participatory processes will really ensure that poor countries have ownership of their policies and that their governments will be accountable. Are governments gen-uinely willing to let civil society influence the decisionmaking process, and how does this will fit in with the conditionalities internalized in the current aid framework? Second, they ask whether the content of policies has changed and whether countries can meet the goals that have been set; in particular, the authors are concerned that most PRSPs still fail to address the link between poverty and inequality. Finally, they express deep concern that the HIPC/PRSP process lacks effective monitoring and evaluation systems.

Institutions

In recent years, discussions about institutional reforms have moved to the center of the development debate, with a corresponding shift away from a static, technocratic approach toward a more dynamic perspective on state transformation. This shift is reflected in the first three papers in this section, as Mariano Tommasi, Mushtaq Khan, and David Dunham outline the complexities involved in institutional reforms. A dynamic perspective also calls for historical analysis, and the two final contribu-tions shed new light on how a society's history and resource endowments affect the choices that it makes.

Tommasi examines analytically the claim that crises may make introducing insti-tutional reforms easier. In recent years this view has evolved into the conventional wisdom, but Tommasi sketches out a more nuanced picture of this interaction, taking Argentina as an illustration. In particular, he argues that a crisis does not necessarily induce changes at the deeper politico-institutional level, even though it may facilitate the introduction of some policy reforms. Moreover, because the implementation of policy changes—for example, in the areas of privatization, taxation, and monetary stabilization—depends strongly on the fundamental institutions, crises are partly endogenous to bad institutions. Tommasi also emphasizes that no universal set of good policies exists. Policies are contingent responses to underlying states of the world, and as a result, what works in a given country at a given time may not work well elsewhere or at another time. In addition, the relationship between policies and outcomes is extremely complex; hence Tommasi stresses that the development debate should move beyond a discussion based on the "titles" of policies and focus instead on the details of their implementation.

Khan distinguishes between two completely different views of what the state does: the service delivery view and the social transformation view. The service delivery approach defines the state's role as providing basic public goods and services. By contrast, the social transformation approach sees the state as a dynamic entity that intervenes in property rights and devises rent management systems to accelerate the transition to capitalism and the diffusion of new technologies. Khan sees the service delivery view as the consensus approach in the development debate. It fits in nicely with theories that have a well-functioning market economy as the benchmark, and empirically, it is supported by a number of econometric studies that have established a systematic relationship between governance variables—such as measures of corruption, stability of property rights, and democracy—and developmental outcomes. However, Khan argues that governments in developing countries play a much more critical role than the service delivery model suggests. Bolstering his argument with a review of the experiences of China, the Republic of Korea, and Taiwan (China) and a critique of the robustness of the econometric work in this area, he maintains that state success is not related in any simple way to the state's neutrality in upholding preexisting property rights and delivering basic services. Development demands political restructuring of the organization of power to promote growth and political stability. Within this framework, Khan argues, the challenge is to propose feasible institutional reforms for particular countries, taking into account preexisting political arrangements, prior capitalist development, and capitalists' technological capacities.

Dunham highlights the danger that extensive economic policy reforms can erode social and political institutions and set off a downward spiral into crisis and offers a more nuanced view of the relationship between the state and the reform process that emphasizes social dynamics. The history of the country, the societal context, the motives and commitment of the leadership, the broader economic and political program, and the state's management capacity are as important as the specific elements of any reform package, Dunham argues. In the case of Sri Lanka, with its history of social tension, the liberalization process was part of a much broader program with distinct, ethnically-biased political purposes. Dunham suggests that even though the economic reforms contributed to considerable growth, they also initiated processes that subverted political institutions, and in the end caused large-scale violence.

Development researchers continue to debate the relative importance of geography and institutions as the fundamental causes of differences in prosperity between countries (see, for example, Acemoglu, Johnson, and Robinson 2002; Sachs and Warner 1997). In this context, considering how factor endowments and geography might affect how institutions evolve is important. Based on a study of the history of the New World, Stanley Engerman and Kenneth Sokoloff argue that initial differences in the degree of inequality in colonized countries—caused largely by differences in factor endowments—had profound effects on the development paths of different economies. For example, colonies established in Brazil and the Caribbean developed extreme levels of inequality, because geographic conditions made large, slave-owning plantations a natural adaptation in those environments. Elites were able to establish a legal framework that assured them a disproportionate share of political power, thereby making inequality persistent. By contrast, climatic conditions made smaller family farms the rule in the colonies of the North American mainland, resulting in institutions that provided more equal treatment and opportunities in society. Thus initial differences in climatic conditions led to systematic differences in the ways institutions evolved, which may help explain why the first group of countries has suffered persistently higher inequality and achieved lower long-run growth rates.

What are the obstacles to the evolution of legal institutions in transition economies? Karla Hoff and Joseph Stiglitz examine this question using development in Russia in the 1990s as their point of departure. In 1992–94 Russia underwent mass privatization, a process that might have been expected to spur a demand-driven evolution of institutions toward the rule of law, but no such evolution occurred. Hoff and Stiglitz suggest a multiple-equilibria model that may explain this nonevent. The key purpose of the model is to clarify the role of externalities mediated by the political environment. Even when a majority of asset-holders would benefit from the establishment of the rule of law, demand for the rule of law may not be the equilibrium outcome if individuals believe (correctly) that it is unlikely to be established. In this case, many individuals will rationally choose to strip assets, which then gives them an interest in prolonging the absence of the rule of law so that they can enjoy the fruits of asset stripping. The model may also highlight why Russia's Soviet legacy weakens the equilibrium demand for legal institutions. During the long period of Soviet rule, informal structures were established that raised the return to asset stripping relative to building value.

Globalization

International trade and international mobility of capital and labor have had an enormous impact on global development, but the gains from increased integration have not been distributed equally. For example, in recent years Sub-Saharan Africa has only received about 1 percent of the foreign direct investment in the world, and the region may be losing as much as US$4 billion a year because of the emigration of top professionals seeking better jobs abroad. At the same time, the 1997–98 East Asian crises reminded us that globalization is both more complex and more fragile than it once seemed, and that knowledge about and discussion on how to structure international economic activity are urgently needed. The papers in this section contribute to this debate.

No one anticipated the East Asian debacle of 1997–98, and consensus on how to characterize it has yet to be reached. Jomo Sundaram assesses opposing views on the nature of the crisis. He concludes that investor panic was the proximate cause of the crisis in a region in which financial liberalization had undermined monetary and financial governance. Jomo draws the lesson that financial markets are driven by sentiment as much as by fundamentals. This argument is consistent with the absence of the usual sources of currency stress at the outbreak of the crisis and underlines the risks involved in financing current account deficits with short-term capital flows. Jomo also critiques the role of the International Monetary Fund in the evolution of the crisis, and more generally reviews the role of international financial markets in allocating capital among countries and providing instruments for risk management. Finally, the author offers six lessons for reforming the international financial system.

John Dunning discusses how the world economic slowdown has affected international firms' strategies in relation to location. He cites figures that show that in the late 1990s, global foreign direct investment flows shifted markedly to the industrial regions of the world. Dunning attributes this shift largely to a huge, cross-border merger and acquisition boom; the growth of regional integration schemes; the slowdown in economic growth in China; and the crisis in other East Asian economies in 1997–98. He argues that governments seeking to attract multinational enterprises will need to recognize the location-specific advantages that mobile investors seek. For poor countries, this mainly means the availability of cheap labor; natural resources; and, in some cases, market access, combined with political stability and an institutional framework that supports private enterprises and competition.

The paper by Antonio Spilimbergo, Juan Luis Londoño, and Miguel Székely is a revised version of a paper first published in the *Journal of Development Economics* (1999). It is printed here in tribute to Juan Luis Londoño, who died tragically on February 6, 2003. Londoño presented related work at the conference in Oslo, but never had the opportunity to revise the presentation for this book. The joint paper with Spilimbergo and Székely is an interesting empirical study of the effects of trade openness on inequality. In recent years, many poor countries have implemented radical trade reforms, which have led to complex changes in resource allocation across society. The final effect on income distribution is not clear from a theoretical point of view, and hence careful empirical studies are needed. Spilimbergo, Londoño, and Székely find that the effect of trade openness on inequality depends on factor endowments: trade openness reduces inequality in capital-abundant countries and increases inequality in skill-abundant countries.

Andrés Solimano takes on several conceptual and policy issues related to international flows of human capital. The magnitude and impact of the outflow of human capital on poor countries varies from region to region, as Solimano illustrates with examples from Africa, China, and India. In general, he sees a disturbing picture. By way of illustration, Solimano reports that developing countries account for only 16 percent of global research and development spending, even though they account for 78 percent of world population and 39 percent of world gross national product. Many developing countries are trapped in a self-reinforcing cycle of low research and development investments and high levels of outmigration of scientists and technical experts, who prefer to work in countries that have a critical mass of scientific activity. Hence, even though various sorts of migration may result in global efficiency gains, the uneven distribution of these gains suggests a need for remedial action. Solimano urges the governments of poor countries to give greater priority to knowledge generation at home, while arguing that the industrial countries should increase their knowledge transfer to poor countries and should realign foreign aid priorities toward science and technology.

Oded Stark closes this section with a paper that turns the brain drain concern on its head. Using a formal model incorporating externalities in human capital productivity, Stark shows that the possibility of migration to a richer country may induce individuals to invest in a socially desirable level of human capital. Stark identifies conditions under which per capita output and the level of welfare of all workers are higher with migration than without it. Therefore, Stark argues, a controlled and restrictive migration policy may actually benefit poor countries, notwithstanding the standard view of the brain drain literature.

Concluding Remarks

Research gatherings like this conference are about exchanging ideas rather than formulating a specific set of policies to which all participants would subscribe. So it is a sign of the success of the conference that so many different, well-considered views were represented. Nevertheless, we would argue that it is possible to draw some lessons from the discussion along the same thematic lines as used in this volume.

First, we now know much more about what types of institutional structures support the productive use of aid. The donor community should focus on providing and allocating aid in ways that reinforce those structures rather than undermining them.

Second, we are continually learning more about how to promote institutional development. Building sound institutions—those that offer a framework for economic growth and the inclusion of poor people—should be a major part of the domestic policy agenda for developing countries, and supporting those efforts should be a leading goal of aid donors.

Finally, we have learned that if poor economies can successfully integrate into world markets, this is likely to accelerate their development. The issue is therefore not whether globalization should take place, or whether developing countries should accede to it. Instead, the focus should be on how they should best take advantage of globalization to promote the lives of poor people.

References

Acemoglu, Daron, Simon Johnson, and James A. Robinson. 2002. "Reversal of Fortune: Geography and Institutions in the Making of the Modern World Income Distribution." *Quarterly Journal of Economics* 117(4): 1231–94.

Burnside, Craig, and David Dollar. 2000. "Aid, Policies, and Growth." *American Economic Review* 90(4): 847–68.

Sachs, Jeffrey, and Andrew Warner. 1997. "Fundamental Sources of Long-Run Growth." *American Economic Review* 87(2): 184–88.

Spilimbergo, Antonio, Juan Luis Londoño, and Miguel Székely. 1999. "Income Distribution, Factor Endowments, and Trade Openness." *Journal of Development Economics* 59: 77–101.

Part I. Aid

Scaling Up: The Challenge of Monterrey

NICHOLAS STERN

The most urgent problem the world confronts today is absolute poverty, in all its dimensions. Poverty embodies or exacerbates hunger, illiteracy, and communicable disease, as well as state failure and civil and international conflict. Poor people not only endure deprivation in relation to income and human development, but also suffer from great income insecurity. They are profoundly constrained in their ability to shape their own lives. The challenge of fighting poverty is one of tremendous scale. In terms of income poverty, some 1.2 billion people must subsist on less than US$1 per day and 2.8 billion, nearly half the world's population, must survive on less than US$2 per day. In terms of health, each year some 3 million people die as a result of AIDS and a million die of malaria, with Sub-Saharan Africa accounting for more than 75 percent of the AIDS deaths and 90 percent of the deaths from malaria. The overall life expectancy for the developing world remains 14 years below that of the rich countries, while the under 5 mortality rate is 14 times as high. In relation to education, more than 100 million children of primary school age do not attend school, while a third of adult women in the developing world are illiterate. The problem of poverty is urgent, because with the addition of 2 billion people in the developing world over the next 30 years, the scale of the problem could grow if we do not act now, forcefully and reflectively. But it is also urgent because of the private suffering of all those afflicted by poverty and the opportunities for human development that are lost every day.

Fortunately, the global community has begun to come to grips with the extent of the problem, and we have reason for hope. The United Nations meeting on Financing for Development, held in Monterrey, Mexico, in March 2002, was the latest and clearest indicator that developing and industrial nations have committed to trying to

At the time of the conference, Nicholas Stern was senior vice president Development Economics and chief economist at the World Bank. He is currently head of the Government Economic Service and second permanent secretary to the U.K. Treasury.

Annual World Bank Conference on Development Economics—Europe 2003
© 2004 The International Bank for Reconstruction and Development/The World Bank

attain ambitious global development targets with some degree of mutual accountability. The international community agreed on targets at the United Nations Millennium Summit; has agreed to increase aid resources, even if not yet to a level commensurate with the challenge; and has agreed broadly on the approach necessary to reach the goals.

Even if the commitment is sustained and strong, however, do we have the knowledge necessary to meet the development goals? In this paper I argue that even though development is a constant process of learning and change, we do have the knowledge for effective action now. We have already greatly increased our understanding of development and the effectiveness of development assistance in key respects. We have gone beyond some of the less constructive arguments, which set planning against the market, statist against neoliberal, reform against revolution. We understand that sustained growth over a long period must be market driven, but also that markets cannot function well without good governance and a well-functioning state. That leaves a great deal to study and learn, as well as room for many different strategies, but our current understanding does provide a platform for action, and we have already disposed of a good deal of obstructive intellectual debris. As long as we are willing to continue investing in experimentation, research, and evaluation and to build on this knowledge base, we will be able to meet the development challenge.

We know that for all their diversity, countries that have developed successfully have shared two main characteristics. First, they have taken charge of their own development, launching reforms and building institutions primarily for their own reasons, rather than because they have been induced to do so by promises of aid from outside. Second, they have generally constructed their economies on two pillars of development: they have improved the domestic environment for investment, productivity, and job creation; and they have invested in and empowered people, including poor people, to participate in growth. Both these pillars embody processes. Promoting poverty reduction is not primarily about redistributing fixed assets to either investors or the poor, but about putting in place the mechanisms to encourage innovation and entrepreneurship, to include all who can contribute to growth and development, and to protect those who cannot. In promoting development, our task is to act in ways that encourage these dynamic processes. To achieve this, we must constantly act in ways that allow us to learn more about change and how to promote it.

This paper has two main objectives. First, it attempts to show that we, the development community, have made great progress both in understanding development and poverty reduction and in applying the lessons learned. Second, it attempts to provide a map for a way forward. It outlines the development challenge, as summarized in the Millennium Development Goals (MDGs), and makes the case that meeting that challenge will depend on "scaling up" the international community's development efforts. For donors, this means not just increasing the quantities of assistance, but more important, changing qualitatively from past modes of doing business. This change is already under way, and I sketch out some ways in which the World Bank has reoriented itself for scaling up. Nevertheless, much remains to be done, and better measurement and evaluation for both learning and management must lie at the heart of our actions.

Understanding Development and Applying the Lessons Learned

We have learned a great deal from experience with development strategies and approaches. One lesson is that development, including advancement along multiple dimensions of human welfare, is possible. In recent decades, development progress has taken place at unprecedented rates in poorer regions and countries (Goldin, Rogers, and Stern 2002):

- *Health*. Over the past 40 years, life expectancy at birth in developing countries has increased by 20 years. The previous 20-year increase in longevity probably took millennia. This increase had a number of causes, including higher incomes and better education, particularly of women and girls; investments in infrastructure, particularly for water; and improvements in knowledge and understanding about the prevention and treatment of disease along with new programs to share this knowledge and put it into practice.

- *Education*. Over the past 30 years, illiteracy in the developing world has been cut nearly in half, from 47 percent of all adults to 25 percent. Steady expansion of school enrollments worldwide and increases in educational quality made key contributions to this improvement, as did better infrastructure and nutrition.

- *Income poverty*. The number of people subsisting on less than US$1 per day (measured in constant dollars) rose steadily for nearly two centuries, from the early 19th century, the earliest period for which we have data, to the late 20th century, but in the past 20 years this number has begun to fall. As a result of better and more market-oriented economic policies through much of the developing world—but especially in China and India—the number of poor people worldwide has fallen by 200 million or more since 1980, even as the world's population has risen by about 1.6 billion.

This progress in the fields of health, education, and income is not accidental. With the support of the development community and nongovernmental organizations (NGOs), governments have accelerated growth and poverty reduction by improving their policies, institutions, and governance and by undertaking well-designed projects and programs. For example, programs like Bolsa Escola in Brazil and PROGRESA (recently renamed Oportunidades) in Mexico have used financial incentives and parental involvement in school management to induce families to keep their children in school, thereby substantially raising school enrollments among the poorest children. In West Africa, targeted action by a global public-private partnership has eliminated river blindness (onchocerciasis) from much of the region, following the global community's earlier success in eradicating smallpox from the planet. In Bangladesh, local NGOs and outside donors have helped cut infant mortality in half, from 140 to 71 per 1,000 live births, in the past 30 years; reduce fertility sharply, from 7 births per woman in 1970 to 3.2 births in 1999; and achieve almost universal primary enrollment for girls in an environment where they historically faced high barriers.

But major setbacks have also occurred. Some regions and countries have grown extremely slowly or declined in recent decades. Most notably, Sub-Saharan Africa saw no increase in per capita incomes between 1965 and 1999, despite some improvement in the 1990s. Even though Africa did make steady progress on health and education indicators during much of that period—despite the lack of income growth—the AIDS epidemic has sharply reversed progress on life expectancy. For the region as a whole, life expectancy fell from 50 years in 1990 to 47 years in 1999, and several countries have suffered double-digit declines in life expectancy. Nor is Africa the only region that has struggled. Many of the transition economies in Central Asia and Eastern Europe suffered deep declines in living standards and sharp rises in poverty during the 1990s.

The challenge is to extend the progress that has improved the well-being of so many people to all regions and countries. To do so, the development community must learn from past failures as well as understand the origins of successes. Like aid recipients, who have often followed weak policies or allowed institutions to deteriorate, donors have also contributed to mistakes that slowed development.

Learning Lessons about Development and Development Assistance

Achieving the goal of globally shared development depends on understanding how policy, institutions, and governance promote development, as well as how development assistance and the external environment can contribute. We have various sources of understanding to guide us here. First, we have in-depth studies of particular countries, those that have been both more and less successful. Research at the micro level is of special interest to me, because of my own first-hand experience with both the difficulties and the potential payoffs of detailed research at this level. Second, we have comparative cross-country analyses of experience. This includes cross-country regressions, though they are not at the top of my list of ways to learn. Third, we have the project and program experience of the World Bank and other development institutions. Finally, we have examinations of the role of global structures (in such areas as trade and finance, knowledge, and cross-border environmental and health issues) and global action (in such areas as agricultural research and vaccine development) in promoting development.

What do we learn from looking in greater detail at these experiences? Above all, we learn that the prime mover of development must be the country itself. Evidence has shown that the country's own initiative, capacity, and political readiness are what drive policy change and institutional reform, rather than foreign assistance and associated loan conditionality (Dollar and Svensson 2000; World Bank 1998a). Heavy reliance on conditionality is ineffective for several reasons, namely: whether a government has actually fulfilled the conditions can be difficult to monitor, particularly when external shocks muddy the picture; governments may revert to their old practices as soon as the money has been disbursed; and when assessments are subjective, donors may have an incentive to emphasize progress to keep programs moving. Without country ownership, lending has not only failed to support reforms, but has probably contributed to their delay. For example, case studies of the Democratic Republic of Congo, Côte d'Ivoire, Kenya, Nigeria, and Tanzania all concluded that the availability of aid money in the 1980s postponed much-needed reforms (Devarajan, Dollar, and Holmgren 2001).

Where country commitment to reform exists, development assistance can be, and has been, extremely effective in supporting development. Country case studies show that in countries as diverse as China, India, Mozambique, Uganda, and Vietnam, development assistance—whether in the form of knowledge sharing, capacity building, or finance—has helped the country solidify and build on its reform momentum. Cross-country empirical evidence reveals that the targeting of aid toward poverty reduction has improved over the past decade with the decline in Cold War political pressures to lend to nonreforming countries. Financial assistance is now channeled primarily to countries with good enough policies and high enough levels of poverty to make aid effective at poverty reduction. At the program and project level, World Bank evaluations show impressive and rising economic rates of return, at least for the large subset of projects for which rates of return are calculated, as well as tangible results in human development outcomes. At the global level, a number of programs have yielded abundant returns, such as the Consultative Group for International Agricultural Research program supporting agricultural research and innovation, which has helped develop and spread green revolution technologies. While each of the approaches for gauging the effects of development assistance has its analytical problems, and none of them is above challenge, all four provide evidence that assistance has made a difference, and together they provide a basis for optimism about what can be achieved.

Goals and Approaches to Development: The Evolution in Thinking

To understand the extent of the success or otherwise of development assistance, we must first have goals against which to assess it. Because our understanding of development has evolved in this respect, we have been aiming at a moving target, but it has moved in the right direction. The development community now widely accepts that poverty reduction efforts should address poverty in all its dimensions—not only lack of income, but also the lack of health and education, the vulnerability to shocks, and the lack of control over one's own life. In some cases, this understanding of poverty implies different approaches from those used in the past, for example, an increased focus on access to public services for vulnerable groups and greater attention to early disclosure of information that poor people can use. The multidimensionality of poverty is embodied in the MDGs, which heads of state adopted at a United Nations summit in 2000.

Our understanding about which broad development approaches are effective and which are less so has also improved. Experience has shown that neither the central planning approach that many countries followed in the 1950s and 1960s nor the minimal government, free market approach that many people advocated in the 1980s and early 1990s is likely to deliver on the scale embodied in the MDGs. While the private sector will lead most effective approaches to development, sustained growth and poverty reduction depend on sound governance, facilitation or provision of physical infrastructure, human capital investments, and social cohesion. All these factors for success depend heavily on institutional development, a subject that past policy discussions have too often neglected, but that development practitioners now recognize is essential for sustained poverty reduction.

In my opinion, in the examination of the effectiveness of different approaches to development, the notion of achieving the correct balance between state and market is not helpful. This concept assumes that states and markets are substitutes for each other, whereas in reality they are essentially complementary. For example, the lack of property titles can hamper poor people's ability to accumulate and use assets. Private infrastructure will not perform effectively without a clear and well-designed regulatory framework. In securities markets, as recent events in the United States have demonstrated, better regulation can improve the functioning of markets and increase the volume of private sector activity, and an efficient bond market can lower the government's costs of borrowing, thereby reducing the share of the government's budget devoted to paying interest and, at least potentially, freeing up resources for health, education, or other public services.

A Strategy for Development: Building the Investment Climate and Empowering People

While the broad principles for effective development are clear, there is no single road to follow. Countries must devise their own strategies and approaches appropriate for their particular circumstances and goals. Nevertheless, the development community has learned much about the sources of growth and poverty reduction, and an examination of the evidence reveals certain patterns. The evidence on country policies, institutions, and governance can be summarized as follows: development depends on two pillars, the investment climate and the empowerment of poor people, which together support sustained growth and poverty reduction (Stern 2001).

Providing a good investment climate means providing an environment in which the private sector will invest and produce efficiently in a way that generates jobs and productivity growth. The investment climate consists of all the factors that have the greatest influence on private sector decisions and economic activity, including macroeconomic stability and openness, governance and institutions, and infrastructure. The private sector should be understood not only to include large firms and multinationals, but also—indeed, first and foremost from the point of view of generating opportunities for poor people—farmers and small and medium enterprises.

Empowering and investing in poor people means not only overcoming poverty directly in terms of health, education, and the ability to shape one's own life, but also enabling participation in growth. We know that sustained growth is essential for poverty reduction, so the focus on the investment climate is itself a tool for poverty reduction. At the same time, providing opportunities for poor people to acquire the tools necessary to participate in growth, such as education and health and access to infrastructure and financial services, itself drives the growth process. Direct actions by governments, international organizations, NGOs, and the private sector can and should be powerful forces for promoting empowerment.

Promoting the investment climate and empowerment implies an active and challenging role for governments. From this perspective, there is no sense in which this role should be seen as minimal. Many countries have built up these two pillars in recent decades and have reaped rewards in terms of more rapid growth and poverty reduction. Although many countries continue to fall behind economically, most of the developing world's population lives in countries that have grown rapidly and are closing the gap with the rich countries (World Bank 2002). Even the countries that have stagnated economically have, for the most part, seen material improvements in social indicators, such as health and education measures (Becker, Philipson, and Soares 2002; World Bank 1998b). For example, in 1950 the average country with a per capita income of US$8,000 (measured in 1995 dollars) would have had an infant mortality rate of 45 per 1,000 live births, but by 1995 the average country at the same level of real income would have had an infant mortality rate of just 15 per 1,000 live births, a reduction of two-thirds. Large reductions in mortality occurred all along the income spectrum, so any given income level was associated with much higher infant survival rates than in the past.

Applying the Lessons on Development Effectiveness

Development effectiveness depends not only on learning from experience, but also on ensuring that the knowledge gained is translated into changes in development practice. That is, effectiveness depends on trying, learning, reworking, and trying again. The World Bank, or any aid bureaucracy, must typically accumulate a considerable body of evidence before it changes course. That is probably as it should be, because we cannot afford to shift course with every change in the winds of intellectual fashion; however, we have proven not only that we work to generate and understand evidence, but also that when that evidence accumulates, we do reorient ourselves in a more productive direction.

Lesson 1: Allocating Aid Well

At the economy-wide level, the evidence suggests strongly that aid promotes development if the aid is provided under the right circumstances and is correctly designed (World Bank 1998a). In general, official development assistance (ODA) has historically delivered substantial poverty reduction, and the poverty-reducing impact of ODA has increased in the past decade because of improved design and allocation. Empirical studies have shown, first, that well-targeted aid increases investment (Dollar and Easterly 1999). The results suggest that each US$1 of assistance provided through the World Bank's concessional lending arm, the International Development Association (IDA), leads to nearly US$2 of additional private investment, including 60 cents of additional foreign direct investment (Collier, Devarajan, and Dollar 2001). Thus aid draws in private investment rather than crowding it out. Second, the evidence shows that well-targeted aid has high overall economic payoffs. Because aid creates new economic possibilities, its economy-wide returns extend far more broadly than the poverty reduction returns expressed in terms of the number of people who move across a particular poverty line. The overall rate of return to IDA lending exceeds even the strong returns estimated at the project level (Collier, Devarajan, and Dollar 2001).

Allocating aid to countries with better policies and institutions has become easier over time, because the average economic performance of developing countries has improved in significant ways. The 1980s and 1990s were periods of major policy reforms throughout the developing world. We can see this clearly, for example, in the areas of macroeconomic stability and openness. Developing countries cut their median inflation rate in half between 1982 and 1997, from about 15 to 7 percent. The improvements were even greater in low-income countries. By the end of the 1990s, only 5 percent of developing countries had inflation above 10 percent. Average tariff rates have also declined sharply in all developing regions. In South Asia, for example, the unweighted average tariff rate fell from about 65 percent in 1980–85 to 30 percent in 1996–98, and in Latin American and the Caribbean, it fell from 30 percent to less than 15 percent. Tariff averages are an imperfect measure of openness, but the black market exchange rate premium, which is an indicator of macroeconomic instability and of the restrictiveness of the trade or capital market regime, has declined even more. Governance has also improved in some key respects. Most notably, the share of the world's countries that are democracies rose from less than one-third in 1974 to nearly two-thirds in 1998, with democratically elected governments coming to power across Eastern Europe, Latin America, and Sub-Saharan Africa (World Bank 1999).[1]

Aid in general has become far better targeted toward poverty reduction in recent years. With the end of the Cold War, donors became less interested in using aid to achieve geopolitical goals and more interested in using aid to promote development. Large-scale financial assistance is increasingly allocated to countries that have reasonably good policies and institutions, that is, the countries that can best use aid for poverty reduction. At the same time, the improvements in developing countries' policies mean that within a given country the effectiveness of aid for poverty reduction is likely to have increased. With these shifts, the estimated poverty reduction effectiveness of ODA—that is, the marginal productivity of aid in terms of poverty reduction—nearly tripled during the 1990s (Collier, Devarajan, and Dollar 2001). The Bank's IDA lending is targeted even more effectively than other concessional aid, both because a somewhat larger share goes to countries with good policies and because a larger share goes to high-poverty countries.

Lesson 2: Working to Improve Policies

Thus aid is increasingly going to countries that can use it well. This implies that countries that cannot use aid well—those with weak institutions, policies, and governance—are receiving a smaller share of aid budgets. This is a hard consequence of the lessons of experience, but it is the right policy. Aid budgets are too constrained and development needs are too vast to allow the massive waste that has sometimes come with the misallocation of aid. As a reminder, we need think only of Zaire (now the Democratic Republic of Congo): the country received more than US$10 billion in ODA in the past 40 years, mostly during the rule of President Mobutu (1965–97), while income declined by a factor of four between 1974 and 1996 (calculated from World Bank databases). Keeping the aid spigot open did not serve the goal of long-term poverty reduction.

Yet, as critics of the aid effectiveness literature have pointed out, the international community cannot simply abandon people who live in countries that lack the policies, institutions, and governance necessary for effective use of aid. Poor people in these countries are among the poorest in the world and face the greatest hurdles in improving their lives. The World Bank and other institutions are now investing more resources to work out the best approaches for helping people in these countries. Experience suggests that technical assistance for capacity building efforts, even when combined with the promise of greater financial assistance if policies, institutions, and governance improve, is often insufficient to enable these countries to initiate and sustain reform.

The Bank's analysis of the potential role of development assistance for these countries has, so far, pointed in the following directions. Of the two or three dozen countries with the poorest institutions and policies, over the last two decades only a few have made major improvements in the environment for growth and poverty reduction. Ethiopia, Mozambique, and Uganda are unusual among these countries in having achieved significant progress. Others have seen few advances, and the performance of the Bank lending portfolio in this group has been poor: projects have failed at double the rate for other countries.

Approaches that work in the typical low-income country may not be appropriate in these poor-policy countries, as they typically lack the basis for country leadership of reform, and traditional lending conditionality has not worked well in inducing and supporting reform. Given the weaknesses in governance and central institutions, at times the development community may have a role to play in becoming more directly involved in the provision of basic health and education services.

The poor-policy countries vary widely in their problems and opportunities. As is the case for the better performing countries, no single strategy will be appropriate for all nations with poor policies and institutions: each country has its specific challenges. Nevertheless, distinguishing between approaches in poor-policy countries and those that will work in countries with better policies, institutions, and governance is useful.

- Large-scale financial transfers are unlikely to work well in poor-policy countries, because absorptive capacity is limited in these environments.

- Donors should instead focus on knowledge transfer and capacity building to facilitate change. Given the constraints on government capacity, such efforts should concentrate on a limited reform agenda that is both sensible in economic terms (that is, mindful of sequencing issues) and feasible from a sociopolitical standpoint. Only when they develop greater capacity, and when early gains demonstrate the benefits of reform, will the poor-policy countries generally be able to make good use of large-scale aid. In some cases, the appropriate arena for these early demonstration reforms will be important regions with more reform-minded governments.

- Donors may see a need for using aid to improve basic health and education services in poor-policy countries. To be effective, however, funding should probably be directed through channels other than the central government. A recent World

Bank task force suggested structures whereby a donor-monitored wholesaling organization contracts with multiple channels of retail provision, such as the private sector, NGOs, and local governments.

- Humanitarian aid remains necessary in some countries with the worst policies and institutions. A recent example is the provision of food aid to Zimbabwe, a country with urgent needs, but few prospects for using longer-term development assistance well at this point.

Lesson 3: *Changing the Way We Do Business*

A third lesson concerns how development agencies work with client countries, and the last decade has seen significant change in this regard. This change complements the shift toward improved targeting of large-scale lending. The development community should work to support reform that is led by a country and not attempt to impose it from outside. Externally mandated reforms are not only offensive, but also ineffective in most cases. Furthermore, in offering its support, the outside development community should respect local knowledge and priorities if the outside assistance is to be effective.

One of the areas in which the mode of engagement is particularly important is adjustment lending. This in an area in which the international community learned from flawed early rounds in the 1980s and early 1990s, and it has begun to incorporate those lessons into current practice. Adjustment lending emerged in the 1980s in response to a real problem: it was intended to address major imbalances and shortcomings in the macroeconomic environments of developing countries, which often rendered project-level assistance ineffective. The evidence shows that adjustment lending can indeed help countries undertake reforms and smooth the transition costs associated with adjusting to economic shocks, but only if critical reforms are actually carried out and are tailored to local conditions. The record of World Bank adjustment lending is mixed in this regard. It includes some success stories, such as adjustment in Uganda and Vietnam, but also other cases where adjustment lending was not followed by reform implementation or where the design neglected social concerns and local conditions. As noted earlier, heavy reliance on conditionality was usually ineffective, with the large number of conditions doing nothing to strengthen borrower ownership of the reforms.

The World Bank has applied these lessons through targeting adjustment loans more effectively; attempting to use conditionality more judiciously; and paying greater attention to governance, institutional, structural, and social issues. As with overall lending, the Bank has increasingly focused adjustment lending on borrowers with a satisfactory track record. The increasing performance-based selectivity in World Bank (IDA and International Bank for Reconstruction and Development) lending decisions meant that by 1995–2000, 72 percent of adjustment loans went to countries with above average performance on a broad range of policies (as measured by the Bank's country policy and institutional assessments).[2] The Bank and other lenders have also attempted to move toward lighter use of conditionality, a trend that in low-income countries is reflected in the introduction of more participatory processes designed to encourage country ownership of the entire reform program, known as the poverty reduction strategy paper (PRSP) process. The result of these changes has been a sharp increase in the effectiveness of adjustment lending, as evaluated by the World Bank's independent Operations Evaluation Department.[3]

Effectiveness of Global Action: Rationale and Experience

In addition to the lessons for country economic policies and for the design, allocation, and delivery of development assistance to particular countries, another arena for action by the development community exists that is beyond the level of the individual country. Individual countries cannot handle global development challenges—such as the spread of infectious diseases, the challenge of building an international trade and financial architecture, the loss of biodiversity, the outcomes of deforestation, and the implications of climate change—that therefore require multilateral action. The Bank has contributed to such global programs through financing, through advocacy, and through alignment with its country programs. The following two examples illustrate the far-reaching potential and large returns of such global initiatives:

- The West African Onchocerciasis Control Program is a collaborative effort by multilateral agencies, governments, NGOs, and the private sector. Since it was launched in 1974, the program has largely eliminated the scourge of river blindness from 11 countries in West Africa. As a result, it has prevented an estimated 600,000 cases of blindness and added an estimated 5 million years of productive labor to the 11 countries' economies.

- The Consultative Group for International Agricultural Research (CGIAR), a network of research centers, has created and promoted crop improvements in developing countries over the last 30 years, enhancing productivity and nutrition and reducing rural poverty. These centers have produced more than 500 varieties of grain now planted in poor countries and have helped to increase average yields in target grains by 75 percent over three decades.

At the same time, there have been major setbacks in some areas where global action is clearly warranted. For instance, the international community failed to respond rapidly to AIDS in the early years of the epidemic and to work to persuade developing country governments to take action. Malaria is another scourge against which international response has been insufficient. When I began my field research in the village of Palanpur, India, in the mid-1970s, the general assumption was that malaria would soon go the way of smallpox. Some 30 years later, malaria continues to afflict 300 million to 500 million people each year and to kill about 1 million of them.

Priorities for Global Action: The Case of Trade

The examples of past global action remain relevant, but we should also ask what the other priority areas are for global action today. In my view, the trade agenda belongs near the top of the list. The international trade architecture is considerably more conducive to development than it was 40 years ago, but it could and should improve further. The Doha Development Agenda provides a framework for progress, but the road ahead will be a difficult one to travel. To move forward, we must win arguments in both rich and poor countries about the benefits of openness to trade and investment. Rich countries in particular must be willing to make the trade-related adjustments that they often urge on poorer countries. Unfortunately, recent policy steps by some donor countries cast some doubt on political leaders' willingness to provide leadership on this issue, notwithstanding their brave words at Doha and Monterrey.

As concerns trade-related adjustments, a number of priorities spring to mind. The first priority would be for rich countries to reduce protectionism in agriculture and textiles, both areas of special importance to poor countries. According to World Bank calculations, on average, poor people face tariffs for their exports that are twice as high as those rich people face (World Bank 2001a). Nontariff barriers also remain a problem, such as when phyto-sanitary regulations are used for protectionist purposes. For example, the European Union requires that for camel cheese imported from Mauritania, one of the poorest countries in the world, the camels must be milked mechanically (Wilson 2002). A second priority for trade architecture is revising the intellectual property regime to increase its benefits to developing countries. In agreeing on revisions, rich countries should think of the long-term benefits of promoting development and expanding markets, rather than focusing on profits in the short to medium term. A third priority would be for the global community to promote development by further opening to trade in services, including the temporary movement of workers to supply services in rich countries. Some argue that labor should not be treated the same as other commodities, and that allowing a completely free flow of labor would undermine the very notion of the nation-state. However, temporary movements of workers would not have such far-reaching, noneconomic effects, but would allow developing countries to exploit an area of comparative advantage (as industrial countries do when they send expatriate managers to oversee multinational operations). At the same time, allowing expanded trade in services could give those developing country workers additional skills and ideas that they could bring home with them, as well as capital to finance the application of those ideas.

Achieving Goals: What Is Scaling Up and Why Is It Necessary?

Winning the fight against poverty will depend on scaling up, that is, increasing our effectiveness and efforts to a level commensurate with the challenge. This section describes further what scaling up means and what it will entail. To provide the necessary context for that discussion, however, we first need to understand the development targets to which the international community has committed.

The Millennium Development Goals

Development agencies, including the World Bank, and governments around the world are dedicated to fighting poverty, but what do we mean by this and how will we know whether we are making headway? To help answer these questions, and to draw attention to the urgent need for action on poverty reduction, most of the world's governments have signed on to the MDGs adopted at the Millennium Summit of the United Nations General Assembly in 2000. These goals not only commit the world's governments—in both developing and developed countries—to work together to eradicate extreme poverty, but they also set specific targets in several areas.[4]

The MDGs commit the international community to a target of halving the proportion of people living in absolute poverty (defined as subsisting on less than US$1 per day in purchasing power parity terms) by 2015. In health and education, the MDGs require cutting child mortality by two-thirds and achieving universal primary education by 2015, while at the same time eliminating gender disparities in schooling by 2005. The MDGs also commit the international community to beginning to reverse the spread of HIV/AIDS and malaria, as well as the loss of environmental resources by 2015. These and the other MDGs are ambitious, at least in light of historical trends on these dimensions. Attaining them will require both decisive action and further investment in learning.

The MDGs are multidimensional and multisectoral, covering income, gender, education, health, and the environment. This is a much broader definition of objectives than we would have seen 15 years ago, and it embodies a deeper understanding of the nature of poverty. The multidimensionality is crucial, not only in concept, but also in action: confronting poverty will require collaboration by partners, each with their own comparative advantages and skills, as well as an understanding of how income, education, health, gender, the environment, and other aspects of the development of the economy and of society interact. Resources cannot be wasted through uncoordinated efforts. The measurable results to which the MDGs point can help us to manage, allocate, and coordinate our activities and resources more effectively. Equally important is the sense of urgency provided by the deadlines specified in the MDGs.

The MDGs are also becoming embodied in country-specific goals set by the developing countries themselves, including through the PRSP process. It is important that each developing country set its own targets and that rigid or formulaic external attempts to impose specific objectives are avoided: without country ownership of objectives, country commitment to specific actions or approaches is unlikely to materialize. At the same time, however, the international community has a role to play in raising awareness about the importance of recognizing poverty as a multidimensional problem. This is relevant for policy because pushing for income growth of the poor, with the hope that health, education, and other welfare indicators will follow, is not enough. Historically, even though income and nonincome welfare improvements have been correlated, major advances and declines in nonincome indicators have been observed that have been independent of income. At the same time, projected income growth alone will not be enough to achieve nonincome targets at acceptably rapid rates. Specific and focused action to achieve the other goals is required, over and above efforts to promote income growth.

Taking the Measure of the Poverty Challenge

Achieving these ambitious goals will require that we scale up our efforts. By scaling up I do not mean only increasing the resources devoted to the problem, although increased aid is surely an element, and has indeed been recognized as a piece of the puzzle. The magnitude of the challenge embodied in the MDGs is such that we must get more out of each dollar spent on development assistance. In the remainder of this paper, I will outline how we can achieve this.

As I noted at the outset, the MDGs are a great challenge. That the bar is high is implied not only by current income poverty and population growth figures, that is, the 1.2 billion people living on less than US$1 per day, the 2.8 billion living on less than US$2 per day, and the 2 billion additional people who will be added to the world's population over the next 30 years. The current forecasts for the MDG indicators also indicate the extent of the challenge. The distance from our development goals is not only great overall, but also varies tremendously across dimensions and across populations. Based on current trends and growth forecasts, the world is likely to just meet the global target for income poverty, thanks to continued strong growth in East Asia, but at a region by region level, the income poverty forecasts are not reassuring (table 1). Only two of the six developing regions are projected to meet the target of halving the share of their populations living in income poverty, and Sub-Saharan Africa is projected to fall far short.

In the nonincome poverty dimensions, based on historical income elasticities of health and education advances, growth alone is clearly insufficient to meet the challenge. With the growth rates now forecast for the developing world, an implementation focus on income alone will not do enough; we must also act directly to achieve health, education, and other goals (Devarajan, Miller, and Swanson 2002). Table 2 illustrates this point, by showing how far growth alone, without any further initiatives, can be expected to take us toward reaching the MDG health and education goals.

Education indicators, and especially health indicators, would likely fall well short of the MDGs on the basis of growth only forecasts. The shortfall is large: for example, education outcomes in Africa are far from reaching their targets under a growth-only strategy. Even if per capita income growth in Sub-Saharan Africa were three times as rapid as forecast and the region therefore met the income poverty goal, it would still fall short of the education and child mortality goals in the absence of more direct interventions in those areas. Therefore to meet the MDGs related to human development, the focus of implementation must go well beyond income growth.

Scale of Resources and the Meaning of Scaling Up

In assessing the challenge, we must also recognize that aid flows are small relative to the scale of the challenge. Moreover, the World Bank is a small player, even in relation to flows to developing countries. Consider these figures: total aid flows are about US$50 billion per year, and the Bank's aggregate flows (largely lending) amount to about US$16 billion per year. By comparison, flows of foreign direct investment to developing countries have averaged about US$160 billion per year in recent years, and total investment in developing countries is approximately US$1.5 trillion per year. That is, World Bank lending only accounts for about 1 percent of total

TABLE 1. Income by Region, Selected Years

Region	Population, 2000 (millions)	GDP per capita, 2000 (current US$)	Average annual rate of change in GDP per capita (%)		Poverty (%)			
			1990–2000	1995–2015	Population in extreme poverty, 1990	Population in extreme poverty, 1999	Target, 2015	Growth alone[a]
East Asia and the Pacific	1,855	1,110	5.9	5.6	27.6	14.2	13.8	7.4
Europe and Central Asia	474	1,986	–1.7	4.8	1.6	3.6	0.8	2.1
Latin America and the Caribbean	516	3,879	1.7	3.0	16.8	15.1	8.4	8.4
Middle East and North Africa	295	2,235	0.9	1.4	2.4	2.3	1.2	1.8
South Asia	1,355	440	3.6	3.7	44.0	36.9	22.0	25.4
Sub-Saharan Africa	659	490	–0.1	1.4	47.7	46.7	23.9	40.6

GDP Gross domestic product.

a. Growth alone projections are constructed from forecast growth rates and simple assumptions about income distribution. The growth alone calculations take two effects into account: the productivity of the increased public expenditure that growth permits and the increased demand for services and other behavioral changes that result from income growth.

Source: World Bank (2001a, b).

TABLE 2. Health and Education, by Region, Selected Years

Region	Under-five mortality rate (per 1,000 live births)			Net primary school enrollment rate (%)		
	2000	Target, 2015	Growth alone[a]	1998	Target, 2015	Growth alone[a]
East Asia and the Pacific	44.7	18.2	38.9	97	100	127
Europe and Central Asia	25.2	11.2	23.4	93	100	117
Latin America and the Caribbean	36.7	16.2	35.6	94	100	108
Middle East and North Africa	53.9	23.4	52.4	86	100	92
South Asia	96.5	39.9	91.2	73	100	87
Sub-Saharan Africa	161.6	51.2	154.2	60	100	64

a. Growth alone is constructed from forecast growth rates and a growth elasticity that can be found in Pritchett and Summers (1996) and Schultz (1987). The challenge of meeting targets specified in terms of primary school completion rates is much more difficult than meeting enrollment targets (see World Bank Development Committee 2002).

Sources: Pritchett and Summers (1996); Schultz (1987); World Bank (2001a,b); United Nations Educational, Scientific, and Cultural Organization, Institute for Statistics (online database);. World Development Indicators.

investment in developing countries. Another way of calibrating the aid flows is to note that total aid flows from the industrial countries are equivalent to only a fifth to a sixth of the amount of agricultural subsidies they pay to support their own small farming sectors, which amount to some US$300 billion per year. In education, the Bank lends approximately US$2 billion, compared with a total education budget in developing countries of around US$250 billion. With the exception of some small and extremely poor countries—most notably in Sub-Saharan Africa, where aid inflows approach 5 percent of income—aid itself is small relative to gross national income, that is, less than 0.5 percent of income, for countries where a majority of the developing world's population lives (tables 3 and 4).

The implications of these numbers are simply this: even if we were to double the current level of development assistance, thereby going far beyond the increases announced by donor countries at the Monterrey conference, resources alone would be unlikely to allow us to reach our goals. While increasing resources must be part of a successful effort to reach the goals, if we are to create outcomes commensurate with the large scale of the goals and challenges—in other words, if we are to scale up effectively—we must go beyond simple resource expansion. We must find ways of getting much more out of both current resources and any increases in aid. We are going to have to apply the lessons we have learned even more effectively.

Ideas and knowledge are central to scaling up. As Thomas Jefferson pointed out: "He who receives an idea from me, receives instruction himself without lessening mine; as he who lights his taper at mine, receives light without darkening me" (cited in World Bank 1998b, p. 16). In the jargon of economics, ideas are nonrival and are a public good. Developing countries themselves can take forward ideas about what works in development and what does not. They can scale up good ideas, which they can discover from their own experience or that of others, and development agencies

TABLE 3. Aid Recipients' Characteristics by Level of Aid Received

| | Atlas[a] | | | | Purchasing power parity | | | |
| | 1995–2000 average | | 2000 | | 1995–2000 average | | 2000 | |
	No. of countries with data	GNI per capita (current US$)	GNI (current US$ billions)	Population (millions)	No. of countries with data	GNI per capita (current US$)	GNI (current US$ billions)	Population (millions)
Aid (as a percentage of GNI, Atlas)					Aid (as a percentage of GNI, PPP)			
>20	13	270	16.9	63.5	>20	0	n.a	n.a	n.a
10–20	30	272	69.8	257.6	10–20	3	670	10.1	14.3
5.0–10	19	503	89.9	179.4	5.0–10	15	854	90.6	98.6
2.0–5.0	19	606	249.6	369.7	2.0–5.0	36	1,375	346.7	238.0
1.0–2.0	17	1,461	511.7	346.3	1.0–2.0	17	1,969	372.6	179.2
0.5–1.0	16	1,193	641.0	610.0	0.5–1.0	19	2,840	1,424.3	452.6
0–0.5	28	1,508	4,791.0	3,077.5	0–0.5	48	4,078	18,081.9	3,992.1
<0	3	7,950	506.2	71.0	<0	3	3,921	875.4	71.0
Low- and middle-income countries	130	1,248	6,099.3	4,929.2	Low- and middle-income countries	128	3,541	19,297.9	4,929.1
High-income countries	13	15,344	776.7	45.8	High-income countries	13	20,076	1,028.4	45.8

GNI   Gross national income.

n.a.   Not applicable.

PPP   Purchasing power parity.

a. The Atlas conversion factor—used in calculating GNI—is the average of a country's exchange rate (or alternative conversion factor) for that year and its exchange rates for the two preceding years, adjusted for the difference between the rate of inflation in the country and that in the Group of Five countries. PPP GNI is gross national income converted to international dollars using purchasing power parity rates. An international dollar has the same purchasing power of GNI as a U.S. dollar has in the United States. Unallocated/unspecified aid is not included. Data are shown only for countries reported by the Organisation for Economic Co-operation and Development, Development Assistance Committee as aid recipients. Less than 0 percent refers to recipients with negative net disbursements.

Source: World Bank (2001b).

TABLE 4. Aid by Region

Region	Atlas 1995–2000 average			Purchasing power parity 1995–2000 average		
	Aid (as a percentage of GNI, Atlas)	GNI per capita (current US$)	Population, 2000 (millions)	Aid (as a percentage of GNI, PPP)	GNI per capita (current US$)	Population, 2000 (millions)
East Asia and the Pacific	0.4	1,038	1,785	0.1	3,542	1,785
Europe and Central Asia	0.8	2,093	474	0.2	6,002	460
Latin America and the Caribbean	0.3	3,678	501	0.1	6,605	501
Middle East and North Africa	1.0	1,975	267	0.4	4,898	261
South Asia	0.9	417	1,329	0.2	1,977	1,329
Sub-Saharan Africa	4.4	510	647	1.5	1,518	647
Low- and middle-income countries	1.0	1,227	5,154	0.3	3,507	5,154
High-income countries	0.0	27,023	903	0.0	25,088	903

GNI   Gross national income.

PPP   Purchasing power parity.

Note: For Atlas and PPP definitions see table 3. The aggregates include unallocated/unspecified aid. The GNI per capita and population data refer to the entire region, including countries that receive no aid or are net donors.

Source: World Bank (2001b).

have a key role to play here, both in promoting learning within a country and in bringing in new ideas from elsewhere.

China's dramatic turnaround of the past quarter of a century is an excellent example of learning and scaling up. Even though Western aid resources played some role early in China's takeoff, they were relatively small compared with the size of China's economy. The key way the development community has contributed has been by bringing in ideas. These have gone far beyond ideas about the benefits of openness, the role of competition, the principles of good macroeconomic management, and so on, and range from tendering techniques, to road planning, to dry-land farming systems. Of special importance have been ideas and learning about how to reform economic institutions. These ideas, completely reworked by the Chinese and therefore owned by them, are at the heart of China's remarkable growth and poverty reduction.

Ideas are not at their most effective as disembodied knowledge. Usually they are most useful when they are blended with practical partnership and with supporting resources. In situations where the value of the idea can be hard to gauge, a donor's commitment of resources to the idea and to joint learning can serve as a credible signal of quality and commitment. Often resources will be necessary to meet the costs of the change involved in putting the idea into practice.

Why Now?

As I have described it, scaling up—changing the way countries do business and harnessing the transformative power of ideas and learning—must always be a good idea, so why should we place special emphasis on scaling up now? I would argue that despite the global economic slowdown, the medium-term outlook for development is unusually promising, and that we therefore have both a unique opportunity and a responsibility to make genuine advances in the fight against poverty. This spirit motivated the proceedings at the recent Monterrey development assistance and Doha trade conferences, which have provided a foundation on which to build.

Specifically, I would argue that we now have

- *A shared recognition of the importance of the poverty challenge.* Both Monterrey and Doha signaled that political leaders across a broad spectrum of countries recognize that, from a moral standpoint, the poverty challenge is the greatest mission of our times. Translating this moral clarity into sustained action is another matter, but signs of progress are evident on that front too.

- *An agreed, multidimensional set of targets.* In particular, we have the MDGs themselves. As outcome targets, they focus attention on the desired ends of our development efforts, and they command broad international agreement. In both these senses, they represent an advance over input targets, such as the oft-cited goal of increasing aid flows from the industrial countries to 0.7 percent of their gross domestic product (GDP). Moreover, as discussed earlier, the MDGs embody a newly acquired recognition of the multidimensional nature of poverty.

- *A history of achievements.* The advances of the past 40 or 50 years, such as the reductions in income poverty rates and the advances in health and education, are becoming more widely known. Recognition is growing that the developing world has not only made considerable progress, but has also used development assistance to accelerate it. Even those who have historically been the most skeptical of aid are now taking a more nuanced position, recognizing that the effectiveness of aid depends on the conditions under which it is provided.

- *A set of lessons learned about effectiveness.* Perhaps the most important lessons we have learned concern the conditions for effective use of aid and the importance of ownership. Most donors have already incorporated these lessons in their practices through better aid allocation and the adoption of the Comprehensive Development Framework/PRSP approach stressing country ownership.[5]

- *An acceptance of responsibility, commitment, and mutual accountability.* Developing countries have accepted that their own actions—their policies, institutions, and governance—will be the primary determinants of the pace of their development, no matter what external forces may have contributed to their underdevelopment in the past. The New Partnership for Africa's Development is a concrete statement of this acceptance of responsibility. At the same time, the wealthier nations have committed to doing their part for development through increased aid and a more open trading regime.

All this builds on the foundation of improved policies in developing countries. Together, these developments point to prospects for development over the next several years, and for the productivity of development assistance during that period, that are brighter than they have been for decades.

How Do We Scale Up?

The conditions are ripe for scaling up. I have already pointed to the importance of both resources and ideas. If resources and ideas are to translate into effective action, we shall need to place greater reliance on partnership, on the one hand, and on better use of the variety of instruments available to us, on the other.

Partnership

We have begun to recognize the need to base our development approach more solidly on partnership. Given the scale of the challenge, the development community must work together to build public support and raise aid resources, to make use of complementary skills, and to share ideas. The contributions of different partners will be diverse, but coherence is also necessary. First, we need to sustain and deepen the mutual commitment to shared goals. Second, countries need to maintain their commitment to improving policies, governance, and institutions, which provide the foundations for all partnership efforts. Third, donor country governments and international institutions must increase their support, in terms of both quantity and quality, for change and capacity building. Fourth, we must create a supportive external environment for development. This includes encouraging a development-oriented trade regime, promoting vigorous knowledge creation, maintaining financial and environmental stability, controlling communicable diseases, and restricting international flows of drugs and crime. Finally, donors must harmonize aid and take other steps necessary to relieve developing countries of the excessive administrative and other burdens that they now face.

Instruments for Change

Different organizations have developed their own instruments and areas of comparative advantage. Consider, for example, the instruments that the World Bank can bring to bear in this context of partnership. These are, or should be, instruments for change—change that is strategically oriented toward poverty reduction based on the strategy proposed here. These are tools for, first, improving the investment climate, and second, empowering and investing in poor people. Probably most important, as indicated in the discussion of scaling up, are the analysis and ideas that the Bank and other development agencies bring to the table, but these ideas are of limited utility without country capacity to adapt and implement them. That capacity is embodied in institutions and people; thus the second instrument is capacity building.

Neither of these first two instruments emphasizes the transfer of financial resources, but of course financial support is an important tool for development assistance. Much financial support should be provided through programmatic support for change, that is, multiyear lending with the flexibility to direct resources toward reforms across a significant part of the economy. Therefore, in its essence, this instrument works on a large scale commensurate with the scale of the challenge. This programmatic approach to lending contrasts with the narrower project-level support that the Bank focused on during its early decades. It is an approach to building institutions and strengthening governance across an economy and society. It could apply to a sector such as health, education, or power that affects the entire economy, or it could apply to an adjustment program for the management of the whole economy.

Not all financial support should be provided through programmatic lending. This approach can be complemented powerfully by demonstration projects. These are projects designed to develop new approaches, to show how ideas can be put into practice, and to encourage scaling up. Whether or not such a project succeeds depends primarily not on the direct project outcomes, but on whether it yields knowledge that is developed and replicated at a much larger scale elsewhere. If we are to be convincing that the project really does embody strong lessons, evaluation must play a key role in learning from demonstration projects. Such evaluation has strong public good characteristics, in that its benefits are nonrival in use, and so financing or carrying out evaluation is a highly appropriate role for international institutions and governments. To be effective, evaluation must be built into a project from the start. From the perspective of development effectiveness and scaling up, evaluation is not a desirable add-on to a project, but a central component.

Finally, there is merit in considering necessary steps, often called conditionality, as a separate instrument, though these are typically packaged with programmatic lending. Most development agencies are working to make necessary steps simpler and more country specific in design, compared with much conditionality in the past. When selected and designed judiciously, these necessary steps can promote reform. They are not a substitute for country commitment. If they are to be effective, they must act to support country commitment.

Underlying all these instruments should be one guiding principle: the international community should provide finance for change, not finance for not changing. We must recognize that in the past, often for political reasons, the international community has often financed the cost of not changing, as in Mobutu's Zaire.

What the World Bank Is Doing

The Bank has been working to combine these two strands, with increased emphasis on partnership and on using its lending and nonlending instruments as outlined. The PRSP approach, based on the Comprehensive Development Framework concept, provides a relatively new vehicle for coherent partnership in support of change in low-income countries. It brings together donor support under a common framework that, much more than in the past, is set by the developing country itself in a participatory process.

As noted, ideas for promoting change are central to efforts to scale up. For example, new thinking is essential in supporting the countries with the weakest policies, institutions, and governance. The research on aid effectiveness, to which the Bank contributed heavily, has led to a warranted reduction in the share of aid flows going to countries with policies and institutions that are unlikely to support poverty reduction. At the same time, the Bank is developing ideas on how to promote change in these countries.

A second example is the Education for All Fast Track program. This is a new approach aimed at scaling up primary school participation to help countries meet the MDG of attaining universal primary education by 2015. With more than 100 million children of primary school age who do not attend school, the need for action is urgent. The Education for All Fast Track program focuses on identifying low-income countries that are committed to meeting this goal, helping them to identify the main obstacles to universal enrollment, and then committing the Bank to a long-term program of finance for education. The innovation here is that every country that satisfies the criteria of a PRSP approach and has a credible education plan will be eligible to receive this support.

The World Bank is indeed a bank, and lending is central to its business. As noted previously, the Bank's financial resources play a major role in development finance for Sub-Saharan Africa, where concessional flows are large (table 4), amounting to some 4.4 percent of the recipient countries' GDP. Of course, some countries exceed the average by a considerable margin, for example, at US$600 million per year, projected IDA programs in Ethiopia would represent some 10 percent of GDP.

Some observers have questioned whether the poorest countries, including many in Africa, can absorb additional flows. They point to dangers such as currency appreciation of the Dutch disease type, as well as the inability of weak government bureaucracies to make good use of new money. Clearly any program of external support will have to take a country's absorptive capacity into consideration. Cross-country evidence suggests that aid in a given country has diminishing returns and that marginal returns tail off earlier in countries with low institutional capacity and poor policies (Collier and Dollar 2002). The risk of saddling extremely poor populations with debts they cannot pay should always figure prominently in our discussions with these countries. Moreover, we have seen that aid can actually delay progress in countries whose governments are not committed to reform. These are strong arguments for reducing flows to the poorest performers and for shifting further toward grant financing in the more marginal countries.

Nevertheless, preliminary calculations based on the experiences of the Bank and other donors suggest that the scope for expanded aid flows is already considerable, thanks in part to the improvement in policies in recent years. The risk of Dutch disease does not appear to be severe in countries with some reform momentum. The evidence suggests that if aid can support improvements that reduce supply bottlenecks, this can apparently more than offset the pressures toward currency appreciation (Hjertholm and Lauresen 2000; Nyoni 1998). Cross-country regressions suggest that in countries that have achieved reasonable levels of policy, resource flows could often remain effective even if they expanded to 15 to 20 percent of national income, or even more in a postconflict situation (Collier and Hoeffler 2002). Thus our thoughts about ideas, financial flows, and development need to be tailored to country circumstances. In some countries, contributing ideas that catalyze domestic reforms will be the predominant contribution of outside assistance, while in other countries, particularly in Sub-Saharan Africa, an increase in financial flows will also be crucial.

New ideas can be more credible, and more effectively implemented, if they are accompanied by finance. From a credibility standpoint, a donor's willingness to commit its money and reputation to an idea can signal its belief in a new idea and its willingness to help make that idea work, whether this involves establishing a public works program or implementing a macroeconomic stabilization plan. In addition, the implementation of new ideas sometimes involves an up-front investment, the money for which may be available to the recipient country only through aid. Bank research shows that when its projects are preceded by relevant analytical work, they have significantly higher success rates than do other projects (Deininger, Squire, and Basu 1998). Thus packaging lending and knowledge is often the most effective way of supporting development, and the Bank has great experience and a comparative advantage in preparing such packages.[6]

The Role of Measurement in Scaling up

How will we know if we have succeeded in scaling up? As I emphasized earlier, the test of scaling up is not the volume of external assistance delivered, but the change that results from it. In the past, the Bank and other donors too often tended to equate effectiveness with the volume of lending that goes out the door. Instead, all partners—developing countries, donor countries, and international financial institutions—need to do a better job of assessing change and measuring results. These include the ultimate goals, such as those enshrined in the MDGs, as well as the intermediate indicators that can serve as gauges of progress.

Measurement and Developing Countries

Measurement starts with the developing countries themselves. After the country sets its own objectives, whether in the context of the PRSP process or of some other such exercise, it will need clear indicators of whether it is reaching those objectives. Like the goals themselves, the metrics of success will generally be multidimensional, encompassing not just growth and income poverty measures, but also health, education, environmental, and other indicators.

Measuring ultimate outcome indicators is not enough, however. Suppose that those measures show that poverty rates are flat, because income growth is unimpressive. This highlights a problem, but gives little guidance on how to solve it; "raise growth rates" hardly constitutes a concrete policy direction. Therefore countries need indicators of intermediate goals that reflect processes and measures leading toward the ultimate goals. These include measures of the investment climate, governance indicators, and measures of the degree of participation by poor people in growth. The World Bank is helping countries to obtain numerical assessments of these processes, most recently by upgrading its program of micro-level surveys. In the past, the Bank has led the way in developing careful, comparable household surveys to help measure key outcomes, such as consumption, employment, and poverty reduction. More recently, it has launched systematic programs to develop surveys of key factors in the processes driving development. In particular, these involve investment climate surveys of firms aimed at understanding where the major constraints to growth are and surveys of the processes shaping basic services, which assess the quantity and quality of services actually available and delivered. These process indicators complement the household surveys by providing insight into the processes that generate poverty reduction. The coordination of these three sets of surveys is providing an extraordinarily powerful instrument for understanding the drivers of development.[7]

When we measure to understand sectoral outcomes, that does not mean measurement only within that sector. We have learned that development outcomes have diverse determinants, many of which are not narrowly tied to the sector of outcomes. For example, children's health outcomes are influenced strongly by the education levels of their mothers, by family incomes, by the availability of clean water, and by the quality of transportation services, as well as by public health interventions and medical inputs. Similarly, education levels are influenced not only by schools, teachers, and textbooks, but also by income level, nutrition, availability of fuel and water (especially in the case of girls' education), transport, and electricity. The effectiveness of health and education services also depends in large part on the manner of delivery and the degree of participation by beneficiaries. For these reasons, intermediate and process indicators need to range well beyond the sector immediately associated with an ultimate goal, such as education or health.

Measurement to Improve Donor Performance

International financial institutions and other donors are participating, as indeed they should, in this increased emphasis on measurement. For donors, as for developing country governments, hard-nosed analysis of what works is crucial to scaling up. Evaluation, whether formal or informal, permits scaling up by identifying ideas that can be adapted for use elsewhere. Note that this is different from measurement for accountability, though that too has a role, and that tensions between the two will sometimes arise. Learning involves experimentation, and therefore sometimes failure. This is especially true for international institutions, one of whose roles is to pilot promising new approaches that may have a significant risk of failure. Demonstration projects contribute to the international public good of knowledge about whether a given approach will work. The more innovative an approach is, the greater the potential learning externalities from trying it. This points to a role for public institutions, especially international public institutions. But these more innovative approaches will often fail, and the international financial institutions must be allowed room for some failure as long as their successes yield large enough returns to offset the failures, and as long as they work to understand and explain the reasons for failures. The World Bank's project success rates have risen steadily over the past decade to 80 percent or more; however, if they were ever to reach 100 percent, that would be a sign of timidity, and therefore of ineffectiveness.

Whether for learning or for accountability, good measurement of the success of interventions is crucial. Evaluation, if it is to work well, should be designed into a project or program from the beginning as part of its substance and output. Surveillance and monitoring systems have been crucial to tracking progress in health interventions, for example, in fighting malaria in Vietnam; HIV/AIDS in Senegal, Thailand, and Uganda; and measles in Malawi. Less formal evaluation has also proven successful in scaling up reforms, as in the regional experimentation and nationwide replication used by China during its 1980s reforms.

Development evaluation has recently taken an important step forward with the increased emphasis on randomized trials (Kremer 2002). One widely cited example is Mexico's PROGRESA (now Oportunidades) program, which provides cash transfers to poor rural families on condition that children remain in school and are given preventive health care. The program was phased into communities on a randomized basis so that it could be evaluated properly. After evaluation revealed large development effects, the program was expanded throughout the country, and similar programs are now being adopted in other parts of Latin America. Here evaluation was important not only because it provided clear results for learning purposes, but also because it provided a measure of protection in the political arena: the results were so clearly positive that even a change in governing party at the national level would be unlikely to derail the program's expansion.

A truly randomized approach is not always feasible. Yet even if comparing a randomly assigned treatment group with a control group is impossible, for example, because withholding the treatment would be unethical, then sometimes the treatment can at least be rolled out in a randomized fashion. That is, if budget or other constraints prevent the project from being implemented simultaneously for the entire target population, project managers can introduce it to households or communities in a randomized sequence. They can then gauge the effects of the program by comparing early-treatment groups with late-treatment groups (Kremer 2002). Where even a randomized rollout is impossible, careful statistical analysis can help in project evaluation. If the probability of participation in the benefits of a project can be modeled on the basis of some variable, then we can try to evaluate the effects of an intervention (Bourguignon, Pereira da Silva, and Stern forthcoming).

Project- and program-level evaluation is an element of increased measurement for learning, but international financial institutions also need to be concerned with progress at the wider sectoral and economy-wide levels. They should have action plans with outcome benchmarks in each area, such as education and health. Even though international financial institutions are unlikely to be the primary force behind achieving or missing those benchmarks, they need to know whether the programs they are supporting are making adequate progress. The recent agreement on the replenishment of IDA, which moves strongly toward such benchmarks, is an encouraging sign of a shared approach. At the same time, we must recognize that any measure is partial, and we should not allow those measures that can most easily be made quantitative to dominate the allocation and management of efforts.

Measurement and the Responsibilities of Rich Countries

Finally, measurement and learning can help in assessing and improving those policies and institutions of the rich countries that affect the developing world. This is part of the mutual accountability discussed earlier. The list of such policies and institutions is a long one, and it reflects the key role of the international environment in determining the extent of traction that developing countries can gain with improved policies and institutions of their own. The international community should carry out mutual assessment of how actions by rich countries are affecting the development, as well as the actions, of poor countries. Relevant areas for measurement include the following, in which rich countries can take positive steps to promote development, and which have a strong influence on the international flows of goods, aid, capital, knowledge, and people:

- Volume and efficiency of aid, including the degree of harmonization of policies and procedures among donor countries

- Openness of rich countries' markets and extent of both tariff and nontariff barriers to exports from developing countries

- International financial architecture and financial stability

- Extent of knowledge transfer from rich countries and effectiveness of capacity building

- Intellectual property regime and whether it primarily benefits or harms different parts of the developing world

- Migration policies.

In addition, rich countries can and should increase their efforts to prevent cross-border flows of the following damaging international flows:

- Environmental degradation

- Communicable diseases

- Drugs and organized crime networks

- Arms

- Conflict, which can be fueled by external forces, for example, through the purchase of so-called conflict diamonds

- Corruption, which in developing countries can be fed by bribes from firms in rich countries.

In these areas, measurement and learning are essential to progress. The fact that most donor countries are democratic probably increases the scope for knowledge to affect policy. Sometimes, measurement can lead to strong and well-organized domestic constituencies for policy improvement in rich countries, as in the case of the Jubilee 2000 debt cancellation campaign. Figures comparing debt repayment with government expenditures on human development were powerful spurs to action by church groups and other NGOs. While not all the statistics cited in that campaign were equally illuminating, the overall effect was to cancel debt that was constraining the growth of the world's poorest countries. Some of the measurement will no doubt prove embarrassing to industrial country governments. If such public knowledge of actions influences policies, then it will have made a real contribution to development.

Conclusion

Delivering on the promise of Monterrey and meeting the MDGs depends on scaling up our development efforts. In doing so, we can build on both past learning and a record of applying that learning. We have learned much about the meaning and dimensions of development, in particular, recognizing that it may be multidimensional. We have achieved a stronger understanding of the drivers of development, including the key role of the domestic investment climate and of strategies for empowerment. Developing countries have been improving their policies and institutions and have seen results in terms of poverty reduction. Sadly, such progress has been far from universal.

We have also learned more about the circumstances under which development assistance can be and has been effective, especially about the importance of a country's commitment to sound and improving policies and institutions. In addition to this learning, the international community has shown some ability to incorporate these lessons into practice. For example, in response to the post-Cold War decline in politically motivated aid and the increased understanding of aid effectiveness, donors have shifted their aid toward those countries most able to use it effectively.

We still have much to learn. For example, we need to know more about how improvements in the investment climate lead to sustained, increasing returns; about the sources and effects of empowerment and inclusion; and about the role of changing preferences and behavior in development (Stern 2002). We must build learning and evaluation into our actions.

Yet despite these gaps in our knowledge, we are already well equipped to move forward on scaling up, that is, to achieve results on a scale commensurate with the challenge. Our understanding of what works, both in relation to domestic development strategy and to development assistance, provides a basis for action. At Monterrey and Doha, donor and recipient countries agreed on their mutual obligations in this regard. While it has far to go, the international community has increasingly shown that it recognizes the importance of partnership, and I believe that it also has an increased understanding of the fundamental role of ideas and knowledge in generating the change that is necessary for scaling up.

Not only can we act now, but we must. With billions of people still living in poverty and 2 billion more to be added to the world's population in the coming generation, the scale of the poverty challenge is so great that we cannot afford to postpone action. We have never had as great an opportunity, or as daunting a responsibility, to make major advances in development as we do today.

Notes

1. Of course, democracy is only one element of governance, and it may not be the most important one for growth. China and Vietnam—both of which underwent rapid growth and poverty reduction in the 1990s—have made less progress on democratic governance than on some other aspects of governance.

2. The country policy and institutional assessments (CPIAs) rate 20 dimensions of countries' policies and institutions categorized into four broad groups: economic management, structural policies, public sector management and institutions, and policies for social inclusion and equity. The first three categories relate closely to the investment climate and the last one to empowerment. The CPIAs should no doubt be refined, but they nevertheless do provide a useful working framework. As noted earlier, country policies have improved in recent years: between 1995 and 2001, the overall CPIA index for developing countries increased significantly, rising nearly half a point in the six-point index.

3. The Operations Evaluation Department's outcome ratings typically measure the extent to which an operation has achieved its objectives, and thus provide a good indicator of the strength of the link between adjustment lending and the implementation of the program being supported by the loans. The share of operations rated as satisfactory in outcome increased from 68 percent in fiscal 1990–94 to 86 percent in fiscal 1999–2000. Weighted by lending volumes, the increase was even more pronounced, from 73 percent satisfactory in fiscal 1990–94 to 97 percent in fiscal 1999–2000. The department's ratings of long-term sustainability (an assessment of resilience to risk) and of institutional development (the contribution of operations to capacity building) also increased during the same period.

4. For details on the MDGs, see http://www.developmentgoals.org.

5. The PRSPs embody the principles of the Comprehensive Development Framework approach, which lays out the following principles for assisting developing countries: partnership among recipient countries and donors; comprehensive diagnosis and vision, encompassing not only economic policies, but institution building and human development;

and country ownership of development approaches. (Information is available at http://www.worldbank.org/cdf.)

6. Some critics have argued that the reverse is true, that is, when finance is in the mix, borrowing countries go through the motions of being interested in the outside ideas, when all that really motivates their engagement with the Bank is the prospect of money. Certainly this can happen, but streamlined use of conditionality and better country ownership of reforms can and do remove much of the incentive for such game playing by recipients.

7. The Bank's country policy and institutional assessment ratings of country policies and institutions, described earlier, are another tool for measuring many of the intermediate variables that point to development progress, from macroeconomic policies, to governance, to social inclusion.

References

The word "processed" describes informally reproduced works that may not be commonly available in libraries.

Becker, Gary, Tomas Philipson, and Rodrigo Soares. 2002. "Growth and Mortality in Less Developed Nations." University of Chicago. Processed.

Bourguignon, François, Luiz Pereira da Silva, and Nicholas Stern. Forthcoming. "Evaluating the Poverty Impact of Policies: Some Analytical Challenges." In Catherine Pattillo and Ashoka Mody, eds., *Proceedings of an IMF Conference on Macroeconomic Policies and Poverty*. Washington, D.C.: International Monetary Fund.

Collier, Paul, and David Dollar. 2002. "Aid Allocation and Poverty Reduction." *European Economic Review* 46(8): 1475–1500.

Collier, Paul, and Anke Hoeffler. 2002. "Aid, Policy, and Growth in Postconflict Societies." Policy Research Working Paper no. 2902. World Bank, Washington, D.C.

Collier, Paul, Shantayanan Devarajan, and David R. Dollar. 2001. "Measuring IDA's Effectiveness." World Bank, Washington, D.C. Processed.

Deininger, Klaus, Lyn Squire, and Swati Basu. 1998. "Does Economic Analysis Improve the Quality of Foreign Assistance?" *World Bank Economic Review* 12(3): 385–418.

Devarajan, Shantayanan, David R. Dollar, and Torgny Holmgren. 2001. *Aid and Reform in Africa*. Washington, D.C.: World Bank.

Devarajan, Shantayanan, Margaret J. Miller, and Eric V. Swanson. 2002. "Goals for Development: History, Prospects, and Costs." World Bank, Washington, D.C. Processed.

Dollar, David, and William Easterly. 1999. "The Search for the Key: Aid, Investment, and Policies in Africa." *Journal of African Economies* 8(4): 546–77.

Dollar, David, and Jakob Svensson. 2000. "What Explains the Success or Failure of Structural Adjustment Programmes?" *Economic Journal* 110(466): 894–917.

Goldin, Ian, Halsey Rogers, and Nicholas Stern. 2002. "The Role and Effectiveness of Development Assistance: Lessons from World Bank Experience." In *The Case for Aid*. Washington, D.C.: World Bank.

Hjertholm, P., and J. Lauresen. 2000. "Macroeconomic Issues in Foreign Aid." Institute of Economics Discussion Paper. University of Copenhagen, Copenhagen.

Kremer, Michael. 2002. "Incentives, Institutions, and Development Assistance." Paper presented at the U.S. Agency for International Development/Center for Institutional Reform and the Informal Sector Forum Series on the Role of Institutions in Promoting Growth, January 11, Washington, D.C.

Nyoni, T. 1998. "Foreign Aid and Economic Performance in Tanzania." *World Development* 26.

Pritchett, Lant, and Lawrence H. Summers. 1996. "Wealthier Is Healthier." *Journal of Human Resources* 31(4): 841–68.

Schultz, T. Paul. 1987. *Education Investments and Returns in Economic Development.* Discussion Paper no. 115. New Haven, Conn.: Yale University, Economic Growth Center.

Stern, Nicholas. 2001. *A Strategy for Development.* Washington, D.C.: World Bank.

———. 2002. "Dynamic Development: Innovation and Inclusion." Presented at the Munich Lectures in Economics, November 19–21, University of Munich, Center for Economic Studies.

Wilson, John S. 2002. "Standards, Regulation, and Trade: WTO Rules and Developing Country Concerns." In Bernard M. Hoekman, Philip English, and Aaditya Mattoo, eds., *Development, Trade, and the WTO: A Handbook.* Washington, D.C.: World Bank.

World Bank. 1998a. *Assessing Aid: What Works, What Doesn't, and Why.* Washington, D.C.

———. 1998b. *World Development Report 1998/99: Knowledge for Development.* New York: Oxford University Press.

———. 1999. *World Development Report 1999/2000: Entering the 21st Century.* New York: Oxford University Press.

———. 2001a. *Global Economic Prospects 2002: Making Trade Work for the World's Poor.* Washington, D.C.

———. 2001b. *World Development Indicators.* Washington, D.C.

———. 2002. *Globalization, Growth, and Poverty: Building an Inclusive World Economy.* Washington, D.C.: Oxford University Press and the World Bank.

World Bank Development Committee. 2002. *Education for Dynamic Economies: Action Plan to Accelerate Progress Toward Education for All.* Washington, D.C.: World Bank.

New Perspectives on Aid Effectiveness

DAVID ROLAND-HOLST AND FINN TARP

Foreign aid has undergone many fundamental shifts since the middle of the last century. During the 1960s and 1970s, the international development community added a multilateral agenda of development goals, institutions, and procedures to traditional bilateralism. Thinking about development policy was drastically modified from the early 1980s onward, and the evolving donor-recipient relationship as it exists today can best be described as uncertain and circumspect. In parallel, the global economic context in which foreign aid is implemented has been transformed in ways unimagined at the time of the Bretton Woods Conference.

Emerging from debates about the "micro-macro" paradox in the 1980s, the analysis of aid effectiveness became dominated by macro-econometric approaches during the 1990s. Convincing evidence appeared that aid works at both the macroeconomic and microeconomic levels, but the putative lessons learned from this inference vary greatly, and disagreements persist about necessary and sufficient conditions for effective economic assistance. This is true both with reference to more narrow debates about appropriate economic policy and to the wider institutional context within which aid is implemented. Since the mid-1990s, the donor-driven nature of many aid programs has inspired repeated calls for a new kind of partnership (Helleiner 2000). One response has been the increased use of the concept of ownership in the rhetoric of aid policy, but what this means in theory and practice is not entirely clear.

After a historical survey of the aid effectiveness literature, this paper turns to a brief empirical narrative on the changing relative importance of aid in the present era of globalization. As a modest contribution to renewing perspectives on development assistance, this is followed by a set of five guidelines for effective aid relationships in the future before conclusions are drawn.

This is an updated version of the paper presented at the Annual Bank Conference on Development Economics. David Roland-Holst is director of the Rural Development Research Consortium at the University of California, Berkeley, and James Irvine Professor of Economics at Mills College, Oakland, California. Finn Tarp is professor of development economics and coordinator of the Development Economics Research Group at the University of Copenhagen.

Annual World Bank Conference on Development Economics—Europe 2003

Retrospective

Economic development has been spectacular since the middle of the last century.[1] Encouraging examples of development successes abound, yet the evidence also points to a widening gap between the most and the least successful countries. Too many nations lag behind, particularly in Africa, and around 1.2 billion people have to manage their lives with an income of less than US$1 a day. Political leaders have repeatedly asserted that widespread poverty and existing imbalances in socioeconomic conditions are unacceptable and should be corrected through urgent and concerted action. In parallel, foreign aid commitments are under political pressure, and economic analysts questioned their usefulness during the 1990s.

The roots of foreign aid can be traced back to at least the 19th century, but the economic and social development of the developing world was clearly not a policy objective of colonial rulers before World War II. As Thorbecke (in Tarp 2000) argues, such an objective would have been inconsistent with the underlying division of labor and trading patterns within and among colonial blocks. Thorbecke also outlines how the concept of foreign aid as a contributing factor to development evolved within the broader framework of development theory and strategy during the last five decades of the 20th century.

In the aftermath of World War II, Europe faced an acute need for reconstruction and a critical shortage of capital. The response was the Marshall Plan, implemented from 1948 to 1953 and driven in part by a fear of communism and the desire of the United States to secure American hegemony in global trade and investment. The plan was massive even by today's standards, and was also extremely effective. It helped mitigate an acute scarcity of foreign exchange in Europe and gave rise to many of the elements of the existing system of aid delivery. However, the needs of the developing areas of the world were not yet in focus. The International Bank for Reconstruction and Development, established at the Bretton Woods Conference in 1944, was originally concerned with reconstruction in Europe, and the International Development Association, used to channel resources to the poorest countries on "soft" conditions, was only created in 1960. Developing regions did receive support from the colonial powers before 1960, notably from France and the United Kingdom, and the volume of French aid as a share of gross national product (GNP) actually amounted to more than 1 percent during the early 1960s. A major part of the rapidly increasing bilateral flows during the 1950s came from the United States, whose ratio of aid to GNP grew from very little to well above 0.5 percent, but colonial ties were strong and influential, and considerable continuity from colonial to postcolonial institutions was characteristic (Hjertholm and White in Tarp 2000).

After the success of the Marshall Plan, the industrial countries' attention increasingly turned to the developing countries, many of which became independent around 1960. Hjertholm and White note that this created a constituency for aid, and that the first meeting of the nonaligned movement in 1955 gave a focus to this voice, as did the various organs of the United Nations, notably the United Nations Conference on Trade and Development. The transition toward somewhat more independent, multilateral relations, as opposed to the traditional bilateralism inherited from colonialism, was beginning to emerge. In parallel, the 1960s saw a distinct increase in the share of multilateral aid, and the role of aid started shifting toward a broader agenda of socioeconomic goals that clearly went beyond the exclusive focus on promoting economic growth that was characteristic of the 1950s. The Economic Commission for Africa came into being in 1958, and the first of the three regional development banks, the Inter-American Development Bank, was established in 1959. The multilateralism of aid became even more pronounced in the 1970s, which saw an increased focus on employment, income distribution, and poverty alleviation as essential objectives of development, and indeed of aid.

During the 1960s and 1970s, economic progress was visible in much of the developing world. Adelman (in Tarp 2000) refers to this as the golden age of economic growth, but this era came to an abrupt end when crisis set in at the beginning of the 1980s. It soon became evident that the downturn was of a more permanent nature, not temporary as in 1973, and both development analysts and practitioners gradually recognized that the development strategies of the previous decades were no longer sustainable. Economic circumstances in the developing countries and the relations between North and South had changed radically, and adjustments were needed in economic policies. Achieving macroeconomic balance (externally and internally) appeared to be an essential prerequisite for renewed development. Thus macroeconomic stabilization and adjustment became important, and in much of the rhetoric of the day, nearly synonymous with economic transformation and development. The World Bank and others emphasized a reliance on market forces; an outward orientation; and the role of the private sector, including nongovernmental organizations (NGOs). In parallel, poverty alleviation somehow slipped out of view in mainstream agendas for economic reform, while still remaining at the center of attention in, for example, the adjustment with a human face approach of the United Nations Children's Fund.

At the same time, bilateral donors and international agencies such as the World Bank grappled with how to channel resources to the developing world. Net aid flows were seriously affected by flows related to recurrent indebtedness, and by the late 1970s, channeling fresh resources to many developing countries had become increasingly difficult. The various kinds of macroeconomic program assistance, such as balance of payments support and sector budget support, which were not tied to investment projects, and which could be justified under the headings of stabilization and adjustment, appeared to be an ideal solution to this dilemma. Financial program aid and adjustment loans became fashionable and policy conditionality became more widespread.[2] A rationale had been found for maintaining the flow of resources, which corresponded well with the major tenets of the ongoing "neoclassical counterrevolution" and the guidelines for good policy summarized by the Washington consensus. Aid continued to grow in real terms until the early 1990s, and as a rising share of the growing GNP of the donor community more than tripled during 1970–90 (figure 1).[3] However, after 1990, total aid flows started to decline both in absolute terms and as a share of GNP.

Many reasons account for the fall in aggregate flows, including the decline of communism and the end of the Cold War. Weakening patron-client relationships among

FIGURE 1. Ratios of Aid to Trade, Gross Domestic Product, and Population, Developing Countries, 1970–99
(index, 1970 = 1)

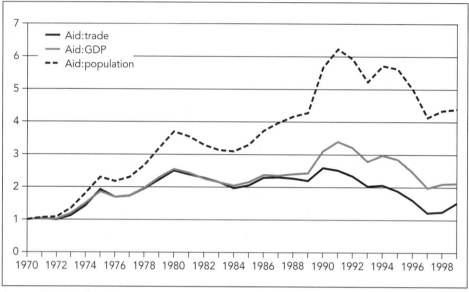

Sources: OECD (2002); World Bank (2001).

the developing countries and their former colonial masters also certainly played a role, and the traditional support of development aid by vocal interest groups in the industrial countries receded. Other concerns, including a distrust of bilateral and multilateral agencies on the part of developing countries, came in focus. These institutions were subjected to criticism, and at times were characterized as blunt instruments of commercial interests in the industrial world or as self-interested, rent-seeking bureaucracies. Moreover, acute awareness in donor countries of cases of bad governance, corruption, and so-called crony capitalism led during the 1990s to skepticism about the sincerity and credibility of governments receiving aid and the role aid might have played in underpinning economically or socially irresponsible regimes.

Hopkins (in Tarp 2000) points out that the use of governments to transfer resources has become less legitimate as governments have become less trusted on the part of both donors and recipients. One could argue that because more countries have democratized, this should mean that their governments are now more legitimate recipients of aid than they were in the past when they were one-party states. In any case, a first and superficial look at the available data does indeed seem to suggest that aid was ineffective in promoting growth, and a sense of ambivalence, and even failure, spread during the 1990s. While we have more to say about this later, aid fatigue became common, and prevalent perceptions clearly represented a serious challenge to any economic development rationale for aid. Such reservations should not undermine the primary ethical impetus for aid, that is, the betterment of basic human circumstances, but they do justify more rigorous thinking about the design and implementation of aid. After all, even though aid has generally fallen in relation to other resource flows it still represents a sizable amount of resources whose impact should be maximized.

Throughout its history, foreign aid has been subjected to close scrutiny by both academic researchers and other interested observers, as demonstrated by a huge outpouring of studies for several decades that in many cases have been characterized by the lack of a clear delineation of the boundary between policy advocacy and research. At some point, most development economists and aid practitioners have come across Mosley's (1987) so-called micro-macro paradox. He suggests that while aid seems to be effective at the microeconomic level, identifying any positive impact of aid at the macroeconomic level is harder, or even impossible. Much of this thinking was spurred by the focus in the 1980s on assessing the impact of stabilization and structural adjustment packages. Along with adjustment programs, the use of a wider variety of analytical tools to assess the impact of aid became common. Evaluation methods such as calculating the internal rate of return of projects came under severe criticism as the perception spread that aid channeled through sovereign governments is fully fungible. The internal rate of return approach also became problematic as donors started to embrace goals for aid, such as environmental sustainability and broader social objectives.[4] At the same time, discussions arose about the difficulties of macroeconomic evaluation of the before and after and with project and without project type, and methodological issues gradually came to play an important role in the aid effectiveness debate.

In parallel with all this, aid fatigue persisted. Donors' strong faith in the operation of markets reinforced this circumspection. After all, foreign aid has to a large extent always involved state-to-state relationships rather than market-based types of interaction. Fatigue was also influenced by the fear that foreign aid was generating aid dependency relationships and would therefore have negative incentive effects. The increasing perception that conditionality was failing to promote policy reform started to creep in at the turn of the century, and those involved realized that the relationship between donors and recipients left much to be desired. Kanbur (in Tarp 2000) argues that the accounts of failure are legion and presents a fascinating summary of both the background and the current state of affairs. He notes that while the donor-recipient relationship can be viewed as one of unequal power, imposing conditionality is, in practice, much more subtle, and that there is strength in the weakness of the recipients and weakness in the strength of the donors. Kanbur suggests that this is primarily because donors and recipients are so enmeshed—at the level of governments, agencies, and individuals—that where the strengths and weaknesses actually lie is not clear. Conditionality was no doubt imposed on unwilling recipients at the time of signing adjustment documents, but "the recipients know, the donors know, and in fact everybody knows, that these are paper conditions; the outcome will be driven by the need of both sides to maintain normal relations and the flow of aid" (Kanbur in Tarp 2000, p. 416).

All this prompted renewed interest in new kinds of donor-recipient relationships and in the effectiveness of aid. The outcome was calls for increased national ownership of aid programs, and both World Bank and other researchers started digging into the aid-growth relationship.[5] This was facilitated in part by the availability of much better data than in the past, and in part by insights emerging from new growth theory and the rapidly increasing number of empirical studies of growth. Early work in this area by Boone (1996) suggested that aid does not work and is simply a waste of resources. This was followed up with an analysis by Burnside and Dollar (1997, 2000).[6] They argue that some aid does work, and provided an attractive and seemingly self-evident solution to the micro-macro paradox, that is, aid works, but only in countries with "good policy." They based this on an aid-policy interaction term that emerged as statistically significant in their macro-econometric analyses of the relationship between aid and growth.

Burnside and Dollar, and more recently Collier (2002), have used the foregoing framework as a basis for suggesting that aid should be directed to good policy countries to improve aid's impact on poverty alleviation. This is partly justified by reference to the seeming inability of aid to change policy, a finding that has emerged from other Bank-funded research (Devarajan, Dollar, and Holmgren 2001). While the Bank's Monterrey document (World Bank 2002) toned down these recommendations, the basic thrust is still that macroeconomic performance evaluation and policy criteria (established by the World Bank) should play a key role in aid allocation. In an apparent rhetorical parallel, the president of the World Bank has on many occasions asserted that a development program must be owned by the country, not by donors or the World Bank.

The work of Burnside, Collier, and Dollar has led to heated discussions about what constitutes good policy. In many ways these discussions are extensions of more general debates and views about development strategy and policy, and the World Bank has gradually expanded the good policy concept to include a much wider and more complex set of characteristics than originally considered. Discussions have centered around what can be learned from the cross-country growth regressions that underlie much of the recent empirical work on aid effectiveness,[7] and academic debate on aid effectiveness has certainly covered new and important territory in relation to issues of empirical methodology and interpretation. Generally speaking, the robustness of methodological choices and data is a thorny issue that should not be taken lightly when research is used for formulating policy.

Dalgaard, Hansen, and Tarp (2002) offer an up-to-date account of the many contributions to this debate, which for reasons of space cannot be reviewed here.[8] They note that the single most common result of recent empirical studies is that aid has a positive impact on real gross domestic product (GDP) per capita growth, but displays diminishing returns. They go on to point out that political decisions to curb aid at the macroeconomic level cannot be justified, arguing that aid has no impact on growth. The accumulated research evidence is encouraging, and it suggests that the focus should now turn to how the effectiveness of aid can and should be improved rather than concentrating on whether aid works. In trying to move forward, it is hard not to be struck by the realization that the inferences drawn and putative lessons learned during the past 5 to 10 years vary greatly. What we have learned about what aid can do, what aid should do, and how to provide it remains clouded, and the gap between rhetoric and practice in aid relations continues to worry many independent observers and analysts.[9]

In sum, while the last 50 years of the 20th century saw a move away from colonial to postcolonial aid and increasing multilateralism, the early 21st century is best characterized as an era of uncertainty. Today's evolving donor-recipient relationships are unclear and circumspect. A particular dimension of this is that fungibility and crowding out remain important, implying that the macroeconomic impact of aid may well be different from expectations based on microeconomic perceptions, depending on specific country circumstances and characteristics.[10]

Aid and Globalization

During the period discussed in the previous section the world economy changed in unprecedented and irreversible ways. Most notable in the context of this discussion has been the rapid proliferation of international trade relations that have been built on a layer of open multilateralism. Regional and global agreements to liberalize international commerce have changed the economic landscape and nearly every economic policy agenda in ways that are pervasive and still only partially understood. Thus a reasonable question is how the mission of aid can best be pursued in an era of globalization. Without offering any definitive answers, this section provides a brief historical narrative to elucidate this question.

The growth of trade and developing economies and their interaction in recent decades have inspired volumes of statistical tables, policy analysis, and academic research. Here we adopt a more narrow focus on the components of economic change that might be more relevant to aid's place in the global economy. Even though much work has been done on this narrower topic, we believe that a new perspective on the facts and prior analysis is beneficial.

Consider, for example, the animated debate about absolute levels of global development assistance as measured by flows of official development assistance. While we believe that even greater levels of commitment to the world's poor are necessary to secure sustainable progress for them and for the rich, as figure 1 shows, historical data indicate that global aid levels have kept pace with both incomes and population in the developing world.

The figure shows total aid rising steadily in relation to income and population until the early 1990s, but stagnating thereafter. While some might note with satisfaction that the ratio of aid to GDP is now twice what it was in the early 1970s and that of aid to population has quadrupled, the international composition of these ratios varies tremendously between the high- and low-growth economies of the South. Perhaps the most revealing aspect in this context is the lack of net progress in these indicators over the last two decades.

How does all this relate to globalization? The ratios of aid to total world exports and imports and GDP reveal that trade has been growing faster than GDP, and despite a recent upturn, aid flows are about the same magnitude relative to trade as they were in the 1970s. Thus the trends indicate that flourishing international private commerce has not been associated with a boom in charitable activity, a link often observed in domestic economic cycles.

Although trade can facilitate poverty alleviation, it operates in completely different ways than aid and has a different mission. A primary impetus of aid is real and social investment, and its mission can generally be characterized as an effort to facilitate better living standards by making direct transfers, encouraging investment, and overcoming institutional and market failures. From this perspective, aid more closely resembles activities on the capital account, including one dramatically emergent phenomenon, foreign direct investment (FDI). While FDI is a private sector activity, and is therefore stimulated by different primary objectives than aid, it has conferred many benefits on developing economies that are consistent with the objectives of aid, including human resource development, technology diffusion, and, ultimately, poverty alleviation and more sustainable growth.[11] In this sense, the potential complementarities between private FDI and official development assistance to developing countries have long been recognized.[12]

The extent to which the complementarities matter depends on their real and potential economic significance. The trends revealed in figure 2 illustrate this notion. The most arresting feature of the data is the meteoric rise of inbound FDI, which has increased almost exactly 100-fold over the last three decades (while remaining unequally distributed across countries). This trend inspires reflection on the appropriate strategy for public foreign investment or development assistance in the future, especially as we seem to have already entered what can be termed the age of complementarity in relation to development assistance. This is a new era in which aid strategies must be focused more tightly on their core missions, with many

FIGURE 2. Macroeconomic Trends, Non–Organisation for Economic Co-operation and Development Countries, 1970–99
(index, 1970 = 1, based on constant U.S. dollars)

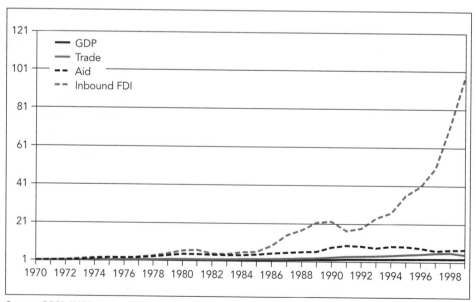

Sources: OECD (2002); UNCTAD (various years); World Bank (2001).

components of the grander aid agendas of the 1960s and 1970s being pared away. At the same time, aid institutions must allocate new resources to more strategic partnerships that can leverage private financial resources to advance socially beneficial objectives in recipient countries. This does not, of course, imply that tying aid to private investment from donor countries is appropriate. Tied aid represents a postcolonial anachronism that contradicts the efficiency principles of aid effectiveness as well as of domestic and external market liberalization. As such, tied aid remains an anti-competitive export promotion technique.

In consequence, we believe that perspectives on aid must change in two ways to deal with this situation. First, awareness of the implications of coexistence between public and private investment in developing countries must be broader and more refined. A better understanding of the primary behavioral drivers and institutional mechanisms behind private investment, especially ownership and contracts, will be particularly important. The World Bank and others have drawn public attention to the concept of ownership, but the real microeconomics of property rights and entitlement in the marketplace is more complicated than rhetoric about stake-holding and community participation.

Second, official multilateral initiatives to improve public-private communication on development priorities would help promote more effective aid complementarities. Obviously institutions such as the International Monetary Fund have been contending with this "partnership" for a long time, but whether more traditional bilateral and multilateral aid agencies have awakened to the realities of aid and globalization or made the strategic adjustments necessary to exploit complementarities with private capital markets more fully is not clear. Indeed, multilateral coordination of public aid alone is still a significant challenge. To date, public-private coordination has remained primarily a domestic policy matter, with trade and commerce ministries simply working to promote market access abroad.

Let us review two examples of how this strategy might develop. Consider one of the primary missions of development assistance in its earliest days: providing liquidity for public investment in the absence of well-developed international capital markets. While this kind of capital market failure is quite different today, it has not disappeared. Even though investment resources are now available for an enormous spectrum of activities in the developing world, the public sector must still take the initiative in certain areas. These areas include the traditional social investment activities and long-term infrastructure projects, such as public health in rural areas, that offer low and/or highly uncertain private rates of return, but are nevertheless essential to the most economically disadvantaged. This is what we mean by refocusing on the core mission of assistance.

At the other extreme, we see private entities stampeding into infrastructure investments in the media, telecommunications, and energy. In situations like this, private markets appear to be delivering technological progress to developing countries rapidly and relatively efficiently, and one might reasonably question the need for public assistance. To do so is to underestimate the potential of complementarity, however. In the case of the media, for example, countries of the Organisation for Economic Co-operation and Development have long histories of regulatory evolution that can be conferred to developing countries, thereby helping them to use the resources of private sector development more effectively for socially beneficial ends. Aid certainly has a potential role here, and in this way bilaterals and multilaterals could influence the quality, if not the quantity, of inbound investment and its ultimate social impact. The same logic applies to public and private provision of health services, pharmaceuticals, food safety inspections, and so on.

Five Guidelines for Increased Aid Effectiveness

The previous two sections clearly indicate that the role and context of aid has evolved rapidly in recent years in response to a combination of economic and political forces. Even though aid no longer serves quite the same objectives or enjoys the prominence it once did, it can still be a potent catalyst for poverty alleviation around the world. We agree with Healey and Killick (in Tarp 2000), who argue convincingly that aid can be used to reduce poverty. Similarly, as Morrissey (in Tarp 2000) points out, aid can be used to promote international integration. Given its diminished political and economic significance on a global scale, however, the effectiveness of aid design and implementation is more important than ever, thus this section surveys five areas that can provide more insight in this regard.

The topics addressed here represent only a subset of the many issues relevant to improving the effectiveness of aid. We have omitted a variety of better known and more obvious suggestions. For example, we strongly subscribe to the view that the cause of aid effectiveness could be advanced dramatically if bilateral donors would simply improve their own policy coherence and better harmonize their domestic economic management, trade policy, and development assistance agendas. In what follows, we will not elaborate on this, concentrating instead on suggestions that offer fresh perspectives, with a particular emphasis on microeconomic issues.

Macroeconomic Perspectives

We begin by looking at aid issues from an economy-wide perspective, which includes, for example, macroeconomic topics and performance criteria as reviewed by Hansen and Tarp (2000).

Reconsidering Macroeconomic Evaluation and Allocation Criteria

Macroeconomic performance in general, and aggregate real income growth in particular, are certainly high priorities for development policy. Yet we believe that macroeconomic criteria cannot and should not stand alone in evaluating the effectiveness of development assistance. Whether or not, and under what circumstances, macroeconomic growth and poverty alleviation might be correlated is an interesting and policy-relevant empirical issue. Poverty itself, however, is a microeconomic phenomenon and needs to be addressed as such with a significant component of development assistance.[13] Ultimately, the target beneficiaries of aid intended for poverty alleviation are microeconomic institutions: small enterprises, households, and individuals. Macroeconomic metrics, let alone heuristic and quasi-political rules of thumb such as good or bad government policies, cannot effectively assess their creditworthiness and need-worthiness. In countries with poor macroeconomic conditions, including adverse business cycles and weak or compromised policy institutions, many creditworthy and need-worthy candidates are ineligible for credit they might be able to use effectively.[14] At the same time, a macroeconomic bias in favor of other countries would promote substandard credit allocation at the microeconomic level. In other words, rationing credit by means of macroeconomic criteria inevitably screens out creditworthy or need-worthy recipients, and many beneficiaries in attractive macroeconomic settings may be less deserving.

The literature on aid effectiveness, as well as the institutions supporting much of this research, clearly indicates that sovereign credit relationships reinforce a macroeconomic bias. Bilateral and multilateral institutions generally enter into aid relationships with national entities, and therein arises the preoccupation with quantitative and qualitative macroeconomic policy criteria. Our essential argument is that much greater care should be taken when applying macroeconomic performance evaluation to development assistance. This approach increases the risk that aid will be politicized and allocated inefficiently. Using generic government policy ratings to assess economies carries similar misallocation risks. Simplistic macroeconomic rules of thumb not only compromise more rigorous credit and need standards, but reinforce the adversity facing those living under substandard governance. Many of the world's poorest people live in conditions of substandard national, regional, and/or local governance, and unlike their enfranchised counterparts in countries of the Organisation for Economic Co-operation and Development, lack any tenable means of changing these institutions.[15] For aid agencies to compound the misfortunes of these people with discriminatory aid allocation would be ironic.

Assisting poor people in complex, poor policy and bad governance environments is clearly far from easy; however, donors should not use this as an excuse to turn away from these challenges, especially because aid may well be one of a limited number of viable instruments that could help promote change. Few would probably disagree that sustained aid to NGOs during the apartheid regime in South Africa played a significant role in furthering change. Similarly, in most environments much can be done to pursue social investments in the area of education and health, both of which directly benefit poor people.

Finally, the use of the ownership concept is often misplaced in the national (government) macroeconomic context. Nothing is wrong with the concept of ownership as such, but governments have varying degrees of ownership over policies and do not "own" some at all. Indeed, many governments do not even provide a single policy line. Different parts of the government adhere to different policies depending on how close they are to donors and on the preferences of state actors in each ministry. What genuine ownership entails is therefore neither obvious nor transparent,[16] particularly when microeconomic actors are omitted, yet it is precisely these actors whose incentives and interests will determine much of aid's real effectiveness.

Assessing Foreign Exchange Risk, Local Currency Credit, and Macroeconomic Moral Hazard

Two critically important focal points in the context of sustained development assistance—as opposed to short-term macroeconomic stabilization—are quality of contracts and microeconomic appraisal. While we discuss both these issues from a microeconomic perspective later, the nature of sovereign relations makes contract quality just as important at the macroeconomic level. Better contracts, particularly those that capture the realities of incentive problems endemic to principal-agent relationships, can improve aid effectiveness at both the macroeconomic and microeconomic levels and can potentially help infuse the ownership concept with genuine meaning. They would also facilitate more truly independent monitoring of aid relations, as advocated by, for example, Helleiner (2000).

As a macroeconomic example, consider the currency of denomination for development assistance loans. Many critics of foreign assistance have argued that credit denominated in dollars or other hard currency has conferred excessive foreign exchange risk upon poor borrowers. Some have even asserted that this risk amounts to a subsidy for hard currency donors, because borrowers are obliged to accumulate debt in foreign currency, effectively financing the lenders' current account deficits. In response to this and other criticisms, a significant interest in promoting local currency aid and other commercial finance is emerging. For example, at its most recent annual meeting the Asian Development Bank floated the idea of converting its future assistance to local currency bond finance. This would achieve at least two objectives: transferring foreign exchange risk to the lender and promoting the development of domestic financial markets in the borrowing country.

While such objectives seem laudable, they ignore a serious problem of moral hazard that arises in the macroeconomic management context. Countries with substantial aid obligations of this type would be sorely tempted to mitigate their external liabilities with inflationary policies. With this in mind, developing a middle ground for aid finance using a weighted basket of currencies to overcome incentive problems on the part of both lenders and borrowers might be advisable.

Microeconomic Perspectives

In reality, and despite all the rhetoric of the aid community, aid and lending relationships involve complex contractual and agency relationships that are essentially microeconomic in nature. Even though the beneficiary signatories to aid agreements or contracts often have macroeconomic authority, they behave like microeconomic agents and their strategic environment is often partially in conflict with that of the donor or lender. Nowhere is this incentive paradox more apparent than in lending for development assistance.

This section discusses aspects of contract theory that may contribute to overcoming these incentive problems.[17] In many cases we emphasize the idea of ownership, particularly the localization of ownership. By this we do not mean abstract or rhetorical notions of stakeholding or community participation, but contractual ownership, with its appurtenant entitlements and responsibilities. Whether because of its paternalistic, bilateral tradition or the bias of sovereign lending arrangements, the aid relationship has been relatively weak in relation to the recognition of local ownership principles. We believe this has been detrimental to aid effectiveness for many reasons, not least of which because it has diluted accountability and promoted such practices as rent-seeking, fungibility, and aid arbitrage.

Decentralizing Sovereign Credit

Bilaterals, and especially multilaterals, often find themselves facing the dilemma of extending 15- to 30-year credit to governments that are clearly influenced by more short-run (3- to 5-year) policy priorities. This reinforces the macroeconomic, heuristic rule biases discussed earlier, because national governments have the authority to barter longer-term repayment commitments for short-term liquidity or political gain. Sovereignty is obviously not negotiable, but ways may be available to restructure lending agreements to limit the uncertainty associated with political transition. The point is that an aid contract must identify a good local partner and decisionmaker that both understands the benefits and is responsible for obligations. In many cases the central government may not be the best choice, so an attractive approach is decentralization, whereby those providing loans and performance-based grants enlist the help of regional and local agencies and do so within clear, statutory contract mechanisms.[18] Ideally, these would include both performance criteria and direct financial responsibility, such as co-payment provisions and even collateral.[19] Most decentralization entails the conferral of local authority, and in the case of co-payment might require new systems of domestic entitlement, including direct income that can be taxed for debt service.[20]

For example, an upland water retention scheme could be coupled with local water resale rights to finance co-payment. National, and even regional, governments might not favor such statutory reforms, but provisions of this kind have two important virtues: they help overcome the primary aid incentive problem and they improve domestic policy coherence by better aligning real entitlements with financial responsibility and performance. Lenders and donors might complain that regional and local governments are even more unpredictable than national governments. Our response is that creditworthiness and need-worthiness should be assessed at the beneficiary level and despite its relative convenience, national accountability often fails to meet the necessary standards.

Reconsidering Micro-Credit

Micro-credit can be viewed as one of the most extreme forms of aid decentralization, extending both assistance and fiduciary responsibility directly to the microeconomic level. Moreover, we argue that the much touted success micro-credit has enjoyed is directly attributable to the microeconomic nature of the contracts that underlie this form of assistance. Eligibility, evaluation, and financial accountability (as well as ownership) are based on the individual, and this aligns incentives to produce superior performance characteristics. This provides important lessons for designing aid contracts at the community, regional, and national levels.

This said, experience with micro-credit has not been uniformly positive. Indeed, recent experience in Bangladesh and elsewhere has revealed substandard loan port-folios and serious risks beyond recognized loan loss provisions. We believe these cases justify a reconsideration of the appropriate role and design of micro-credit schemes. Like many forms of aid, micro-credit is most appropriate when designed to overcome market failure. The failure in question here is that of the local capital mar-ket, which results in credit rationing. However, most micro-credit programs focus on both credit provision and interest rate mitigation,[21] but the latter creates a new source of policy risk. While credit is often rationed at the local level in developing countries, empirical evidence on what is or should be the real local risk premium or market rate of return is negligible. For this reason, assuming that local lending rates are too high, as is often done, may not make sense. Thus well-intentioned micro-credit schemes may overallocate credit and accumulate loan losses at unsustainable rates. In this context, note that the rates of nonperforming loans are not by them-selves a problem; the pricing of risk is what is critical. A financial aid scheme that presumes to increase credit allocation and fix prices at the same time assumes a great deal about the quality of its administrator's expectations.

Micro-credit policies should focus on overcoming quantity constraints, especially by facilitating market-based financial intermediation. This approach is currently working well in promoting commercial bank participation in the remittance market (see IDB 2001 for details).[22] Finally, credit institutions in countries receiving aid and their clients must not be led to believe they will be bailed out in case of financial problems. This may be hard for altruistically-minded donors, but this guideline should be taken much more seriously than in the past if unnecessary losses are to be avoided.

Comparing Grants and Negative Interest Rates

Discussion about increasing the grant proportion of development assistance has recently been extensive, both in terms of converting future aid from loans to grants and by forgiving outstanding loans. While loan forgiveness has many advocates, par-ticularly on behalf of the poorest and most indebted countries, opposition to large-scale loan to grant conversion is significant and influential. The main objection is that development assistance funds represent a kind of global commons, or community credit pool, that should be managed on a renewable basis. We instinctively side with the opponents of large-scale conversion, sharing their concerns about the sustainabil-ity of assistance, but we also believe that both sides in this debate are ignoring behav-ioral fundamentals. As long as an artificial dichotomy between grant and loan aid is maintained, significant inefficiencies in global aid allocation will persist. A better long-term approach would be a comprehensive and standardized set of guidelines for concessional assistance, supported by a continuous spectrum of aid schemes, ranging from outright grants to commercially-rated credit, so that the grant element is clear-ly identifiable. This can best be achieved by means of standardized aid contracts that stipulate interest rates varying from -100 percent, that is, pure grant aid, to LIBOR plus some commercial margin.[23]

Negative interest rates are an obvious efficiency refinement of the concept of concessional credit, while contract standardization would help to harmonize public and private credit instruments, and, eventually, to facilitate interaction between the two. Moreover, such transparency might help clarify the respective roles of different donors. In practice, donors' operations often overlap in ways that are seldom easy to relate to the underlying differences in aid and lending instruments and conditions.[24] Finally, while the idea of continuous aid pricing (positive and negative interest rates) can easily be defended on efficiency grounds, it does not by itself provide any guidance about what kind of projects should qualify for which interest rates. We therefore want to highlight the argument for public goods in extremely poor countries. In this situation, we strongly believe that outright grants dominate subsidies.

Conclusions

This paper was originally motivated by informal discussions about how changes in the global economy have influenced the development process and, inevitably, must inform the strategies of those who seek to promote development. A searching examination of the literature on historical aid practices revealed important insights about what has been accomplished. We also observed that the relative significance of public development assistance is much smaller than it once was. To be effective as a relatively smaller player in this new environment, public aid agencies must recognize they have entered an age of complementarity. For this reason, we argue that aid agencies should focus on core priorities; sharpen their implementation skills; and develop new strategic capacity for complementary relationships with, among others, private capital markets and NGOs.

The ideas presented here are part of a work in progress. We remain relatively agnostic about the political implications of our analysis and recommendations, striving foremost to stimulate rethinking and new debate. With this in mind, we stress that poverty and its attendant experiences are microeconomic phenomena. For this reason alone, most aid research and resources should be focused at this level. However, we also believe that paying more attention to the microeconomic properties of development aid will improve its effectiveness. In this context, we view decentralization in the context of economic accountability, including ownership—in the literal sense of contractual entitlement and responsibility down to the local level—as critical, in part because this more concrete approach to ownership is likely to significantly improve the incentive characteristics of development aid. In parallel, we advocate a more flexible approach to the grant versus loan dichotomy and more generous grants for public goods provision in the poorest countries.

In sum, we suggest a selected set of five guidelines for the design and implementation of more effective development assistance. In addition, bilateral donors should make much greater efforts to achieve policy coherence by reconciling, or at least clarifying, many policies that are in partial or direct conflict with generally accepted principles of development aid. These include domestic agricultural support, tied aid, and strategic assistance. If the ideas presented here are allowed to evolve in the aid policy environment, the aid community will also see more robust and dynamic links between public and private finance in the developing world. Aid agreements with better private incentive (ownership) characteristics, coupled with the steadying influence of private capital market discipline, may bring us closer to the dual goals of social progress and economic efficiency. If this happens, both the developing and the industrial world will benefit.

Notes

1. In what follows we draw in part upon many of the papers published in Tarp (2000). This edited volume synthesized contributions from some 29 authors and also contains extensive references to other contributions to the aid literature. For other overview volumes and further references see, for example, Cassen and Associates (1994); Mosley (1987); and World Bank (1998, 2002).

2. Mosley and Eeckhout (in Tarp 2000) describe the movement from project to program assistance in detail, and Andersen (in Tarp 2000) provides a sector perspective on these issues.

3. This trend prevailed even though as a share of GNP, U.S. assistance had already started falling in the mid-1960s, reaching less than 0.2 percent by the end of the century.

4. If analysts cannot value, for example, environmental costs and benefits, accounting for them in rate of return calculations is difficult. The same goes for valuing participation by communities in the design of projects at the local level.

5. See http://www.wider.unu.edu/research/research.htm for World Institute for Development Economic Research papers on the issue of reform ownership and development (research project 2.2/2000-2001).

6. The work by Burnside and Dollar formed the analytical core of an important World Bank (1998) study on the subject.

7. Solow (2001) suggests focusing more directly on total factor productivity or factor augmentation functions as the proper left-hand-side variables in empirical work and thinking more seriously about legitimate right-hand-side variables. In his view, current practice is much too haphazard.

8. See, for example, the August 2001 special issue of the *Journal of Development Studies* (volume 37, number 6) with contributions by many authorities in this area. Draft versions of many of these contributions were originally put out as working papers by the University of Nottingham's Centre for Research in Economic Development and International Trade. Easterly, Levine, and Roodman (2003) is the most recent study of the aid-policy interaction postulated by Burnside and Dollar and deepens their analysis by extending the time period and sample size.

9. In discussing current aid modalities, Helleiner (2000, p. 23) notes that "a curious 'disconnect' between donors' general rhetoric on these issues and actual practice on the ground" still persists.

10. In this sense the micro-macro paradox remains unresolved, even if those involved agree that aid works at the macroeconomic level.

11. An extensive literature deals with the impact of FDI on developing countries. See, for example, Borensztein, de Gregorio, and Lee (1998); de Mello (1997, 1999); Fung, Zeng, and Zhu (1999); Nair-Reichert and Weinhold (2001); UNCTAD (1999); and Zhang (2001) for a focus on empirical analysis of FDI and growth.

12. Mozambique is an excellent example of the complementarity of aid and FDI. If aid had not been used to stabilize the postwar economy and to help start rebuilding institutions, Mozambique is unlikely to have received as much FDI as it has in recent years.

13. Thus while growth should certainly be promoted, it is seldom enough to alleviate poverty. The pattern of growth remains critically important. See, for example, http://www.wider.unu.edu/conference/conference-2001-1/conference1.htm for papers from a World Institute for Development Economic Research conference on growth and poverty.

14. Caution against the overuse of macroeconomic criteria is especially warranted in post-conflict societies. Addison (in Tarp 2000) addresses the complex issues related to aid and conflict, and simplistic rules of thumb would certainly rule out aid to such postconflict countries as Afghanistan and Timor-Leste at present, but these are precisely the countries that need better macroeconomic policy institutions. The ongoing debate about the allocation of the so-called U.S. Millennium Challenge Account illustrates that the overuse of macroeconomic criteria is equally an issue in noncrisis situations (see, for example, Hiebert 2003).

15. For those interested in cross-country empirical approaches, see Dalgaard, Hansen, and Tarp (2002) for an elaboration of why the endogeneity of policies and institutions should be taken more seriously than in much of the existing analytical work.

16. A large literature is available on microeconomic institutions in development (see, for example, Altonji, Hayashi, and Kotlikoff 1989; Fafchamps 1992), but relatively little work has been done on the potential to link them more directly with aid relationships.

17. The issues raised here are supported by an extensive parallel theoretical literature, although it has only been partially directed at the aid effectiveness debate. Good examples include Gjesdal (1982); Mace (1991); Rogerson (1985); Rosenzweig (1988); Spear and Srivastava (1987); and Thomas and Worrall (1990).

18. The microeconomic literature on these issues extends back to early work on agency problems in agriculture. See, for example, Allen (1985); Bardhan (1980); Basu (1989); Bell (1988); Bhaduri (1973); and Stiglitz (1974).

19. In this context one could also argue that perhaps donor sanctions could be more credible at the local level, thereby increasing the likelihood that recipients will adhere to the terms of the contract.

20. A small but emergent literature pertains to this issue, including Atkeson (1991) and Besley (1988).

21. For more background on this issue, see Braverman and Stiglitz (1982): Stiglitz (1974); and Stiglitz and Weiss (1981). From an applied perspective, see Binswanger and others (1984, 1985); Rosenzweig and Binswanger (1993); and Udry (1990).

22. For further information see http://www.wider.unu.edu/research/research.htm on World Institute for Development Economic Research project number 3.2/2000-2001.

23. Large-scale conversion of development lending to a scheme of this kind would need to be supported by more comprehensive sovereign and other credit rating in developing countries, but this trend is already under way, and could be extended through a variety of public-private partnerships in global capital markets.

24. Making aid-related credit contracts more efficient, particularly in concert with decentralization, will require greater attention to intertemporal microeconomic behavior. Fortunately, a large literature is now available to support this analysis, for example, Deaton (1992); Deaton and Paxson (1994); Green (1987); Hayashi (1987); and Hayashi, Altonji, and Kotlikoff (1996) in the context of households and villages, and more generally, Prescott and Wallace (1987). Also relevant are Altug and Miller (1990) and Atkeson and Lucas (1992).

References

Allen, Franklin. 1985. "On the Fixed Nature of Sharecropping Contracts." *Economic Journal* 95(377): 30–48.

Altonji, Joseph G., Fumio Hayashi, and Laurence J. Kotlikoff. 1989. "Is the Extended Family Altruistically Linked?" Working Paper no. 3046. National Bureau of Economic Research, Cambridge, Mass.

Altug, Sumru, and Robert A. Miller. 1990. "Household Choices in Equilibrium." *Econometrica* 58(3): 543–70.

Atkeson, A. 1991. "International Lending with Moral Hazard and Risk of Repudiation." *Econometrica* 59(4): 1069–89.

Atkeson, A., and Robert E. Lucas, Jr. 1992. "On Efficient Distribution with Private Information." *Review of Economic Studies* 59(3): 427–53.

Bardhan, Pranab K. 1980. "Interlocking Factor Markets and Agrarian Development: A Review of the Issues." *Oxford Economic Papers* 32(1): 82–98.

Basu, Kaushik. 1989. "Technological Stagnation, Tenurial Laws, and Adverse Selection." *American Economic Review* 79(1): 251–55.

Bell, Christopher R. 1988. "Credit Markets and Interlinked Transactions." In H. Chenery and T. Srinivasan, eds., *Handbook of Development Economics,* vol. I. Amsterdam: Elsevier Science.

Besley, Timothy J. 1988. "Tied-in Credit with a Monopoly Credit Market." *Economics Letters* 28(2): 105–08.

Bhaduri, Amit. 1973. "Agricultural Backwardness under Semi-Feudalism." *Economic Journal* 83(329): 120–37.

Binswanger, Hans P., T. Balaramaiah, V. B. Rao, M. J. Bhende, and K. G. Kshirsagar. 1985. "Credit Markets in South India: Theoretical Issues and Empirical Analysis." Discussion Paper no. ARU 45. World Bank, Washington, D.C.

Binswanger, Hans P., V. S. Doherty, T. Balaramaiah, M. J. Bhende, K. G. Kshirsagar, B. Rao, and P. S. Raju. 1984. "Common Features and Contrasts in Labor Relations in the Semi-arid Tropics of India." In H. P. Binswanger and M. R. Rosenzweig, eds., *Contractual Arrangements, Employment, and Wages in Rural Labor Markets in Asia.* New Haven, Conn.: Yale University Press.

Boone, Peter. 1996. "Politics and the Effectiveness of Foreign Aid." *European Economic Review* 40(2): 289–329.

Borensztein, Eduardo, Jose de Gregorio, and Jong Wha Lee. 1998. "How Does Foreign Direct Investment Affect Economic Growth?" *Journal of International Economics* 45(1): 115–35.

Braverman, Avishav, and Joseph E. Stiglitz. 1982. "Sharecropping and the Interlinking of Agrarian Markets." *American Economic Review* 72(4): 695–715.

Burnside, Craig, and David Dollar. 1997. "Aid, Policies, and Growth." Policy Research Working Paper no. 1777. World Bank, Development Research Group, Washington, D.C.

————. 2000. "Aid, Policies, and Growth." *American Economic Review* 90(4): 847–68.

Cassen, Robert, and Associates. 1994. *Does Aid Work?.* Report to an intergovernmental task force. Library of Political Economy Series. Oxford and New York: Oxford University Press and Clarendon Press.

Collier, Paul. 2002. "Making Aid Smart: Institutional Incentives Facing Donor Organizations and Their Implications for Aid Effectiveness." Paper presented at the U.S. Agency for International Development Forum Series on the Role of Institutions in Promoting Growth, February 25, Washington, D.C.

Dalgaard, Carl-Johan, Henrik Hansen, and Finn Tarp. 2002. "On the Empirics of Foreign Aid and Growth." Working Paper no. 02/08. University of Nottingham, Centre for Research in Economic Development and International Trade, Nottingham, U.K.

Deaton, Angus. 1992. *Understanding Consumption*. Oxford, U.K.: Clarendon Press.

Deaton, Angus, and Christina Paxson. 1994. "Intertemporal Choice and Inequality." *Journal of Political Economy* 102(3): 437–67.

De Mello, Luiz R. 1997. "Foreign Direct Investment in Developing Countries and Growth: A Selective Survey." *Journal of Development Studies* 34(1): 1–34.

_____. 1999. "Foreign Direct Investment-Led Growth: Evidence from Time-Series and Panel Data." *Oxford Economic Papers* 51(1): 133–51.

Devarajan, Shantayanan, David Dollar, and Torgny Holmgren, eds. 2001. *Aid and Reform in Africa*. Washington, D.C.: World Bank.

Easterly, William, Ross Levine, and David Roodman. 2003. "New Data, New Doubts: Revisiting 'Aid, Policies, and Growth'." Working Paper no. 26. Center for Global Development, Washington, D.C.

Fafchamps, Marcel. 1992. "Solidarity Networks in Preindustrial Societies: Rational Peasants with a Moral Economy." *Economic Development and Cultural Change* 41(1): 147–74.

Fung, Michael K. Y., Jinli Zeng, and Lijing Zhu. 1999. "Foreign Capital, Urban Unemployment, and Economic Growth." *Review of International Economics* 7(4): 651–64.

Gjesdal, Frovstein. 1982. "Information and Incentives: The Agency Information Problem." *Review of Economic Studies* 49(3): 373–90.

Green, Edward J. 1987. "Lending and Smoothing of Uninsurable Income." In E. C. Prescott and N. Wallace, eds., *Contractual Arrangements for Intertemporal Trade*. Minneapolis, Minn.: University of Minnesota Press.

Hansen, Henrik, and Finn Tarp. 2000. "Aid Effectiveness Disputed." *Journal of International Development* 12(3): 375–98.

_____. 2001. "Aid and Growth Regressions." *Journal of Development Economics* 64(2): 547–70.

Hayashi, Fumio. 1987. "Tests for Liquidity Constraints: A Survey and Some New Observations." In T. F. Bewley, ed., *Advances in Economic Theory, Fifth World Congress*. Cambridge, U.K.: Cambridge University Press.

Hayashi, Fumio, Joseph G. Altonji, and Laurence J. Kotlikoff. 1996. "Risk Sharing between and within Families." *Econometrica* 64(2): 261–94.

Helleiner, Gerry. 2000. "Towards Balance in Aid Relationships: Donor Performance Monitoring in Low-Income Countries." *Cooperation South Journal* 6(2): 21–35.

Hiebert, Murray. 2003. "More Aid, but New Strings." *Far Eastern Economic Review* 166(7): 12–14.

IDB (Inter-American Development Bank). 2001. *Remittances as a Development Tool: A Regional Conference*. Proceedings of the Inter-American Development Bank conference, May 17–18. Washington, D.C.

Mace, Barbara J. 1991. "Full Insurance in the Presence of Aggregate Uncertainty." *Journal of Political Economy* 99(5): 928–56.

Mosley, Paul. 1987. *Overseas Aid: Its Defence and Reform*. Brighton, U.K.: Wheatsheaf Books.

Nair-Reichert, Nair, and Diana Weinhold. 2001. "Causality Tests for Cross-Country Panels: A New Look at FDI and Economic Growth in Developing Countries." *Oxford Bulletin of Economics and Statistics* 63(2): 153–71.

OECD (Organisation for Economic Co-operation and Development). 2002. *International Development Statistics 2002.* Paris.

Prescott, Edward C., and Neil Wallace, eds. 1987. *Contractual Arrangements for Intertemporal Trade.* Minneapolis, Minn.: University of Minnesota Press.

Rogerson, William P. 1985. "Repeated Moral Hazard." *Econometrica* 53(1): 69–76.

Rosenzweig, Mark R. 1988. "Risk, Implicit Contracts, and the Family in Rural Areas of Low-Income Countries." *Economic Journal* 98(393): 1148–70.

Rosenzweig, Mark R., and Hans P. Binswanger. 1993. "Wealth, Weather Risk, and the Composition and Profitability of Agricultural Investments." *Economic Journal* 103(416): 56–78.

Solow, Robert. 2001. "Applying Growth Theory across Countries." *World Bank Economic Review* 15(2): 283–88.

Spear, Steve E., and Sanjav Srivastava. 1987. "On Repeated Moral Hazard with Discounting." *Review of Economic Studies* 54(4): 599–618.

Stiglitz, Joseph E. 1974. "Incentives and Risk Sharing in Sharecropping." *Review of Economic Studies* 41(2): 219–55.

Stiglitz, Joseph E., and Andrew Weiss. 1981. "Credit Rationing in Markets with Imperfect Information." *American Economic Review* 71(3): 393–410

Tarp, Finn, ed. 2000. *Foreign Aid and Development: Lessons Learnt and Directions for the Future.* London and New York: Routledge.

Thomas, Jonathan, and Tim Worrall. 1990. "Income Fluctuation and Asymmetric Information: An Example of a Repeated Principal-Agent Problem." *Journal of Economic Theory* 51(2): 367–90.

Udry, Christopher. 1990. "Credit Markets in Northern Nigeria: Credit as Insurance in a Rural Economy." *World Bank Economic Review* 4(3): 251–69.

UNCTAD (United Conference on Trade and Development). 1999. *World Investment Report: Foreign Direct Investment and the Challenge of Development—Overview.* New York and Geneva: United Nations.

———. Various years. *World Investment Report.* New York and Geneva: United Nations.

World Bank. 1998. *Assessing Aid: What Works, What Doesn't, and Why.* New York: Oxford University Press.

———. 2001. *World Development Indicators 2001 CD-Rom.* Washington, D.C.

———. 2002. *A Case for Aid: Building a Consensus for Development Assistance.* Washington, D.C.

Zhang, Kevin H. 2001. "Does Foreign Direct Investment Promote Economic Growth? Evidence from East Asia and Latin America." *Contemporary Economic Policy* 19(2): 175–85.

In Search of the Holy Grail: How to Achieve Pro-Poor Growth?

STEPHAN KLASEN

Recent policy and research documents from various institutions, researchers, and organizations have identified pro-poor growth as the most important ingredient for achieving sustainable poverty reduction (for example, Ravallion 2002; Thomas and others 2000; U.N. 2000; World Bank 2000b). As poverty reduction has become the central objective of development efforts—as evidenced by the Millennium Declaration, the poverty reduction strategy paper (PRSP) process, and the associated lending instruments by the International Monetary Fund and the World Bank—achieving pro-poor growth is today's most important development challenge.

Even though it is rarely spelt out, the usual implication is that pro-poor growth refers to growth that leads to significant poverty reduction (U.N. 2000; World Bank 2000b). What is less clear is how one defines significant reductions in poverty, and thus how one should monitor the extent to which countries are succeeding in achieving pro-poor growth. The policy implications of a call for pro-poor growth are even less clear. There are debates about the linkages between pro-poor growth and its constituent elements, the growth of mean incomes and redistribution (Bourguignon 2001; Dollar and Kraay 2002; Ravallion 2002; Thomas and others 2000); the sectoral, regional, and functional composition of pro-poor growth (Ames and others 2000; Ravallion and Datt 2002); and the precise policy measures under the control of governments or of international development partners that can generate pro-poor growth. Particular areas of dispute include the macroeconomic field, policies for addressing inequality, and sectoral and regional policies. Despite the centrality of pro-poor growth for the formulation and implementation of poverty reduction strategies, few policy documents comprehensively tackle this set of issues.[1]

This paper addresses these issues by defining the terms of the debate and by identifying areas of policy consensus and remaining disagreements. It examines the

Stephan Klasen is professor of economics at the University of Göttingen in Germany. This paper is a revised version of a paper commissioned by Deutsche Gesellschaft für Technische Zusammenarbeit for the Growth and Equity Task Team of the Strategic Partnership with Africa.

Annual World Bank Conference on Development Economics—Europe 2003

measurement of pro-poor growth; looks at the linkages between growth, inequality, and poverty reduction, thereby focusing on macro linkages; examines the microeconomic links between the sectoral, regional, and functional distribution of growth and poverty reduction; and distills policy messages with particular regard to Sub-Saharan African countries before concluding.

Defining and Measuring Pro-Poor Growth

While a number of suggested definitions of pro-poor growth have been circulated, official documents from the international agencies involved with the International Development Goals and the Millennium Development Goals have not included a precise definition or associated measures of pro-poor growth. Policy documents usually imply that pro-poor growth is growth that benefits the poor and give them more access to economic opportunities (OECD 2001; U.N. 2000). These statements are vague and give little guidance to policymakers about how to achieve and monitor success in achieving pro-poor growth.

Academic researchers have suggested a number of measures of pro-poor growth (Hanmer and Booth 2001; Kakwani and Pernia 2000; McCulloch and Baulch 1999; Ravallion and Chen 2003; Ravallion and Datt 2002; White and Anderson 2000). Rather than discussing the merits of each of those contributions, I will begin by suggesting a definition and a few desirable requirements of a measure and then propose a simple measure that would meet these requirements.[2]

In the spirit of the policy documents cited and the academic debate on the issue, pro-poor growth should at a minimum involve disproportionate growth of the incomes of the poor. Thus it must involve absolute growth of the incomes of the poor and, at least in a relative sense, growth disproportionately benefiting the poor, that is, the income growth rate of the poor must exceed the growth rate of the non-poor.[3] To move from such a definition to a precise measure of pro-poor growth, further requirements need to be specified.

A first requirement of such a measure is that it should clearly differentiate between pro-poor growth and other types of economic growth, while at the same time it should indicate the *amount* of pro-poor growth, that is, it should answer the following questions: Was growth pro-poor? How large was pro-poor growth? This requirement rules out the proposals by McCulloch and Baulch (1999), who compare actual income distribution with income distribution that would result from distribution-neutral growth, and Kakwani and Pernia (2000), whose pro-poor growth index is the ratio of total poverty reduction to poverty reduction in the case of distribution-neutral growth, because both only provide a clear answer to the first, but not to the second question.

A second requirement is that the measure should be sensitive to the distribution of incomes among the poor in the sense of giving greater weight to the poorest of the poor. The much used elasticity of the poverty rate with respect to the mean growth rate (the so-called poverty elasticity of growth) would not meet this requirement, because it does not consider information about the distribution of incomes among the poor.[4] Indeed, a high poverty elasticity of growth might often just mean that many poor who were close to the poverty line were lifted above it rather than high income growth among the severely poor, who should be of particular concern.

A third requirement is that the measure should not be sensitive to the particular choice of poverty line. This requirement rules out the poverty elasticity of growth, which is highly sensitive to the choice of poverty line, but also the measure proposed by Ravallion and Chen (2003), who suggest a measure of pro-poor growth that integrates the growth rates of the poorest quantiles up to the poverty line in the initial period.

Finally, the definition should allow an overall assessment of economic performance while giving more weight to the poor, and should therefore not be exclusively focused on the fortunes of the poor. The proposal by Ravallion and Chen (2003) would also not meet this requirement.[5]

Two simple measures that would meet all these requirements are the population- and poverty-weighted growth rates proposed by Ahluwhalia and Chenery (1974). The former is an arithmetic average of the growth rates of different income groups, for example, deciles, quintiles, or centiles. By treating everyone's income growth rates (rather than absolute increments) the same, it gives more implicit weight to the absolute income growth of the poor than to the average income growth rate, which depends largely on income growth rates in the richest two quintiles (Ahluwalia and Chenery 1974; Klasen 1994). The poverty-weighted growth rate puts greater weight on the income growth rate of the poorest quintiles and declining weights on the income growth rates of richer quintiles, and may therefore be the most suitable measure of pro-poor growth (Klasen 1994).[6] If either of these measures exceeded the average income growth rate, growth would be pro-poor,[7] and the amount of pro-poor growth is simply the population-weighted or poverty-weighted growth rate. An added advantage would be that these measures consider growth and distribution jointly, and thus emphasize, as do the proponents of pro-poor growth, that the two cannot easily be separated, either analytically or from a policy point of view (Ahluwalia and Chenery 1974; Klasen 1994).[8]

The definition and the proposed monitoring tool are focused on the income dimension of poverty. While most recent studies have emphasized the multidimensionality of poverty and highlighted the importance of health, education, and gender equity (U.N. 2000; World Bank 2000b), no corresponding indicators have been proposed for capturing pro-poor growth in this wider dimension, although one could easily think of candidates (Bardhan and Klasen 1999; Klasen 2000).[9]

Fortunately, causal linkages (with causality running both ways) exist between income poverty and most other nonincome measures of well-being. In particular, if the poor have access to better health and education and their access is equal for both genders, this will improve their chances of escaping income poverty. Conversely, higher incomes will typically allow the poor to obtain greater access to health and education services. However, these linkages are far from perfect, so that monitoring progress on these nonincome dimensions separately is also important (Drèze and Sen 1989; Klasen 2000, 2002b; U.N. 2000).

Poverty, Inequality, and Pro-Poor Growth

Recent years have seen a wealth of studies on the linkages between poverty, inequality, and economic growth. Without reviewing them all, the following points highlight some of the most important conclusions and caveats:

- Sustained economic growth tends to reduce poverty (Ames and others 2000; Bruno, Squire, and Ravallion 1998; Christiaensen, Demery, and Paternostro 2002; Dollar and Kraay 2002; Thomas and others 2000; White and Anderson 2000; World Bank 2000b). While this is the case on average and in the long term, examples abound of short-term growth episodes in individual countries that have had little, or even a negative, impact on poverty (Bourguignon 2003; Ravallion 2002).

- While comparable data on inequality across space and time are still rare and error prone, inequality seems to have remained fairly stable across most countries (Deininger and Squire 1998; Li, Squire, and Zhou 1998). Thus most growth has not been explicitly pro-poor, but has given all income groups, including the poor, roughly proportional increases in their incomes (Dollar and Kraay 2002). Important exceptions are the transition countries, the United Kingdom, and the United States, where inequality has sharply increased over the past two decades (Grün and Klasen 2001, 2003). In addition, significant short-term variations in inequality greatly affect poverty. For example, Bourguignon (2003) shows that short-term changes in poverty are due in roughly equal amounts to changes in mean incomes and changes in income distribution. The relative long-term stability might often be due to offsetting trends rather than to the absence of significant changes. For example, Bourguignon (2001) shows that in Brazil and Indonesia, demographic trends that lowered inequality offset labor market trends that increased inequality, leaving a net effect of little change.[10] This suggests that the average stability in distribution need not continue and is not immune to policy interventions.

- Higher income inequality reduces the poverty impact of growth regardless of the poverty measure chosen, because the absolute increments of (even proportional) increases in income of the poor are much smaller in a high inequality environment (Ravallion 2002; World Bank 2000b, Thomas and others 2000). In addition, in an environment of high inequality, the poor are further away from a poverty line, thus even the same absolute increments would lead to less poverty reduction (measured by the poverty rate or headcount ratio).[11] Thus the payoff to reduced initial inequality is twofold: it will immediately reduce poverty by giving the poor more resources and it will increase the poverty impact of subsequent growth (Bourguignon 2003).

- Lower initial income or asset inequality also seems to result in a growth payoff (Alesina and Rodrik 1994; Christiaensen, Demery, and Paternostro 2002; Deininger and Squire 1998; Lundberg and Squire 1999; Rodrik 1999; World Bank 2000b). Cross-country studies show that countries with lower initial inequality, particularly low inequality in land, appear to experience higher subsequent growth.[12] Such countries also appear to be better able to manage external shocks and reduce latent social conflict (Rodrik 1999). Moreover, household panel studies show that households with few physical and human assets are often caught in a poverty trap that sharply reduces their chance of economic advancement, and therefore harms the overall economic performance of an economy (Christiaensen, Demery, and Paternostro 2002; Woolard and Klasen 2002). Thus lower initial inequality yields a growth payoff, resulting in a triple effect of reduced inequality on poverty, that is, it seems to reduce poverty immediately, increase growth, and enhance the poverty impact of such growth.[13]

- The last two findings are also relevant in the context of gender inequality. Higher gender inequality appears to increase poverty and to reduce other welfare measures, because women appear to allocate more resources to food, health care, and their children's education than men do, and researchers have found that female literacy is one of the most important determinants of the effects of growth on income poverty (Ravallion and Datt 2002; Thomas 1997; World Bank 2001b). Moreover, gender inequality, particularly in education, in access to technology, and probably also in employment, reduces economic growth, because the economy fails to make adequate use of female resources (Blackden and Bhanu 1999; Klasen 2002a; Klasen and Lamanna 2003; Knowles, Lorgelly, and Owen 2002; World Bank 2000a, 2001b). Thus reduced gender inequality would boost both economic growth and the economic impact of growth on poverty reduction, that is, it would generate more growth and more pro-poor growth.

Apart from supporting a traditional emphasis on furthering economic growth, these findings suggest that pro-poor growth policy should emphasize the reduction of inequalities, particularly asset and gender inequalities, to benefit from the triple payoff to redistribution. While this has been recognized in theory (Ravallion 2002; World Bank 2000b, 2001b), no clear policy agenda for enhancing equality has been spelt out, particularly for high-inequality countries, where such an agenda is most urgent to further pro-poor growth.

The Sectoral, Regional, and Functional Distribution of Pro-Poor Growth

While the previous section examined aggregate linkages between growth, distribution, and poverty reduction, this section takes a more disaggregated look at the determinants of pro-poor growth. As the poor are not distributed evenly throughout the economy, the sectoral, regional, and functional distribution of growth matters for poverty reduction. Analytically, economic growth can be pro-poor in two ways. The first, or direct, way is a pattern of growth that immediately raises the incomes of the poor. This must be growth that favors those sectors and regions where the poor live (or are moving to) and must use the factors of production that they possess or are able to acquire. While this is probably the most sustainable way of ensuring that the poor benefit disproportionately from economic growth, it carries the risk that they will also suffer, possibly disproportionately, from economic contractions and high volatility.[14] The second way in which economic growth can be pro-poor, the indirect way, operates via public redistributive policies, especially via taxes, transfers, and other government spending. High growth of any sort could, in principle, be made pro-poor if it involved progressive taxation and targeted government spending on the poor. The government spending on the poor could either try to promote their inclusion in economic growth, and thereby improve the direct linkage between growth and poverty reduction (Thomas and others 2000), or it could simply provide transfer payments to the poor through a safety net that could become increasingly generous with the increase in economic growth. The former is clearly preferable to the latter, although the existence of some kind of safety net is important for the poor, and indeed, can ensure that they become direct beneficiaries of economic growth by allowing them to take greater risks and therefore reap higher rewards (Atkinson 1999; World Bank 2000b).

In relation to the direct way in which economic growth can be pro-poor, pro-poor growth that directly reduces poverty must obviously be in those sectors where the poor are and must use the factors of production they possess. The vast majority of the poor live in rural areas; most depend directly or indirectly on agriculture for their livelihoods; and the factor of production the poor possess and use most is labor, sometimes land, and even more rarely human capital (see Alderman and others 2000a; Ames and others 2000; Eastwood and Lipton 2000; Ravallion and Datt 2002; World Bank 2000b). Thus pro-poor growth must focus on rural areas, improve incomes in agriculture, and make intensive use of labor. While conceptually quite obvious, these points are often forgotten and are not reflected in public policies or in the allocation of public funds by national governments or donors (Lipton 1977; World Bank 2000a), yet most empirical analyses of these linkages have confirmed the importance of these relationships (for surveys, see Eastwood and Lipton 2000; Lipton and Ravallion 1995). Virtually all cases of successful development indicate that rapid growth and poverty reduction always involve an emphasis on improving productivity and incomes in agricultural and nonfarm rural occupations (Lipton and Ravallion 1995; Timmer 1988; World Bank 2000a).

In the longer term, growth can also be pro-poor through indirect linkages between sectors, regions, and factors of production. For example, over time high and labor-intensive growth in manufacturing and services can lead to a migration response from poor rural areas and increase the incomes of both poor migrants and those poor left behind and/or lead to improved opportunities for nonfarm rural growth. Similarly, growth that is intensive in skilled labor by the non-poor might, in due course, increase the demand for unskilled labor, as the two are often complementary. Or as the poor improve their human capital, growth can be pro-poor if it becomes more intensive in human capital rather than simply in unskilled labor. While simply assuming the existence of these longer-term linkages and basing poverty reduction strategies on them (which has been rightly criticized as a trickle-down view of development) would be unwise, those devising long-term development strategies to reduce poverty must bear these longer-term linkages in mind.[15]

Studies by Ravallion and Datt (1996, 2002) on the impact of the sectoral composition of growth in India highlight some interesting further linkages. First, they find that rural growth indeed reduced poverty in both rural and urban areas, while urban growth only had some impact on urban poverty. By sector, they show that output growth in the primary and tertiary sectors reduced poverty in rural and urban areas, presumably because those sectors are where the poor are and make heavy use of their labor (see also White and Anderson 2000 for a similar finding in a cross-country context). In a later study, Ravallion and Datt (2002) find that farm output has the same large impact on poverty reduction everywhere in India, but that nonfarm output has a variable impact on poverty reduction. This variability depends largely on the levels of female literacy, urbanization, urban-rural disparities, and farm yields. States with high female literacy, high urbanization, low disparities, and high initial farm yields experience a higher elasticity of poverty to nonfarm output, with the effect of female literacy being by far the strongest. These findings not only confirm the importance of agricultural development and reductions in gender inequality for poverty reduction, but also the complementarity between income and gender inequality and poverty reduction, particularly in relation to nonfarm rural growth. Related analyses in Eastwood and Lipton (2000) confirm that in both country studies and in cross-country analyses, improvements in labor productivity in agriculture have been more pro-poor than improvements in other sectors. However, cross-country analyses suggest that such improvements in agriculture may have a much smaller, or even negligible, effect in high-inequality countries, further emphasizing the need to tackle distributional issues.

While the just discussed sectoral and regional distributions of growth overlap considerably, the two concerns are not identical. Most backward regions are rural and need agricultural and nonfarm rural growth, but the regional distribution of growth is also concerned with differences in poverty that go beyond the rural-urban and sectoral divide and focus on pockets of deep poverty in particularly backward areas. Examples are northeastern Brazil, western China, and the former homelands in South Africa. A high concentration of poor people can often lead to persistent poverty traps, when concentrations of poverty generate negative spillovers through credit, land, or labor markets; through the quality of public institutions, for example, those involved in health and education; through the failure of an agglomeration dynamic to take hold; through too little public investment; or through sheer remoteness from markets (Christiaensen, Demery, and Paternostro 2002; Jalan and Ravallion 2000; Ray 1998).

Pro-poor growth must therefore try to stimulate economic activity in precisely these pockets of poverty (or encourage migration out of them to richer areas). Given the dynamics of poverty traps in such areas, reliance on the private sector is unlikely to succeed. Instead, strong government involvement is typically required, combined with incentives to encourage private sector activities. Recent policy documents on poverty give relatively little guidance on such policies beyond some focus on infrastructure investments and the targeting of safety net programs (Christiaensen, Demery, and Paternostro 2002; Thomas and others 2000; World Bank 2000b).

Regarding the functional distribution of income, growth is pro-poor if it makes use of the factors of production the poor possess. These are primarily labor, predominantly unskilled, and in some contexts land if the poor have adequate access to land. The poverty reduction records of countries such as China, India, and the rapidly growing East Asian countries show that poverty reduction was largest when growth made use of the assets the poor possess (see, for example, Drèze and Sen 1989; Ravallion and Datt 1996). While poverty can be reduced somewhat by simply reallocating the functional distribution of income, for instance, through high mandated wages or interventions to raise the returns to land, such static redistributions are unlikely to reduce poverty significantly unless they are also compatible with, or even foster, economic growth (Dollar and Kraay 2002). Some interventions are likely to be compatible with sustained economic growth, such as productivity enhancements in agriculture that raise the returns to land, while others are unlikely to foster economic growth in most contexts, like measures to artificially raise formal sector wages beyond market clearing levels.

The extent to which growth will be pro-poor will also depend on the amount of human capital the poor possess. As the empirical growth literature has demonstrated, growth is highly contingent on the state of human capital in a country. Thus growth of any variety is higher in countries with greater human capital (Barro 1991; Klasen 2002a; Mankiw, Roemer, and Weil 1992). Consequently, many of the returns to growth accrue primarily to those with high human capital, although some trickledown to the less skilled may occur over time. Indeed, the combination of high returns to education and high inequality in education is probably one of the most important reasons why growth is less pro-poor in countries with high income inequality (Deininger and Squire 1998; Thomas and others 2000). Conversely, it is one of the most important ways through which inequality appears to have a negative effect on economic growth (Deininger and Squire 1998; Klasen 2002a; Thomas and others 2000).

Thus heavy investment in the human capital of the poor will yield two benefits in relation to poverty reduction: it will increase economic growth and it will make growth more pro-poor. The record of East Asia, where high human capital accumulation (and rapidly shrinking disparity in human capital) promoted growth and poverty reduction, is an important illustration of these linkages (Drèze and Sen 1989; Thomas and others 2000; World Bank 1993).

This is true in accentuated fashion for gender inequality in human capital. Research suggests that gender inequality in human capital could boost economic growth and increase the poverty impact of economic growth. As estimated by Klasen (2002a), had Sub-Saharan Africa had East Asia's record in initial gender inequality in education and closed the gap at the same speed East Asia had, real per capita annual growth between 1960 and 1992 would have been between 0.4 and 0.6 percent faster. In South Asia, where gender gaps are more pervasive and closed even slower, growth would have been 0.7 to 1 percent faster. These effects only relate to gender inequality in education, and are thus in addition to the effects of average human capital on growth (Klasen 2002a; see also Blackden and Bhanu 1999; Dollar and Gatti 1999; Knowles, Lorgelly, and Owen 2002; World Bank 2001b).[16]

Regarding the indirect linkages between economic growth and poverty reduction, economic growth clearly provides opportunities for dynamic redistribution that can have a significant impact on poverty. Such dynamic redistributions are typically easier to achieve, because they will only focus on redistributing the gains from growth rather than involve potentially painful and politically difficult static redistributions of income (Ahluwalia and Chenery 1974; Bourguignon 2000). Successful examples of such dynamic redistributions include, for example, the policies the Malaysian government adopted to reduce poverty and increase the share of economic activity for the Malay population (Lindauer and Roemer 1994).

One way this indirect linkage can work is if growth enables the necessary fiscal resources to expand investments in the assets of the poor. The success of the East Asian economies in using the resources generated by growth to expand mass education among the poor, and especially among women, is a case in point (Klasen 2002a; Lindauer and Roemer 1994; World Bank 1993).

Finally, growth can generate the resources to expand transfers and safety nets for the poor. Such transfers and safety nets are clearly important from a welfare perspective and can also strengthen the economic self-reliance of the poor, as they will allow greater risk taking, and will therefore allow them to reap the benefits of more risky but rewarding income-earning opportunities (Atkinson 1999; Ray 1998; World Bank 2000b). Too great a reliance on such programs can, however, generate poverty traps and welfare dependency, especially in the case of tightly targeted transfers that are sharply reduced as soon as self-earned incomes increase, and thus constitute high implicit taxes on the economic activities of the poor (Atkinson 1999).

Note that all these indirect mechanisms, while potentially important elements of pro-poor growth, are contingent on a policy process that actually brings about these redistributions. If this policy process is absent or lacks the necessary political resolve, these opportunities will not be exploited. While the direct strategies will immediately translate into gains to the poor, the indirect strategies are not automatic and are mediated by contentious battles over the distribution of resources generated by growth.

In sum, this discussion suggests that pro-poor growth must, in the first instance, focus on growth in agriculture and nonfarm rural growth, must be labor intensive and land intensive where the poor have access to land, and must be concentrated in geographic pockets of deep poverty. Reducing inequalities in human capital by income and gender will both boost growth and make it more pro-poor. In the longer term, strategies will also need to take account of indirect linkages between the sectors and regions where the poor currently are and to which they may be drawn as economic growth takes hold. Indirect mechanisms to turn growth into pro-poor growth are also feasible, but depend critically on effective redistributive processes.

Policy Issues for Pro-Poor Growth

The discussion so far (and in documents such as Thomas and others 2000; World Bank 2000b) has focused on the state of research on the aggregate and disaggregated determinants of pro-poor growth. While this is helpful and clarifies many policy debates, discussing specific policies that are likely to promote high and pro-poor economic growth is critical. This task is difficult, mainly because researchers and policymakers continue to disagree on this topic. While the discussion will mostly be applicable to all developing regions, it will focus on Sub-Saharan Africa, where the poverty problems appear to be the most intractable.

We start with a brief discussion of past efforts to raise growth and reduce poverty in Africa, especially by means of the structural adjustment programs (SAPs) that were implemented throughout Africa in the 1980s and 1990s. After nearly 20 years of experience, it is now clear that, with some exceptions, SAPs in Africa did not have the intended outcome.[17] All empirical studies seem to suggest that the impact of SAPs on growth was typically negligible, nonexistent, or not statistically significant (Easterly 2000 and the literature cited therein; Mosley, Harrington, and Toye 1995). Debate on whether this was due to insufficient implementation (Christiaensen, Demery, and Paternostro 2002; Mosley, Harrington, and Toye 1995; World Bank 1994), external factors (Collier and Gunning 1999; World Bank 1994, 2000a), or inappropriate policies included in the SAPs (Cornia and Helleiner 1995; Mkandawire and Soludo 1999) is intense. Beyond this by now somewhat tedious, though obviously important, debate, however, proponents and critics of structural adjustment appear to have reached some consensus that a combination of the three factors is at work. In particular, there is now little debate about the increasingly unfavorable external environment for primary producers (Mkandawire and Soludo 1999; World Bank 2000a); about the less than full implementation in many countries, particularly those that were opposed to some aspects of the reforms and only partly implemented conditionalities so as to continue to receive funds (Mosley, Harrington, and Toye 1995; World Bank 2001a); and about some of the policies being insufficient, improperly sequenced, or too focused on short-term problems, thereby compromising longer-term development (Cornia and Helleiner 1995; World Bank 2000a).

As SAPs have, in general, not delivered higher growth (with some notable exceptions, such as Ethiopia, Mozambique, and Uganda), and as the distributional effects of SAPs appear to have canceled each other out, with some poor (typically some rural poor, especially those involved in agricultural production for exports) winning and some poor (those in remote areas and the urban poor) losing (Christiaensen, Demery, and Paternostro 2002; World Bank 1994, 2000a;), SAPs have had only a small impact on poverty despite their initial claims that they would reduce poverty (World Bank 1981).[18]

Given the mixed to disappointing experiences of SAPs in Africa, the outcome of the debates on the merits and problems of structural adjustment, and the findings on pro-poor growth mentioned earlier, what light do they throw on the appropriate policies for achieving pro-poor growth? While many disagreements prevail, it is argued that the debates on structural adjustment and on pro-poor growth have generated a core policy consensus on how to achieve pro-poor growth. Tables 1 and 2 try to summarize this policy consensus that many participants in these debates agree on and distinguish it from remaining disagreements and areas for further research. Table 1 focuses on policy issues and table 2 on process issues.

TABLE 1. Policies to Promote Pro-Poor Growth: Research Findings, Consensus Policies, and Remaining Debates

Policy issue	Research finding	Agreed policy implication	Areas of debate
Macroeconomic stability (see also individual areas of macroeconomic policy)	Macroeconomic stability is a critical (though insufficient) condition for pro-poor growth. The poor are hurt particularly hard by high inflation and high macroeconomic volatility.	Monetary and exchange rate policy should aim for low inflation and competitive exchange rates. Fiscal policy should aim for low budget deficits.	Should exchange rate policy principally be used to fight inflation? How quickly should stabilization occur in order to avoid a recession?
Monetary and exchange rate policy	Overvalued exchange rates and high black market premiums hurt economic growth and tend to be anti-poor.	A competitive and possibly undervalued exchange rate is a critical ingredient to ensure macroeconomic stability. Government intervention is necessary to manage capital inflows.	Fixed or floating rates? What is the role of capital controls to manage inflows and outflows during crises? Should undervaluation be a goal?
Fiscal stance	Large budget deficits hurt growth and are unsustainable. Rapid expenditure cuts can often undermine the delivery and quality of such critical services as health and education and hurt the poor.	Governments should aim for moderate budget deficits by broadening the tax base and, if necessary, refocusing expenditures (especially by cutting subsidies to state-owned enterprises and unproductive sectors). During crises, cutting expenditures rapidly is neither feasible nor desirable.	Mix of tax increases, tax broadening, and expenditure cuts?
Privatization	Loss-making, state-owned enterprises undermine fiscal stability, with negative implications for the poor. Some privatizations have been captured by local elites and have not led to better services for the poor.	Reform of loss-making, state-owned enterprises and parastatals is critical. Privatization processes must be transparent and competitive.	How to ensure and finance expansion of services for the poor? Should cross-subsidies be used to ensure access to the poor?
Financial sector	Severe financial repression hurts savings and promotes capital flight. Poorly sequenced financial sector reforms can be counterproductive and destabilizing.	Capital account and financial sector reform should be phased slowly; be implemented only if macroeconomic stability has been achieved; and be accompanied by tight regulation, competition policies, and policies to improve access by the poor.	Should the state allocate credit to priority sectors? Should the state be involved in the provision of credit for the poor? What policies should be adopted to mobilize domestic savings?

(Continues on next page)

TABLE 1. (Continued)

Policy issue	Research finding	Agreed policy implication	Areas of debate
Trade policy	An anti-export bias hurts growth and the poor, while import liberalization can be anti-poor and insufficient to generate a supply response. Diversification is essential for long-term growth.	Focus on removal of any anti-export bias (competitive exchange rate, duty draw-back schemes, and so on) and provide infrastructure to assist exports, especially for export diversification.	Is more activist state intervention (for instance, export subsidies or subsidized credit for exporters) needed to boost nontraditional exports?
Agriculture	Raising agricultural productivity is critical for pro-poor growth. Removal of price distortions is necessary, but insufficient in the presence of other market failures. Protection and subsidies in the North hurt the poor in the South.	A renewed emphasis on agricultural research and extension, rural infrastructure, and competitive marketing and input supplies is needed. Open access to OECD markets and removal of OECD subsidies is critical.	How can nontraditional agricultural exports be stimulated? What is the role of subsidies to promote new seeds and fertilizer use?
Industrial policy	Removal of distortions is necessary but insufficient for a vibrant industrial sector, especially small and medium enterprises.	Focus on providing infrastructure and services to the industrial sector.	Activist industrial policy? State credit or subsidies? Cluster initiatives?
Human capital	Lack of human capital by the poor hurts growth and poverty reduction. Education and health services have suffered greatly during economic crises and structural adjustment programs. Credit constraints and high costs for health are significant deterrents for the poor.	Increase investment in education and health, particularly basic education and primary health care; place more emphasis on quality; and reallocate public spending to the poor, lowering the costs of primary health care and education through greater subsidies (demand- and supply-side subsidies) and the use of subsidized community insurance.	How to finance the expansion of primary education and health care (especially in Africa)? Should all user fees for primary health care and (primary and secondary) education be phased out?
Asset inequality	Inequality of assets, especially land, reduces economic growth and the poverty impact of growth.	In relation to land inequality: remove subsidies to large landowners. In relation to other asset inequalities: provide microcredit and subsidies for infrastructure for the poor, such as hookups to electricity.	In relation to land inequality: What are the roles of market- and subsidy-based land reform versus quick one-off (partly) confiscatory land reform? How can land taxes contribute to speed land reform? In relation to other asset inequalities: what is the role of land and inheritance taxes in reducing asset inequality?

Income inequality	High income inequality is associated with higher poverty and lower poverty impact of growth. High initial income inequality may reduce subsequent growth.	Safety nets, social funds, and some targeted cash and in-kind transfers to the poor.	Increasing progressivity of tax system (for example, luxury value added tax and import duties, greater reliance on personal income tax for those employed in the formal sector)? Scaling up of redistributive transfer programs such as PROGRESA in Mexico?
Gender inequality	Gender inequality reduces growth and makes growth less pro-poor.	A greater supply of education for girls plus targeted subsidies to boost enrollments, removal of restrictions on female control of other assets, and political empowerment of women.	How should the expansion of female education be funded? What is the role of affirmative action policies in the labor market?
Regional inequality	Regional inequality can sharply reduce the impact of growth on poverty. There is a possibility of regional poverty traps.	Target state transfer programs and safety nets on regions with a high poverty concentration, focus on improving infrastructure, consider regional inequality in decentralization and fiscal equalization programs.	How should economic growth be promoted in backward regions? What is the role of regionally targeted industrial policy? What is the role of incentives to move industries or people?
Population policy	High fertility among the poor constrains pro-poor growth. Inequality reduction is often a result of fertility decline among the poor.	Emphasize female education and employment and access to reproductive health services.	What is the role of family planning policies? How should incentives for large families among the poor be altered?
Security	Physical and social security is essential for pro-poor growth.	Safety nets and greater physical security are essential measures to promote pro-poor growth.	What are the public and private sectors' roles in safety net provision, for example, in relation to credit and insurance? How extensive are these roles? How should they be funded?

OECD   Organisation for Economic Co-operation and Development.

Source: Author's compilation.

TABLE 2. Process Issues in Promoting Pro-Poor Growth: Research Findings, Consensus Policies, and Remaining Debates

Policy issue	Research finding	Agreed policy implications	Areas of debate
Governance	Poor governance, corruption, political instability, and civil strife are major deterrents to investment, growth, and poverty reduction. The poor suffer more than others under poor governance.	Reduce incentives and possibilities for corruption by simplifying rules and regulations that invite rent-seeking behavior; adopt merit-based pay and recruitment; and increase public accountability through greater transparency, better institutional oversight of governments (parliaments, independent boards), and decentralization. Donor support for conflict prevention, resolution, and postconflict reconstruction is critical.	What is the role of privatization in improving governance? How should governance be improved when the public sector is contracting? What is the state's role where state capacity is weak? Should countries rely on parliaments or extraparliamentary means for public oversight? How can countries ensure that decentralization reduces incentives and possibilities for corruption?
Private sector	An indigenous private sector is critical for employment growth and a dynamic economy.	Provide state assistance with capacity building and finance (especially microfinance) and promote dialogue between the state and the domestic private sector.	What is the role of national versus multinational companies? Should there be preferences for national companies?
Political economy of reform	The domestic political economy is crucial for success. Pro-poor coalitions are necessary to implement reforms.	Dialogue is needed to replace donor conditionality. Empowerment of the poor and local analytical and research capacity are critical for implementation.	What is the role of financial aid and conditionality under some circumstances? Is empowerment from outside possible or desirable?
Donor policies	Donors can assist with pro-poor growth when aid and advice is focused on the poorest countries and those with the highest poverty impact of policies.	Aid should be focused on the poorest countries that promote pro-poor growth, should flow through the budget and be accounted for using national processes, and should respect country leadership.	What should be done in poor countries with poor policies? Under which conditions should donors bypass governments and interact directly with civil society? How should accountability for resources be ensured?

Source: Author's compilation.

Beginning with policy issues, consensus that macroeconomic stability is a prerequisite for pro-poor growth is now widespread (see, for example, Ames and others 2000; Mkandawire and Soludo 1999; World Bank 2000b). This implies both that short-term stabilization measures are necessary in the case of a fiscal, financial, or balance of payments crisis, and that, more important, macroeconomic policy should aim for stability that would reduce the likelihood of such crises. In particular, investigators have repeatedly found that high inflation, particularly above about 10 percent, hurts the poor (and economic growth), and that large budget and current account deficits will eventually lead to crises in which the poor will suffer disproportionately (Ames and others 2000; Chen and Ravallion 2000; World Bank 2000b).

There is also some consensus on how to achieve such stability. In particular, most investigators agree that monetary and exchange rate policy must be coordinated to ensure low inflation, and that governments should avoid an overvalued real exchange rate at all costs because it will destroy efforts to boost exports, generate a balance of payment crisis in time, and is typically anti-poor because the rich have a much higher propensity to import. While the World Bank tends to favor a competitive exchange rate, some argue that governments should manage capital flows to generate an undervalued exchange rate so as to provide incentives to export and to build up cushions against inevitable external shocks (Ames and others 2000; Herr and Priewe 2001; World Bank 2000a). This was the policy stance that supported export-led growth in many East Asian economies and continues to be the policy stance in China. Given the success in these countries, it is well worth emulating (Rodrik 1995; World Bank 1994). In light of recent financial crises in several parts of the developing world, debates about the appropriate exchange rate regime (for example, currency board, fixed, floating, intermediate solutions) continue, and the outcome depends greatly on the country context, the nature of anticipated shocks, and the stance toward capital inflows.[19]

Regarding fiscal policy, the consensus is that governments should aim for low budget deficits, as only those will support macroeconomic stability and avoid disruptions and distortions to financial markets, all of which tend to hurt the poor disproportionately. Nevertheless, considerable disagreements remain about the precise mix of tax increases and expenditure cuts, on the extent of fiscal tightening during stabilization, and on what size of budget deficits are "low enough." However, the views of the international financial institutions appear to have shifted quite a bit from a traditional focus on quick and radical tightening via expenditure cuts in response to a crisis toward those of the proponents of alternatives to adjustment policies, which call for a more gradual approach that emphasizes broadening the tax base and greater toleration of short-term deficits during stabilization. This way, the deep contractions that have typically characterized the international financial institutions' response to crises might be mitigated (Ames and others 2000; Bevan and Adam 2001; Cornia and Helleiner 1995; Mkandawire and Soludo 1999; World Bank 2000a). More work is needed to determine the options for a return to a balanced fiscal policy in response to a crisis that reduces the danger of severe contractions or recessionary spirals.

Once a country has achieved stabilization, the fiscal room for maneuver has increased, and it should emphasize returning to those levels of public expenditures required to provide essential human capital and infrastructure for sustained pro-poor economic growth (Bevan and Adam 2001; Cornia and Helleiner 1995). To what extent this room for maneuver should be further enhanced via more revenue measures or used via increased spending remains a subject of disagreement and needs to be explored (see Bevan and Adam 2001 for a careful discussion of these and related fiscal and budgetary issues).

Regarding the role of privatization in public enterprise reform, most policy research agrees that loss-making state enterprises are a source of serious inefficiency, distort markets, often fail poor consumers, and divert resources from priority pro-poor investments. This was the main reason why SAPs pushed hard for state divestiture from most productive enterprises. At the same time, privatizations have often been captured by political elites, have yielded low fiscal benefits to the government, and have increased the costs of services for some poor. For a pro-poor agenda, loss-making state enterprises must be reformed through corporatization or private sector participation, private sector participation in public utilities must ensure that services are extended to poor households, and the process must be managed in a transparent and competitive manner. To what extent corporatization versus privatization is able to deliver remains controversial and depends on the country context. The use of cross-subsidies to subsidize services to the poor also continues to be an area of contention (Mkandawire and Soludo 1999; World Bank 1997, 2002, 2003).

Liberalized capital accounts and domestic financial markets used to be a key ingredient of SAPs, but here opinion appears to have shifted considerably. Liberalized capital accounts have often led to capital flight or high volatility in capital flows, particularly in countries where other macroeconomic imbalances persisted. Liberalized financial markets have not delivered higher savings or financial deepening as promised, but have often led to high spreads and high real interest rates (World Bank 2000a). The new consensus that appears to be emerging is that the capital account should be liberalized only gradually and only in an environment of overall macroeconomic stability. Financial liberalization should also come after some reforms, notably, reduced budget deficits to lower the public's demand for funds in the domestic capital markets, and should include proactive measures to improve domestic savings, access by the poor to financial services, measures to foster competition, and better regulation. To what extent the state should directly intervene to promote savings (for example, through forced savings schemes or through a public financial system) remains controversial.

A new consensus also seems to be emerging in relation to trade policy. In traditional SAPs, trade liberalization, especially a sharp reduction of import tariffs, the abolition of quotas, and the abolition of export taxes and marketing boards, was a centerpiece of reform efforts. However, recent policy documents suggest that the emphasis on rapid import liberalization threatened to undermine what little industrial capacity existed without giving enough impetus to the development of new export sectors (Mkandawire and Soludo 1999). Such liberalization has also hurt the rural poor, especially food producers, in some countries, and has created fiscal problems in others (Milanovic 2002; World Bank 2000b). Recent World Bank documents now seem to focus more on removing any anti-export bias rather than liberalizing imports.[20] This will surely involve removing some of the most egregious distortions in tariffs and quotas, lowering or abolishing export taxes, and reforming or abolishing state marketing boards, but does not require outright, across-the-board import liberalization. Instead, duty draw-back schemes for exporters and a competitive exchange rate are emphasized (World Bank 2000a). The remaining disagreement is about proactive policies to promote exporters, such as export subsidies and preferential allocation of credit, which were a standard tool of export promotion in East Asian countries (Cornia and Helleiner 1995; Mkandawire and Soludo 1999; Rodrik 1995; World Bank 1994). However, the renewed emphasis on infrastructure, human capital, technology, and perceived risks also supports the idea that simply providing the right prices does not generate a vibrant export sector (Mkandawire and Soludo 1999; World Bank 2000a). Clearly governments have a role to play in providing the necessary support—infrastructure, credit, technology, and possibly outright subsidies—for nascent exporters.

Regarding agricultural policies, clear consensus exists that pro-poor policies must focus on improving agricultural productivity and incomes, because the poor depend disproportionately on agriculture. Most observers also tend to agree that past policies failed because they did not provide sufficient incentives and were strongly biased against agriculture (Mkandawire and Soludo 1999; World Bank 2000a). SAPs have attempted to alter the incentives, primarily through promoting devaluations, abolishing marketing boards, and reducing export taxes, and have had some success in doing so (Christiaensen, Demery, and Paternostro 2002; World Bank 1994). However, because of other market failures, it is now widely recognized that a change in price incentives sometimes does not filter down to individual farmers, or that improving price incentives is insufficient for a dynamic agriculture sector. Moreover, a reliance on improving price incentives might well help poor agricultural producers, but will hurt poor food consumers, so the net impact on poverty can be small. To achieve a significant poverty impact, much greater emphasis must be placed on improving agricultural productivity (Eastwood and Lipton 2000). To achieve this, more public investment in agriculture, including basic and applied research, extension, rural infrastructure, irrigation, and rural credit, is urgently needed. Observers also agree about the burden of agricultural protectionism in the North on agricultural incomes in developing countries (Eastwood and Lipton 2000; World Bank 2000a), but disagreements remain about the extent of state activism in the promotion of non-traditional agricultural exports, the role of input subsidies, and the measures to ensure successful extension services.

While past efforts at industrial policy in many developing countries were unable to generate a vibrant and competitive industrial sector, relied heavily on fiscal transfers and protection, and benefited mostly the non-poor, clearly a long-term strategy for pro-poor growth must support the emergence at least of a labor-intensive, small-to medium-scale industrial sector. The experience of East Asia, where state policy strongly supported labor-intensive, export-led industrialization, shows that successful industrial policy can help deliver high growth and rapid poverty reduction. Providing a neutral policy stance is insufficient in most countries in the face of many structural bottlenecks, including poor infrastructure, poor financial systems, high risk, and strong international competition from established producers (Collier and Gunning 1999). Consensus is emerging on the need for state support in the form of improving infrastructure, information, and financial systems, while some call for more activist industrial policy of the type used in East Asia, including subsidies, subsidized credit, and some time-limited protection, although it is unclear whether many African governments have the capacity to provide such support effectively (Mkandawire and Soludo 1999; World Bank 1997, 2000a).

Agreement on policies to promote the human capital of the poor is also near universal. In particular, expenditure switching, especially in health and education, needs to focus scarce public funds on improving access by the poor to these vital assets (Bevan and Adam 2001; Thomas and others 2000; World Bank 2000a,b, 2003). Despite some progress, much more needs to be done, and this is a major focus of current PRSP processes. Instead of the earlier calls for user fees for health and education to mobilize resources, the new policy emphasis is on lowering barriers to participation by the poor, which clearly goes against raising user fees, particularly for primary health care or education (World Bank 2000b). At the same time, the full implication of these policies has not been spelt out. Should user fees in primary education (and secondary education?) be abolished for everyone or just for the poor? What is the role for demand-side subsidies? How should tertiary education be financed? Thus the policy direction appears to be clear, but the implications need to be considered carefully, and the hope is that they will be clarified in the ongoing PRSP discussions (see also World Bank 2003 for a full discussion of these issues).

As discussed above, there appears to be a triple payoff of redistribution for poverty reduction (reducing poverty immediately, increasing the poverty impact of growth, and promoting growth). As a result, equity issues are receiving much greater emphasis in policy documents than in the past, as well as in the PRSP processes (Thomas and others 2000; World Bank 2000a,b, 2002). Development practitioners disagree, however, on whether to target the asset and income base of the poor or to target inequality reduction as such. While both policies have obvious overlaps, they are not identical.[21]

Moreover, policy discussion on how to reduce asset inequalities is surprisingly infrequent. While land reform in countries with a highly unequal distribution of land, such as most of Latin America and southern Africa, is back on the policy agenda, the World Bank usually only advocates market-based land reforms, where the poor receive subsidies to purchase land from willing sellers (Alderman and others 2000a,b; World Bank 2000a,b). Despite some compelling arguments in favor of such an approach, the high fiscal costs of the subsidies sharply reduce the pace and scope of such reforms. Moreover, the redistributive impact of market-based land reform is minor, the efficiency gain may be modest, and the poorest are often excluded (Banerjee 1999; Binswanger, Deininger, and Feder 1995; Klasen 2002b; Zimmermann 2000). Virtually no discussion of partially confiscatory reforms has taken place, despite their great success in some East Asian economies (Binswanger, Deininger, and Feder 1995; Thomas and others 2000; World Bank 2000b).[22]

Similarly, policy discussions rarely consider other forms of asset redistribution, such as land or inheritance taxes. While tackling taxes of this type clearly involves administrative difficulties, such taxes could be among the most effective and nondistortionary policies for asset redistribution (Eastwood and Lipton 2000).[23] In the case of land taxes, progressive land taxes could also greatly help to speed up market-based land reforms. Apart from these unanswered questions, most observers agree that countries could use targeted subsidies to improve the poor's access to financial assets, for instance, subsidies for microlenders' operating costs, or to other important productive assets, such as one-time subsidies for electricity hook-ups or clean water access).

In relation to policies to reduce income inequality, consensus exists on safety nets, social funds, microcredit, and targeted cash and in-kind programs, especially in health and education (Thomas and others 2000; World Bank 2000a,b, 2003). While these policies are likely to help the poor in high-inequality countries, the scale of income redistribution through such measures is usually limited because of the small size of most of these programs. Finer targeting, often seen as the best way to increase the flow of resources to the poor, carries the risk of high implicit taxes when benefits are withdrawn as poor people increase their incomes. Thus research on the extent to which these programs could be scaled up to levels that would have a serious impact on redistribution is urgently needed. Moreover, using the tax and expenditure system for explicitly redistributive policies remains controversial, although there appears to be some scope for doing so, for example, luxury value added tax rates and import duties, greater reliance on personal income taxation, or greater scale of redistributive transfer programs (see Bourguignon 1998 for a discussion).

Regarding policies to reduce gender inequality, consensus exists on reducing gender inequality in education and in access to land, inputs, and technology, while affirmative action policies to improve labor market access for women are more controversial (Blackden and Bhanu 1999; World Bank 2001b). Comparatively little work has been carried out on combating regional inequality. That done has focused mostly on regionally targeted transfers, fiscal equalization, and infrastructure development for remote areas. Consequently, there is little discussion on the merits and problems of activist policies to remove regional inequality, such as regionally focused industrial policies or other policies that encourage populations to move away from the remotest areas to areas where poverty reduction is easier. Given the large regional disparities in poverty, this is another area of policy research where more direction is needed.

The role of population policy in pro-poor growth is rarely discussed, despite the research finding that high fertility among the poor can become a poverty trap and that smaller family sizes among the poor have been one of the most powerful ways to reduce inequality in developing countries (Bourguignon 2001; Eastwood and Lipton 2000; Kremer and Chen 2002). Nevertheless, broad consensus exists on the importance of female education and good access to reproductive health services in reducing fertility rates. The role of family planning programs and the issue of altering the incentives for large family sizes among the poor remain controversial (Pritchett 1995).

Apart from increasing average incomes, awareness has increased that the incomes of the poor are more volatile than those of the non-poor. Because the poor are so close to subsistence, they cannot tolerate risk, and therefore engage in activities that reduce risk at the cost of lowering their returns (Ray 1998; World Bank 2000b). While most development research agrees that disaster relief, public safety nets, public works, and state support for microcredit and insurance can help the poor manage risk, serious disagreements remain about such initiatives as crop insurance and social health insurance and the extent of state support for such ventures.

Turning to process issues (table 2), a critical ingredient of pro-poor policies relates to the need for improved governance. Delivering even the agreed-on policy proposals, let alone the more activist approaches advocated by some, requires peace, political stability, absence of corruption, and high levels of state capacity in policy formulation and implementation. Thus consensus has emerged that a functioning state lies at the heart of pro-poor policies (Mkandawire and Soludo 1999; World Bank 1997, 2002). During the SAP era, development institutions tended to see the state as a central part of the problem, and the recommended solution was to shrink the size of the public service, divest from state enterprises, and sharply reduce state interventions in most aspects of the economy. More recently, the state was seen as corrupt, clientelist, and an obstacle to good governance (Engelbert 2000; Mkandawire and Soludo 1999). While many of the past problems of the state persist in many African countries, and some may be deep-rooted and related to the colonial legacy (Engelbert 2000), the new consensus indicates that attempts to shrink the state have created serious new problems, including a weakening state capacity; a demoralized civil service more prone to poor governance, which appears to hurt the poor the most (Thomas and others 2000); and a private sector that can take advantage of weak state capacity in economic affairs (Mkandawire and Soludo 1999; Thomas and others 2000; World Bank 1997).

Given these results and the urgent need for a strong and functioning state to implement the pro-poor agenda, emphasis on strengthening state capacity and on expanding its role in selected aspects of the economy has been renewed. In addition, a new focus has emerged on improving governance by strengthening the state's democratic accountability and the role of civil society in monitoring governance and state performance and by using transparent meritocratic hiring and promotion policies and competitive salaries (World Bank 1997). Beyond this consensus, disagreements remain on the extent of state intervention given current capacity. While most agree that, unlike much state intervention in the past, the state should focus more on providing a facilitating, catalyzing, and regulating role for private sector activity rather than replacing or crowding out the private sector, some argue that particularly weak states in many poor countries should limit their involvement to providing the most essential public goods (World Bank 1997). Others, however, call for a greatly expanded role for the state and argue that if this is not the case, the pro-poor agenda cannot be implemented successfully (Mkandawire and Soludo 1999). Not enough is known about the best ways to improve state capacity, especially when starting from weak states with poor capacity. While much is made of the lessons learned from the role the state played in East Asia, how nations can move from the current situation in many African countries to the situation prevailing in East Asia is not clear (Lindauer and Roemer 1994).

There is also a corresponding new appreciation of the indigenous private sector and the large informal economy that will be critical in diversifying the economy and generating a labor-absorbing growth path. Both were viewed with great suspicion in the era of state-led development and both sectors suffered as a consequence (Mkandawire and Soludo 1999). SAPs have often improved the conditions for private enterprise, but have not typically emphasized indigenous enterprises and the informal economy. Observers increasingly recognize that the indigenous private sector and the informal economy play a vital role in pro-poor growth, because they are typically highly employment intensive, are less footloose than foreign enterprises, and are a critical ingredient of civil society that has been recognized as vital for pro-poor growth and better governance. As a result, emphasis has been renewed on improving the conditions under which indigenous companies operate; addressing finance, capacity, and regulation problems; and taking indigenous companies' views, complaints, and constraints more seriously than in the past (Mkandawire and Soludo 1999; World Bank 2000a). In addition, some are calling for a much improved dialogue and possibly state-led or facilitated coordination of private sector activities (Mkandawire and Soludo 1999).

Lastly, clear consensus seems to be emerging on the role of aid in relation to reforms to deliver pro-poor growth. One important lesson of the SAP era was that trying to drive policy reform from outside using aid conditionality was problematic and unsuccessful (Mosley, Harrington, and Toye 1995; World Bank 1994). This realization, combined with the emergence of the debt crisis in the 1990s and the increasing pressure from nongovernmental organizations in both the North and South, led to the new approach to aid that is embodied in the Heavily Indebted Poor Countries Initiative and the PRSP process.

In this context, recent policy documents have revealed a new direction for donor policies. First, rich countries must open their economies more to exports from poor countries, particularly agricultural exports (World Bank 2000b). Second, debt relief is critical to improve macroeconomic stability, reduce the drain on scarce resources, and allow investments in such priority sectors as health and education. Third, aid should be allocated to areas and countries where poverty is highest and the impact of aid on poverty is the largest (World Bank 1998). Fourth, countries should determine their strategic priorities and aid should merely support rather than drive these processes. Fifth, the administration of aid should be channeled through governments and make use of regular government accounting mechanisms to avoid the duplication of reporting, the balkanization of the development budget, and the excessive claims on the time of top government officials (Tumisiime-Mutebile 2001, World Bank 2003).

This survey suggests that proponents and critics of structural adjustment appear to have adopted a new postadjustment agenda for pro-poor growth. The disappointing experience with adjustment and constructive debate among proponents and critics of adjustment have generated a new middle ground of policies that could foster pro-poor growth. While this new consensus in many policy areas is encouraging, it is not enough. First, sizable disagreements remain that have not yet been tackled, especially in relation to activist state policies and policies to tackle inequality. Second, recent policy documents (World Bank and IMF 2002) have said too little about trade-offs and proper sequencing (see Bevan and Adam 2001 for a discussion of these and related issues). Governments should ideally be able to focus on policies that have the largest marginal effect on pro-poor growth. Some policies have a large effect on growth, but may not be particularly pro-poor; others do not have such a large effect on growth, but are extremely pro-poor. The best policies are obviously those that have a large effect on both, but not enough is known about which policies fall into what category.[24] In addition, implementing a package of policies is sometimes critical when individual policies may be insufficient. Here more work is clearly needed, as the current wish-list for pro-poor growth is long, and some kind of sequencing, prioritizing, and packaging is critical. Finally, differences between policy papers and actual operational work continue to be considerable, particularly among the World Bank, the International Monetary Fund, and many other donors, where many elements of this new consensus are apparent in recent policy work, but operational policies and procedures have changed only slowly. For example, only some of the new thinking about policy reform has influenced the first generation of PRSPs and the associated lending policies (World Bank and IMF 2002). Also many donors continue to rely on project-based support instead of program-based funding, and many trade-distorting policies in the North persist (World Bank and IMF 2002, World Bank 2003).

Conclusion

This broad and necessarily cursory survey has tried to move the debate on pro-poor growth forward by pointing, on the one hand, to the substantial body of knowledge and policy that appears to form part of the new policy agenda, and on the other hand, by highlighting the remaining substantial disagreements, unfinished agendas, and insufficient research in many areas. In particular, the critical policy areas of inequality reduction and the scale and scope of activist state policies to support pro-poor growth remain controversial, and further research and policy work is urgently needed.

This policy discussion has been largely from a technocratic point of view, focusing on the critical components of a strategy to promote pro-poor growth, setting aside the political economy of such policy reforms. One of the important outcomes of the debates about structural adjustment has been, however, that one can only ignore political economy constraints at one's peril. For example, an interesting review of the political economy of aid and reform in Africa (World Bank 2001a) suggests that despite conditionalities by donors, the success of economic reforms in African countries depended largely on domestic political considerations (see also Mosley, Harrington, and Toye 1995; World Bank 1994). In particular, successful reform was particularly likely in countries that faced severe economic crises with few economic options. These countries built up a consensus for change prior to reforms, had substantial indigenous technical capacity at their disposal, and used aid and technical advice to sustain the reforms. Donors were able to assist successful reformers, although donor aid sometimes also delayed reforms in other countries or reduced the ownership of reforms through excessive conditionalities.

Moreover, policies to promote pro-poor growth will inevitably depend on the strength of what the World Bank calls pro-poor coalitions (World Bank 2000b, 2003). Promoting pro-poor growth in countries with high inequality and where the poor are politically and economically marginalized is likely to be difficult. As a result, success in implementing pro-poor policies will depend greatly on creating and strengthening pro-poor coalitions, which can involve parts of governments, nongovernmental organizations, donors, and civil society. A free press, democratic institutions, and accountable governments will clearly help strengthen such coalitions, particularly in countries where the poor are the majority (World Bank 2003).

Thus the agenda for pro-poor growth should be viewed as much as a process as a set of policy rules, because success will ultimately depend on the domestic political economy of individual countries. In that sense, the PRSP process, which is also largely a process-oriented approach to policymaking, but makes, at least in theory, high demands on inclusiveness and country leadership, might be precisely the vehicle for moving forward the pro-poor agenda as it has been outlined in this paper.

While the PRSP process thus offers the opportunity to advance the pro-poor agenda within the domestic political economy of each country, the experience with the first round of PRSPs, while showing considerable promise overall, has also shown clear limitations. In particular, many PRSPs did not go far beyond poverty-oriented, often unrealistic, goal-setting exercises; lacked country-specific research to define a new policy agenda along the lines outlined here; and focused excessively on pro-poor budget policies rather than on a comprehensive economic policy framework that includes all aspects of the economy related to poverty reduction (Demery 2002; World Bank and IMF 2002). In addition, there are further pitfalls to be concerned about. First, by virtue of their poverty, the poor are typically poorly organized, and who will champion their cause in the PRSP process in not clear, particularly against possible resistance by more organized groups. Thus even adequate representation and input from civil society will not necessarily strengthen pro-poor coalitions. Second, to date the PRSP process appears to have focused mainly on the budget, and particularly on expenditure issues. While these are clearly important, this survey has suggested that a pro-poor agenda must consider the entire range of economic policies with impacts on the poor, and must therefore become centrally involved in macroeconomic, sectoral, and regional policy issues.

Notes

1. Despite being at the forefront of the PRSP process and having provided substantial analysis and documentation in the *PRSP Sourcebook*, the World Bank decided to drop earlier plans to include a chapter in the sourcebook that would explicitly address pro-poor growth. For some discussion documents by researchers from within or related to major development partners, see Eastwood and Lipton 2000; Edgren 2001; Hanmer and Booth 2001; and White and Anderson 2000.

2. For another possible approach to defining and measuring pro-poor growth that is grounded in traditional poverty measurement theory, see Ravallion and Chen (2003).

3. This would ensure that the relative gap between the non-poor and the poor would fall over time. A stronger requirement would be that the absolute income growth of the poor must exceed the absolute income growth of the non-poor; however, this would be an extremely high standard to meet, as it would mean that the income growth rate of the poor would have to be much larger than the income growth rate of the non-poor. Nevertheless, this would ensure not only that the relative, but also the absolute, gap between rich and poor would decline. As White and Anderson (2000) show, less than 3 percent of actual growth episodes in past decades would meet this latter more stringent definition.

4. Some measures, such as the one proposed by Kakwani and Pernia (2000), could accommodate this requirement if they were based on the poverty severity measure rather than the poverty headcount.

5. They wanted a measure that focused exclusively on the performance of the poor, thus they did not intend it to be a measure of aggregate performance.

6. For an empirical application of these measures see Klasen (1994). Welfare measures implied by the class of Atkinson inequality measures is quite similar to this formulation. For a discussion and application, see Grün and Klasen (2001, 2003).

7. One can construct, albeit somewhat unlikely, cases where the population-weighted growth rate in particular exceeds the average income growth rate, yet the poor have lower growth than the average because of particularly high income growth among middle-income groups. Except in extreme cases, this would not happen if poverty-weighted growth rates were used, which give greater weight to the growth rates of the poor.

8. There is a close relationship between the proposal by Ravallion and Chen (2003) and these growth rates. Ravallion and Chen use a population-weighted growth rate applied to centiles and just focus on the poor, while the Ahluwalia and Chenery measures are more aggregative and give some weight to growth by the non-poor. Both measures also share the feature that they consider the growth rates of quantiles of the income distribution, which may not contain the same people in two periods. Thus none of the measures are able to say much about the mobility of people in and out of poverty, for which different types of data (panel data) and different measures (mobility measures) are needed.

9. The Millennium Development Goals and the related International Development Goals (OECD 1996) include improvements in education and health and propose separate indicators. This is one way to address the issue. Another is to propose indicators that capture the multidimensionality of poverty in a single indicator (Klasen 2000).

10. For a related paper on the relationship between demographics and inequality, see Kremer and Chen (2002), who show that high-inequality countries have large fertility differences between rich and poor that tend to reproduce inequality.

11. An illustration of these two effects may be helpful. Two countries have per capita annual income of US$300, 5 percent average income growth, and 10 percent income growth of the poor (and thus exhibit pro-poor growth). In country A the poor have a per capita

annual income of US$100 and the rich have US$500. In country B the poor have a per capita annual income of US$50 and the rich have US$550. The poverty line stands at US$110. In country A, pro-poor growth will mean that all the poor attain a per capita annual income of US$110 and poverty, measured using the headcount, the poverty gap, or the squared poverty gap, is eradicated. In country B, the poor only attain a per capita annual income of US$55, thus poverty remains substantial (indeed, it does not change using the headcount ratio and is reduced only slightly using the poverty gap or severity measure). This numerical example also illustrates how the findings by Dollar and Kraay (2002) can be reconciled with the finding that the same amount of growth yields larger poverty reduction in countries with low inequality (Ravallion 2002; World Bank 2000b). Dollar and Kraay only relate average income growth to the proportionate income growth rate of the poor and find that the two are closely correlated, but this still means that poverty reduction will be easier in countries where inequality is lower, because their proportionate income gains are larger in absolute terms.

12. In contrast, Forbes (2000), using a fixed effects specification, finds that changes in inequality appear to be positively correlated with growth in the subsequent five years, but her panel regressions with fixed effects depend greatly on interpreting minute changes in inequality in countries. Given the poor quality of the data, the signal to noise ratio in such an analysis is likely to be substantial. For a discussion of related issues, see Atkinson and Brandolini (2001); Banerjee and Duflo (2003); and Barro (2000). Easterly (2000) finds that not all types of inequality harm growth, but a small middle class appears to be particularly detrimental. See also Rodrik (1999).

13. While the cross-sectional findings about the negative impact of existing inequality and growth are fairly robust, whether reducing inequality in a particular country will boost growth in all cases is somewhat less clear. Forbes (2000) finds that it would reduce growth, at least in the short term; Barro (2000) finds that it would increase growth in poor countries; Banerjee and Duflo (2003) find that any change in inequality (improvement or worsening) appears to reduce growth; and Eastwood and Lipton (2000) argue that growth depends on the type of inequality. Clearly, more research is needed, especially empirical investigation of specific causal pathways from changes in inequality to economic growth.

14. This may be one of the reasons why the poor suffered badly during the 1997 Asian crisis (Chen and Ravallion 2000). Targeted safety nets and automatic stabilizers are one way to ensure asymmetry in the linkage between growth and poverty reduction between expansions and contractions. For a related discussion, see Christiaensen, Demery, and Paternostro (2002) and Easterly (2000).

15. Recent innovations in generating detailed and precise poverty profiles have an in-built bias to focus on static views of poverty and may neglect these dynamic options for the poor to participate in economic growth in a multitude of ways that cannot easily be deciphered from such poverty profiles. These dynamic responses by the poor can be captured using microsimulation or dynamic computable general equilibrium techniques. Such analyses should complement the static poverty profiles.

16. These studies do not include the growth impact of reduced gender inequality in employment or access to assets and technology, which have been found to be significant (Blackden and Bhanu 1999; Klasen and Lamanna 2003).

17. Some studies, most notably Christiaensen, Demery, and Paternostro (2002) and World Bank (1994), argue that SAPs have induced growth and reduced poverty in those countries where they were successfully implemented. The usual indicators used to measure successful structural adjustment are measures of macroeconomic policy outcomes, such as competitive exchange rates, low inflation, and low external and internal imbalances.

These findings are not as revealing as one might think at first sight for several reasons. First, SAPs asked countries to do much more than simply adjust a few macroeconomic variables, so the latter are not really an indicator of the way SAPs were implemented. Second, they do not clearly link macroeconomic policies undertaken as part of SAPs and macroeconomic outcomes measured. Third, they essentially only reproduce the well-known finding from the empirical growth literature that macroeconomic stability is good for growth and poverty reduction. Lastly, they beg the question of why some countries adjusted successfully but most did not, despite all having agreed to SAPs. Several interesting studies have taken up this last issue (Mosley, Harrington, and Toye 1995; World Bank 2001b).

18. Proponents of SAPs had claimed that with their emphasis on improving incentives for agriculture, they should sharply reduce poverty by raising the incomes of poor rural dwellers. Easterly (2000) claims that the SAPs have had no aggregate impact on poverty, but interacted negatively with growth, in the sense that in countries with SAPs, poverty was reduced less if there was growth and increased less if there were contractions. Christiaensen, Demery, and Paternostro (2002) find that contractions have been strongly pro-poor and expansions have been mildly pro-poor in most African countries with the exception of Zambia. The finding that contractions are pro-poor might well be related to the use of consumption as the measure of poverty. During contractions, the poor will try to stabilize their consumption by eating into their assets, and their greater stability in consumption might come at the expense of reduced assets, and thus of reduced opportunities to escape poverty.

19. While some still argue for fixed exchange rates and the use of the exchange rate as a nominal anchor (Herr and Priewe 2001), the experiences of recent decades have shown that fixed exchange rate regimes have much greater difficulties in coping with external shocks (Fisher 2001; World Bank 1994) and are prone to speculative attacks unless they are backed by a currency board (which creates its own problems, as the 2002 crisis in Argentina demonstrated). At the same time, full flexibility is also not desirable given the large volatility that may result, but a managed flexibility, such as that which has characterized South Africa's exchange rate policy in the past few years (where the Reserve Bank does not announce an exchange rate target, but occasionally intervenes to reduce sharp fluctuations), might be more or less the right approach for many countries. Such managed flexibility becomes much easier if a country is aiming for an undervalued exchange rate. Keeping the exchange rate undervalued requires careful management of capital account liberalization and capital inflows, particularly short-term ones, and the type of policies that Chile has been using to manage such flows might be advisable. During a currency crisis, the option to resort to short-term capital controls, as Malaysia did during the Asian crisis, is also firmly back as an option on the policy agenda, although the extent of reliance on such a measure remains controversial (IMF 1999a,b; Lane 1999).

20. Actual trade policy reforms in many countries do not yet seem to bear out this shift in emphasis.

21. Conceptually, the main difference is that a poverty-focused policy will only indirectly be inequality reducing to the extent that it finances poverty-reducing policies through overall taxation and favors the poor in other policy arenas. A policy targeting inequality directly would focus on inequality and use policy instruments to address this. In practice, many policies would serve both ends, but policies targeting inequality would typically be broader in scope and intensity, as they not only seek to overcome specific barriers the poor face, but also to alter the distribution of resources in society. Given that high inequality poses a problem for poverty reduction, clearly even those who are focused on absolute poverty reduction (as exemplified by the first Millennium Development Goal) need to worry about inequality reduction to achieve this goal, particularly in countries with high inequality.

22. The *World Development Report* on poverty (World Bank 2000b) explicitly cautions against confiscatory land reform and argues that it lacks political support. Given that the World Bank has been willing to advocate and enforce such policies as structural adjustment, which similarly lacked political support in many countries, this caution is somewhat surprising.

23. Eastwood and Lipton (2000) distinguish between ascribed (for example, inherited) and achieved (earned) inequality and argue that the former is particularly harmful for growth. Land reform, as well as land taxes and inheritance taxes, would directly address such ascribed inequality.

24. The World Bank has developed a set of tools as part of its poverty and social impact analysis that allows a partial assessment of this important issue.

References

The word "processed" describes informally reproduced works that may not be commonly available in libraries.

Ahluwhalia, M., and H. Chenery. 1974. *Redistribution with Growth.* Oxford, U.K.: Oxford University Press.

Alderman, H., and others. 2000a. "Rural Poverty." In World Bank, *PRSP Sourcebook,* August 29 version. Washington, D.C.: World Bank.

Alderman, H., and others. 2000b. "Technical Note 1." In World Bank, *PRSP Sourcebook,* August 29 version. Washington, D.C.: World Bank.

Alesina, A., and D. Rodrik. 1994. "Distributive Policies and Economic Growth." *Quarterly Journal of Economics* 109(2): 465–90.

Ames, B., W. Brown, S. Devarajan, and A. Izquierdo. 2000. In World Bank, *PRSP Sourcebook,* September 21 version. Washington, D.C.: World Bank.

Atkinson, A. B. 1999. *The Economic Consequences of Rolling Back the Welfare State.* Cambridge, Mass.: MIT Press.

Atkinson, A. B., and A. Brandolini. 2001. "Promise and Pitfalls in the Use of Secondary Data Sets." *Journal of Economic Literature* 39(3): 771–99.

Banerjee, A. 1999. "Land Reforms: Prospects and Strategies." Massachusetts Institute of Technology, Cambridge, Mass. Processed.

Banerjee, A., and E. Duflo. 2003. "Inequality and Growth: What Can the Data Say?" *Journal of Economic Growth* 8(3): 267–99.

Bardhan, K., and S. Klasen. 1999. "UNDP's Gender-Related Indices; A Critical Review." *World Development* 27(6): 985–1010.

Barro, R. 1991. "Economic Growth in a Cross-Section of Countries." *Quarterly Journal of Economics* 106(2): 407–41.

_____. 2000. "Inequality and Growth in a Panel of Countries." *Journal of Economic Growth* 5(1): 5–32.

Bevan, D., and C. Adam. 2001. "Poverty Reduction Strategies and the Macroeconomic Policy Framework." Department of Economics, Oxford, U.K. Processed.

Binswanger, H., K. Deininger, and G. Feder. 1995. "Power, Distortions, Revolt, and Reform in Agricultural Land Relations." In J. Behrman and T. N. Srinivasan, eds., *Handbook of Development Economics,* vol. 3b. Amsterdam: North-Holland.

Blackden, M., and C. Bhanu. 1999. *Gender, Growth, and Poverty Reduction.* Technical Paper no. 428. Washington, D.C.: World Bank.

Bourguignon, F. 1998. "Redistribution and Development." Delta, Paris. Processed.

———. 2000. "Can Redistribution Accelerate Growth and Development?" Paper presented at the Annual World Bank Conference on Development Economics–Europe, June 26–28.

———. 2001. "The Distributional Effects of Growth: Micro vs. Macro Approaches." Delta, Paris. Processed.

———. 2003. "The Growth Elasticity of Poverty Reduction." In T. Eicher and S. Turnovsky, eds., *Inequality and Growth: Theory and Policy Implications*. Cambridge, Mass.: MIT Press.

Bruno, M., L. Squire, and M. Ravallion. 1998. "Equity and Growth in Developing Countries: Old and New Perspectives on the Policy Issues." In V. Tanzi and K. Chu, eds., *Income Distribution and High-Quality Growth*. Cambridge, Mass.: MIT Press.

Chen, S., and M. Ravallion. 2000. "How Did the World's Poorest Fare in the 1990s?" World Bank, Washington, D.C. Processed.

Christiaensen, L., L. Demery, and S. Paternostro. 2002. "Reforms, Economic Growth, and Poverty Reduction in Africa: Messages from the 1990s." World Bank, Washington, D.C. Processed.

Collier, P., and J. W. Gunning. 1999. "Explaining African Economic Performance." *Journal of Economic Literature* 37(1): 61–111.

Cornia, G., and G. Helleiner. 1995. *From Adjustment to Development In Africa*. New York: Oxford University Press.

Deininger, K., and L. Squire. 1998. "New Ways of Looking at Old Issues: Inequality and Growth." *Journal of Development Economics* 57(2): 259–87.

Demery, L. 2002. "Review of Poverty Diagnostics in African PRSPs." World Bank, Washington, D.C. Processed.

Dollar, D., and R. Gatti. 1999. "Gender Inequality, Income, and Growth: Are Good Times Good for Women?" Policy Research Report Working Paper no. 1. World Bank, Washington, D.C.

Dollar, D., and A. Kraay. 2002. "Growth Is Good for the Poor." *Journal of Economic Growth* 7(3): 195–225.

Drèze, J., and A. Sen. 1989. *Hunger and Public Action*. New York: Oxford University Press.

Easterly, W. 2000. "The Effect of IMF and World Bank Programs on Poverty." World Bank, Washington, D.C. Processed.

Eastwood, R., and M. Lipton. 2000. "Pro-Poor Growth and Pro-Growth Poverty Reduction: Meaning, Evidence, and Policy Implications." *Asian Development Review* 18(2): 1–37.

Edgren, G. 2001. "Pro-Poor Growth: A Review of Evidence and Policy Conclusions." Swedish International Development Agency, Stockholm. Processed.

Engelbert, J. 2000. "Solving the Mystery of the Africa Dummy." *World Development* 28(10): 1821–35.

Fisher, S. 2001. "Exchange Rates Regimes: Is the Bipolar View Correct?" *Finance and Development* 38(2).

Forbes, K. 2000. "A Reassessment of the Relationship between Inequality and Growth." *American Economic Review* 90(4): 869–87.

Grün, C., and S. Klasen. 2001. "Growth, Inequality, and Well-Being in Transition Countries." *Economics of Transition* 9(2): 359–94.

———. 2003. "Growth, Income Distribution, and Well-Being: Intertemporal and Global Comparisons." *CESifo Economic Studies* 49(4): 617–59.

Hanmer, L., and D. Booth. 2001. "Pro-Poor Growth: Why Do We Need It?" Overseas Development Institute, London: Processed.

Herr, H., and J. Priewe. 2001. "The Macroeconomic Framework of Poverty Reeducation." Berlin. Processed.

IMF (International Monetary Fund). 1999a. *International Capital Markets September 1999*. Washington, D.C.

_____. 1999b. *World Economic Outlook May 1999*. Washington, D.C.

Jalan, J., and M. Ravallion. 2000. "Geographic Poverty Traps? A Micro Model of Consumption Growth in Rural China." World Bank, Washington, D.C. Processed.

Kakwani, N., and E. Pernia. 2000. "What Is Pro-poor Growth?" *Asian Development Review* 18(1): 1–16.

Klasen, S. 1994. "Inequality and Growth: Introducing Inequality-Weighted Growth Rates to Reassess Postwar U.S. Economic Performance." *Review of Income and Wealth* 40(3): 251–72.

_____. 2000. "Measuring Poverty and Deprivation in South Africa." *Review of Income and Wealth* 46(1): 33–58.

_____. 2002a. "Low Schooling for Girls, Slower Growth for All?" *World Bank Economic Review* 16: 345–73.

_____. 2002b. "Social, Economic, and Environmental Limits for the Newly Enfranchised in South Africa?" *Economic Development and Cultural Change* 50(3): 607–42.

Klasen, S., and F. Lamanna. 2003. "The Impact of Gender Inequality in Education and Employment on Economic Growth in the Middle East and North Africa." University of Munich Department of Economics. Processed.

Knowles, S., P. Lorgelly, and D. Owen. 2002. "Are Educational Gender Gaps a Brake on Development?" *Oxford Economic Papers* 54(1): 118–49.

Kremer, M., and D. Chen. 2002. "Income Distribution Dynamics with Endogenous Fertility." *Journal of Economic Growth* 7: 227–58.

Lane, T. 1999. "The Asian Financial Crisis." *Finance and Development* 36(3): 44–47.

Li, H., L. Squire, and H. Zhou. 1998. "Explaining International and Intertemporal Variations in Income Inequality." *Economic Journal* 108(1): 26–43.

Lindauer, D., and M. Roemer. 1994. *Asia and Africa: Legacies and Opportunities in Development*. New York: Oxford University Press.

Lipton, M. 1977. *Why Poor People Stay Poor: Urban Bias in World Development*. Cambridge, Mass.: Harvard University Press.

Lipton, M., and M. Ravallion. 1995. "Poverty and Policy." In J. Behrman and T. N. Srinivasan, eds., *Handbook of Development Economics*, vol 3b. Amsterdam: North-Holland.

Lundberg, M., and L. Squire. 1999. "The Simultaneous Evolution of Growth and Inequality." World Bank, Washington, D.C. Processed.

Mankiw, N. G., J. Roemer, and P. Weil. 1992. "A Contribution to the Empirics of Economic Growth." *Quarterly Journal of Economics* 107(2): 407–37.

McCulloch, N., and B. Baulch. 1999. *Tracking Pro-Poor Growth*. ID21 Insights no. 31. Brighton, U.K.: Institute of Development Studies.

Milanovic, B. 2002. "Can We Discern the Effect of Globalization on Income Distribution?" Policy Research Department Working Paper no. 2876. World Bank, Washington, D.C.

Mkandawire, T., and C. Soludo. 1999. *Our Continent, Our Future*. Asmara, Eritrea: Africa World Press.

Mosley, J., J. Harrington, and J. Toye. 1995. *Aid and Power,* 2nd ed. London: Routledge.

OECD (Organisation for Economic Co-operation and Development). 1996. *Shaping the 21st Century: The Role of Development Cooperation.* Paris.

———. 2001. "Rising to the Global Challenge: Partnership for Reducing World Poverty." Statement by the Development Assistance Committee High-Level Meeting, April 25–26. Paris.

Pritchett, L. 1995. "Desired Fertility and the Impact of Population Policy." *Population and Development Review* 20(1): 1–55.

Ravallion, M. 2002. "Growth, Inequality, and Poverty: Looking beyond Averages." World Bank, Washington, D.C. Processed.

Ravallion, M., and S. Chen. 2003. "Measuring Pro-Poor Growth." *Economics Letters* 78(1): 93–99.

Ravallion, M., and G. Datt. 1996. "How Important to India's Poor Is the Sectoral Composition of Economic Growth?" *World Bank Economic Review* 10(1): 1–25.

———. 2002. "Why Has Economic Growth Been more Pro-Poor in Some States of India Than Others?" *Journal of Development Economics* 68(2): 381–400.

Ray, D. 1998. *Development Economics.* Princeton, N.J.: Princeton University Press.

Rodrik, D. 1995. "Trade and Industrial Policy Reform." In J. Behrman and T. N. Srinivasan, eds., *Handbook of Development Economics,* vol 3b. Amsterdam: North-Holland.

———. 1999. "Where Did all the Growth go? External Shocks, Social Conflict, and Growth Collapses." *Journal of Economic Growth* 4(4): 385–412.

Thomas, D. 1997. "Incomes, Expenditures, and Health Outcomes." In J. Haddad, J. Hoddinott, and H. Alderman, eds., *Intrahousehold Resource Allocation in Developing Countries.* Baltimore, Md.: The Johns Hopkins University Press.

Thomas, V., M. Dailami, A. Dhareshwar, D. Kaufmann, N. Kishor, R. López, and Y. Wang. 2000. *The Quality of Growth.* New York: Oxford University Press.

Timmer, P. 1988. "The Agricultural Transformation." In H. Chenery and T. N. Srinivasan, eds., *Handbook of Development Economics,* vol. 1. Amsterdam: North-Holland.

Tumisiime-Mutebile, E. 2001. "The Role of the International Development Goals in Uganda's Development Strategy." Paper prepared for the World Bank Conference on International Development Goals, March 19–20, Washington, D.C.

U.N. (United Nations). 2000. *A Better World for All.* New York.

White, Howard, and Edward Anderson. 2000. "Growth Versus Distribution: Does the Pattern of Growth Matter?" Brighton, U.K.: Institute of Development Studies. Processed.

Woolard, I., and S. Klasen. 2002. "Income Mobility and Household Dynamics in South Africa." Paper presented at the International Association of Research in Income and Wealth conference, August 18–24, Stockholm.

World Bank. 1981. *Sub-Saharan Africa: From Crisis to Sustainable Growth.* Washington, D.C.

———. 1993. *The East Asian Miracle.* Washington, D.C.

———. 1994. *Adjustment in Africa: Reforms, Results, and the Road Ahead.* New York: Oxford University Press.

———. 1997. *World Development Report: The State in a Changing World.* New York: Oxford University Press.

———. 1998. *Assessing Aid.* New York: Oxford University Press.

———. 2000a. *Can Africa Claim the 21st Century?* New York: Oxford University Press.

_____. 2000b. *World Development Report: The State in a Changing World*. New York: Oxford University Press.

_____. 2001a. *Aid and Growth in Africa*. New York: Oxford University Press.

_____. 2001b. *Engendering Development*. New York: Oxford University Press.

_____. 2002. *World Development Report: Building Institutions for Markets*. New York: Oxford University Press.

_____. 2003. *World Development Report 2004: Making Services Work for Poor People*. New York: Oxford University Press.

World Bank and IMF (International Monetary Fund). 2002. "Review of the Poverty Reduction Strategy Papers Approach: Main Findings." World Bank, Washington, D.C. Processed.

Zimmermann, F. 2000. "Barriers to Participation of the Poor in South Africa's Land Redistribution." *World Development* 28(8): 1439–60.

Aid and Growth Revisited: Policy, Economic Vulnerability, and Political Instability

LISA CHAUVET AND PATRICK GUILLAUMONT

The paper by Burnside and Dollar (2000), followed by the publication of *Assessing Aid* (World Bank 1998), gave rise to intense debate about the impact of aid on growth and poverty reduction (see, in particular, Berg 2002; Beynon 2001; Hansen and Tarp 2000, 2001). This is a clear instance of when strong policy recommendations were drawn from econometric results, that is, the finding that the effectiveness of aid depends on the quality of domestic policies in the recipient countries has engendered a selectivity principle in favor of countries considered as pursuing good policies. Simplifying, a significantly positive coefficient of the aid × policy interaction term in a growth regression has induced a significant international reallocation of aid. Collier and Dollar (2001, 2002) take an additional step by presenting a so-called poverty-efficient aid allocation model. Relying on a model of the Burnside and Dollar type, they argue that poverty could be halved if aid were targeted to countries with severe poverty and good policies. Even though aid also affects poverty in ways other than through growth—an issue that Collier and Dollar do not consider—the bulk of the effect of aid on poverty reduction depends on its effect on growth.[1] Thus the impact of aid on growth remains crucial in understanding its impact on poverty.

The results and implications of a Burnside-Dollar type of model have been debated in relation to several points. As broad as this debate has been, it focuses mainly on methodological issues and policy conclusions rather than on the relevance of the conceptual framework. Major contributions have challenged the robustness of the aid and policy interaction on growth, and as such, have mainly discussed the specification of the model, for instance, aid squared versus aid interacted with policy, and the sample composition, especially the influence of outliers.

Regarding the conceptual framework, four main issues need to be considered more than they have actually been insofar as they affect the adequacy of the Burnside-Dollar

Lisa Chauvet is an assistant researcher at the Centre d'Etudes et de Recherches sur le Développement International (CERDI) in Clermont-Ferrand, France. Patrick Guillaumont is a professor at the University of Auvergne in France and is president of CERDI.

Annual World Bank Conference on Development Economics—Europe 2003
© 2004 The International Bank for Reconstruction and Development/The World Bank

model in assessing the effectiveness of aid at the macroeconomic level. For simplicity, the empirical model developed by Burnside and Dollar and elaborated on by Collier and Dollar and others will be referred to here as the standard model.

The first issue to consider is the effect of aid on policy itself. The standard model assumes no effect, which is debatable. The second issue is the potential impact of external shocks on the effectiveness of aid: by omitting external shocks from the analysis, the standard model implicitly assumes that these shocks have no effect. A third and more tricky issue is that of the relationship between aid effectiveness, policy, and political instability. Finally, a fourth issue is the possible limits on the effectiveness of aid caused by the lack of absorptive capacity.

This paper tackles these four issues and formulates additional hypotheses that are introduced in the standard model of aid and growth. If some of these assumptions are not rejected by the econometric test implemented, they may have policy implications in relation to aid effectiveness and allocation. Note that as in the standard model, the following analysis considers aid as an aggregate independently of its characteristics, which obviously matter.

Aid and Policy

An important underlying assumption of the standard model is that aid has no impact on policy. The World Bank initiated a study to analyze and possibly confirm this assumption (Devarajan, Dollar, and Holmgrem 2001). If it is valid, this assumption has a direct implication, namely, when a country's economic policies are considered to be poor, then financial aid should be replaced by technical assistance and the diffusion of ideas. As one might have expected, the picture arising from the World Bank study is less clear than the original assumption. Evidence from several case studies (Côte d'Ivoire, Ghana, and Mali) suggests that aid had actually influenced policy (as Berg 2002 notes). For instance, in Côte d'Ivoire before the devaluation of the CFA franc in 1994, several important reforms aimed at increasing competitiveness had been implemented under pressure from donors; in Mali, the main reforms in the area of grain marketing and trade liberalization were also introduced with the support of foreign aid; and in Ghana, "Aid *was* an important part of the decision to reform as the government anticipated that aid would enable it to meet its economic and political objectives" (Tsikata 2001, p. 89). Of course, aid conditionality has often not worked (see, for instance, Collier and others 1997), but in many cases, especially when the initial conditions had hindered reforms and when these conditions were likely to change, aid was a significant and sometimes major factor in improvements in policy.

The influence of aid on policy depends on whether the aid is program or project aid. Program aid influences policy through the conditionality of macroeconomic support, with more room for improvement the lower the initial level of policy. Project aid influences policy through the design and implementation of specific public expenditures on projects, and the improvement in the quality of public projects or expenditures induced by aid is likely to be greater the poorer their current design, whatever the degree of fungibility between them. This assumption is consistent with the Burnside-Dollar result that aid is more effective in a good policy environment; however, it underlines that the scope for policy improvement brought about by aid is greater the poorer the initial policy.

Thus in modeling the effect of aid on policy, we have to assume that the present level of any index of policy (P_t) depends (negatively) on an interactive term between aid (A_t) and the past level of the policy (P_{t-1}). This assumption may help explain why in the growth literature the interactive aid × policy variable appears with an uncertain sign (either positive or negative or insignificant). Indeed, to assess the impact of policy on aid effectiveness accurately, the dynamic relationship between aid and policy has to be taken into account. In our econometric analysis, the policy × aid term ($A_t \cdot P_t$) only appears to be positively significant in the growth regressions when we control for these dynamics through the interactive term between aid and the past level of policy index ($A_t \cdot P_{t-1}$).

Aid Effectiveness and Economic Vulnerability

In a previous paper we argue that the effectiveness of aid depends more clearly on economic vulnerability to exogenous shocks than on policy (Guillaumont and Chauvet 2001). Indeed, foreign aid has a greater impact in developing countries affected by external or climatic shocks, insofar as it prevents growth from being interrupted: it has often reduced the probability of an economic collapse following an exogenous shock, and more generally, it allows a country to face such shocks without reversing policy reforms (for example, through quantitative restrictions on imports or deficit financing). In other words, aid contributes to the sustainability of growth and reforms in vulnerable countries. This effect has to be considered in addition to the negative effect of vulnerability on growth, which has been demonstrated elsewhere (see, for instance, Guillaumont, Guillaumont Jeanneney, and Brun 1999).

The results tested in Guillaumont and Chauvet (2001) using a composite index of economic vulnerability supported the view that the effectiveness of aid depends on economic vulnerability rather than on policy. A recent paper by Collier and Dehn (2001) that focused on terms of trade shocks makes a similar assumption, and underlines that aid is more effective when a country faces export price shortfalls.

Here we rely on the assumption that the effectiveness of aid depends on economic vulnerability, using a concept narrower than in Guillaumont and Chauvet (2001), but broader than the shock concept Collier and Dehn (2001) use. Leaving aside climatic shocks, like Collier and Dehn we focus on external shocks, but we consider both the instability of exports of goods and services weighted by the average exports to gross domestic product (GDP) ratio (an indication of exposure to the shocks) and the trend of the terms of trade.

Taking vulnerability into account in the aid effectiveness issue seems particularly relevant today for at least two reasons. First, vulnerability matters not only for the effectiveness of aid in relation to growth, but also its effectiveness in terms of poverty reduction, because of the specific effect of vulnerability on poverty (at both the macroeconomic and microeconomic levels) (World Bank 2000). Second, the United

Nations recently adopted economic vulnerability as one of the three criteria for identifying the least developed countries (the other two being GDP per capita and the
level of human resources) (Guillaumont 2000b; United Nations 2000). Insofar as aid
appears to be more effective in more vulnerable countries, it gives some rationale to
the specific aid targets for the least developed countries adopted by the international
community.

Aid Effectiveness and Political Instability

Given the prevalence of political instability in many developing countries, any discussion of the effectiveness of aid needs to take this instability variable into account.
Not surprisingly, the negative effect of political instability on growth (and investment) is well documented in the literature (see, for instance, Alesina and Perotti
1996; Alesina and others 1996);[2] however, the impact of political instability on the
effectiveness of aid on growth and on the factors of this effectiveness, in particular,
the quality of policy, has not been considered to anything like the same extent.

We tentatively advance the following hypotheses. Political instability may influence
the effectiveness of aid in two opposite directions. Indeed, political instability could
be viewed like economic vulnerability, that is, as an exogenous negative shock likely
to be compensated for (or insured against) by foreign aid. But precisely because this
instability is political rather than economic and endogenous rather than exogenous,
its effects are less likely to be compensated for by a resource inflow. Political instability is more likely to work in the opposite direction and negatively influence the effectiveness of aid. Thus in a troubled environment, with violence, frequently changing
governments, coups d'état, riots, and so on, aid may contribute little to growth.

Aid Effectiveness and Absorptive Capacity

Absorptive capacity has for a long time been a popular concept in the aid literature,
used to explain precisely why the effectiveness of aid may decline sharply beyond a
certain level of aid inflow (see, for instance, Chenery and Strout 1966; Millikan and
Rostow 1957; Rosenstein-Rodan 1961). The main factors identified as limiting
absorptive capacity are related both to the level of human capital and to the quality of
infrastructure. Cases abound of aid wasted, or simply not used, because of a lack of
domestic capacity or of appropriate physical infrastructure. Of course, good policies
and a stable political environment can also be viewed as components of absorptive
capacity, but in our conceptual framework, the latter only captures those factors that
are not already taken into account by the policy and political instability indicators.

Thus we focus on the two components of absorptive capacity previously mentioned: the quality of infrastructure and the level of education. Insofar as these factors appear to significantly influence growth, they can be combined in a composite
index of absorptive capacity that can be introduced in the growth regression both
additively and in interaction with the aid variable (that is, as an independent factor
of growth and as a factor influencing the effectiveness of aid, respectively). Moreover,
the composite index of absorptive capacity includes factors, in particular, human

capital, that may have a positive influence on the quality of policy. In this way, absorptive capacity may also influence the effectiveness of aid.

An Augmented Model of Aid Effectiveness

The starting point of our analysis is the standard model of aid effectiveness as estimated by Burnside and Dollar (2000) and others, which can be written as follows:

$$g_t = f(X_{gt}, P_t, A_t, A_t \cdot P_t), \tag{1}$$

with g_t denoting growth of income per capita, X_{gt} being a vector of structural factors, A_t denoting aid (as a percentage of income), and P_t denoting present policy.

The analysis presented in this paper leads us to formulate an augmented model of aid effectiveness that includes three additional variables (economic vulnerability, EV_t; socio-political instability, SPI_t; and absorptive capacity, AC_t) and three variables corresponding to their respective interaction with aid ($A_t \cdot EV_t$, $A_t \cdot SPI_t$, and $A_t \cdot AC_t$). Moreover, we have introduced the dynamics of the aid-policy relationship. To capture the effect of aid going through its effect on policy and depending on the previous level of policy, we have added in the standard model the level of past policy (P_{t-1}) and its interaction with aid ($A_t \cdot P_{t-1}$). The augmented model can then be written as follows:[3]

$$g_t = f(X_{gt}, P_t, P_{t-1}, EV_t, SPI_t, AC_t, A_t, A_t \cdot P_t, A_t \cdot P_{t-1}, A_t \cdot EV_t, A_t \cdot SPI_t, A_t \cdot AC_t)$$
$$ + \quad + \quad - \quad - \quad + \quad ? \quad + \quad - \quad + \quad - \quad + \tag{2}$$

The marginal effect of aid on growth is given by:

$$\frac{\partial g_t}{\partial A_t} = f(P_t, P_{t-1}, EV_t, SPI_t, AC_t)$$
$$\phantom{\frac{\partial g_t}{\partial A_t} = f(} + \quad - \quad + \quad - \quad +$$

Thus the effectiveness of aid is expected to depend

- Positively on the level of present policy (the standard model assumption)
- Negatively on the previous level of policy (policy catching up caused by aid)
- Positively on economic vulnerability (insurance effect of aid)
- Negatively on political instability (obstacle to the effects of aid)
- Positively on absorptive capacity.

Estimation Methodology and Data Description

The first step of the econometric analysis is to construct the four composite indicators: policy, economic vulnerability, political instability, and absorptive capacity. Following the standard model, the policy index is constructed by weighting an inflation variable and an openness policy variable by their respective effects on growth.[4,5] Burnside and Dollar use the Sachs and Warner (1995) openness dummy variable, which with the exception of Rodriguez and Rodrik (1999) has rarely been debated in the literature. However, observed openness cannot be employed as a policy indicator, because it depends to a large extent on structural factors. Thus we measure openness policy as that part of observed openness that is not explained by structural factors, namely, the size of the population, the extent of mining and oil resources, the level of development, and the costs of transportation (an indicator used in several previous papers, especially Combes and others 2000).

The economic vulnerability index is constructed as the weighted sum of the trend of the terms of trade and the instability of exports of goods and services (weighted by the ratio of exports to GDP). As for the policy index, these two variables are weighted by their relative impact on growth.

The political instability index is a weighted sum of the number of coups d'état, of the number of demonstrations per million people (both variables are from Banks 1996), and of a dummy equal to 1 when a civil war breaks out (Chauvet 2001).[6] Thus the aim of this composite index of socio-political instability is to capture extremely violent instability, less violent mass instability, and elite instability.

The absorptive capacity index is a weighted sum of the electricity generating capacity in kilowatts (Canning 1998) and of the completion of secondary education of the total population aged 15 and over (Barro and Lee 2000).

Finally, growth is measured by the growth rate of per capita GDP (Summers and Heston 1991, updated in the Global Development Network database) and aid is the ratio of official development assistance to the gross national product (from the Organisation for Economic Co-operation and Development-Development Assistance Committee). Note that time dummies are introduced in all regressions to capture business cycles.

Growth and policy equations are estimated on five-year subperiods from 1965 to 1999 for 59 developing countries, which include 18 Sub-Saharan African countries. Estimations are performed using the Arellano and Bond (1991) application of the generalized method of moments estimator. The model is estimated in first differences to eliminate the country-specific fixed effect. The right-hand–side, first-differenced variables are then instrumented with their lagged levels from $t - 2$.[7] Using these instruments requires no second-order auto-correlation of the residuals in the first-differenced equation. An auto-correlation test of the residuals and a Sargan over-identification test are used to make sure that the instruments are valid. Arellano and Bond (1991) propose a two-step estimation; however, they underline that a small sample bias in the two-step estimations leads to underestimated standard errors. The results therefore include both first-step (corrected for heteroscedasticity) and two-step estimations. A variable is considered significant if, and only if, it is significant in the first-step estimation.

Econometric Results

Growth estimations were used to construct the four indicators. One constraint was obtaining the weights for all four indicators from the same regression, so that the impact of each variable on growth is purged from the impact of the other variables. Note that all variables (except per capita GDP) are normalized on a scale from 0 to 100 so that the coefficients can be compared. The inflation rate, which has a negative impact on growth, and the terms of trade, which have a positive impact on growth, are also measured on a reverse scale so that all variables in the same indicator have the same sign (to make interpretation easier). The coefficients from the two-step estimations are used to construct the four indicators.[8] Thus the composite indicators constructed from a growth regression are as follows:

Policy = 0.0023. Ln inflation + 0.0012. Openness policy

Economic vulnerability = 0.0023. Instability of exports + 0.0017. Trend of terms of trade

Political instability = 0.0011. Coups d'état + 0.0009. Civil war + 0.0016. Demonstration

Absorptive capacity = 0.0043. Electricity capacity + 0.0044. Education

---

The weight of each variable corresponds to the coefficient of this variable in a growth regression including policy, economic vulnerability, political instability, and absorptive capacity variables, all of them being significant.

These indicators are then introduced into the growth regression, as is foreign aid. Regressions (1) and (2) of table 1 show that the four indicators have the expected and significant impact on growth, whereas aid is not significant.[9]

Regressions (3) to (6) in table 1 also show a set of results regarding the interaction terms between aid and the four variables: policy, economic vulnerability, political instability, and absorptive capacity. First, the aid × vulnerability term is positively significant, confirming Guillaumont and Chauvet's (2001) results, that is, aid is more effective in countries facing adverse external shocks. This relationship is significant in all regressions, whatever the specification.

Second, the aid × political instability interaction term is negative and significant in all regressions of table 1, except in regression (5) (p-value = 0.128). This result suggests that contrary to the compensation mechanisms of foreign aid at work when economic vulnerability is high, there is no compensation mechanism regarding political instability. The effectiveness of aid is negatively influenced by political instability, that is, an unstable and uncertain political environment hinders the impact of aid on growth. Note that the political instability variable is no longer significant when this interaction term is introduced in regressions (5) and (6).

Third, the aid × absorptive capacity interaction term is positive (aid may be more effective when absorptive capacity is high), but is barely significant in the first-step regressions (p-values are 0.121 and 0.103 in regressions [3] and [5], respectively).

Fourth, whereas the policy index has a significantly positive impact on growth, the aid-policy interaction term is not significant and even has a negative sign (regressions [3] and [4]), contrary to Burnside and Dollar's findings. We argue that this result stems from the fact that the impact of aid on policy was not taken into account.

We have assumed that the poorer the initial policy, the stronger the potential positive effect of aid on the level of policy. The regressions in table 2 explore these dynamics. The present level of policy is estimated as a function of its previous level,

TABLE 1. Growth Regressions, 1965–99
(dependent variable Ln Income per capita$_t$)

GMM estimations	1-step (1)	2-step (2)	1-step (3)	2-step (4)	1-step (5)	2-step (6)
Ln income per capita$_{t-1}$	0.700*** (0.000)	0.675*** (0.000)	0.697*** (0.000)	0.646*** (0.000)	0.595*** (0.000)	0.581*** (0.000)
Economic policy$_t$ (POL$_t$)	1.055*** (0.000)	1.074*** (0.000)	1.286*** (0.000)	1.248*** (0.000)	0.523° (0.102)	0.579*** (0.000)
Economic policy$_{t-1}$ (POL$_{t-1}$)					0.947** (0.040)	1.005*** (0.000)
Political instability (SPI)	−0.751*** (0.001)	−0.744*** (0.000)	−0.556* (0.089)	−0.629*** (0.000)	−0.060 (0.883)	0.116 (0.677)
Economic vulnerability (EV)	−1.090*** (0.001)	−1.419*** (0.000)	−1.843*** (0.001)	−2.273*** (0.000)	−1.818*** (0.000)	−1.971*** (0.000)
Absorptive capacity (AC)	0.800** (0.020)	0.960*** (0.000)	0.708** (0.045)	1.055*** (0.000)	0.463 (0.303)	0.491*** (0.001)
ODA/GNP	−0.282 (0.165)	−0.275** (0.011)	−1.413* (0.093)	−1.979*** (0.000)	−1.539 (0.165)	−2.139*** (0.004)
ODA/GNP × POL$_t$			−0.686 (0.738)	−1.225 (0.408)	7.117* (0.073)	7.622** (0.012)
ODA/GNP × POL$_{t-1}$					−7.742** (0.034)	−7.131*** (0.003)
ODA/GNP × SPI			−6.889* (0.066)	−4.841** (0.027)	−13.473° (0.128)	−16.165** (0.011)
ODA/GNP × EV			15.290* (0.085)	25.768*** (0.000)	14.687* (0.063)	19.918** (0.012)
ODA × AC			14.549° (0.121)	17.758*** (0.009)	17.700° (0.103)	17.818*** (0.000)

Constant	0.071**	0.073***	0.076**	0.074***	0.022**	0.022***
	(0.012)	(0.000)	(0.014)	(0.000)	(0.042)	(0.000)
Number of observations	262	262	262	262	224	224
Number of countries	59	59	59	59	57	57
AR(1)[a]	0.001	0.0007	0.002	0.002	0.0007	0.0001
AR(2)[a]	0.597	0.715	0.799	0.912	0.628	0.499
Number of Instruments	146	146	149	149	150	150
Sargan[b]		52.1 (133)		45.7 (132)		46.9 (131)

AR(1)   First-order correlation test.

AR(2)   Second-order correlation test.

GNP   Gross national product.

GMM   Generalized method of moments.

ODA   Official development assistance.

***Significant at the 1 percent level.

**Significant at the 5 percent level.

*Significant at the 10 percent level.

°Significant at the 15 percent level.

Note: Time dummies are introduced in all regressions, but the corresponding results are not reported in this table (the full results are available on request). Robust p-values are in parentheses.

a. p-value.

b. χ_2, degrees of freedom in parentheses.

Source: Authors.

Table 2. Economic Policy Regressions, 1970–99

Economic policy$_t$	1-step (1)	2-step (2)
Economic policy$_{t-1}$ (POL$_{t-1}$)	0.516**	0.495***
	0.031	0.000
Political instability (SPI)	−6.336**	−5.514***
	0.028	0.000
Absorptive capacity (AC)	0.632	0.404*
	0.162	0.085
ODA/GNP	0.694*	0.742***
	0.059	0.000
ODA/GNP × POL$_{t-1}$	−2.592**	−2.651***
	0.029	0.000
SPI × POL$_{t-1}$	0.226**	0.198***
	0.029	0.000
AC × POL$_{t-1}$	−0.024*	−1.673**
	0.082	0.024
Constant	0.002	0.003***
	0.386	0.000
Number of observations	229	229
Number of countries	57	57
AR(1)[a]	0.003	0.005
AR(2)[a]	0.329	0.354
Number of instruments	83	83
Sargan[b]		38.4 (69)
Nested test EV	0.404	0.004
Nested test EV · POL$_{t-1}$[c]	0.448	0.051
Nested test ODA · ISP	0.286	0.000
Nested test ODA · EV[c]	0.453	0.000
Nested test ODA · AC	0.636	0.201

EV   Economic vulnerability.

GNP   Gross national product.

ODA   Official development assistance.

***Significant at the 1 percent level.

**Significant at the 5 percent level.

*Significant at the 10 percent level.

°Significant at the 15 percent level.

Note: Time dummies are introduced in all regressions, but the corresponding results are not reported in this table (the full results are available on request). Robust p-values are in parentheses.

a. p-value.

b. χ_2, degrees of freedom in parentheses.

c. EV is also introduced in the regression for this test.

Source: Authors.

as well as of political instability, absorptive capacity, aid, and interaction terms.[10] Foreign aid appears to have a significant positive impact on the level of policy, and the aid × past policy interaction term is significantly negative, which means that aid improves policy relatively more when its initial level is poor.[11]

Turning back to the growth regressions of table 1, the dynamic aid-policy relationships are introduced in regressions (5) and (6) through the lagged policy index (P_{t-1}), and this lagged index is interacted with aid ($A_t \cdot P_{t-1}$). Thus in regressions (5) and (6), both policy at time t and policy at time t − 1, as well as their respective interaction terms with aid, are introduced in the regressions to estimate equation (2). First, both policy at time t and policy at time t − 1 have a positive effect on growth. Second, and more important, these regressions confirm that the effectiveness of aid is greater when past policy is poor: policy at time t − 1 interacted with aid has a negative (and significant) impact on growth. At the same time, policy at time t interacted with aid has a positive (and significant) impact on growth: the policy × aid variable, which was not significant in regressions (3) and (4), is now significant (and positive), because the dynamic negative effect of past policy on the effectiveness of aid has been taken into account. Thus it seems that the effectiveness of aid with respect to growth is enhanced when initial policy is poor.

Conclusions

Aid matters for growth, and thus for poverty reduction. The analysis in this paper indicates that the debate about the significance and robustness of the effects of policy on aid effectiveness does not suggest that present policy has no positive impact on aid effectiveness, but that the effectiveness of aid has to be examined in a broader context than that of the standard model. Estimations of an augmented growth model— taking into account the dynamic relationship between aid, policy, and growth, as well as the influence on aid effectiveness of economic vulnerability, socio-political instability, and absorptive capacity—lead to the following conclusions.

First, as several case studies demonstrate, aid may influence policy. According to our hypothesis, which is not rejected by our econometric estimations, the poorer previous policy is, the stronger the improvement of policy induced by a given amount of aid. Consistently, aid appears simultaneously more efficient when present policy is good, but also when past policy was poor (that is, likely to be improved under the influence of aid). Omitting to take into account the previous level of policy and its possible improvements brought about by aid may lead to erroneous conclusions about the influence of policy on the effectiveness of aid.

Second, economic vulnerability to external shocks, which is by itself a negative factor of growth, is a factor that enhances the effectiveness of aid (which is higher in more vulnerable economies). Therefore retaining economic vulnerability as one of the criteria for aid allocation is necessary to maximize the effects of aid on growth, and consequently on poverty reduction. It is all the more needed given that poverty, for a given average growth rate, is likely to be higher when growth is volatile, which is the case in vulnerable countries.

Third, political instability, while also by itself a negative factor of growth, lowers the effectiveness of aid. If aid cannot be expected to promote growth in troubled countries, it can, however, be used efficiently to prevent political instability. Of course, it also may help countries make up for lost time once stability has returned.

Fourth, absorptive capacity still matters. Human capital and physical infrastructure are significant positive factors of growth. Absorptive capacity may also improve the effectiveness of aid, but according to the somewhat restrictive measure used in this paper, such an effect does not appear to be particularly significant.

In summary, the main lesson to be drawn from the econometric exercise presented in this paper is not to deny the role of policy in relation to the effectiveness of aid, but to consider its role in a dynamic and broader context. However, we readily admit that precisely because we rely on econometric estimations with their own data constraints, the scope of this study is still too narrow. It does not tackle the direct effectiveness of aid in terms of poverty reduction; it still relies on an index of economic policy that, even though revised with regard to previous similar exercises, should be extended; and it does not consider the impact of aid on socio-political instability, which may be significant, as documented in the case of civil war (Arcand and Chauvet 2001; Collier and Hoeffler 2000). The conceptual framework of this paper can still be extended to include these crucial factors.

Notes

1. Dollar and Kraay (2001) emphasize the link between growth and poverty reduction. The main assumptions of the Collier-Dollar model are discussed elsewhere (Guillaumont 2000a).

2. The mixed effects of socio-political instability on aid allocation (depending on the kind of instability) have also recently been examined (Chauvet 2003).

3. We also estimate the effect of aid on policy using the following model: $P_t = f(X_{pt}, P_{t-1}, A_t, A_t \cdot P_{t-1})$.

4. A budget surplus variable is also included in the standard model. It is not introduced here because of the following measurement problems: (a) a budget surplus excluding grants artificially augments the deficit in countries receiving large amounts of grants (expenditures are higher), and (b) a budget surplus including grants means that grants are being introduced twice in the regressions with aid.

5. All data sources and definitions are provided in more detail in a longer version of the paper that is available at http://wbln0018.worldbank.org/EURVP/web.nsf/Pages/ABCDE +2002-Papers.

6. Coups d'état are updated from 1995 to 1999 from the Centre d'Etudes et de Recherches sur le Développement International database. Regarding civil wars, we distinguish between the onset and the duration of the war; however, the latter was never significant.

7. Economic policy, economic vulnerability, political instability, absorptive capacity, and aid are instrumented along with the lagged GDP per capita variable.

8. All coefficients are significant in the first-step estimation, but for the coups d'état variable, the p-value is only 0.114.

9. Note that added alone in a Burnside-Dollar type of regression, aid × policy is not significant (result not reported).

10. Economic vulnerability has also been introduced in the regressions of table 2, but it was not significant (p-values are presented in the last rows of the table).

11. Note that a similar argument can be made regarding both political instability, which has a negative impact on policy, and absorptive capacity, which has a positive impact on policy. The interactive term of past policy with political instability (absorptive capacity) is significantly positive (negative), suggesting that the negative (positive) impact of political instability (absorptive capacity) is stronger when the initial policy is poor.

References

The word "processed" describes informally reproduced works that may not be commonly available in libraries.

Alesina, Alberto, and Roberto Perotti. 1996. "Income Distribution, Political Instability, and Investment." *European Economic Review* 40(6): 1203–28.

Alesina, Alberto, Sule Ozler, Nouriel Roubini, and Phillip Swagel. 1996. "Political Instability and Economic Growth." *Journal of Economic Growth* 1: 193–215.

Arcand, Jean-Louis, and Lisa Chauvet. 2001. "Foreign Aid, Rent-Seeking Behaviour, and Civil War." Centre d'Etudes et de Recherches sur le Développement International, Clermont-Ferrand, France. Processed.

Arellano, Manuel, and Stephen Bond. 1991. "Some Tests of Specification for Panel Data: Monte Carlo Evidence and an Application to Employment Equations." *Review of Economic Studies* 58(2): 277–97.

Banks, Arthur. 1996. *Cross-National Time Series Data.* Binghamton, N.Y.: State University of New York.

Barro, Robert, and Jong-Wha Lee. 2000. "International Data on Educational Attainment: Updates and Implications." Harvard University, Cambridge, Mass. Processed.

Berg, Elliot. 2002. "Increasing the Effectiveness of Aid: A Critique of Some Current Views." Paper prepared for the Expert Group Meeting, Department of Economic and Social Affairs, January 24–25, United Nations, New York.

Beynon, Jonathan. 2001. "Policy Implications for Aid Allocation of Recent Research on Aid Effectiveness and Selectivity." Paper presented at the Joint Development Centre and Development Assistance Committee Experts Seminar on Aid Effectiveness, Selectivity, and Poor Performers, January 17, Organisation for Economic Co-operation and Development, Paris.

Burnside, Craig, and David Dollar. 2000. "Aid, Policies, and Growth." *American Economic Review* 90(4): 847–68.

Canning, David. 1998. "A Database of World Infrastructure Stocks 1950–1995." *World Bank Economic Review* 12(3): 529–47.

Chauvet, Lisa. 2001. "Les guerres civiles de 1960 à 1999. Synthèse et mise à jour." Centre d'Etudes et de Recherches sur le Développement International, Clermont-Ferrand, France. Processed.

_____. 2003. "Socio-Political Instability and the Allocation of International Aid by Donors." *European Journal of Political Economy* 19(1): 33–59.

Chenery, H. B., and A. Strout. 1966. "Foreign Assistance and Economic Development." *American Economic Review* 56(4), part I: 679–735.

Collier, Paul, and Jan Dehn. 2001. "Aid, Shocks, and Growth." Policy Research Working Paper no. 2688. World Bank, Washington, D.C.

Collier, Paul, and David Dollar. 2001. "Can the World Cut Poverty in Half? How Policy Reform and Effective Aid Can Meet International Development Goals." *World Development* 29(11): 1787–1802.

———. 2002. "Aid Allocation and Poverty Reduction." *European Economic Review* 46(8): 1475–1500.

Collier, Paul, and Anke Hoeffler. 2000. "Aid, Policy, and Peace." World Bank, Development Research Group, Washington, D.C.

Collier, Paul, Patrick Guillaumont, Sylviane Guillaumont Jeanneney, and Jan W. Gunning. 1997. "Redesigning Conditionality." *World Development* 25(9): 1399–1407.

Combes, Jean-Louis, Patrick Guillaumont, Sylviane Guillaumont Jeanneney, and Pascale Motel Combes. 2000. "Ouverture sur l'extérieur et instabilité des taux de croissance." *Revue Française d'Economie* 15(1): 3–33.

Devarajan, Shantayanan, David Dollar, and Torgny Holmgrem, eds. 2001. *Aid and Reform in Africa*. Washington, D.C.: World Bank.

Dollar, David, and Aart Kraay. 2001. "Growth Is Good for the Poor." Policy Research Working Paper no. 2587. World Bank, Washington, D.C.

Guillaumont, Patrick. 2000a. "Making Aid more Effective in Reducing Poverty. Comment." In Conseil d'Analyse Economique and World Bank, eds., *Governance Equity and Global Markets*. Proceedings of the Annual World Bank Conference on Development Economics—Europe. Paris: La Documentation Française.

———. 2000b. *On the Economic Vulnerability of Low Income Countries*. Clermont-Ferrand, France: Centre d'Etudes et de Recherches sur le Développement International.

Guillaumont, Patrick, and Lisa Chauvet. 2001. "Aid and Performance: A Reassessment." *Journal of Development Studies* 37(6): 66–92.

Guillaumont, Patrick, Sylviane Guillaumont Jeanneney, and Jean-François Brun. 1999. "How Instability Lowers African Growth." *Journal of African Economies* 8(1): 87–107.

Hansen, Henrik, and Finn Tarp. 2000. "Aid Effectiveness Disputed." *Journal of International Development* 12(3): 375–98.

———. 2001. "Aid and Growth Regressions." *Journal of Development Economics* 64(2): 547–70.

Millikan, M. F., and W. W. Rostow. 1957. *A Proposal: Key to an Effective Foreign Policy*. New York: Harper and Row.

Rodriguez, Francisco, and Dani Rodrik. 1999. "Trade, Policy, and Economic Growth: A Skeptic's Guide to Cross National Evidence." Working Paper no. 7081. National Bureau of Economic Research, Cambridge, Mass.

Rosenstein-Rodan, P. N. 1961. "International Aid for Underdeveloped Countries." *Review of Economics and Statistics* 43(2): 107–138.

Sachs Jeffrey D., and Andrew M. Warner. 1995. "Economic Reform and the Process of Global Integration." *Brooking Papers on Economic Activity* 1: 1–118.

Summers, Robert, and Alan Heston. 1991. "The Penn World Tables (Mark 5): An Expanded Set of International Comparisons, 1950–1988." *Quarterly Journal of Economics* 106(2): 327–68.

Tsikata, Yvonne M. 2001. "Ghana." In S. Devarajan, D. Dollar, and T. Holmgrem, eds., *Aid and Reform in Africa*. Washington, D.C.: World Bank.

United Nations. 2000. *Poverty amidst Riches: The Need for Change*. Report of the Committee for Development Policy on the second session, April 3–7. New York.

World Bank. 1998. *Assessing Aid: What Works, What Doesn't, and Why*. New York: Oxford University Press.

_____. 2000. *World Development Report 2000–2001. Attacking Poverty*. New York: Oxford University Press.

New Poverty Reduction Strategies: Old Wine in New Bottles?

JEAN-PIERRE CLING, MIREILLE RAZAFINDRAKOTO,
AND FRANÇOIS ROUBAUD

Another idea has now appeared which fires the enthusiasm of some Northern economists, that of eradicating poverty—a phenomenon which, apparently, they have just discovered. Who could refuse to fight against poverty? . . . But is this possible outside the context of development and an enlightened international cooperation policy?

R. Prebisch (1979, pp. 1–2)

At the end of the last decade, the World Bank and the International Monetary Fund (IMF) were forced to change their attitude and renew their approaches and practices toward developing countries. Acute awareness about the increase in the incidence of poverty in many parts of the world contributed significantly to this evolution, as did the failure of structural adjustment policies in most countries and the questioning of the Washington consensus on which they were based. These various elements resulted in a crisis of legitimacy among the Bretton Woods institutions (BWIs), which faced increasing criticism from civil society, various protest movements, and the phenomenon of "aid fatigue."

The BWIs reacted by launching a joint initiative at the end of 1999 that positioned the fight against poverty at the core of development policies. Under this initiative, low-income countries wishing to apply for financial aid from either the World Bank or the IMF or for debt relief under the Heavily Indebted Poor Countries (HIPC) initiative are required to draw up poverty reduction programs known as poverty reduction strategy papers (PRSPs).[1] Since then, the BWIs have mobilized considerable human and financial resources to implement the initiative and to ensure its success.

Jean-Pierre Cling is director of Développement et Insertion Internationale (DIAL) in Paris and a member of the Croissance, Inégalités, Population et Rôle de l'Etat (CIPRE) research unit of the Institut de Recherche pour le Développement (IRD). Mireille Razafindrakoto is an economist at DIAL, a member of the CIPRE research unit, and an IRD researcher. François Roubaud is an economist at DIAL and director of the CIPRE research unit. This is a revised version of the paper presented at the ABCDE-Europe conference.

Annual World Bank Conference on Development Economics—Europe 2003
© 2004 The International Bank for Reconstruction and Development/The World Bank

FIGURE 1. A Comparison of the Main Characteristics of Structural Adjustment
Programs and Poverty Reduction Strategy Papers

Main objective	Structural adjustment programs	Poverty reduction strategy papers	New principles
Instruments	- Policy framework papers (World Bank) - Country assistance strategy (World Bank) - Enhanced structural adjustment facility (IMF)	- Poverty reduction strategy papers (BWIs, countries) - Poverty reduction support credit (World Bank) - Poverty reduction and growth facility (IMF)	- Ownership - Participation - Donor coordination
Handling of debt	- Indirect (Paris Club)	- Debt alleviation (HIPC, BWIs)	- Donor coordination
Preparation	- Policies imposed from outside - Top-down decisions - Secretive	- Nationally prepared policies - Bottom-up approach - Transparent	- Ownership - Participation/ empowerment - Accountability
Accounting for country specificity	- Weak	- Strong	- Ownership
Funding	- Project aid a priority	- Budget support a priority	- Ownership - Donor coordination
Monitoring indicators/ conditionalities	- Means indicators	- Results indicators	- Accountability

Source: Cling, Razafindrakoto, and Roubaud (2003).

Other donors rapidly decided to follow suit and link their aid policies to the PRSP initiative. The new poverty reduction programs now channel all official international aid resources destined for low-income countries, that is, almost all these countries' external resources.

As figure 1 shows, the principles on which PRSPs are based represent a fundamental break with past practice in relation to the way policies are designed and their content, their funding, and their performance indicators. In all these aspects, the failure of previous strategies required the BWIs to formulate policies based on radically different principles. In this context, three major innovations should be recognized.

First, the BWIs' placement of poverty reduction, and not structural adjustment, at the core of their strategies is a welcome shift. Indeed, the quotation from Prebisch at the beginning of this paper reminds us that poverty reduction is an objective that was first affirmed in the 1970s, but was largely set aside during the structural adjustment era.[2] In particular, the fact that this initiative helps to secure social expenditures is one result that deserves to be emphasized.

Second, adopting a participatory process for defining and monitoring the PRSPs is an innovation drawn from experience with various forms of participatory democracy in an increasing number of countries. It certainly has great potential for strengthening democracy in countries where people generally have few ways to make themselves heard.

Third, the objective of increased coordination of aid is one of the main principles of PRSPs. Indeed, the PRSP/HIPC approach does lead to better coherence between donors, including between the BWIs themselves: the major donors are aligned in relation to this framework, and debt relief granted within the HIPC initiative is managed collectively. This is a major change, because foreign aid has traditionally been criticized for its incoherence.

It might be too soon to assess the entire scope of the new poverty reduction initiative, especially because to date it has mainly initiated dialogue on development strategies, and gradual improvements are supposed to take place in the future through an ongoing process. Nevertheless, alongside some positive features that can be considered as steps forward, this new initiative clearly also has many weaknesses and contradictions that need to be addressed.

This paper aims at presenting a first diagnosis of the PRSPs and is based on an indepth analysis summarized in Cling, Razafindrakoto, and Roubaud (2003). It focuses on three main questions related to the PRSPs' basic components—participatory process, poverty reduction strategy, and monitoring and evaluation system—as defined by the World Bank (Klugman 2002). First, will the participatory process really result in ownership of policies by developing countries and will it enhance their governments' accountability and their people's empowerment? Second, has the content of policies changed and are they able to meet the goals that have been set? Third, what are the available means for monitoring and assessing these new policies?

New Relationships between Stakeholders

In an attempt to break with previous practices that, under structural adjustment, tended to take responsibility away from the countries receiving development aid, the new approach clearly emphasizes that each country has the primary responsibility for its own development. While also acknowledging fault, in a report prepared for the United Nations International Conference on Financing for Development, held in Monterrey in March 2002, the World Bank stated:

> One lesson from experience is that reform does not usually succeed without strong local ownership and a broad-based approach, which includes a consideration of institutions, governance, and stakeholder participation—a lesson that has provided the impetus for the Poverty Reduction Strategy Paper (PRSP) process. (World Bank 2002b, p. 46)

Learning from experience, the new approach, outlined by the World Bank (Klugman 2002), recommends active involvement by all stakeholders and the establishment of new relationships between them.

The objective of the PRSPs is to respect the following principles:

- *Ownership.* If governments are responsible for preparing PRSPs and for conducting participatory processes, this should increase their commitment to undertake the actions set out in the PRSP efficiently, while participation by civil society, not only in defining policies, but also in monitoring them, should ensure wide support for reforms.

- *Empowerment.* The intent of the participatory process is to improve the quality of the political debate and to help define strategies that better meet real social needs. By offering the poor a way to express themselves and to influence policies affecting their living conditions, this approach also aims to fight social exclusion, which is one dimension of poverty.

- *Accountability.* Through participation, all stakeholders are invited to discuss government policies and governments are made accountable to all citizens. Accountability applies to government policies in general (have the policies actually been implemented and to what effect?), and more specifically to the use of resources, especially foreign aid, and public expenditure management.

The current PRSPs and their chances of success can be analyzed using a flow chart (figure 2) that identifies the key stakeholders and shows how they interact (convergence of interests, tactical alliances, power relationships, sources of tension, open conflicts, and so on). As a first approximation, each actor may be decomposed into two subgroups, the one dominant and the other dominated: the state, in its broadest sense, differentiating between the ministry of finance and other public institutions (technical ministries, local administrations); civil society at large, differentiating between organized intermediate groups and the citizenry (whose opinions are supposed to be relayed through public opinion), especially the poor; and the donors (which now refer to themselves as development partners), separating the BWIs from other donors (multilateral and bilateral). The objective is to synthesize the intensity and the nature of relationships that generally characterize these three groups (the state, civil society, and donors) today.

Our analysis focuses on the new relationships between stakeholders, particularly the position of donors whose aim is to promote ownership of poverty reduction strategies, and on the potential impact on democracy of the participatory process, which requires the effective application of both empowerment and accountability concepts.

Donors' New Attitude toward Increased Ownership

PRSPs promote the establishment of new relationships between donors and developing countries aimed at making recipient countries more aware of their responsibilities in relation to both the definition of policies and their application. The BWIs now adopt, in principle at least, a more humble attitude concerning the countries in which they intervene. PRSPs are supposed to be written by the countries themselves,

FIGURE 2. New Relationships between the State, Civil Society, and Donors

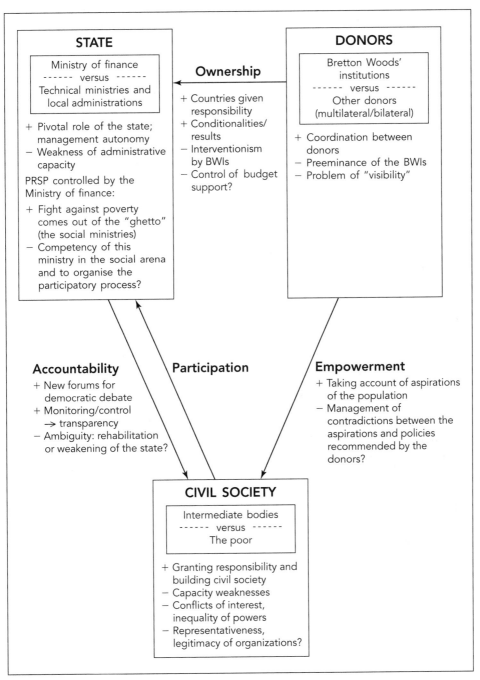

+   Positive points.
−   Weak points, problems.

Source: Cling, Razafindrakoto, and Roubaud (2003).

whereas the World Bank's policy framework papers were mostly written in Washington. In parallel, the BWIs also seek better coordination between themselves and between other donors. This new approach is supposed to go hand-in-hand with a transformation of conditionalities attached to funding, which are now considered to be a major impediment to increased ownership.

The structural adjustment period was marked by the burgeoning of intrusive conditionalities imposed by the BWIs. According to Chavagneux (2001), the number of structural conditions included in IMF facilities linked to structural reforms grew from an average of 2 in 1987 to 17 in 1997, before falling to 13 in 1999. Officially, this process has now been abandoned.[3] Indeed, as the IMF points out, streamlining structural conditionality is necessary to increase ownership (Khan and Sharma 2002).

The principles underlying the PRSPs should lead to the growth of budget support at the expense of project aid. Whereas project aid precludes all policy ownership, the PRSPs assume that policy ownership becomes easier with budget support. This is justified by the fact that funds released by debt relief within the PRSP framework lead to savings in public debt servicing, and as such constitute budget support. In addition, promoting aid ownership by the recipient countries has as its corollary the granting of greater management control over these funds, which is inherent in budget support. The counterpart should be greater aid selectivity, but debt relief within the HIPC initiative is granted according to purely financial criteria, without taking into account the quality of governance or financial needs.

Conditionality criteria have changed in that they no longer concern only the measures to be adopted, but also, and above all, the outcomes regarding poverty reduction. The extent of the changes should not be underestimated. Rather than encouraging developing country governments to act out a pantomime by stressing the formal aspects of their respect for their commitments, for the first time the PRSPs are also emphasizing the fundamentals, that is, policy results, which is a sensible principle for assessing any policy, whatever the field. However, putting these principles into practice will be far more difficult than it seems to be, as the analysis of monitoring and evaluation presented later demonstrates.

Conceived as a holistic development strategy, PRSPs also aim to improve the coherence of donors' interventions. Insofar as all donor countries are also shareholders in the BWIs, approvals of programs naturally lead to their incorporation in each country's aid policy, which is exactly what has happened in recent years. However, the risk remains that greater practical cohesion masks an alignment of all donors, whether bilateral or multilateral, behind a strategy defined and applied by the BWIs without consultation with other donors.[4] The fact that the major donors consider the PRSPs to be the basis of their interventions in low-income countries reinforces the importance of PRSPs as a condition for receiving foreign aid.

Thus conditionalities have not disappeared from the PRSP framework. They are merely "internalized," because to obtain debt relief, countries are required to define homegrown economic strategies that the BWIs subsequently validate. As such, the principles of ownership and conditionality appear antithetic. Thus in practice, the principle extolling national sovereignty remains largely illusory: the international financial community remains dependent, to a great extent, on intervention by means of coercion. PRSPs are, above all, conditions imposed by the BWIs for granting new financial aid. Furthermore, the predominance of donors in providing funding for developing countries with no access to private capital flows has increased with the introduction of PRSPs, because these have now become essential instruments in relations between developing countries and the donor community as a precondition both for debt relief and for access to new concessional lending by the BWIs. This biases the process of national ownership from the start. Because the BWIs must ratify the countries' strategies, the respect for conditionalities and policies suggested by the BWIs take precedence over those judged adequate by national players.

The Participatory Process as a Factor in Strengthening Democracy

One of the main innovations of the PRSP approach is the participation of civil society in the definition and monitoring of policies with the goal of strengthening the democratic debate and, as such, enhancing the legitimacy and efficiency of policies. Paradoxically, criticisms against this new principle come from all sides of the political scene. On the one hand, some critics underline the inevitable interference with politics inferred by the participatory process, claiming that the promotion of citizen involvement by those other than the democratically elected government risks fragmenting young democracies (Summers 2001). On the other hand, some critics are suspicious of what they perceive as the BWIs' duplicity, claiming that they have just adopted a slogan, but have neither the will nor the competence (seeing as how they are staffed primarily by economists) to intervene in the political arena and to conduct a participatory process (Chavagneux 2001).

Despite numerous difficulties and imperfections, as underscored in the many reviews undertaken by nongovernmental organizations (NGOs) as well as by experts and BWI staff (IDA and IMF 2002; ODI 2001; Whaites 2002), we have no doubt that this initiative should be encouraged. Few countries engaged in defining and implementing PRSPs are truly democratic, and unlike in long-standing democracies, intermediate civil society bodies, such as political parties, trade unions, associations, and NGOs, are extremely fragile, if not entirely absent; yet it is such bodies that are supposed to ensure democratic control between elections by means of lobbying groups, petitions, demonstrations, and so on. Thus little or no mediation takes place between the elected powers and the people, especially the most disadvantaged among them. Under such conditions, the participatory process principle is a potentially positive factor because it may help reinforce intermediate institutions (social capital), have a positive influence on the accountability of the state, enlarge the democratic debate, and improve the circulation of information. It also provides a forum for the expression of problems and opinions that did not exist before, and is therefore a means for empowering the poor.

This is not to say that the processes established in recent years are satisfactory. Observers have noted numerous deficiencies caused by such factors as inexperience and lack of good will or capacity on the part of some of the actors in the process. The sidelining of elected assemblies in several cases is particularly questionable (McGee, Levene, and Hughes 2002). Participation has also been incomplete because some governments are reluctant to accept suggestions from civil society groups. For example, in Cambodia only the final version of the interim PRSP was made available in Khmer (Whaites 2002). Thinking that PRSPs would generate a civil society if one were not already organized is naive. Simply organizing a participatory process is difficult, especially given poor countries' limitations and time constraints: poor countries need debt relief urgently, which requires them to complete their PRSPs rapidly.

This gives rise to two questions. First, what are the preliminary criteria that allow civil society representatives to take part in defining economic policies? While NGOs are generally considered as the only representatives of civil society, they frequently lack representativeness, legitimacy, and capacity, which according to the World Bank are the three main criteria essential for ensuring effective participation. The central role NGOs play (by default in the absence of other representative organizations) risks increasing the normal perverse effects arising from their function as "development brokers" (seeking development rents) or as fronts for the administration (Lautier 2001; Raffinot and Roubaud 2001; Winter 2001). For example, trade unions are often excluded from the process, as is the private sector, which is theoretically considered to be part of civil society, but which is not always explicitly involved in the participatory process.

Does this mean that participation by civil society is useless, or even that it biases the functioning of democracy? Clearly the lack of coordination and organization of civil society in poor countries constitutes a serious handicap for the success of the process, but in most countries the process must above all be viewed as a means of strengthening civil society. The benefits of this approach will be manifested only when it leads to the preparation of a feasible and ultimately successful PRSP. However, the elaboration of economic policies to alleviate poverty is a difficult exercise, both for national leaders and for civil society, and for most of them it will be their first experience with such an exercise. Capacity weaknesses, a lack of training, and inadequate information prevent them from proposing concrete policies that can withstand rigorous analysis or be defended against donors. Ownership, as an objective, risks coming up against this problem of inadequate capacity with, in consequence, a return to policy definition by the donors.

The second question is whether genuine will exists to allow civil society to have an effective influence on decisionmaking. In Nicaragua, the macroeconomic framework was not open to debate, partly because it was determined by a separate IMF Poverty Reduction Growth Facility program being negotiated at the same time (Panos Institute 2002). Implementation of the principle of accountability also leads us to question the management of conflicts of interest within civil society and how policy definition takes the outcome of the participatory process into account. The choice between a purely consultative process or a process that actually contributes to decisionmaking is not explicit, even if in practice the trend is toward the former alternative, which tends to generate frustration among the participants (McGee, Levene, and Hughes 2002). The situation could hardly be otherwise, as the principle of the participatory process as described by the World Bank (Klugman 2002) does not permit resolving conflicts of interest. By and large, as was the case with the *World Development Report 2000/2001: Attacking Poverty* (World Bank 2000a), which inspired this new approach, PRSPs neither take into account the need for arbitration when defining a poverty reduction strategy nor all the implications of this strategy for the state in general. In this sense, the participatory process concept may be considered "utopian" (Lautier 2001).

Political Economy versus Economic Policy

Recent years have witnessed intense debate about the reasons behind the general outcome of structural adjustment policies in developing countries, whose failure is especially obvious in Africa. On the one hand, the imperfections of policy design are notably pointed out by Stiglitz (2002) and UNCTAD (2002) in general, and more specifically by Berg (2000) concerning public sector reform. On the other hand, the deficiencies in the implementation of reform (whose quality has been extremely unequal) are widely recognized (Collier 1997; van de Walle 2001). Nevertheless, according to Killick (1996), nearly half the IMF programs conducted in developing countries between 1979 and 1993 were completed during the loan period. If this is true, then why have these countries not been able to register sustained economic growth and poverty reduction since that time?

The BWIs have undoubtedly chosen their side in this debate: they ascribe most of the blame to the developing countries' failure to implement these economic policies rather than to their content. Therefore according to the BWIs, changing the methods for elaborating and applying policies, that is, by promoting ownership, participation, and accountability, would be enough to ensure their success without necessarily having to review their appropriateness or adequacy. As a consequence, the PRSP process currently underestimates the necessary change required in the orientation of economic policy, even though most economists agree that at least some aspects of these policies need to be reexamined. This especially concerns the need for a better balance between state and markets to take specific national and local contexts into account and the shortcomings of liberalization (see the paper by Klasen in this volume).

Our diagnosis of the content of PRSPs is based on an examination of interim and final PRSPs prepared by the end of 2002, paying particular attention to those countries that have finalized arrangements,[5] as well as to the BWIs' joint staff assessments and PRSP review (IDA and IMF 2002) and assessments by various other institutions (Thin, Underwood, and Gilling 2001; Whaites 2002). Our goal is not to undertake an exhaustive review of the strengths and weaknesses of the documents. Rather, we seek to highlight a number of oversights that have implications for efficient poverty reduction and that appear to have been inadequately addressed to date.

PRSPs Share Some Shortcomings

Detailed analysis of PRSPs shows that their content is of unequal quality, depending on the country concerned. Those where poverty alleviation programs have been in preparation for several years, such as Honduras, Mozambique, and Uganda, and those that have received significant external technical assistance, Bolivia in particular, are distinguished by relatively elaborate PRSPs.[6] By contrast, PRSPs are more basic and superficial for countries that prepared them under a strict time constraint and lacked adequate experience with poverty alleviation, for instance, Burkina Faso, Mauritania, and Tanzania.

Nevertheless, despite these differences most countries' strategies consist of simple recycling of previous policies with minimal adjustments to establish a link with poverty. To obtain the international funding they badly need, poor countries adjust their strategies to what they know the BWIs expect from them. This process of homogenization is reinforced by the wide availability of PRSPs, notably on the World Bank web site, which generates a cascading, mimetic effect.

The emphasis on the fight against poverty and the establishment of a participatory process, while supposed to promote an appreciation of people's needs and of the characteristics of each country, appear to have little influence on the content of programs. The translation of general orientations into concrete operational measures raises several difficulties, in particular, because of the problem of the lack of capacity in poor countries and because of the underestimation of these human and financial resource constraints, which are generally not even acknowledged. The lack of well-defined priorities reflects this underestimation of capacity constraints, yet the need for priorities is especially crucial, as the objectives that have been set are extremely ambitious, and perhaps even unrealistic. For example, most African countries will clearly be far from reaching the Millennium Development Goals set down in their PRSPs that they are to achieve by 2015 (World Bank 2002a,c).

The diagnosis that states' institutional capacities need to be strengthened is not clearly assessed, although managing poverty reduction strategies is even more complex and more demanding than managing past stabilization or adjustment programs. The World Bank itself recognizes that this problem is especially acute in Africa. According to a World Bank (2000b, p. 37) report:

> [T]he adjustment decades also saw a substantial deterioration in the quality of public institutions, a demoralization of public servants, and a decline in the effectiveness of service delivery in many countries. Together with falling incomes, these effects—which cannot be speedily reversed—translated into falling social indicators and capabilities in many countries and to losses of human capital, especially (though not exclusively) in the public service.

The same negligence is apparent in relation to strengthening the capacities of civil society: the PRSPs do not address the issue of empowerment, that is, the consolidation of civil society organizations.

Failure to Address the Link between Poverty and Inequality

Given that PRSPs are inspired and validated by the BWIs, their inadequacies reflect, above all, the inadequacies of these institutions (Cling 2003). This section discusses how PRSPs gloss over the links between poverty and inequality, which we consider to be one of their main analytical shortcomings. As Bourguignon (2003, p. 1) argues:

> Part of the ongoing debate on poverty reduction strategies bears on the issue of the actual contribution of economic growth to poverty reduction. There is no doubt that faster economic growth is associated with faster poverty reduction. But what is the corresponding elasticity? If it is reasonably high, then poverty reduction strategies almost exclusively relying on economic growth are probably justified. If it is low, however, ambitious poverty reduction strategies might have to combine both economic growth and some kind of redistribution.

In practice, the impact of growth on poverty depends to a great extent on initial inequality. Higher income inequality reduces the impact of growth, because the poor are further away from the poverty line and their income increases start from a lower base (Ravallion 2002). According to the World Bank (2000a), a 1 percent increase in average per capita consumption reduces the incidence of extreme poverty (the proportion of people living on less than US$1 a day) by around 1.5 percent in a country with an initial Gini coefficient of 0.6 (the inequality index staying constant). The equivalent reduction is doubled (3 percent) if the Gini coefficient is 0.2. Because of this relationship, income redistribution has a dual payoff in poverty reduction: it reduces poverty instantaneously by giving the poor higher incomes and it contributes to a permanent increase in the elasticity of poverty reduction with respect to growth, and therefore to an acceleration of poverty reduction for a given rate of economic growth (Bourguignon 2003). Thus if "growth is good for the poor," as the title of a widely quoted World Bank study (Dollar and Kraay 2002) claims, it certainly is not sufficient to reduce poverty significantly in the near future, especially in developing countries where high levels of poverty are found in combination with inequality.[7]

One would expect poverty reduction strategies to take these conclusions into account, especially as countries' PRSPs assign extremely ambitious objectives as far as poverty reduction is concerned, such as halving extreme poverty by 2015 (which is the first of the eight Millennium Development Goals). In practice, most PRSPs do not address the issue of inequalities and redistribution. A detailed analysis of PRSPs available at the time this paper was written reveals that, with the exception of Bolivia's PRSP, they rarely use the word redistribution, and that concepts related to inequality are only mentioned occasionally, with just Vietnam effectively emphasizing this subject.[8] No doubt most PRSPs wish to avoid head-on conflicts of interest between different population groups, but at the same time they avoid addressing the social cohesion that the participatory process is meant to build or to reinforce.

This general lack of interest in the inequality issue is hardly surprising given the World Bank's overall neglect of social inequality. Contrary to the United Nations Development Programme, for example, the World Bank views the fight against inequalities as a means and not as an end in itself (Klugman 2002).[9] Whether the intent is to promote a policy aimed at reducing inequality or not, PRSPs always follow the same instrumental approach. For instance, even though Guyana is a middle-income country, its PRSP reaffirms the following:

> With per capita income of less than US$3 per day, there is very little scope for income redistribution as a mechanism for poverty reduction . . . Given the evidence of a strong correlation between growth and poverty reduction, income redistribution is not a viable option.

On the contrary, the PRSPs of Bolivia, Mauritania, and Zambia suggest improving income distribution to accelerate growth, and ultimately to reduce poverty faster.

Poverty alleviation strategies necessarily imply arbitration between conflicting interests that is almost never explicitly stated. For example, the principle of universal social protection is implicitly queried in some PRSPs (Lautier 2001), which raises questions about the position to be adopted regarding the non-poor or the less poor among the poor. In the same way, in many countries access to land by the poor would require the application of a land redistribution policy to the detriment of better-off population groups, but measures recommended in PRSPs in this connection are generally limited to guarantees of tenure. Finally, with few exceptions—notably Bolivia, Mauritania, and Uganda—fiscal policies are not mentioned as instruments to be used in promoting income redistribution in favor of the most impoverished.

The Challenge of Building an Efficient Monitoring and Evaluation System

Despite the neglect of these in the past, monitoring and evaluation systems are now a built-in component of PRSPs. They are supposed to guide action in real time, with their findings used as a basis for redirecting policies. In addition, the emphasis on citizen participation in defining policies and in leading reforms implies wider access to information about problems and about the actual or expected impacts of implemented or planned options. Policy evaluation becomes all the more crucial because of the changes in the types of conditionality criteria noted earlier. The relative growth of budget support demands the establishment of results-based indicators, which are also a way to control the use of external funds, because permanent monitoring as applied to project aid is no longer feasible.[10]

Currently, however, one of the main weaknesses in the current process is the lack of innovations in relation to monitoring and evaluation systems (IDA and IMF 2002). To date, monitoring and evaluation systems proposed in PRSPs are, in general, nothing more than an extension of past systems, with in some cases an effort being made to measure indicators directly linked to the Millennium Development Goals. Clearly much remains to be done, and even to be devised, in this area. Even though the poor countries have implemented policies—albeit not necessarily good or effective ones—the policies have seldom been monitored, and even more rarely have they been rigorously evaluated. Many countries' statistical systems are in ruins (the most recent estimates of poverty based on survey data are often more than 10 years old), political demands for indicators and analytical results are insignificant, and providing the general public with economic and social information is problematic. As for policy evaluation, it faces intrinsic methodological problems. Even though these problems are not specific to developing countries, given their serious deficiencies in even the most elementary information systems and lack of reliable, relevant data, they make assessing the impact of policies difficult, if not impossible.

Acquiring Relevant Monitoring Systems

A critical review of the indicators proposed in the final PRSPs for five African countries reveals a number of shortcomings (Brilleau 2002): they fail to address the issue of monitoring systems; they often propose inadequate indicators for tracking the progress of suggested policies and actions and evaluating their results; they pay too little attention to intermediate indicators, which are easier to measure than final indicators; they focus too much on monetary poverty and on indicators of access to health and education services, neglecting those dealing with the population's level of satisfaction; they fail to include indicators to measure the share of state spending toward rural areas; and they do not take into account the lack of data and the human and financial constraints affecting the collection of data.

In relation to final indicators measuring monetary poverty, we come to the paradoxical conclusion that the proliferation of household surveys during the last decade has not led to a better understanding of the evolution of poverty (Razafindrakoto and Roubaud 2003b). This is due to the inadequacy and inconsistency of survey design and of indicators and to poor—if not unacceptable—reliability of statistical data, which in African countries continues to deteriorate (Deaton 1995; Naudet 2000; Srinivasan 2001). While the analyses based on these data carried out by academics from the industrial countries and from international institutions have become increasingly sophisticated in relation to poverty (chronic and transient) and inequality, the results are rarely communicated to poor countries. In the latter, at best only extremely basic analyses are conducted, which are largely underutilized by decisionmakers and rarely made available to civil society (for the example of Mali, see Dante, Marouani, and Raffinot 2003). In such conditions, the absence of linkages between diagnoses on characteristics and causality of poverty, established on the basis of poverty profiles, and strategies proposed in most PRSPs is not surprising.

The introduction of reliable methods of poverty monitoring within the framework of new policies and their evaluation calls for a radical break with past practice. This break must take place on two closely connected fronts: first, technically, in terms of the production and analysis of statistics (methodology for ensuring consistency in sequential monitoring indicators, fieldwork, and procedures for ensuring data quality); and second, institutionally (capacity building, wage issues, mobility, career management, training, access to information) to reinforce the public institutions responsible for economic and social information systems in the South. While the list of recommendations may seem to be based on simple common sense, experience nonetheless shows that they are not generally adhered to. This catalogue of good practice constitutes a minimum requirement for offsetting the effects resulting from the deterioration in data quality and institutional capacity over the last 15 years. This is especially true given that the new generation of surveys, launched rapidly to finalize the PRSPs, bodes ill for a rapid improvement in the situation.

Widening the Scope of Monitoring Indicators

As regards monitoring indicators, numerous paths must be explored to reach beyond the narrow framework of traditional indicators (on monetary poverty, education, and health) and to take into account new concepts concerned with the multiple dimensions of poverty, especially those related to vulnerability, empowerment, and participation versus exclusion. This is particularly important because the various dimensions of poverty do not overlap. According to Razafindrakoto and Roubaud (2003a), while nearly 80 percent of the population in Antananarivo, the capital of Madagascar, fall into at least one of seven categories of poverty related to monetary and nonmonetary poverty, including subjective poverty, only 2.4 percent fall in all seven categories (table 1).

An adequate monitoring and evaluation system must explore and aim for a better understanding of the interactions between various dimensions of development strategies, such as the level of growth; the distribution of income and assets; the quality of institutions, particularly public institutions; the type of political regime; and the society's value system. The objectives pertain to the collection of information as well as to the evaluation methods to be put in place.

TABLE 1. Percentage of the Population Found in Different Categories of Poverty, Antananarivo, Madagascar, 1998

Category of poverty	Percentage of the population
Monetary poverty (consumption of less than US$1 a day per capita)	32.0
Nonmonetary "objective" poverty	
In terms of living conditions (existential poverty)	35.0
In terms of human capital	32.6
In terms of social exclusion	34.6
"Subjective" poverty	
General perception	33.0
Nonsatisfaction of needs considered to be vital	34.5
Financial difficulties	33.9
Fall into all seven poverty categories	2.4
Fall into all four objective categories of poverty (monetary poverty and objective poverty)	7.1
Fall into all three nonmonetary objective categories of poverty	8.9
Fall into all three categories of subjective poverty	11.9
Falling into at least one of the poverty categories	77.7

Source: Razafindrakoto and Roubaud (2003a).

Statistical surveys are a way to listen to the voices of the poor and to provide quantitative information that decisionmakers can use. In countries where not only are the authorities not yet held substantially accountable for their actions and performance, but the bridging organizations through which the poorest groups in the population can promote their interests (that is, organized civil society) are virtually nonexistent, representative surveys constitute a unique opportunity for the poor to express their opinions and influence public policy. They also provide precise and relevant information about the quality of governance, which donors are still urgently seeking (Kaufmann, Kraay, and Zoido-Lobaton 2002). Three types of information can be collected and combined by means of household surveys: subjective perceptions and values (poll surveys); objective data on socio-political practices (political and social participation, access to public services, violence, corruption, and so on); and classical economic variables (education, occupation, income, consumption, and so on).

An example of the application of this kind of approach in selected African countries shows that with the exception of Abidjan, most people living in the capital cities believe that policies currently being implemented by their governments do not take their aspirations into account and do not believe that they are clearly contributing to poverty reduction (figure 3).[11]

According to these household surveys, the poor have a strong need for the state and for public regulation, which reflects a strong need for protection. This result

FIGURE 3. People's Opinions About Policies Implemented by Their Governments, Five African Capitals, 2001–02

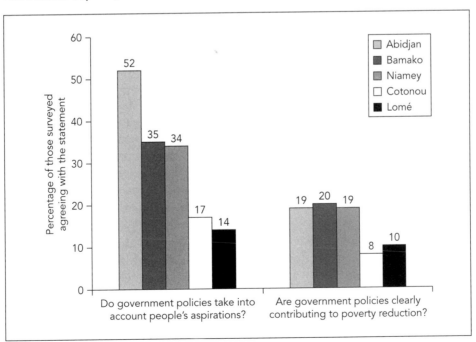

Source: 1-2-3 surveys; national statistical offices; authors' calculations.

presents a problem for the BWIs: how can they integrate such an aspiration for a welfare state (Cling, Razafindrakoto, and Roubaud 2003)? The broad consensus about the measures that should be taken to reform public services, such as linking salaries to performance and reinforcing a system for penalizing incompetent employees, confirms the possibility for creating pro-reform coalitions and the legitimacy of these types of measures. Empirical evidence also highlights a link between an improvement in civil servants' wages in Madagascar and a sharp drop in the incidence of corruption (Razafindrakoto and Roubaud 2001). Despite their potential contribution to decisionmaking, measurement of these types of indicators remains the exception in poor countries.

Evaluating Policy

Defining an effective strategy to fight poverty requires, in particular, a careful assessment of the distributive impact of economic policies that are planned or implemented. The World Bank's and IMF's poverty and social impact analysis programs respond to this need. These recent programs represent an immense project in terms of operational research and applications (Bourguignon, Pereira da Silva, and Stern 2002). However, the first evaluation of the PRSP process by the BWIs found that poverty and social impact analysis remains nonexistent:

> Poverty and Social Impact Analysis (PSIA) of major policies and programs has typically not been undertaken as part of PRSPs, for reasons to do with national capacity constraints and its inherent technical difficulties. The data and capacity needs are formidable and serious methodological issues remain unresolved, despite some analytical advances in this area. (IDA and IMF 2002, p. 13)

The natural order of things would have been to use these techniques from the beginning when drawing up the PRSPs and defining policy priorities, but the PRSP system was set up in such haste that this was not possible. More fundamentally, currently no instruments are available to enable precise assessment (ex ante and ex post) of the impact of the policies on poverty. Certain innovative paths of research, such as microsimulations, represent promising methodological progress in this direction (Cogneau, Grimm, and Robilliard 2003), but two fundamental problems remain unsolved: how can the multidimensional nature of poverty be taken into account when analyzing policies' redistributive effects and how can the impact of alternative policies be measured in terms of poverty. For example, with a given budget, should a country construct rural roads or improve the quality of primary schooling? To try to answer these questions, we need an analysis of what are still widely unknown interactions between the different forms of poverty and the wide range of alternative policies.

Assuming that researchers solve these analytical difficulties and that the data required to implement the new methods are provided, the constraints of local technical and institutional capabilities will still need to be overcome and the means of dialogue between those "in the know" and society will need to be rethought to realize the key principles of ownership and participation. Although this ambitious project is clearly unattainable in the short term, making a firm commitment in this direction is nonetheless vital. Creating and transferring the appropriate instruments to be mobilized for this project will be a final challenge.

Conclusion

A review of the goals set by the new poverty reduction strategies, crystallized in PRSPs, clearly demonstrate the weaknesses of the process currently under way in connection with poverty reduction. In the coming years, the challenges will concern both the validity of the policies adopted and the ability to implement them, and tools will be required to monitor them and assess their results. At all three levels, participation is supposed to play a key role. It is also the main unknown factor.

The principle of the participatory process is to make public choices explicit and increase transparency in the management of state affairs, while offering the different players in society the possibility of exerting pressure, or even of taking sanctions in the case of policy failure. In short, accountability is at stake. But most players do not seem to be fully aware of these new prospects because they lack guidelines and are used to being excluded from decisionmaking circles. The real influence of the participatory process on economic policy decisions has yet to be defined.

The recognition of the role of the political economy in development strategies is laudable. Ownership of and participation in the process of designing and implementing policies are important, yet the process cannot by itself bridge the gap in terms of economic policy. Perhaps the BWIs' emphasis on the process is intended to mask their inability to identify viable and coherent alternative economic options?

Arrangements for measuring poverty are about to play a crucial part in drafting, monitoring, and evaluating new international development policies, but neither national nor international institutions have yet fully addressed the complete spectrum of deficiencies in poor countries' statistical systems. The diagnosis and recommendations given here are clearly fragmented, and a deeper and more systematic evaluation of existing statistical systems is necessary. Only in this way can methods for monitoring and evaluating policies stand a chance of responding effectively to the ambitious objectives assigned to them by the PRSPs.

In any event, the PRSP initiative has opened up new paths for development strategies. It offers a genuine opportunity for realizing changes in the nature of public policies and international aid in a manner that favors development and calls for greater participation by citizens. Of course, nothing guarantees that this opportunity will actually be grasped. This will depend on the ability of social forces, in local contexts, to work to this end, but the formal conditions allowing these new voices to emerge have never been as favorable. Nevertheless, whether the numerous obstacles and constraints that still exist can be overcome, and whether the different players at the national and international levels are aware of the actual stakes involved and are ready to mobilize the resources needed to make the process a success, remains to be seen.

Notes

1. The original HIPC initiative was launched in 1996, but never actually took off. The enhanced HIPC initiative—whereby the criteria for debt relief were softened and a strong link with poverty reduction was established—was launched in 1999 at the Group of Seven summit in Cologne.

2. During the presidency of Robert McNamara (1968–81), the World Bank emphasized the importance of poverty reduction. During the following decade, the United Nations Children's Fund demonstrated the negative social impact of structural adjustment (Cornia, Jolly, and Stewart 1987), which prompted the World Bank to launch the Social Dimensions of Adjustment Program.

3. Nonetheless, a case study of six poor countries (Albania, Ghana, Kenya, Mozambique, Vietnam, and Zambia) concludes that the streamlining of conditionality within the new instruments put in place by means of the PRSP initiative is limited to the IMF. This streamlining is narrowly conceived and restricted to structural, but not macroeconomic, conditions. Moreover, what may happen is that many of the more important structural conditions dropped by the IMF will be taken up in World Bank programs (Killick 2002).

4. For example, the United Nations Development Programme has long experience with the fight against poverty, but the BWIs have taken little account of it, in terms of either concepts or country strategies, as shown by a field study on Mali (Dante, Marouani, and Raffinot 2003). The same study shows that the BWIs did not allow European countries to participate in the negotiations on the PRSP with the Malian government.

5. These countries are Albania, Bolivia, Burkina Faso, The Gambia, Guinea, Guyana, Honduras, Mauritania, Mozambique, Nicaragua, Niger, Tanzania, Uganda, Vietnam, and Zambia.

6. Bolivia and Uganda were among the pilot countries involved in the establishment of the Comprehensive Development Framework.

7. Cling and others (2003) have simulated the evolution of poverty in developing countries by 2015 based on assumptions about income distribution (log-normal hypothesis) and about the growth pattern (neutral, pro-poor, and anti-poor growth). According to their estimates, pro-poor growth could reduce poverty significantly in India, for example, but would only have a slight impact on poverty in Africa, which combines slow growth with high levels of poverty and inequality.

8. These "concepts" refers to the following words: equity/inequity, equality/inequality, equal/unequal, equitable/inequitable, and redistribution. The PRSPs of the four Central and South America countries, which are also the most inegalitarian, mention these concepts, on average, every other page, whereas the eight African countries, which are much poorer, but also generally less inegalitarian, use them only once every three pages. Vietnam, whose socialist regime makes it more inequality conscious, mentions these concepts frequently (every one-and-a-half pages), whereas Albania, despite its high and rapidly increasing inequalities, only refers to these concepts about once every five pages.

9. Maxwell (2001) regrets that the reduction of social inequalities is not listed among the Millennium Development Goals.

10. However, the application of this idea will be more difficult than it appears to be because of the weakness of policy evaluation tools. What would happen if, for example, the path followed by a country differs from its goals for exogenous reasons, such as the AIDS epidemic, which has reduced life expectancy in several African countries, or a prolonged slump in the prices of primary export commodities?

11. Roubaud (2003) provides a provisional analysis of the results of a regional program of opinions surveys in the capitals of seven West African countries, focusing on Côte d'Ivoire. Similar surveys have been regularly conducted in Antananarivo, Madagascar, since 1995 (Razafindrakoto and Roubaud 2001).

References

The word "processed" describes informally reproduced works that may not be commonly available in libraries.

Berg, Elliott. 2000. "Aid Failure: The Case of Public Sector Reform." In Finn Tarp, ed., *Foreign Aid and Development: Lessons Learnt and Directions of the Future*. London and New York: Routledge.

Bourguignon, François. 2003. "The Growth Elasticity of Poverty Reduction: Explaining Heterogeneity across Countries and Time Periods." In Theo Eicher and Stephen Turnovsky, eds., *Inequality and Growth. Theory and Policy Implications*. Cambridge, Mass.: MIT Press.

Bourguignon, François, Luiz Pereira da Silva, and Nicholas Stern. 2002. "Evaluating the Poverty Impact of Economic Policies: Some Analytical Challenges." World Bank, Washington, D.C. Processed.

Brilleau, Alain. 2002. *Etude sur les indicateurs lies à la mise en oeuvre des Cadres Stratégiques de Lutte contre la Pauvreté (CSLP)*. Report for the French Ministry of Foreign Affairs. Paris: Développement et Insertion Internationale.

Chavagneux, Christian. 2001. "Lutte contre la pauvreté; les enjeux politiques d'un slogan." *Politique africaine* (82): 161–68.

Cling, Jean-Pierre. 2003. "A Critical Review of the World Bank's Stance on Poverty Reduction." In Jean-Pierre Cling, Mireille Razafindrakoto, and François Roubaud, eds., *The New International Poverty Reduction Strategies*. London and New York: Routledge,

Cling, Jean-Pierre, Mireille Razafindrakoto, and François Roubaud, eds. 2003. *New International Poverty Reduction Strategies*. London and New York: Routledge. Also available in French: Cling, Jean-Pierre, Mireille Razafindrakoto, and François Roubaud, eds. 2002. *Les nouvelles stratégies internationales de lutte contre la pauvreté*. Paris: Economica.

Cling, Jean-Pierre, Philippe De Vreyer, Mireille Razafindrakoto, and François Roubaud. 2003. "La croissance ne suffit pas pour réduire la pauvreté." *Revue Française d'Economie* XVIII(3): 187–237.

Cogneau, Denis, Michael Grimm, and Anne-Sophie Robilliard. 2003. "Evaluating Poverty Reduction Policies: The Contribution of Micro-Simulation Techniques." In Jean-Pierre Cling, Mireille Razafindrakoto, and François Roubaud, eds., *New International Poverty Reduction Strategies*. London and New York: Routledge.

Collier, Paul. 1997. "The Failure of Conditionality." In C. Gwin and J. Nelson, eds., *Perspectives on Aid and Development*. Policy Essay no. 22. Washington, D.C.: Overseas Development Council.

Cornia, Giovanni Andrea, Richard Jolly, and Frances Stewart, eds. 1987. *Adjustment with a Human Face: Protecting the Vulnerable and Promoting Growth*. Oxford, U.K.: Oxford University Press.

Dante, Idrissa, Mohamed Ali Marouani, and Marc Raffinot. 2003. "Poverty Reduction in Mali: Will the Participatory Process Make a Difference?" In Jean-Pierre Cling, Mireille

Razafindrakoto, and François Roubaud, eds., *The New International Poverty Reduction Strategies*. London and New York: Routledge.

Deaton, Angus. 1995. "Data and Econometric Tools for Development Analysis." In J. Behrman and T. N. Srinivasan, eds., *Handbook of Development Economics,* vol. 3A. Amsterdam: North-Holland.

Dollar, David, and Aart Kraay. 2002. "Growth Is Good for the Poor." *Journal of Economic Growth* 7(3): 195–222.

IDA (International Development Association) and IMF (International Monetary Fund). 2002. *Review of the Poverty Reduction Strategy Paper (PRSP) Approach: Main Findings.* http://www.worldbank.org/poverty/strategies/review.

Kaufmann, Daniel, Aart Kraay, and Pablo Zoido-Lobaton. 2002. "Governance Matters II: Updated Indicators for 2000/01." Policy Research Department Working Paper no. 2195. World Bank, Washington, D.C.

Khan, Mohsin S., and Sunil Sharma. 2002. "IMF Conditionality and Country Ownership of Programs." Working Paper no. WP/01/142. International Monetary Fund, Washington, D.C.

Killick, Tony. 1996. *IMF Programmes in Developing Countries: Design and Impact.* London: Overseas Development Institute.

———. 2002. *The Streamlining of IMF Conditionality: Aspirations, Reality and Repercussion.* A report written for the Department for International Development. London.

Klugman, Jeni. 2002. *A Sourcebook for Poverty Reduction Strategies*. Washington, D.C.: World Bank.

Lautier, Bruno. 2001. "Sous la morale, la politique: la Banque mondiale et la lutte contre la pauvreté." *Politique africaine* (82): 169–76.

Maxwell, Simon. 2001. "Innovative and Important, Yes, but also Instrumental and Incomplete: The Treatment of Redistribution in the New Poverty Agenda." *Journal of International Development* 13: 331–41.

McGee, Rosemary, with Josh Levene and Alexandra Hughes. 2002. *Assessing Participation in Poverty Reduction Strategy Papers: A Desk-Based Synthesis of Experience in Sub-Saharan Africa.* Research Report no. 52. Brighton, U.K.: Institute of Development Studies, Participation Group.

Naudet, Jean-David. 2000. "Les 'guignols de l'info'. Réflexions sur la fragilité de l'information statistique." In J.-P. Jacob, ed., *Sciences sociales en Afrique: les rendez-vous manqués.* Paris and Geneva: Presses universitaires de France.

ODI (Overseas Development Institute). 2001. *PRSP Institutionalisation Study: Final Report.* Submitted to the Strategic Partnership with Africa. London.

Panos Institute. 2002. *Reducing Poverty: Is the World Bank's Strategy Working?* London: Panos Institute.

Prebisch, Raul. 1979. "Aspects of International Cooperation." *Trade and Development: An UNCTAD Review* 1(Spring).

Raffinot, Marc, and François Roubaud. 2001. "Recherche fonctionnaires désespérément." In *Les fonctionnaires du Sud entre deux eaux: sacrifiés ou protégés? Autrepart* (20): 5–10.

Ravallion, Martin. 2003. "Growth, Inequality, and Poverty: Looking beyond Averages." Paper presented at the Annual World Bank Conference on Development Economics—Europe, June 24–26, 2002, Oslo.

Razafindrakoto, Mireille, and François Roubaud. 2001. "Vingt ans de réforme de la fonction publique à Madagascar." *Autrepart* (20): 43–60.

_____. 2003a. "Do They Really Think Differently? The Voice of the Poor through Quantitative Surveys." In Jean-Pierre Cling, Mireille Razafindrakoto, and François Roubaud, eds., *New International Poverty Reduction Strategies*. London and New York: Routledge.

_____. 2003b. "The Existing Tools for Monitoring Poverty: Weaknesses of Traditional Household Surveys." In Jean-Pierre Cling, Mireille Razafindrakoto, and François Roubaud, eds., *New International Poverty Reduction Strategies*. London and New York: Routledge.

Roubaud, François. 2003. "La crise vue d'en bas à Abidjan: ethnicité, gouvernance et démocratie." *Afrique contemporaine* (206): 57–86.

Srinivasan, T. N. 2001. "Croissance et allègement de la pauvreté:les leçons tirées de l'expérience du Développement." *Revue d'Economie du Développement* (1–2): 115–68.

Stiglitz, Joseph. 2002. *Globalisation and its Discontents*. New York and London: W. W. Norton.

Summers, Larry. 2001. Speech at the World Bank country directors' retreat, May. http://www.jubilee2000uk.org/opinion/Larry_summers120601.htm.

Thin, Neil, Mary Underwood, and Jim Gilling. 2001. *Sub-Saharan Africa's Poverty Reduction Strategy Papers from Social Policy and Sustainable Livelihoods Perspectives*. A report for the Department for International Development. Oxford, U.K.: Oxford Policy Management.

UNCTAD (United Nations Conference on Trade and Development). 2002. *Economic Development in Africa—From Adjustment to Poverty Reduction: What Is New?* New York and Geneva: United Nations.

van de Walle, Nicolas. 2001. *African Economies and the Politics of Permanent Crisis, 1979–1999*. Cambridge, U.K.: Cambridge University Press.

Whaites, Alan, ed. 2002. *Masters of Their Own Development? PRSPs and the Prospects for the Poor*. Monrovia, Calif.: World Vision International.

Winter, Gérard, ed. 2001. *Inégalités et politiques publiques en Afrique; pluralité des normes et jeux d'acteurs*. Paris: Karthala-IRD.

World Bank. 2000a. *World Development Report 2000/2001: Attacking Poverty*. New York: Oxford University Press.

_____. 2000b. *Can Africa Claim the 21st Century?* Washington, D.C.

_____. 2002a. *Global Economic Prospects 2003: Investing to Unlock Global Opportunities*. Washington, D.C.

_____. 2002b. *The Role and Effectiveness of Development Assistance: Lessons from World Bank Experience*. Washington, D.C.: Development Economics Vice Presidency.

_____. 2002c.*World Development Indicators 2002*. Washington, D.C.

Part II. Institutions

Crisis, Political Institutions, and Policy Reform: The Good, the Bad, and the Ugly

MARIANO TOMMASI

Having written on crisis and reform in the past, I have lately become rather skeptical about several of the assumptions in some of the discussions on the political economy of reform, of which "crisis and reform" has been one component. In particular, I am inclined to take a more continuous, less episodic, and less heroic view of the policymaking process than that implicit in some discussions of "reform." Furthermore, I question the oft-voiced view that the reforms that countries need to undertake are technically obvious for any half-competent economist, and that it is just a matter of figuring out the political economy of reform. Finally, even beyond definitional problems with regard to what exactly constitutes a crisis, crises are probably not the best times for instrumenting solid, durable reforms with the properties necessary to induce adequate changes in people's behavior, and hence in societal outcomes.

Even though crises might facilitate the introduction of some policy reforms, in general, the quality of the implementation of those policies is conditioned by the overall institutional environment of the country, and crises do not necessarily induce changes at the deeper politico-institutional level. Despite their importance, the so-called first generation of reforms, which were sometimes introduced in the context of crises, were, for the most part, not reforms of the deeper determinants of the qualities of policies. The so-called second-generation reforms, even though they gave some lip service to institutions and governance, do not seem to be generating profound changes either. Thus attention has to be focused not so much on specific policies as on policymaking capabilities. Those capabilities, in turn, are conditioned by the political environment and by the rules of the political game, that is, by political institutions.

Mariano Tommasi is director of the Center of Studies for Institutional Development and professor of economics at the University of San Andrés, both in Buenos Aires, Argentina, and was visiting professor of economics and political science at Yale University, New Haven, Connecticut while reviewing this paper. This paper makes liberal use of earlier accounts of the relationship between economic crises and economic reforms, in particular, Corrales (1998); Drazen (2000); and Tommasi and Velasco (1996). The input of Oslo discussants Jorge Braga de Macedo and Guillermo Perry is gratefully acknowledged.

Annual World Bank Conference on Development Economics—Europe 2003

Let us consider the notion of a hierarchy of rules (this is developed in more detail in Acuña and Tommasi 2000; see also Levy and Spiller 1996). Policies are rules that regulate, say, the behavior of economic agents, for instance, a policy that defines tax bases and tax rates. Let us refer to these as lower-level rules belonging to the set RL. Let us call the rules that determine who has the power, under what procedures, to legislate on tax bases and tax rates intermediate-level rules (RM). These intermediate rules also include, for instance, whether the central bank has statutory independence, the allocation of power to and design of regulatory agencies, and so on. Finally, the high-level rules (RH) are those that determine how RM and RL (as well as their enforcement) are determined. RH are deeper politico-institutional rules that determine the incentives of political actors, and hence political behavior. They include the rules laid down in a country's constitution, electoral rules, and other related (including informal) practices in the polity. Together with a number of contextual and informal elements, RH determine the actual workings of the policymaking system. For instance, is the judiciary independent? Is the bureaucracy professional? Are legislators policy oriented? For brevity, I will use RH (or deep institutional determinants) to include the overall functioning of the political system (Spiller, Stein, and Tommasi 2003 describe the underlying methodology in more detail).

At any given time, the higher-level rules are given, but are themselves a product of history and of previous choices. For instance, they include rules inherited from the history of democracy in the country. In the case of Argentina (Spiller and Tommasi 2003, forthcoming), the many military interruptions of the 20th century left an imprint in several institutional spheres, such as the Supreme Court, the bureaucracy, and federal fiscal arrangements, that cast a long shadow even several years after the return to democracy in 1983.[1]

Using this language, the reforms were reforms in RL (like lowering tariffs) and RM (such as privatization or granting independence to the central bank). RH rules were not necessarily affected. RHs heavily condition not only the choice of lower-level rules, but also the details of their implementation and effectiveness. For example, the political system's capacity to enforce certain rules and to make intertemporal commitments is perhaps more important than the "title" of the policy in RM (such as public enterprises versus regulated private utilities). Even though crises might have facilitated the introduction of reform with good titles, whether they facilitated good implementation of those reforms and of the subsequent policies is not obvious. More generally, whether crises are likely to foster the introduction of deeper reforms is doubtful.

The first three sections of this paper review some of the arguments and implicit assumptions underlying the received wisdom about crisis and reform. The paper then suggests some weaknesses of the received crisis-reform wisdom. The fifth section suggests an alternative approach that focuses on a polity's ability to undertake the political exchanges necessary to instrument good public policies and on political institutions' role as the rules of that game of transactions. The paper concludes with an application of the approach to Argentina.[2]

The Received Wisdom

In recent decades, the notion that economic crises seem either to facilitate or to cause economic reforms has become part of a new conventional wisdom. Large amounts of ink have been devoted to the subject.[3] Rather than reviewing everything that has been said, this section presents a stylized account of the crisis hypothesis.[4]

This conventional wisdom evolved around some specific circumstances the developing countries faced in the 1980s and 1990s. Some of that wisdom might not be too useful in the near future given current circumstances. Crises seem to have led to market-oriented reforms in economies with fairly interventionist policy stances and in an international intellectual atmosphere characterized by the fall of the Berlin Wall. It is not clear what the effect of crises will be now, after countries have already instrumented (more or less well-executed) market-oriented reforms and in an intellectual atmosphere of criticism about the international financial architecture.

The basic "crisis and reform" story is as follows. A set of "bad" policies is in place and the economic situation is poor and possibly deteriorating rapidly. This is supposed to put in motion several mechanisms that lead to the adoption of substantial policy changes and reforms in the "right" direction. The mechanisms linking crisis to reform put forth in the literature are varied. This section reviews, in a nontaxonomic way, some of the most common ones. These mechanisms operate at different stages of the policy process and focus on different actors. Some complement each other, while others are alternatives.

Learning

Economic crises are supposed to contribute to Bayesian learning about the "right" model of the world. A period of intense economic disarray leads to a reassessment of the mapping from policies to outcomes, in particular, to a realization of how costly some previous policies were. Harberger (1993, pp. 15–16) writes:

> [P]ractitioners go around with a certain world view in their heads. All sorts of crazy things happen—like hyperinflations and huge recessions and wrenching debt or exchange rate crises. All of these . . . can occur and still leave seasoned practitioners unruffled, because their worldview already contains sensible explanations for them. Every now and then, however, something happens that does not fit the previous image—something that shakes our Bayesian faith in what we used to think.[5]

The fact that nobody completely understands the possible effects of policies on outcomes, that this mapping is stochastic, and that information about it is subject to various asymmetries leads to a series of policymaking and political gimmicks and tactics that are among the core elements of the policymaking process. The tendency to oversimplify complex messages and to bundle together policy reforms that are not necessarily inseparable from a technical point of view are a consequence of this imperfect knowledge, and have important implications for the path of future policies in political equilibria in which politicians construct messages attempting to differentiate themselves from supposedly bad policies.

The learning view of crises is one of the most important ones and operates at several levels. The foregoing quote by Harberger refers more directly to the technocrats (practitioners), but learning does run through the entire process of "social reasoning," involving experts, policymakers, politicians, the media, and the general public. For instance, Williamson and Haggard (1994, p. 531) write: "[B]elief in the benefits of economic reform is much less widely held among politicians than among economists, and it is even less widely endorsed by the general public, let alone by the specific interests that stand to lose."[6]

This distinction between several layers of the information channel is important to understand several aspects of the dynamics of crisis and reform in particular cases. One important instance of this is the "Nixon goes to China" effect. According to some views, politicians from the left of the political spectrum might have a comparative advantage at convincing people of the long-run need for market-oriented changes, even if those changes have short-term costs for some constituencies (Cukierman and Tommasi 1998a,b).[7] Also the media can play an important role in building public opinion with regard to the diagnosis of a crisis and its possible remedies. Oversimplification of messages and coarsening of information are not uncommon, and are possibly quite risky, for instance, having bundled several market-oriented reforms might now backfire, as politicians and the public might blame the overall package for undesirable outcomes.

Special Politics

"In extreme cases, such as Poland in 1989, the crisis of the ancien regime may be so profound as to create an opening for what Leszek Balcerowitz calls 'extraordinary politics'—a widespread willingness to suspend the usual political rules. These worst of times give rise to the best of opportunities for those who understand the need for fundamental economic reform" (Williamson 1994, p. 20.) "Reform will be easier where the opposition is discredited and disorganized (or repressed)" (Nelson 1990, p. 335).

This line of reasoning contains several ramifications, some emphasizing a temporary reallocation of institutional power, for example, in delegation from the legislature to the executive branch, others emphasizing the temporary or permanent reallocation of effective power among underlying interest groups or the reallocation of space in public debate.

Delegation

Several reform episodes included instances in which, for example, the legislature delegated to the executive branch some unusual legislative prerogatives (see the description in Keeler 1993). Crises create a sense of urgency. Something needs to be done soon, because the crisis requires an urgent resolution, creating room for special politics for a period of time. In that context, Rodrik (1998) emphasizes the agenda-setting role of reformist governments.

The following metaphor illustrates the relationship between crisis and delegation. Imagine a town on fire and people running out of their houses toward the banks of a river flowing past the town. The people meet up at a bridge, which is presumably going to catch fire as well, where a bus is waiting. The bus driver gathers all the people inside the bus and proclaims that he will save them by taking them across the bridge to the other side of the river, a place where, he says, but nobody knows for certain, the fire is not burning and everything is so much better. Jumping into the bus is dangerous: the bridge could collapse, the driver could be a maniac, and nobody knows what things are like on the other side of the river. In addition, boarding the bus means leaving behind all belongings, though sooner or later they would be consumed by the fire anyway. Disregarding the many possible arguments for not boarding the bus, the people accept the bus driver's proposal. In Argentina, the economic, political, and social situation was so dire that both Congress and the population decided to trust President Carlos Menem's promises and embark on actions that, in a normal context, they might not have agreed to.[8]

Weakened or Muted Opposition

Reform efforts at times of crisis are often associated with reconfigurations of dominant coalitions in such a way that the core of the reform coalition is able to mute the opposition. Observers argue that in many cases such reforms have been associated with a relative weakening of, for instance, the labor movement. Alesina and Drazen's (1991) classic war of attrition reform model formalizes what might lie behind the weakening of those who oppose a particular way of instrumenting adjustment and reform. Laban and Sturzenegger (1994) argue that the capitulating group is most likely to be the poor, who have restricted access to financial technologies, and therefore are less able than other groups to protect themselves from the costs of high inflation.

This notion sometimes comes bundled with learning-type arguments. In many policy decisions, the public goods, efficiency, and valence dimensions are intertwined with distributive struggles. Particular groups, say industrialists, build arguments to buttress those policies that protect them. When things are going really badly and somehow people perceive those poor outcomes as related to some preexisting policies, those advocating such policies tend to lose ground in the public debate, and hence supporting such policies becomes less attractive for politicians. For instance, Krueger (1993) argues that economic crises undermine the supporters of the status quo, rendering politics as usual no longer sustainable.

Switch in Equilibrium Behavior

Many actors participate in the policy process. Preexisting, inefficient policies can be seen as a noncooperative outcome in the policymaking game among these actors. Thus crises can be interpreted as situations in which a low expected future payoff of continued noncooperation might induce actors to switch to more cooperative policymaking, which is instrumented through the reform of some institutions. For instance, a reform of fiscal institutions might help to stop subsidies that, even though individually beneficial to each powerful group, were welfare reducing in the aggregate.

Mondino, Sturzenegger, and Tommasi (1996) and Velasco (1998) provide models that capture such dynamics.

Other observers present the converse argument, in which intertemporal cooperation among powerful groups sustained the preexisting, inefficient policies to the disadvantage of the general public. In this view, crises break up such oligopolistic behavior, allowing a reformist government to get rid of the previous policies. For instance, according to Tornell (1995), the reduction of economic rents brought about by an economic crisis destroys the previous "cohabitational equilibrium" among rent-seeking groups. Rather than cooperating among themselves to exploit rents and block reforms, rent-seeking groups turn against each other, with some of them even siding with the executive branch and accepting the costs of reform in order to inflict losses on other groups.

Risk-Taking Behavior

Crisis is often associated with downward economic paths such that if nothing is done, the situation is likely to deteriorate to extremely low levels. In such circumstances, prospect theory (Weyland 1996) argues that risk-taking behavior becomes more likely. According to prospect theory, people tend to engage in highly risky behavior when confronted with threats to their well-being, but are extremely cautious when facing auspicious prospects. Weyland (1996) argues that economic crises (worsening fiscal deficits, sharp external imbalances, or exploding inflation) place the government in the "domain of losses," thus making it more inclined to adopt risky policies, such as market-oriented reforms.[9]

Some Clarifications

The foregoing summary suggests several points that require more precision to operationalize the crisis hypothesis. First, whether the role of crisis should be seen as necessary, as sufficient, or simply as facilitating reform is not clear (Drazen 2000, p. 445). Second, whether we are referring to economic crises in a somewhat narrow sense, as opposed to the total rupture of the social contract that characterizes deeper crises, or whether we include full-blown political and social crises, all of which sometimes come together, is also not clear. Even restricting us to a narrower definition, what is the threshold for declaring a crisis? In a sense, crisis is a mental state related to country-specific aspiration levels, something that is relatively hard to capture in empirical analysis. (Lora [1997, 2000] attempts to implement the notion of crisis empirically.)

In addition, the varied accounts do not always take care to distinguish between different possible origins of crises (and/or the interpretation of the origin of the crisis). Is a particular crisis the outcome of endogenous deterioration induced by preexisting misguided policies (as in Argentina in 1990)? Is it the outcome of savage exogenous shocks that hit a polity that had generally sound policies (as in Argentina in 1994)? Is it largely induced by an endogenous breakup of economic actors' confidence in the sustainability of extant policies (as perhaps in Argentina in 2001)? These three possible reasons for the onset of a crisis—bad policies, bad luck, or bad institutions—might lead to different types of political responses.[10]

The next section looks at the easiest and most benign interpretation with regard to the concerns of the last two paragraphs using the hypothesis that crises are a facilitating factor for reform. Williamson and Haggard (1994, p. 565) argue that "crisis is clearly neither a necessary nor a sufficient condition to initiate reform. It has nevertheless often played a critical role in stimulating reform." The section concentrates on economic crises and identifies a crisis with a deterioration of status quo welfare that is associated with prevailing policies. Nevertheless, the crisis and reform story still contains many "ifs."

Crisis, Reform, and Living Happily Ever After

The following is a stylized account of the steps involved in a crisis and reform story with a happy ending:

1. A set of well-identified, inadequate, preexisting policies is in place.

2. The economic situation deteriorates substantially.

3. The perception is that the deterioration, that is, the crisis, is caused by the preexisting policies, either because they were always inadequate or because they are inadequate to handle some new states of the world.

4. A clear set of "right" prescriptions can take care of the problem.

5. The social learning in relation to 3 and 4 is inadequate.

6. The situation becomes incentive compatible for an agenda-setting leader to act on that.[11]

7. The leader has the political capacity to "play" the reforms through the political process (related to special politics, mentioned earlier).

8. The reforms are sustained throughout the multiple stages of the policy process.

9. The details are dealt with properly (or are unimportant).

10. The economic agents, rather soon, believe in the stability of the new set of policies and react accordingly.

11. As a result, economic outcomes turn out relatively well.

12. The outcomes are sustained politically and no major economic setbacks occur.

13. The end of history.

This highly stylized fable is obviously subject to several caveats. The next section raises some of these, which are relevant to the later discussion.

What Is Wrong with the Fairytale?

The typical account of crisis and reform implicitly focuses on one-shot policy implementation. In reality, policies are complex objects, with multiple stages, and taking reform to full fruition is a process that involves multiple actors through many stages of the policy process and that requires specific responses from economic and social agents, and therefore necessitates several forms of cooperation and positive beliefs about the durability of the policy. That is, policies require a lot more than a magical moment of special politics to produce effective results.

In addition, a universal set of right policies does not exist. Policies are contingent responses to underlying states of the world. What might work at one point in time in a given country might not work in a different place or in the same place at another time. Furthermore, what really matters might not be the broad definition of a policy stance, but the details of implementation. For instance, Rodrik (1995) analyzes six countries that implemented a set of policies that shared the same generic title, export subsidization, but had widely different degrees of success. Rodrik relates their success to such features as the consistency with which the policy was implemented, which office was in charge, how the policy was bundled (or not) with other policy objectives, and how predictable the future of the policy was.[12] This latter point highlights policies' dependence on the expectations and beliefs of economic and social agents for their success. Some of my (mostly indirect) involvement with fiscal issues in Latin America suggests that the success of tax policies is much more a question of accountants, lawyers, and political will than of economists' advice on optimal taxation. Also, a study of the process of "decentralization of education" (a beautiful, Washington-sponsored policy title) reveals enormous variations in performance that depend on many implementation details and on contextual variables (see, for instance, Tommasi 2002, section IV).[13]

The unavailability of universally valid policy recipes is a point that was somewhat forgotten during the reform era of the 1980s and 1990s. Recent work has, rightly, started to emphasize the importance of homegrown development strategies (see, for instance, Evans 2001; Lindauer and Pritchett 2002; North 1994; Pistor 2000).[14] As Mukand and Rodrik (2002) emphasize, countries tend to imitate formulas that have been successful elsewhere too quickly. Even though not the explicit focus of Mukand and Rodrik, I believe that part of the explanation has to do with the informational issues emphasized earlier in this paper. The links between policies and outcomes are complex to understand, as illustrated by the debates among professional economists on the impact of trade liberalization on growth (Edwards 1998; Rodríguez and Rodrik 1999; Srinivasan and Bhagwati 1999) or on poverty reduction (Kanbur 2001). Economic agents, politicians, and policymakers use mental shortcuts to organize the information pertaining to the world around them.[15] That is why the statement "it worked in New Zealand" seems to carry a lot more weight in selling an idea to a politician or to the public than a complex, multivariate analysis that specifies the dependence of optimal policy responses on a large number of difficult to assess variables. These simplifying tendencies seem to be more pronounced among

TABLE 1. The Good, the Bad, and the Ugly as a Response to a Crisis

	Right reform	No reform	Wrong reform
Crisis	Good	Bad	Ugly
No crisis			

Note: The second row is left empty for now, as it was not a concern in the crisis and reform literature.

Source: Author.

the general public than among politicians, among politicians than among so-called policy experts, and among policy experts than among academics specialized in the subject matter.

This multilayered, imperfect knowledge about what the exact impacts of policies are or are likely to be opens the door for manipulation, bundling, oversimplification, and outright lying in policymaking games (Tommasi and Velasco 1996). Some of the bundling and overselling evident during the market-oriented reform era might backfire in a second round of crises, in which the polity might reject sensible policies because they have been unnecessarily bundled with other policies that might have failed. The degree to which such things happen might be a function of the qualities of what Nelson and Tommasi (2001) refer to as the public space of policymaking.

Putting together the notion of policies as titles with the issues of implementation, if a good idea is poorly implemented, whether the public or the political system will be able to tell the difference is not clear, that is, will the "right" social learning take place? In that sense, crises could lead to right reforms (the good), no reforms (the bad), or wrong reforms (the ugly).[16] Adding the fact that reforms (good or bad) could also take place in normal times, we have a two-by-three matrix of possible connections between crisis and reform as depicted in table 1.

Another point that needs more careful consideration is the notion of special politics (delegation, muted opposition, and so on). The fact that reforms are instrumented under forced circumstances imparts some special characteristics to the types of reforms that could emerge. These negative special politics do not seem to be the means for instrumenting deeper institutional reforms. The use of a series of strategic tricks might have a negative impact on the quality of the resulting reforms. This is even more important once we recognize the multistage nature of policy processes: points 8, 9, 10, 11, and 12 of the fairytale, and not just point 7, do matter.

Furthermore, in one sense crises are the worst conditions for enacting good collective choices. As O'Donnell (1994b, p. 170) argues using the example of hyperinflation crises:

> [I]n the context of this crisis it becomes rational for everyone to act 1) at highly disaggregated levels . . .; 2) with extremely short time horizons; and 3) with the assumptions that everyone else will do the same. A gigantic, national level Prisoner's Dilemma emerges . . . The primary basic phenomenon is generalized de-solidarization . . . For players of this game, broad, long-run economic policies, negotiated and implemented with the participation of highly aggregated interest associations, are not important.

Even though O'Donnell focuses on individual economic behavior, much of what he says could be applied to political behavior. That is, crises are perhaps the worst of times to generate the conditions for the deliberative construction of the bargains and consensus needed to sustain quality policies and solid institutional reforms. The capacity for constructing intertemporal cooperation is, beyond the state of crisis or normalcy, heavily affected by the political institutions of the country, the institutional environment RH.

Many aspects of reforms have temporal dimensions that require substantial intertemporal cooperation. These intertemporal dimensions are the political equivalent of the intertemporal characteristics of transactions in transaction cost economics, and as in transaction cost economics are a crucial entry point for the role of institutions, in this case political institutions. Applying such logic to the policy process, we enter the realm of transaction cost politics, which can be viewed as a political version of the Coase theorem. If reforms are so good, why is implementing them so hard? The answer has to include the transaction costs of enforcing the necessary intertemporal compensations.

Rodrik (1996) applies this view to policy reform. He argues that

> Because distributional issues are at the heart of the literature discussed here, we need more progress on understanding why institutions for compensating losers from reform are not more common. There are very few papers where the difficulties of compensation are made endogenous to the analytical framework. This makes the literature somewhat incomplete in its diagnosis of the issues. It also opens up a natural avenue for future research. (Rodrik 1996, p. 39)

Institutions, Policy, and Policy Reform

The reforms usually debated in relation to the reform era are policy reforms (RL) and intermediate-level institutional reforms (RM). The central point of this paper is that what really matters are the deep aspects of the workings of political institutions (RH), which condition not only broad policy choices, including reforms, but, more important, the effectiveness of policy implementation.

What determines a society's capacity to adjust its policies in the face of changed circumstances or the failure of previous policies? What determines a society's ability to sustain policies long enough to create an environment of credibility, and hence to elicit the adequate responses from economic agents? More generally, what determines a society's capacity to decide on and instrument effective polices both in times of crisis and in more normal times?[17]

Rodrik (2000) provides one good entry point for answering that question. His response would be "democracy," or more precisely "participatory politics," or even more precisely "social cooperation." Rodrik emphasizes three channels whereby democracy fosters better policies: (a) deliberation, (b) rules that prevent too much redistribution, and (c) procedural rules that facilitate intertemporal cooperation (my wording).

I believe that Rodrik's answer is basically right, but a little too macro, too general in its depiction of political institutions. Developing a more micro analysis of the effects of political institutions on policy processes would be useful, so that we can move beyond telling a dictatorship "you should become a democracy." What exactly determines the ability to generate the more cooperative societal outcomes that are necessary to sustain effective policies? I believe the answer lies in the general equilibrium interactions of several specific details affecting the workings of the political system.[18]

Here I suggest one possible way of looking at the connection between some detailed aspects of political institutions and the resulting features of public policies and later apply it to the Argentine case. The framework, called a transactions approach to public policy in Spiller and Tommasi (2003), is an elaboration of previous work on transaction cost economics and its application to politics.[19]

Public policies are the outcome of intertemporal transactions among political actors who hold power at different points in time. If the equilibrium of that intertemporal policy game is cooperative, first-best policies could be implemented. First-best policies possess a number of features, such as stability throughout different administrations, adaptability to changing economic and social circumstances (that is, the capacity to instrument reforms), coordination across policymaking units, and sufficient degrees of investment in policymaking capacity.

Whether policies (and processes) with such desirable properties emerge will depend on whether the political institutions (RH) underlying the policy process lead to cooperative behavior. To answer that question, a detailed investigation of the determinants of political cooperation in each polity is necessary. Before turning to the case of Argentina, this section suggests the types of elements pertinent to the abstract description of a policymaking game that need to match observed characteristics of the workings of political institutions. These are drawn from insights of the analysis of intertemporal cooperation in the industrial organization context of oligopoly (for more details and references see Spiller and Tommasi 2003; Spiller, Stein, and Tommasi 2003). The elements are as follows:

- *Payoffs of the stage game.* The elasticity of the per period payoff to alternative spot actions will be an important determinant of whether cooperation is sustainable in equilibrium or not. In repeated games, if the spot payoff from deviating to noncooperation is high, cooperation is less likely. In repeated oligopoly games, this is the case with elasticity to price discounts: if a firm stands to gain large, short-term profits by lowering its price (for instance, because it can steal customers from a large number of competitors), collusive oligopoly is harder to sustain. In the context of the Argentine federal fiscal system (Tommasi 2002), a province's individual payoff to deviate from a cooperative agreement, for instance, by attempting to obtain special benefits from the national government, is quite high, and hence the federal fiscal game has noncooperation as its equilibrium outcome.

- *Number of political actors with power over a given decision.* The theory predicts that the larger the number of players, the smaller the set of other parameters for which cooperation obtains (Fudenberg and Tirole 1991). This is in line with traditional assumptions (such as those in Buchanan and Tullock 1962) that depict the costs of making a decision as increasing with the number of players. It also relates naturally to the previous point, in that in many common pool situations, the intraperiod payoff structure is related to the number of players.[20]

- *Length of the horizons and intertemporal linkages of key political actors.* The intertemporal pattern of interactions among specific individuals in formal political positions, such as legislators, governors, and bureaucrats, matters for developing cooperative outcomes. Having a legislature in which the same individuals interact over extended periods of time is not the same as having a legislature where individuals are drawn at random from given populations (parties, provinces, and so on) and are frequently replaced. Cooperation is less likely in the latter situation. Also historical events, such as past democratic history, can leave a legacy of "short-termism."[21]

- *Timing and observability of moves.* Cooperation is harder to sustain if there is plenty of room for unilateral moves, say by politicians holding executive positions, that are difficult to observe or hard to verify.

- *Delegation.* Other than self-enforcement through repeated play, certain forms of cooperation could be achieved by alternative institutional means. Delegating policy to an independent bureaucracy is one such alternative. Delegation has its problems, but in some cases the cost of those problems will be smaller than the cost of partisan policymaking.

- *Availability of enforcement technologies.* As in transaction cost economics, intertemporal cooperation is easier to achieve if good third-party enforcement is available. The presence and characteristics of a potentially impartial umpire and enforcer of political agreements, such as an independent judiciary, will vary from country to country, resulting in variance in the degree of enforcement of intertemporal political cooperation. Also some countries might have access to external enforcement technologies, such as international treaties or international organizations, at least for some policy areas.

- *Characteristics of the arenas in which key political actors undertake their exchanges.* The complex intertemporal exchanges required to implement effective public policies could be facilitated by the existence of exchange arenas that are organized in ways that make cooperation easier to enforce. Seminal work on the U.S. Congress debates the role that different institutional arrangements have in facilitating legislative bargaining, but observers agree that intertemporal cooperation in political exchanges is (somehow) facilitated (Shepsle and Weingast 1995). Whether the legislature as the arena where these transactions take place is adequately institutionalized or not depends on several factors, including legislators' incentives and capabilities. In some environments legislatures are much weaker than the benchmark U.S. case. If political exchanges are actually undertaken, they take place in settings that are more informal; more uncertain; and harder to monitor, observe, and enforce.

The foregoing list is not a taxonomy, but indicates the types of factors that might characterize the incentives for or against cooperative policymaking in any given polity. Obviously many other factors could be important in specific cases, including a country's historical, cultural, and socioeconomic configurations. Also mapping a set of abstract variables such as those enumerated here into real world political "observables" is not a simple task, and is complicated by the need to look not for the effects of individual variables in partial equilibrium, but for the interactive effects of many institutions on political behavior. This requires a substantial amount of country-specific knowledge. For that reason, the rest of the paper illustrates the general points by looking at a single example: Argentina.

The Argentine Case

This section briefly describes the workings of political institutions, the policy process, and public policies in Argentina. The next section applies this characterization of the Argentine polity in combination with some of the specifics of the 1990s to explain Argentina's trajectory from crisis to reform to crisis again.

Because of its history and the workings of its political institutions (its high-level institutional endowment, RH), Argentina is a polity in which cooperative intertemporal agreements are hard to realize. As a result, even the reform process of the 1990s took on idiosyncratic characteristics. These characteristics, on top of the lack of capacity to make the intertemporal agreements needed to implement good policies, together with several shocks to which the system was unable to adjust, led to the largely endogenous crisis that was still unfolding at the time of writing. From the point of view of this diagnostic, the magic of "crisis, reform, and living happily ever after" is unlikely to operate in the Argentine case this time.

Public policies in Argentina have the following features: (a) they are often too volatile, being changed too easily with sometimes minor changes in political winds; (b) precisely to avoid that opportunistic volatility, rigid mechanisms are frequently put in place to instrument long-term policies;[22] (c) coordination is poor among different government units operating in related policy arenas (levels of government in the federal structure, departments at a given level, subnational governments); (d) some welfare-enhancing reforms are not instrumented; and (e) capacity building for improving public policies suffers from underinvestment (Spiller and Tommasi forthcoming provide evidence of these policy characteristics).

All these features could be explained as the noncooperative outcome of an intertemporal policy game with conflict of interests and alternation in power. (For formal versions of this statement see Spiller and Tommasi forthcoming, and for an application to federal fiscal games see Tommasi, Saiegh, and Sanguinetti 2001). Noncooperative equilibrium play leads coalitions and individual policymakers to behave opportunistically (and individual opportunism leads to poor coordination). To protect themselves from such opportunism, actors embed rigidities into policies, thereby restraining not only opportunistic actions, but also efficient adjustments, and these two elements cannot be separated because of the necessary incompleteness of

legislative contracts. Most relevant reforms have an intertemporal path of implementation that is open to opportunistic moves, and the anticipation of such future
moves often derails reform efforts from the start. Finally, in an environment of weak
political property rights, actors (legislators, subnational politicians, bureaucrats) do
not invest in capacities that could lead to better policies.

Having established the defective properties of Argentine public policies, and having argued that such properties could be explained as the noncooperative outcome of
a policymaking game, the next step is to explore why noncooperation is the outcome
of such a game. Or, in other words, what exactly is the political game played to build
public policies in Argentina?[23]

Argentina shares some basic constitutional characteristics with the United States.
It has a presidential, bicameral, and federal organization of government (24 provinces
with substantial constitutional powers). If a Martian who had read the institutional
literature on American politics were to arrive in Argentina and, without knowing
anything about the country, were to grab a copy of the Constitution, he would form
some expectations that would not be fulfilled upon closer scrutiny.

For instance, our Martian may start by exploring the role of Congress in the
policymaking process. The first thing he would notice is that Congress does not have
an important role in policymaking. The actions and powers that the Martian would
expect to encounter in Congress would fade in the direction of the executive branch,
which is not too surprising in a Latin American context, but also, more surprisingly,
in the direction of provincial governors.

The fact that Congress is not a key policymaking arena is a general equilibrium
result that depends on electoral rules that make legislators weak political actors; on
constitutional rules and historical (and equilibrium) practices that give the executive
branch much leeway to undo or modify legislative agreements, both at a broader legislative stage, as well as at the implementation stage; and on the lack of alternative,
for instance, judicial, enforcement mechanisms for legislative agreements. Perhaps
the most crucial factor for legislative weakness is that electoral rules, broadly defined,
take power away from legislators, voters, and national party leadership and place
that power in the hands of provincial party elites.

National deputies are elected in closed and blocked party lists under a system of
proportional representation, with the provinces being the electoral districts. Provincial party practices mean that provincial party elites play a disproportionately
powerful role in putting together the party lists. (This is especially so when the party
coincides with the provincial executive, as explained in De Luca, Jones, and Tula
2002 and Jones and others 2003).One of the implications of the incentives of provincial party bosses (analyzed in Jones and others 2003) is the frequent rotation of
Argentine legislators, most of whom stay in Congress for only one term, because their
names do not appear on the list for reelection. Thus Argentina's duration figures are
similar to those of countries with term limits. This has the further implication that
legislators do not have the incentive to develop strong legislative institutions, do not
specialize, and are neither important policymaking actors nor do they exert effective
control over the administration (Jones and others 2002).

Congress has the constitutional right to generate national laws. The masters of (most) legislators are the provincial governors, but what do these powerful political actors care about? They care about two related things. One is maintaining their power in the provincial party and in the province, and the other is to obtain resources from central taxes to finance spending in the province. In Argentina, the federal fiscal system (fiscal federalism) is a crucial component of the political game and of the policymaking game, even for policies that, in principle, do not have much of a federal dimension.[24]

In Argentina, the national government is in charge of most taxation, especially of the most productive taxes, such as value added and income taxes, yet provinces are responsible for a large proportion of total spending, especially the most politically "sexy" spending, such as public employment and social programs. This provincial responsibility, in combination with the weaknesses of the national Congress, indicates why the crucial axes of Argentine politics run through the provinces. The large vertical fiscal imbalance between revenue generation and spending obligations is addressed by means of a politically sensitive system of tax sharing and intergovernmental transfers, which generates numerous perverse incentives for provincial and national authorities (see Tommasi 2002 for a detailed analysis). One of the outcomes of this system is a strange symbiosis between fiscal federalism and national policymaking. Whenever the national executive branch needs to pass an important law, it requires the permission of several provincial governors. This permission is usually repaid by means of fiscal favors from the national to provincial treasuries through a variety of instruments and bailouts whose exact form keeps mutating and adapting to the successive "constraints and reforms," usually under the institutional guise of so-called fiscal pacts, attempted under the sponsorship of multilateral organizations (Braun and Tommasi 2002; Tommasi 2002).

All this, plus a series of factors that facilitates executive unilateralism,[25] leaves the central arena of national policymaking in Argentina quite naked, with a group of short-term actors, plus some quite powerful actors that are only tangentially interested in national public goods (including intertemporal investment in policymaking capacities.) Furthermore, a potential enforcer of intertemporal political agreements, the Supreme Court, has tended not to play much of that role in recent Argentine history. For reasons analyzed in Iaryczower, Spiller, and Tommasi (2002), the court has tended to be excessively aligned with the executive branch, and this has led to path-dependent dynamics of diminishing credibility to the point that today the Supreme Court is not an effective warrantor of rights independent of the political configuration of the moment.[26]

A professional bureaucracy, well supervised by Congress, could be another channel for the intertemporal enforcement of political agreements. Argentina, however, in part because of past political instability, but also because of the current incentives of key political players, does not have such a bureaucracy either. A shortsighted Congress has left the bureaucracy without a long-term principal. In the absence of long-term political masters who can provide long-term incentives to invest in developing capabilities, the bureaucracy has become an unresponsive and hard to motivate organization. As a result, political appointees, the so-called parallel bureaucracy, have been used to fill the gap. These appointees, in turn, rotate frequently and do not develop norms of cooperation across departments, thereby contributing to the fragmentation and lack of coordination of public policies (Bambaci, Spiller, and Tommasi 2001).

In sum, and attempting to map back into the game-theoretic language presented earlier, Argentina's polity is configured in a way that fosters noncooperative behavior in the policymaking process. Key actors have either short horizons, wrong incentives, or both. Some potentially important actors, such as legislators, Supreme Court justices, or key civil servants, have extremely short time horizons. The potentially more long-lived and powerful governors have only marginal incentives for providing national public goods. Furthermore, the political configuration of the last two decades has made almost all governors potential veto players, thereby increasing the costs of political transactions (Spiller and Tommasi forthcoming). The executive branch has had excessive leeway to engage in ex post moves that can undo previous agreements, reducing the incentive to work toward those agreements in the first place. Third-party or other enforcement technologies have been missing. The interaction of the capacity for unilateral moves, the history of the country, and the endogenous lack of institutionalization of Congress and of legislators' careers have moved the center of the political scene away from the national legislature and into other arenas. Political bargains take place in executive quarters, in meetings of the president with governors, or occasionally in meetings of national political party leaders. These informal arenas have not been structured for the institutional enforcement of bargains.

To summarize, public policies in Argentina, independently of their titles, have several undesirable properties. This is the outcome of the lack of intertemporal cooperation among political actors, which in turn derives from Argentina's history and higher-level political institutions (RH).

Crisis, Reform, and Crisis Again in Argentina

This section draws on the previous characterization of the Argentine polity to illustrate some of the limitations of the conventional wisdom on crisis and reform.

The Fairytale

In the early 1990s, Argentina was fortunate enough to undergo a process similar to most of the schematic 13 steps presented earlier. In the late 1980s, a deep economic crisis occurred, including hyperinflation and looting, with poverty climbing to a then unprecedented (until the 2002 crisis) 47.3 percent of the population in October 1989. That crisis was interpreted as the terminal stage of the inward-looking, state-led, fiscally irresponsible model of previous decades. Its timing coincided with demonstration effects from other developing countries, abundant international funding and advice, as well as a reasonable amount of consensus among domestic economists on the diagnostic and on the general direction that a way out was supposed to take. A political leader found that steering such a market-oriented reform process was in his best interests. He had the institutional resources to carry it through, including the benefit of some explicit delegation mechanisms as a consequence of the crisis. Thus Argentina underwent a rapid and profound process of economic liberalization that included widespread privatization of public enterprises, substantial trade liberalization, deregulation of several markets, some tax reforms, and a successful inflation stabilization plan that lowered inflation from 4,923 percent in 1989 and 1,343 percent in 1990 to 7.4 percent in 1992 and 3.9 percent in 1993. The outcome was a move away from negative growth in the 1980s to more than 60 percent cumulative growth in the 1990s, even including the so-called Tequila crisis of 1994–95 and the severe downturn that began in mid-1998.

Some Catches

Even though observers had viewed Argentina as a salient case of radical and unconstrained reform, a closer scrutiny of the process shows that the building and maintenance of support for the reforms involved several deviations from an idealized reform blueprint, and that those deviations, which left an important imprint on the economy, were conditioned by the idiosyncrasies of Argentine political institutions and politics (see Bambaci, Saront, and Tommasi 2002 for the economic and political details of the reform process). Furthermore, even those reforms that were actually undertaken were carried out in specific ways that were also derived from the idiosyncrasies of the Argentine political economy, and also cast a long shadow on later events.

Argentina underwent an important transformation in intermediate-level institutions (whether utilities are private or public, for instance), a transformation of such magnitude that it caught the world's attention. Yet no transformation took place in the more fundamental institutions (RH) that are the deeper determinants of how policy actually works. This was reflected in the precise manner in which the transformation was instrumented. For example, there were allegations of corruption in the privatization process, during which utilities went in part to some of the same economic groups that had provided inputs to state monopolies as a way of buying the support of those business groups for the overall reform process. Furthermore, the quality of the ensuing regulatory framework for privatized utilities was uneven and questionable, also for reasons relating to the deeper workings of political, administrative, and judicial institutions in Argentina (Abdala and Spiller 2000). This once again highlights the point that the details of policies (how you regulate) are perhaps more important than the grand titles of policies (privatization, for instance).

The political instrumentation of the reforms could be described as a vote-buying strategy, in which pivotal players for the government coalition received substantial benefits and exemptions throughout the reform process (Bambaci, Saront, and Tommasi 2002). The key pivotal actors were several provinces, mostly from the backward periphery; some union leaders; and some business groups. The concessions in timing and design left an imprint that included insufficient fiscal reform, especially at the provincial level; insufficient labor market reform; no reform of the health sector, which is extremely inefficient and a source of important rents for the unions, some provincial actors, and some business sectors; and no deep reform of the distortive federal fiscal arrangement.[27]

Furthermore, even the reforms that were instrumented took peculiar forms, also as a result of Argentina's political and historical features as already referred to in the example of privatization. In relation to monetary, exchange rate, and stabilization policy, the cornerstone of reform in that realm (and the cornerstone of the entire reform package) was the Convertibility Law, which established one-to-one convertibility between the peso and the U.S. dollar, in effect eliminating almost any monetary or exchange rate policy. Needless to say, that peculiar policy choice had a lot to do with events 10 years later that led to the terrible crisis of 2002. Yet for all the cheap criticism of the regime by "airplane economists," a profound logic underlay that choice of regime and its ex post, costly maintenance throughout the 1990s, a logic that was again grounded in the details of Argentina's political institutions and history (see Galiani, Heymann, and Tommasi 2003).

An institutional change complementary to convertibility was the reform of the central bank's charter to make it an independent institution. Unfortunately, in 2001, the first time that the central bank's independence really collided with the will of the executive branch, the central bank president was dismissed based on some dubious accusations of wrongdoing. This is evidence for the argument about the dependence of lower-level institutions, such as central bank independence (RM), on higher-level political institutions, such as the capacity to enforce such independence (RH).[28]

Fast Forward to the End of the Story

The first administration of President Menem (1989–95) undertook an number of important market-oriented reforms in combination with macroeconomic stabilization in a manner that more or less fits the fairytale scenario outlined earlier. After changing the Constitution in 1994, Menem was reelected in 1995. In his second term, the reformist impetus slowed down, but no major reversal of the main reform measures took place.[29] Clearly no major change in the deep determinants of political practices occurred.

During most of the 1990s, Argentina's economy performed spectacularly by international standards and by comparison with its own history of the second half of the 20th century. Inflation was down from four digits to one digit, and per capita gross domestic product rose from around US$5,000 in the 1980s to some US$9,000 in the 1990s.[30] In the late 1990s, the economy started to show some of the limitations and inconsistencies of the overall macroeconomic framework and was subject to a number of large, negative shocks, including the depreciation of the euro, the real terms of trade shocks, and the capital market shocks of 1998.[31] The hard peg imposed a protracted deflationary adjustment in response to these shocks. Weak fiscal management, especially after 1995, aggravated the imbalances (Perry and Servén 2002). The need to address the rising concern with solvency—given the large debt, the weak primary fiscal balance, and the low level of growth—led to tax hikes and budget cuts in 2000 and 2001 that deepened the economic contraction. The capital flow reversal and increased risk premium in 2001 amplified these problems by requiring a large adjustment in the external current account.

The overall cycle of despair, hope, great expectations, disenchantment, and despair again that Argentina has undergone during the last 13 years is too complex to be resolved in a few paragraphs (Galiani, Heymann, and Tommasi 2003 offer a preliminary step in that direction.) The story is certainly a lot richer and more nuanced than the quick interpretations of "airplane economists" criticizing the unwise choice of exchange rate regime or the lack of accompanying fiscal tightening. The Argentine convertibility experiment was a desperate bet for the economy to find a new growth trend. The role of that monetary system went much beyond its function as a nominal anchor. It was more of an institutional anchor, in which the promise of one peso equals one dollar became the mother of all promises. Over time, more and more contractual promises were predicated on the presumption that the economy could sustain real growth under convertibility. In an economy still haunted by credibility problems, the authorities responded to macroeconomic disturbances by doubling the commitment to the fixed exchange rate and implicitly supporting the dollarization of contracts.

The lack of sustainable compromises among key politico-institutional actors hindered the development of credible alternatives to the rigid monetary regime of the currency board. Judicial, fiscal, monetary, or other institutions that might have alleviated the burden on the exchange rate regime to support the contractual system clearly were not present at the beginning and were not developed over time. Even though attempts were made to establish new fiscal and monetary institutions and to improve the workings of the judicial system, it all proved to be just ink on paper when put to the test: fiscal responsibility laws, federal fiscal pacts, central bank independence, and deposit guarantees were ignored at crucial times. Obviously not all these episodes could be blamed entirely on institutional weaknesses. Negative feedback from the economic situation sometimes pushed political institutions to the limits, and economic instability and broken policy promises reinforced each another in an explosive spiral.

The shortcomings of the policy process, which often relied on the personal influence of particular individuals in the government, became salient during the 2001–02 crisis. While the crisis would have been extremely difficult to handle in any case, the relevant actors, including such international agents as the International Monetary Fund, were unable to establish a precise policy course. At the same time, the urgent problems that emerged in rapid succession frequently led executive authorities to take measures on the spot, sometimes using emergency decrees, without going through a process of detailed discussion and legislative decision, which they judged to be unacceptably slow and uncertain. Parliament passed laws that contravened central elements of economic policies and threatened to create unsolvable dilemmas. The judiciary, which itself lacked a reputation for impartiality, often reversed government decisions. The outcome was that policies did not follow a definite direction, were perceived as arbitrary and lacking in legitimacy, and caused further damage in an already difficult situation.

The Argentine polity showed, once again, a deep incapacity to cooperate to generate the adjustments that might have prevented, or at least mitigated, the effects of the crisis. One of the compounding factors in the final dynamics leading to the implosion were the fiscal pacts signed by the new de la Rúa administration in 1999 and 2000 with provincial governments. To protect themselves from the national government's opportunism, the provinces were able to negotiate some fixed amount transfers out of the national taxation pool. During the steep downturn of 2001, the national government could not deliver on those promises, yet the provinces, most of them held by the then opposition party, stubbornly insisted on those transfers, further damaging the credibility of fiscal adjustment in the eyes of international actors and fueling the downward spiral.[32]

On December 20, 2001, President de la Rúa resigned in the midst of popular protests by the middle classes, whose access to their bank deposits had been blocked, and of the looting of supermarkets and other stores that was partly spontaneous and partly organized by the political machinery of the province of Buenos Aires. De la Rúa was succeeded by a couple of temporary figures until January 1, 2002, when Eduardo Duhalde, the peronist *caudillo* of Buenos Aires who had lost the presidential election to de la Rúa, was named president by Congress. Default on the government's debt was declared in the last week of December, and upon taking office, the Duhalde administration devalued the peso.

By then, the crisis had escalated to a full-blown political and social crisis in the broader sense of a disintegration of some basic aspects of the social contract. At this point, dimensions ignored in the simplified account of the first part of the paper became operational. The world witnessed not just an economic crisis, but a new rupture of the Argentine social contract, which was so fragile that in the last decade it was tied to a particular exchange rate regime.[33] It is still too early, and the situation is still too uncertain, to make any predictions. The game is open again at the level of economic policies and intermediate institutions (will the economy be closed again? will privatized companies be nationalized?).[34] According to some optimistic observers, the crisis is so deep that the higher-level institutional game might also be open. By the reasoning emphasized in the first part of the paper, whether the actual choices, at any given level, will be the best ones is far from obvious.

Table 2 summarizes the dynamics Argentina followed throughout the 1990s in relation to the crisis and reform paradigm. The last step in the temporal sequence

TABLE 2. The Good, the Bad, and the Ugly in Argentina

	Right reform	No reform	Wrong reform
Crisis	Menem, first term (early 1990s)	de la Rúa (2000–01)	Today? (2002–03)
No crisis		Menem second term (late 1990s)	

Source: Author.

implied by the arrows suggests that the Argentine polity might end up doing the wrong type of learning from this experience. There have been hints in that direction in the political discourse since the crisis (although the current government of President Kirchner has so far not reversed any major reform). For instance, Ruben Lo Vuolo, the key economic adviser of one of the 2003 presidential candidates, said: "Argentina was the best pupil of the Washington Consensus, and see where we ended up. We have to change the model" (*Diario Clarín* April 17, 2002).

Conclusion

The purpose of this paper was not to argue that crisis is irrelevant for reform. Under some circumstances a country might be stuck until some form of crisis changes the equilibrium play of the game, or even changes the game, in a positive way. However, the paper presents several caveats. The 13 steps from crisis to happiness represent a special set of circumstances and make several implicit assumptions that are often not true. Furthermore, the reforms to which the fairytale refers are not the deepest-level institutional reforms.

In addition, the details of policies are perhaps more important than their titles, and those details are conditioned by the workings of countries' deeper political institutions. As illustrated in the case of Argentina, the reforms derive features from the underlying policy game. This, in turn, conditions the stochastic path of policies' future success and reflects the fact that underlying political games might still remain the same as those that generated inefficient policies in the first place. Both channels point to potential vulnerabilities of the system. In Argentina, those vulnerabilities manifested themselves a few years later, and in the face of severe shocks the polity was unable to adjust, leading to a second crisis. Whether the 13 magical steps might be operational during this next round is not obvious. On the contrary, several conditions seem to point in the wrong direction. Thus the wisdom developed during the modern economic reform movement might not be that useful for this new round of crises. Furthermore, some of the political and marketing strategies adopted in the previous round might backfire now.

I concur with several authors who emphasize the importance of good institutions for producing good policy outcomes, including policy reform when necessary. I suggest a particular way of operationalizing what good institutions mean, namely, those that facilitate intertemporal political cooperation. Such institutions can help avoid the cycles of crisis and short-lived reform. As the Argentine case illustrates, crises are partly endogenous to bad institutions, to some extent independently of the title of the specific policies in place.

How to go about improving deep institutions and the policymaking process is the million dollar question that I am not ready to answer here. Yet an important step toward that lofty goal will be to recognize that the core of the problem lies in the process of making policies, and that we have to find ways of improving that instead of constantly pushing the "flavor of the month" policy recipe that the development consensus favors at any point. The starting point for that enterprise will certainly be to try to develop better diagnostics of how policymaking processes actually work.

"It is not the policy, it is the polity, stupid." This statement was the original subtitle of this paper. That subtitle was written in a pessimistic mood, which made it sound too deterministic. As conference discussant Jorge Braga de Macedo correctly pointed out, the type of intertemporal cooperation games described here do have a multiplicity of equilibria, and we should not stop our quest for ways out of inefficient equilibria like those that Argentina is suffering.

Notes

1. Furthermore, in some cases past policy choices might themselves become important determinants of political behavior. That is the case, for instance, with federal fiscal rules that in some federal countries are an important determinant of the political and policy incentives of key political actors (see Tommasi 2002 for the case of Argentina). Clearly, feedback effects take place across the policy levels, because the performance of policies in RL can potentially lead to changes in higher-level rules, as has indeed happened throughout the reform crusade, mostly at the level of RM. In the remainder of this paper I will follow the arbitrary convention of reserving the term "institutions" for higher-level rules, and not for policies.

2. The Argentine case might be considered particularly relevant, because while considered a poster child for reform by the Washington establishment throughout the 1990s, it has recently metamorphosed into a basket case (Pastor and Wise 2001). Since its precipitous fall in 2001, Argentina seems to be one of the battlefields in which technical and ideological battles are being fought, often in simplistic and dangerous ways.

3. Bresser Pereira argues that "[w]hen populist leaders in Argentina, Bolivia, Venezuela, Peru and Brazil adopted non-populist policies it was because the crisis in these countries was so deep that even the costs of sticking to populist policies became higher than the costs of adjustment" (1993, p. 57). According to Bates and Krueger: "In all cases, of course, reforms have been undertaken in circumstances in which economic conditions were deteriorating. There is no recorded instance of the beginning of a reform program at a time when economic growth was satisfactory and when the price level and balance of payments situations were stable. Conditions of economic stagnation (and the recognition that it is likely to continue) or continued deterioration are evidently prerequisites for reform efforts" (1993, p. 454). de la Dehesa writes: "[O]nly when the level of reserves was sufficiently low and/or the current account was in large deficit have necessary economic adjustment and structural reform measures been taken" (1994, p. 137). For more systematic accounts see, for instance, Corrales (1998); Nelson (1990); Rodrik (1996); Tommasi and Velasco (1996); and Williamson (1994). Reflecting on a broader notion of crises, Gourevitch (1989, p. 9) says: "[I]t is the crisis years that put systems under stress. Hard times expose strengths and weaknesses to scrutiny, allowing observers to see relationships that are often blurred in prosperous periods, when good times slake the propensity to contest and challenge. The lean years are times when old relationships crumble and new ones have to be constructed."

4. This refers to the crisis hypothesis circulating in the 1980s and 1990s in Washington consensus circles and related literature, or what Stiglitz has dubbed "the modern reform movement" (Stiglitz 2000, p. 551). This hypothesis is heir to a long-standing concern in political science about crisis as an independent variable in explaining policy and political change (see, for instance, Binder 1971; Corrales 1998; Habermas 1975).

5. Bruno (1993, p. 190) describes the Argentine reform process of the early 1990s as the outcome of "a painful and protracted collective learning process." He adds, furthermore, that "[i]t is doubtful, considering the experiences of various countries that we have encountered so far, and given the complexity of Argentina's situation, whether any shortcuts are possible in this process."

6. The Williamson (1994) volume from which the quote is taken is a clear exponent of the most prevalent views on reform at the time. Notice the use of the generic expression "economic reform" to refer to a rather specific set of policies in the direction of market opening and liberalization (on this, see also Stiglitz 2000). Nelson (1997) is an interesting paper that explores some of the complexities in deriving generic propositions about trade reform, and that also emphasizes the asymmetries in understanding and arguing about such complex processes. See also Lohmann (2000), who emphasizes the different degrees of understanding of the details of monetary policy by different audiences.

7. This effect has been dubbed the Nixon goes to China effect on the theory that only someone with impeccable anticommunist credentials like Richard Nixon could have opened the door to a relationship with China without risking his domestic credibility.

8. Using the language of procedural rules in legislatures (Baron and Ferejohn 1989; Moser 1999), the logic of delegation in crises situations can be understood as a switch from open rule to closed rule. It also relates to the standard constitutional practice of granting presidents emergency powers. For more on the logic of delegation see Epstein and O'Halloran (1999). Of course, this delegation has several downsides (see, for instance, O'Donnell 1994a) that could have a negative impact on the quality of the reforms undertaken in crisis scenarios.

9. Although Weyland focuses on the chief executive, the logic can apply to multiple layers of the policymaking process, including public opinion, and even technocrats. This theory seems to apply to the many desperate attempts by Minister Domingo Cavallo in late 2001, when Argentina was entering a crisis of titanic proportions.

10. I refer to the last case as bad institutions in the sense that for most of the decade Argentina seemed to have what the Washington consensus would have called good policies, yet in the end they did not work.

11. The order of these steps is not necessarily chronological. Social learning might be induced by leadership, or more generally by elite domination (Zaller 1992, chapter 12).

12. Some of these policy features are the same as those identified in a more generic approach to public policies in Spiller, Stein, and Tommasi (2003). See also Cox and McCubbins (2001); Sabatier (1999); and Spiller and Tommasi (forthcoming). More theoretically focused studies of the determinants of the effectiveness of polices would be quite useful.

13. Similarly, Murillo (2002) describes the variety of policies undertaken under the title of privatization of utilities in five Latin American countries. She argues that different governments implemented privatization in different ways, depending on their ideological leanings and the nature of the coalitions they forged to make those policies possible.

14. In the words of North (1994, p. 8): "[E]conomies that adopt the formal rules of another economy will have very different performance characteristics than the first economy because of different informal norms and enforcement. The implication is that transferring the formal political and economic rules of successful Western economies to third-world and Eastern European economies is not a sufficient condition for good economic performance." Acuña and Tommasi (2000) make similar points with emphasis on the match between the policies (RL) or lower-level institutional reforms (RM) with the higher-level institutional endowment of the country (RH).

15. For a more detailed elaboration of the notion of mental models, see Denzau and North (1994). They argue that ideologies are the shared framework of mental models that groups

of individuals possess that provide both an interpretation of the environment and a pre-scription as to how that environment should be structured.

16. The latter, again, could relate to learning in reverse, with adequate policies wrongly assigned guilt for poor outcomes.

17. One can also argue that the likelihood of a given polity facing a crisis depends on its insti-tutions and on the more permanent and generic features of its resulting policies.

18. For brevity, I will focus on formal political institutions, which are certainly important, but are by no means the unique determinants of societal outcomes. In particular, the main socioeconomic cleavages and the way they are articulated (or not) via formal political institutions are crucial aspects that need to be studied. More generally, beyond formal political institutions of government we should include the nature of cleavages, corporatist actors, public opinion, social actors, social capital, and so on. Yet the nuts and bolts of professional politics and its determinants are a component of the broader picture as well as a relevant entry point for analysis.

19. Dixit (1996) and North (1990) have labeled transaction cost politics as the use of trans-action cost reasoning to think about politics. While Dixit and North emphasize transac-tions among citizens and politicians, I emphasize transactions among politicians. Related work in political science includes Epstein and O'Halloran (1999); Haggard and McCubbins (2001); Moe (1990a,b); and Moe and Caldwell (1994).

20. The theory also has interesting predictions in terms of the stochastic process generating the exact institutional position of the different players over time. De Figueiredo (2002) and Dixit, Grossman, and Gul (2000) present interesting insights in that regard.

21. Another dimension might relate to the history of the franchise and the type of interaction it tends to induce between citizens and politicians. In countries where large groups of citizens do not have a long tradition of voting, clientelistic practices might be more common, and such practices might induce more myopic behavior from both voters and politicians.

22. A vivid illustration of that was provided by the convertibility regime, which rigidly tied the Argentine peso to the U.S. dollar from April 1991 until its explosion in the first days of 2002. See Galiani, Heymann, and Tommasi (2003) for an analysis of the convertibility experience.

23. For brevity, the paper focuses on formal politico-institutional actors: the president, minis-ters, legislators, provincial governors, party leaders, bureaucrats, and so on. A more com-plete description would include other players, such as unions, business associations, and other socioeconomic actors relevant for the policy game. Also for brevity and simplicity, this paper focuses on the transactional problems among political representatives, leaving aside the quality of representation, that is, the democratic principal-agent problem.

24. "Federal" is used here in the non-U.S. usage to refer to intergovernmental relations and to provincial matters. In Argentina, the federal government is referred to as the national government.

25. These include constitutional features, such as the ability to regulate laws from Congress; path dependency from military times that focused on the executive branch's actions and the expectations of nongovernmental actors that in normal circumstances would have focused on the legislature; general equilibrium implications of the lack of strong Supreme Court enforcement; weakness of Congress; budgetary discretion; and lack of a strong civil service.

26. Iaryczower, Spiller, and Tommasi (2002) show that, historically, the voting patterns of Supreme Court justices in Argentina can be explained with a strategic behavioral model similar to the one used to explain the voting behavior of the U.S. Supreme Court. The cru-cial difference has been in the values of the explanatory variables over time. Because of the many military coups that replaced justices and their subsequent replacement during

democratic restoration, Argentine justices have tended to have short appointments, to be nominated by the ruling executive branch, and to face fairly unified governments.

27. For brevity, I assume that the Washington consensus reform blueprint is the metric from which deviations are measured. Of course, this is an oversimplification, and the point that no effective, universal blueprints are available should be kept in mind (see also Acuña and Tommasi 2000). Nevertheless, the Washington consensus blueprint was the package being promoted throughout this process, perhaps for the signaling abroad reasons argued in Mukand (1999) and Mukand and Rodrik (2002), in combination with the bundling and oversimplification reasons suggested here.

28. For an application of the same logic to fiscal rules, see Braun and Tommasi (2002). For related thoughts with regard to monetary institutions, see Lohmann (2000) and the references therein. This is consistent with the concerns of Posen (1998), who argues that central bank independence merely replaces the credibility of a promise not to inflate with the credibility of a promise to delegate.

29. Several economists who analyzed the Argentine experience ex post argue that the second Menem administration was guilty of not taking additional measures in the macroeconomic realm, which could have prevented, or at least ameliorated, the costs of the later disaster (see, for instance, Perry and Servén 2002).

30. The last number, of course, conflates exchange rate overvaluation with real income growth, but as Galiani, Heymann, and Tommasi (2003) argue, it was a crucial variable for understanding the behavior of the Argentine economy throughout the period.

31. Later on, in the early 2000s, Argentina also had the unlucky timing of falling into a confidence crisis at the time when the United States, and hence the Washington-based multilateral organizations, decided to toughen their stance with countries undergoing financial crises that were in part the outcome of domestic "misbehavior." According to some Argentine economists, Argentina was also partly a victim of the international financial institutions' conversion to the "new" religion of floating exchange rates.

32. For more details about these perverse political and fiscal dynamics, including the peculiar role of the province of Buenos Aires, the largest in the country, which received a disguised bailout during 2001, see Tommasi (2002).

33. That is, of course, quite a weak anchor for a social contract. For related thoughts, see de Macedo, Cohen, and Reisen (2001).

34. The latter may come about not so much because of a vigorous public choice, but because private operators, especially foreign ones, are being scared off by the current scenario. It has pretty much already happened in the banking sector.

References

The word "processed" describes informally reproduced works that may not be commonly available in libraries.

Abdala, M., and P. Spiller. 2000. *Instituciones, Contratos y Regulación en Argentina.* Fundación Gobierno y Sociedad. Buenos Aires: Editorial Temas.

Acuña, C., and M. Tommasi. 2000. "Some Reflections on the Institutional Reforms Required for Latin America." In *Institutional Reforms, Growth and Human Development in Latin America.* Yale Center for International and Areas Studies, vol. 1. New Haven, Conn.: Yale Center for International Area Studies.

Alesina, A., and A. Drazen. 1991. "Why Are Stabilizations Delayed?" *American Economic Review* 81(December): 1170–88.

Bambaci, J., T. Saront, and M. Tommasi. 2002. "The Political Economy of Economic Reforms in Argentina." *Journal of Policy Reform* 5(2): 75–88.

Bambaci, J., P. Spiller, and M. Tommasi. 2001. "Bureaucracy and Public Policy in Argentina." Center of Studies for Institutional Development, Buenos Aires. Processed.

Baron, D., and J. Ferejohn. 1989. "Bargaining in Legislatures." *American Political Science Review* 83(4): 1181–1206.

Bates, R., and A. Krueger. 1993. "Generalizations Arising from the Country Studies." In R. Bates and A. Krueger, eds., *Political and Economic Interactions in Economic Policy Reform: Evidence from Eight Countries*. Oxford, U.K.: Basil Blackwell.

Binder, L. 1971. *Crises and Sequences in Political Development*. Princeton, N.J.: Princeton University Press.

Braun, M., and M. Tommasi. 2002. "Fiscal Rules for Subnational Governments: Some Organizing Principles and Latin American Experiences." Paper presented at the International Monetary Fund and World Bank conference on Fiscal Rules, February 14–16, Oaxaca, Mexico.

Bresser Pereira, L. 1993. "Economic Reforms and Economic Growth: Efficiency and Politics in Latin America." In L. Bresser Pereira, J. M. Maravall, and A. Przeworski, eds., *Economic Reforms in New Democracies: A Social Democratic Approach*. Cambridge, U.K.: Cambridge University Press.

Bruno, M. 1993. *Crisis, Stabilization, and Economic Reform: Therapy by Consensus*. Oxford, U.K.: Oxford University Press.

Buchanan, J., and G. Tullock. 1962. *The Calculus of Consent. Logical Foundations of Constitutional Democracy*. Ann Arbor, Mich.: University of Michigan Press.

Corrales, J. 1998. "Do Economic Crises Contribute to Economic Reform? Argentina and Venezuela in the 1990s." *Political Science Quarterly* 112(4): 617–44.

Cox, G., and M. McCubbins. 2001. "The Institutional Determinants of Policy Outcomes." In S. Haggard and M. McCubbins, eds., *Presidents, Parliaments, and Policy*. Cambridge, U.K.: Cambridge University Press.

Cukierman, A., and M. Tommasi. 1998a. "Credibility of Policymakers and Economic Reforms." In F. Sturzenegger and M. Tommasi, eds., *The Political Economy of Reform*. Cambridge, Mass.: MIT Press.

———. 1998b. "When Does It Take a Nixon to Go to China?" *American Economic Review* 88(1): 180–97.

de Figueiredo, Rui. 2002. "Electoral Competition, Political Uncertainty, and Policy Insulation." *American Political Science Review* 96(2): 321–33.

de la Dehesa, G. 1994. "Spain." In J. Williamson, ed., *The Political Economy of Policy Reform*. Washington, D.C.: Institute for International Economics.

De Luca, M., M. Jones, and M. I. Tula. 2002. "Back Rooms or Ballot Boxes? Candidate Nomination in Argentina." *Comparative Political Studies* 35(4): 413–36.

de Macedo, J. B. de, D. Cohen, and H. Reisen. 2001. *Don't Fix, Don't Float*. Development Centre Study. Paris: Organisation for Economic Co-operation and Development.

Denzau, A., and D. North. 1994. "Shared Mental Models: Ideologies and Institutions." *Kyklos* 47(1): 3–31.

Dixit, A. 1996. *The Making of Economic Policy: A Transaction-Cost Politics Perspective*. Cambridge, Mass.: MIT Press.

Dixit, A., G. Grossman, and F. Gul. 2000. "The Dynamics of Political Compromise." *Journal of Political Economy* 108(3): 531–68.

Drazen, A. 2000. *Political Economy in Macroeconomics*. Princeton, N.J.: Princeton University Press.

Edwards. S. 1998. "Openness, Productivity, and Growth: What Do We Really Know?" *Economic Journal* 108(447): 383–98.

Epstein, D., and S. O'Halloran. 1999. *Delegating Powers: A Transaction Cost Politics Approach to Policy Making under Separate Powers*. Cambridge, U.K.: Cambridge University Press.

Evans, P. 2001. "Beyond 'Institutional Monocropping': Institutions, Capabilities, and Deliberative Development." University of California, Department of Political Science, Berkeley, Calif. Processed.

Fudenberg, D., and J. Tirole. 1991. *Game Theory*. Cambridge, Mass.: MIT Press.

Galiani, S., D. Heymann, and M. Tommasi. 2003. "Great Expectations and Hard Times: The Argentine Convertibility Plan." *Economia: Journal of the Latin American and Caribbean Economic Association* 3(2): 109–60.

Gourevitch, P. 1989. *Politics in Hard Times: Comparative Responses to International Economic Crises*. Ithaca, N.Y.: Cornell University Press.

Habermas, J. 1975. *Legitimation Crisis*. Boston: Beacon Press.

Haggard, S., and M. McCubbins. 2001. *Presidents, Parliaments, and Policy*. Cambridge, U.K.: Cambridge University Press.

Harberger, A. 1993. "The Search for Relevance in Economics (Richard T. Ely Lecture)." *American Economic Review* 83(May): 1–16.

Iaryczower, M., P. Spiller, and M. Tommasi. 2002. "Judicial Decision-Making in Unstable Environments: The Argentine Supreme Court, 1936–1998." *American Journal of Political Science* 46(4): 699–716.

Jones, M., S. Saiegh, P. Spiller, and M. Tommasi. 2002. "Amateur Legislators, Professional Politicians: The Consequences of Party-Centered Electoral Rules in Federal Systems." *American Journal of Political Science* 46(3): 656–69.

————. 2003. "Keeping a Seat in Congress: Provincial Party Bosses and the Survival of Argentine Legislators." Center of Studies for Institutional Development, Buenos Aires. Processed.

Kanbur, R. 2001. "Economic Policy, Distribution, and Poverty: The Nature of Disagreements." Cornell University, Ithaca, N.Y. Processed.

Keeler, J. 1993. "Opening the Window for Reform: Mandates, Crises, and Extraordinary Policy-Making." *Comparative Political Studies* 25(January): 433–86.

Krueger, A. 1993. "Virtuous and Vicious Circles in Economic Development." *American Economic Review* 83(May): 351–55.

Laban, R., and F. Sturzenegger. 1994. "Fiscal Conservatism as a Response to the Debt Crisis." *Journal of Development Economics* 45: 305–24.

Levy, B., and P. Spiller. 1996. "The Institutional Foundations of Regulatory Commitment: A Comparative Analysis of Telecommunications Regulation." *Journal of Law, Economics, and Organization* 10(2): 201–45.

Lindauer, D., and L. Pritchett. 2002. "What Is the Big Idea? The Third Generation of Development Advice." *Economia: Journal of the Latin American and the Caribbean Economic Association* 3(1): 1–40.

Lohmann, S. 2000. "Sollbruchstelle. Deep Uncertainty and the Design of Monetary Institutions." University of California at Los Angeles, Department of Political Science, Los Angeles. Processed.

Lora, E. 1997. "A Decade of Structural Reforms in Latin America: What Has Been Reformed and How to Measure It?" Inter-American Development Bank, Office of the Chief Economist, Washington, D.C. Processed.

———. 2000. "What Makes Reforms Likely? Timing and Sequencing of Structural Reforms in Latin America." Working Paper no. WP-424. Inter-American Development Bank, Office of the Chief Economist, Washington, D.C.

Moe, T. 1990a. "Political Institutions: The Neglected Side of the Story." *Journal of Law, Economics and Organization* 6: 213–53.

———. 1990b. "The Politics of Structural Choice: Toward a Theory of Public Bureaucracy." In O. Williamson, ed., *Organization Theory: From Chester Barnard to the Present and Beyond.* New York: Oxford University Press.

Moe, T., and M. Caldwell. 1994. "The Institutional Foundations of Democratic Government: A Comparison of Presidential and Parliamentary Systems." *Journal of Institutional and Theoretical Economics* 150/1: 171–95.

Mondino, G., F. Sturzenegger, and M. Tommasi. 1996. "Recurrent High Inflation and Stabilization: A Dynamic Game." *International Economic Review* 37(4): 1–16.

Moser, P. 1999. "The Impact of Legislative Institutions on Public Policy: A Survey." *European Journal of Political Economy* 15(1): 1–33.

Mukand, S. 1999. "Globalization and the Confidence Game." Working Paper. Tufts University, Boston.

Mukand, S., and D. Rodrik. 2002. "In Search of the Holy Grail: Policy Convergence, Experimentation, and Economic Performance." Harvard University, Cambridge, Mass. Processed.

Murillo, V. 2002. "Political Biases in Policy Convergence: Privatization Choices in Latin America." Columbia University, New York. Processed.

Nelson, D. 1997. "The Political Economy of Trade Policy Reform: The Problem of Social Complexity." Tulane University, New Orleans. Processed.

Nelson, J., ed. 1990. *Economic Crisis and Policy Choice: The Politics of Adjustment in the Third World.* Princeton, N.J.: Princeton University Press.

Nelson, J., and M. Tommasi. 2001. "Politicians, Public Support, and Social Equity Reforms." Working Paper no. 51. Fundación Gobierno y Sociedad, Center of Studies for Institutional Development, Buenos Aires.

North, D. 1990. "A Transaction-Cost Theory of Politics." *Journal of Theoretical Politics* 2(4): 555–67.

———. 1994. "Economic Performance through Time." *American Economic Review* 84(3): 359–68.

O'Donnell (1994a) "Delegative Democracy." *Journal of Democracy* 5(1): 55–69.

———. 1994b. "The State, Democratization, and Some Conceptual Problems." In W. Smith, C. Acuña, and E. Gamarra, eds., *Latin American Political Economy in the Age of Neoliberal Reforms: Theoretical and Comparative Perspectives for the 1990s.* New Brunswick, N.J.: Transaction Books.

Pastor, M., and C. Wise. 2001. "From Poster Child to Basket Case." Foreign Affairs 80(6): 60–72.

Perry, G., and L. Servén. 2002. "The Anatomy of a Multiple Crisis: Why Was Argentina Special and What Can We Learn from It?" World Bank, Washington, D.C. Processed.

Pistor, K. 2000. "The Standardization of Law and Its Effect on Developing Economies." Discussion Paper 4. Group of 24. Harvard University, Center for International Development, Cambridge, Mass.

Posen, A. 1998. "Do Better Institutions Make Better Policy?" *International Finance* 1(1): 173–205.

Rodríguez, F., and D. Rodrik. 1999. "Trade Policy and Economic Growth: A Skeptic's Guide to the Cross-National Evidence." Harvard University, Cambridge, Mass. Processed.

Rodrik, D. 1995. "Taking Trade Policy Seriously: Export Subsidization as a Case Study in Policy Effectiveness." In A. Deardoff, J. Levinsohn, and R. Stern, eds., *New Directions in Trade Theory.* Ann Arbor, Mich.: University of Michigan Press.

_____. 1996. "Understanding Economic Policy Reform." *Journal of Economic Literature* 34(March): 9–41.

_____. 1998. "The Rush to Free Trade in the Developing World: Why So Late? Why Now? Will It Last?" In F. Sturzenegger and M. Tommasi, eds., *The Political Economy of Reform.* Cambridge, Mass.: MIT Press.

_____. 2000. "Participatory Politics, Social Cooperation, and Economic Stability." Harvard University, Cambridge, Mass. Processed.

Sabatier, P. 1999. *Theories of the Policy Process.* Boulder, Colo.: Westview Press.

Shepsle, K., and B. Weingast. 1995. *Positive Theories of Congressional Institutions.* Ann Arbor, Mich.: University of Michigan Press.

Spiller, P., and M. Tommasi. 2003. "The Institutional Foundations of Public Policy: A Transactions Approach with Application to Argentina." *Journal of Law, Economics, and Organization* 19(2): 281–306.

_____. Forthcoming. *The Institutional Foundations of Public Policy: A Transactions Approach with Application to Argentina.* Cambridge, U.K.: Cambridge University Press.

Spiller, P., E. Stein, and M. Tommasi. 2003. "Political Institutions, Policymaking Processes, and Policy Outcomes. An Intertemporal Transactions Framework." Inter-American Development Bank, Research Department, Washington, D.C. Processed.

Srinivasan, T. N., and J. Bhagwati. 1999. "Outward-Orientation and Development: Are Revisionists Right?" Discussion Paper no. 806. Yale University, Economic Growth Center, New Haven, Conn.

Stiglitz, J. 2000. "Reflections on the Theory and Practice of Reform." In A. Krueger, ed., *Economic Policy Reform: The Second Stage.* Chicago: University of Chicago Press.

Tommasi, M. 2002. "Fiscal Federalism in Argentina and the Reforms of the 1990s." Paper prepared for the Center for Research on Economic Development and Policy Reform (Stanford University) project on Federalism in a Global Environment. Palo Alto, Calif.

Tommasi, M., and A. Velasco. 1996. "Where Are We in the Political Economy of Reform?" *Journal of Policy Reform* 1: 187–238.

Tommasi, M., S. Saiegh, and P. Sanguinetti. 2001. "Fiscal Federalism in Argentina: Politics, Policies, and Institutional Reform." *Economia: Journal of the Latin American and the Caribbean Economic Association* 1(2): 157–201.

Tornell, A. 1995. "Are Economic Crises Necessary for Trade Liberalization and Fiscal Reform? The Mexican Experience." In R. Dornbusch and S. Edwards, eds., *Reform, Recovery, and Growth.* Chicago: University of Chicago Press.

Velasco, A. 1998. "The Common Property Approach to the Political Economy of Fiscal Policy." In F. Sturzenegger and M. Tommasi, eds., *The Political Economy of Reform.* Cambridge, Mass.: MIT Press.

Weyland, K. 1996. "Risk Taking in Latin American Economic Restructuring: Lessons from Prospect Theory." *International Studies Quarterly* 40(June): 185–207.

Williamson, J., ed. 1994. *The Political Economy of Policy Reform*. Washington, D.C.: Institute for International Economics.

Williamson, J., and S. Haggard. 1994. "The Political Conditions for Economic Reform." In J. Williamson, ed., *The Political Economy of Policy Reform*. Washington, D.C.: Institute for International Economics.

Zaller, John R. 1992. *The Nature and Origins of Mass Opinion*. Cambridge, U.K.: Cambridge University Press.

State Failure in Developing Countries and Institutional Reform Strategies

MUSHTAQ H. KHAN

Two radically different theoretical views on the role of the state in economic development have driven policy debates on the location of state failure and the priorities of institutional reform in developing countries. A lack of clarity on this underlying difference has been the source of much confusion. I shall refer to the dominant view, which has underpinned the mainstream consensus on the state, as the service delivery model, and the second view, which looks at the role of the state in the context of the transition to capitalism, as the social transformation model.

The service delivery model focuses on a range of services that states should deliver, in particular, public goods such as law and order, social security, and market regulation, and relies on competitive markets to deliver all other goods and services. The social transformation model looks at the more critical and problematic role the state plays in the transformation of essentially precapitalist and pre-industrial societies into dynamic and essentially industrial, capitalist ones. While states do deliver services, the service delivery model of the state is misleading for poorly performing developing country states undergoing reform. Historically, success in service delivery has generally depended on states' success in pushing social transformation rapidly in the direction of viable capitalist economies. The critical area of state failure has been the absence of adequate institutional and political capacity in developing country states to assist in and accelerate a dynamic transformation. Without strategies to enhance this role of the state, sustained progress on service delivery is also unlikely. Many of the consensus policies on reforming institutions to improve service delivery are based on a partial reading of theory and evidence. They are at best unlikely to work, and at worst could further undermine the state's institutional and political capacity for ensuring a dynamic transformation.

Mushtaq Khan is senior lecturer in economics at the University of London, Department of Economics, School of Oriental and African Studies. This paper is a revised version of the paper presented at the ABCDE-Europe conference.

Annual World Bank Conference on Development Economics—Europe 2003
© 2004 The International Bank for Reconstruction and Development/The World Bank

The state's pivotal role is based on its claim to the monopoly of legitimate violence. The state is the only body in society that can legitimately enforce institutions, collect taxes, redistribute income and wealth, and represent and enforce social cohesion or resolve conflicts, in all cases using force if necessary. All these functions are interdependent and have a role to play in both service delivery and social transformation. This paper cannot look at all these areas, but fortunately, the role of the state in creating and enforcing institutions shows the interdependence between many of these functions.

Institutions are the rules of the game that set incentives, opportunities, and limitations for individuals or organizations. The key institutions the state enforces include the system of property rights; the interventions that define rents and incentive structures, which include taxes and subsidies; and the higher-level political institutions, such as democratic or authoritarian decisionmaking bodies that set the rules for changing rules. Because variations in this set of institutions can potentially have large effects on the quantity and quality of investment, economists agree in general terms that state failure can have a significant effect on growth (see, for instance, Bardhan 2000; Bates 2001; Khan 1995; Lal and Myint 1996; Migdal 1988; North 1981, 1990; Olson 2000; Shleifer and Vishny 1998; Stiglitz 1998b). Therefore adjusting for differences in initial conditions, persistent shortfalls in growth rates compared with similar countries provide initial evidence of state failure and its severity. While this paper does not directly address static redistribution issues, the strong statistical relationship between growth and poverty reduction (Dollar and Kraay 2001; Lal and Myint 1996) also implies that state failure is responsible for poverty in many developing countries. While redistribution can play an important role in any poverty reduction strategy, this paper focuses on the necessary conditions for enabling any economic growth strategy. This is important in a broad discussion of poverty, because growth is a necessary component of poverty reduction in any poor country.

This paper defines state failure in the broadest terms that can loosely incorporate both positions on the role of the state. Based on Krueger's (1990) definition of government failure, state failure is defined here as consisting of both errors of omission, that is, when the state fails to do things that could have improved economic performance, and errors of commission, which is when the state does things that worsen economic performance. While the identification of state failure implies a judgment that better economic performance could have been achieved, the challenge is also to identify the institutions that could achieve this better performance. The service delivery model uses as its benchmark a model of a well-working market economy, loosely referred to here as the liberal market consensus, without implying that everyone within this consensus agrees in all respects. The consensus argues that to generate growth, states have to protect stable property rights, defined by strong contract enforcement, low expropriation risk, and low corruption; they have to ensure undistorted markets defined by low rents; and they have to achieve democratic accountability and civil society participation to keep the state in check. The key service delivery functions of the state are to protect property rights and to deliver democratically decided upon public goods efficiently. It follows that reform should aim to help developing countries attain the appropriate state capacities.

The consensus view has rapidly come to enjoy widespread support because many of the reforms it endorses, such as the pursuit of democratization, the achievement of greater openness and accountability, and the pursuit of anticorruption campaigns, are rightly supported by most people as ends in themselves. However, the new consensus is based on a partial reading of the theory and evidence, and does not address the core issue of social transformation that is a necessary component of any strategy to accelerate growth. As a result, if international agencies give the impression that these reforms are instruments that can overcome state failure and help achieve economic takeoff, a crisis of expectations is likely to occur soon. The benchmark of good institutions described by the new consensus does indeed fit aspects of the institutional structure of advanced countries, and poorly performing developing countries do indeed fail to approach this benchmark. Nevertheless, the reform package that aims to push institutions in developing countries in the direction of a generalized advanced country model is not relevant for helping developing countries carry out the transition from essentially precapitalist societies to dynamic, capitalist ones. The social campaigns to deepen democracy or prevent corruption are legitimate in their own right. The concern here is only whether these reforms can contribute to a serious shift in the growth paths of poorly performing countries.

Theory and evidence can be interpreted to suggest a different and much more demanding reform agenda to combat state failure in developing countries. Development is an ugly and conflict-ridden process, not primarily because of corruption and the lack of democracy, but because social structures are rapidly changing, new classes are emerging, and new wealth is being accumulated at historically unprecedented rates. In the advanced countries, this social and economic transformation took place over centuries. A shock of a similar magnitude has hit the developing countries, but telescoped into a period of decades and, perhaps partly as a result, the transition to capitalism has been much more patchy. Old production systems have collapsed often well before new ones can take over, social conflicts are intense, and stable and productive political constituencies on which viable democracies can be based are often absent. At the same time, political and economic expectations are higher than at any time in the past.

The real question facing developing countries is whether these processes are likely to lead to a viable and dynamic capitalism, as they appear to have done in a few high-growth economies, or whether they will lead merely to the theft of resources by unproductive classes and a descent into anarchy. The institutional reforms identified in the consensus view do not directly address these fundamental challenges facing developing countries during the period of transformation or identify the state capacities required to accelerate the transition in the direction of viable capitalism. Instead it targets some of the symptoms of the transformation period—the prevalence of corruption and the weakness of democracy—and attempts to construct institutions that may not be the most relevant for addressing the problems of transformation that characterize this period. These attempts can prove to be largely irrelevant, but they can also make matters worse by further weakening state capacities, raising unattainable popular expectations, or even by simply diverting attention from more pressing problems. By referring to some of the data, the historical evidence, and the theory that can be brought into play to interpret it, this paper injects a note of caution into the interpretation of this consensus by policymakers. The consequences of yet another round of multilateral-led reform in developing countries running out of steam do not need to be spelled out.

In contrast with the reforms suggested by the liberal market consensus, getting developing economies through this transformation successfully has historically required stronger and more interventionist state capacities. To begin with, states in high-growth countries participated in the transformation of their economies and societies by helping to create a new capitalist class and ensuring that it succeeded in acquiring technology and entrepreneurial capacity. This involved using a range of policies, including active interventions in property rights and management of growth-enhancing rents (Amsden 1989; Aoki, Kim, and Okuno-Fujiwara 1997; Chang 1994; Khan and Jomo 2000; Lall and Teubal 1998; Page 1994; Rodrik 1995, forthcoming; Wade 1990; Woo-Cumings 1999). The conclusion is that policymakers have to focus on these transformation capacities to enable states to push the capitalist transition if they are to address economic underperformance.

In addition, simply describing the transforming role of state intervention in the high-growth economies does not provide directly relevant lessons either, because most developing country states failed to achieve similar goals despite frequent attempts. Here much of the "developmental state" literature on developing countries is also weak in locating the sources of state failure in pushing social transformations. An important aspect of state failure during the transformation is the failure to enforce any institutions, a problem Myrdal (1968) pointed out more than 30 years ago. This paper argues that the distribution and disposition of political power in society is a key determinant of enforcement success, and that the emergence of high-growth states is therefore as much a task of political engineering as it is of institutional engineering to ensure that states are able to enforce painful and socially contested decisions. This explains why institutions that work well in one context may fail badly in another. The evidence supports the claim that the most persistent types of state failure occur when institutions fail because of an inappropriate match between internal political settlements (defined as the distribution of organizational and political power between competing groups and classes) and the institutions and interventions through which states attempt to accelerate transformation and growth (Khan 1995; Rodrik forthcoming).

Policies must recognize that in most cases, political conditions are not conducive for states to acquire and exercise transformation capacities. In such cases, policymakers have to be concerned with how the disposition and organization of political power need to change over time. An unfortunate misconception is that democracy is sufficient to consolidate productive groups and undermine unproductive ones. While direct intervention in the political organization of developing countries is outside the remit of international agencies or researchers, opening up debate about how growth-promoting political coalitions can be constructed is not. On the contrary, by focusing on a set of narrow institutional reforms pertaining to service delivery, international agencies are doing little to prevent the consolidation of unproductive groups in many of the poorest economies.

These concerns suggest that the consensus reforms should not be uncritically supported and indicate other areas where policy-oriented research should focus. The next section looks at the theory and evidence underpinning reforms based on the service delivery model. The following section examines the theory and evidence supporting the need to focus on the capacities of the state that ensure dynamic transformations. The paper concludes with a look at the implications.

The Service Delivery State

The standard textbook list of the state's service delivery functions is well known. These functions include providing law and order, correcting market failures, and, in particular, providing essential public goods and limited welfarist redistributions. Underpinning the service delivery concept of the state is a set of well-developed theories of how a liberal market economy works. The model has three theoretical components that have combined to produce the liberal market consensus underpinning the service delivery view of the state. (While the post-Washington consensus defined by Stiglitz [1998a] strongly criticizes the Washington consensus on the role of the state, both are part of the liberal market consensus in terms of the key policy conclusions discussed below.)

The first component of the model is that efficient markets are rent free and have stable property rights. The standard theory of efficiency in competitive markets has been deepened by new institutional analysis that argues that stable and well-defined property rights are a precondition for efficient exchange and also create incentives for long-term investment (Bates 2001; North 1990). In contrast, rents in markets provide prima facie evidence of restrictions on competition, and if this is achieved through interventions in property rights, they also undermine confidence in the future. Rents are incomes that individuals can earn that are higher than what they can earn in their next-best opportunity, and so rents exist if those in the next-best activities are prevented from acquiring access to particular resources or opportunities. This could be because of protected rights over information, monopoly rights to supply particular markets, rights over subsidies, or even rights over a valuable natural resource. Of all the different types of rents, monopoly profits and special interest subsidies are typically used as examples to argue that efficiency requires rent-free markets. The new information economics critiques this model of the market, but the simpler view still dominates the liberal market consensus on the state. In terms of service delivery, both errors of commission, such as the creation of monopolies, and errors of omission, such as the failure to provide good infrastructure, can be explained in terms of successful attempts to capture such rents.

The second component of the model is that rent-seeking creates rents and destabilizes property rights. The persistence of damaging rents and the associated property right instability is thus explained by the incentives for rent-seeking (Krueger 1974; Posner 1975). Rent-seeking consists of such activities as lobbying and corruption that seek to persuade states to create rents. The literature on rent-seeking has been growing (reviewed in Khan 2000b), and has been extended by a more recent subset of literature addressing the causes and effects of corruption (Andvig and others 2000; Bardhan 1997). Corruption is illegal rent-seeking whereby the rent-seeker uses bribes to influence public officials. One of the most damaging effects of rent-seeking is the destabilization of property rights, because the creation or reallocation of rents always requires appropriate changes in rights.

The third component of the model is that the absence of democracy and a weak bureaucracy allow rent-seeking to continue. To explain why damaging rent-seeking continues even when the majority is hurt by it, the consensus identifies a number of factors. First, the absence of democracy increases the chances that small groups can continue with their socially damaging rent-seeking (Olson 2000, 1997; North 1990). Second, low bureaucratic salaries, a politically appointed (hence "short-termist") bureaucracy, and a weak judiciary can all reduce the expected cost to public officials of accepting bribes, thereby making rent-seeking more likely (World Bank 1997).

Figure 1 shows how these three core components of the liberal market consensus interact to explain how developing countries can become locked into persistent state failure, defined as poor service delivery in such key areas as the protection of stable property rights and the provision of infrastructure, which in turn affect growth. Causality runs in both directions between most of the factors identified. Thus the absence of democracy not only allows rent-seeking to continue, but rent-seeking reinforces the power of special interest groups. In turn rent-seeking not only creates rents, but the presence of rents induces further rent-seeking. Weak bureaucratic capacity and

FIGURE 1. State Failure: The Liberal-Market Consensus

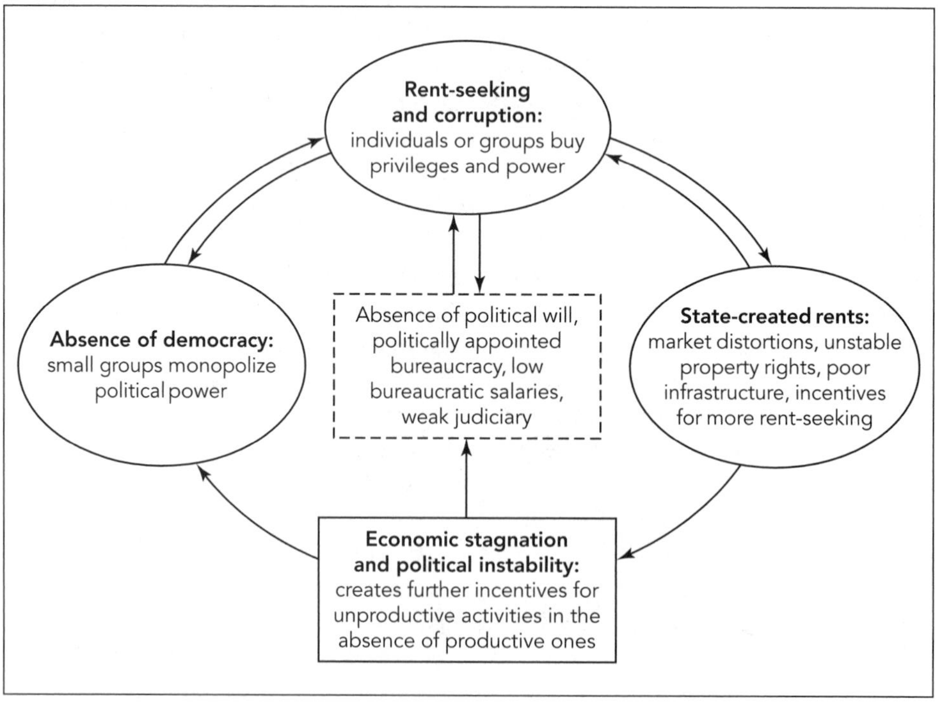

Source: Author.

low salaries not only allow corruption, but corruption makes obtaining the political will to reform the bureaucracy difficult and can make the judiciary corrupt as well. This interdependence means that societies can become locked into undemocratic, highly corrupt, and highly distorted equilibriums (Andvig and Moene 1990; Bardhan 1997; Murphy, Shleifer, and Vishny 1993).

The policy implication of the consensus model is that a number of parallel good governance reforms are required to deal with state failure. Whereas in the past the focus would primarily have been on economic reforms to make markets competitive and rent-free, the liberal market consensus now argues that these policies will not be sustained without simultaneous political and institutional reforms. Political reforms are understood as moves toward democracy and sometimes decentralization, together with encouraging civil society participation, all with the aim of limiting the state's freedom to create arbitrary rents. Institutional reforms include moves to "right size" the state by focusing on service delivery, reducing the state's institutional capacity to create rents, raising bureaucratic salaries, improving civil service recruitment procedures, and making the judiciary more independent. Fighting corruption overlaps with all these reforms and ensures that the incentives to create rents are further reduced. Correcting state failure, according to the liberal market consensus, requires moves on all these fronts simultaneously, because they are preconditions for specific improvements in states' capacity to deliver such services as critical public goods and stable property rights (Asian Development Bank 2000; World Bank 1997).

The Evidence

The most significant support for the consensus view comes from a formidable array of econometric exercises (for instance, Barro 1996; Clague and others 1997; Hall and Jones 1999; Johnson, Kaufmann, and Zoido-Lobatón 1998; Kaufmann, Kraay, and Zoido-Lobatón 1999; Knack and Keefer 1995, 1997; Mauro 1995; World Bank 1997). These studies find that such governance variables as corruption, the stability of property rights, and democracy are correlated with such developmental outcomes as per capita incomes, growth of per capita incomes, investment rates, and direct indicators of poverty (for example, child mortality rates). But has the eagerness to establish that all good things go together colored the measurement and interpretation of the evidence? Some of the data problems are well known and most studies add cautionary statements, but taken together, the data problems suggest that a much higher degree of care is required in interpreting the results.

To begin with, the indexes measuring governance quality are subjective by nature. Corruption, democracy, stability of property rights, and even degree of policy-induced distortion are measured by indexes based on perceptions or on judgments by "competent" observers. Polls are subject to the problem of scaling across countries, while competent observers can have preconceived ideas about what they expect to see. Corruption, instability, and distortions can appear to be less serious in high-growth countries, even to competent observers, simply because things are working well. Finally, corruption, property right instability, and distortions can vary widely in type and seriousness across sectors within an economy. In constructing a composite index, prior expectations can bias the choice of evidence and its weights.

In addition, we do not have satisfactory time-series data for periods that are long enough to test for causality using the same group of countries. To see how governance might affect growth, we need both high- and low-growth countries to test our hypotheses. Most of the high-growth Asian economies began growing sometime in the 1960s, 1970s, or early 1980s, but governance indicators are only available from the mid-1980s onward, and the fuller data sets are only available for the 1990s or later. As high growth is expected to improve governance indicators, to test the causal significance of governance variables we need to have governance indexes for high-growth countries before they began their takeoff. Because such indicators are lacking, growth in the high-growth countries is often misleadingly explained using their ex post governance indicators achieved after their growth has taken off or instrumental variables correlated with them.

Finally, insufficient observations of successful transformation countries are available for satisfactory econometric results. Only a handful of countries were successful developers over the last 40 or 50 years. Even if we had ex ante governance indicators for these countries, in any statistical exercise they are vastly outnumbered by poorly performing developing countries with poor governance indicators on the one hand, and by moderately performing advanced countries with good governance indicators on the other. Thus the characteristics of the critical group of successful transformers are lost as outliers. As a result, the regressions pick up statistical correlations or patterns rather than causality. Incidentally, though small in number, the successful transformers have not been small in terms of population as they include Asian giants like China, but econometric studies do not normally weight observations by population size. This alone might have reversed at least some of the econometric results, even without true ex ante governance indicators being available.

The high-growth developers are particularly important, because even though governance indexes are not available for periods prior to their takeoffs, their governance indexes remain quite poor for a considerable period after their growth took off. For instance, even in the mid-1980s, the averages of the Knack and Keefer (1995) indexes of institutional quality based on quality of bureaucracy, rule of law, expropriation risk, and contract repudiation by the government for the Asian high-growth economies were only a little better than those for many poorly performing countries. Rodrik (1997) points out that while growth within East Asian economies was correlated with the index, only Japan, Singapore, and Taiwan (China) had high scores and none were remotely poor by then. Indonesia scored the same as the Republic of the Congo, Ghana, and Myanmar, while the Republic of Korea, Malaysia, and Thailand were at the same level as Côte d'Ivoire. Nor were most high-growth developers democratic when they began growing or for a considerable period thereafter.

As concerns corruption, table 1 shows the Transparency International corruption index for the 54 countries for which the earliest index is available for the period 1980–85 and growth rates for these countries for 1980–90. While the median growth rates of the East Asian developers were far higher than those of the other two groups, their corruption scores were not significantly better than those of other developing

TABLE 1. Growth and Corruption, 54 Countries, 1980–90

Item	Developing countries (24 observations)	High-growth developers (6 observations)	Advanced countries (24 observations)
Median GDP growth rate, 1980–90	1.9	7.8	2.8
(range)	(−0.4–6.3)	(5.2–9.7)	(1.8–7.1)
Median corruption index, 1980–85	3.5	4.5	8.1
(range)	(0.7–7.4)	(0.2–6.3)	(4.2–8.4)

GDP   Gross domestic product.

Note: The Transparency International corruption index ranges from 0 for the most corrupt countries to 10 for the least corrupt: High-growth developers were separated from the other country groups on the basis of long-term growth rates.

Sources: Transparency International and Göttingen University (2002); World Bank (1999, table 11).

FIGURE 2. Interpreting the Evidence on Governance and Development

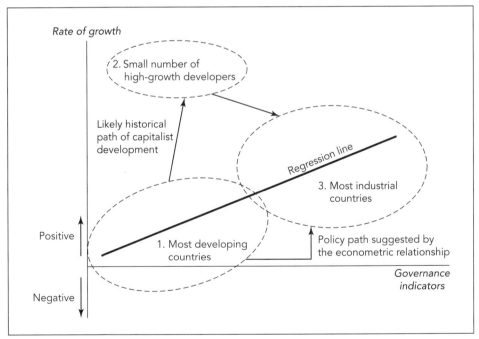

Source: Author.

countries. If governance indexes were available for the periods before growth took off in the high-growth countries, the differences may have been even smaller.

The governance data conform to the general pattern shown in figure 2. Such data provide the typical positive coefficient estimated for governance variables in regression exercises simply because of the numbers of observations in clusters 1 and 3 and the few observations in cluster 2. Taking the earlier discussion into account, two main observations challenge the causality suggested by such a regression exercise.

First, no examples exist of any country that initially improved its governance to advanced country levels to achieve equivalent per capita incomes, growth rates, or other characteristics. Reading this as a possibility from the regression line is misleading. As figure 2 suggests, the route to advanced country status may be quite different.

Second, the growth rates in high-growth developers were associated with governance indicators that were insignificantly or only moderately better than developing country averages. By the 1980s, some of the high-growth countries had been rapidly growing for a few decades, and their relatively high per capita incomes would have allowed governance improvements to happen anyway. In other words, we would expect their ex ante governance indicators to be somewhat worse than the indicators we have for the 1980s, but even using the corruption indexes for the 1980s, the high-growth economies do not have significantly lower corruption. However, this fails to have any effect on the regression simply because the high-growth countries were so few in number. If there were more high-growth countries, we would probably have observed an inverse U relationship as observed in the case of democracy (Barro 1996). The nonlinearity of the data suggests that something else was happening in the high-growth economies that has not been identified or that the main direction of causality has been misunderstood. Saying that countervailing factors, such as high investment rates or high efficiency of investment, operated in the high-growth economies is not enough, because the institutional argument is that good governance has an economic effect precisely by enhancing investment and its efficiency.

In this context note that not all econometric work supports the new consensus models. In particular, Treisman (2000) finds that the effects of democracy and decentralization on corruption are weak, while Burkhart and Lewis-Beck (1994) find that rises in per capita incomes precede the emergence of democracy and not the other way around. However, in the published literature, contrarian results are relatively rare.

These observations do not imply that governance reforms are unimportant. As governance is what states do, and as the state plays a critical role in pushing social transformations, I believe that governance reforms are even more important than the good governance framework suggests. However, the state capacities identified as being critical have little to do with the good governance characteristics derived from an abstraction of the liberal-democratic state observed in advanced capitalist countries. Rather, far from being a precondition for rapid growth, a more consistent interpretation of the historical evidence is that it shows that good governance—in the sense of less corruption and deeper democracy—is typically an outcome of successful economic development.

The correlation exercises are also misleading in a fundamental respect. The claim that if all else remains the same, then higher levels of corruption will lead to poorer economic performance is simply an arithmetic observation that we do not need to question. The point is whether corruption can be reduced sufficiently in failing states to contribute to an economic takeoff. To begin to approach the levels of development of the advanced countries, developing economies have to grow not just at advanced country rates, but much faster. Even if the regression line in figure 2 accurately identified the causality from corruption to growth, reducing corruption to advanced country levels would only allow group 3 countries to grow at group 1 rates. The historic challenge is to approach group 2 growth rates, but the good governance framework does not address this question.

I am not saying that corruption is costless, let alone that it is in any sense functional, nor that democracy is not a fundamental right that people in developing countries strive for. The issue here concerns the degree to which sustainable reductions in corruption or improvements in democracy can be attained before broadly based economic prosperity has been achieved, and even more important, whether these reforms are likely to accelerate economic growth sufficiently to make any impact on poverty (Khan 2002a).

The Social Transformation State

States in developing countries play a much more critical role than the service delivery model suggests. Developing societies are undergoing unprecedented social and economic changes in which states inevitably deploy economic power and violence potential for better or for worse. As rising expectations and social mobilization destroy the political and economic viability of traditional societies, staying still is not an option.

Far from being a service provider, the state is an instrument in the hands of contending classes, groups, and political entrepreneurs, each attempting to capture resources and steer the transformation in specific directions. State institutions and policies are always the outcome of conflict and negotiation between contending forces, but in advanced capitalist countries that already have a dominant capitalist sector, democratic politics usually oscillates around a relatively narrow range of options that seeks to conserve the dynamism of the capitalist sector, and parties usually differ only at the margin in terms of distribution. This reflects two economic facts. First, many of the resources for running the political system come from the capitalist sector, which therefore has considerable influence on policymaking. Second, and more important, the dominance of the capitalist sector means that the immediate welfare of most people, even if they are not capitalists, depends on the health of the capitalist sector. Neither of these restrictions operate to the same extent during the transition to capitalism, when the capitalist sector is, by definition, not dominant. The absence of a dominating feedback loop from the performance of the capitalist sector to the policymaking process in developing countries allows a much greater range of variation in policies and institutions, and makes it possible for sustained state failure to persist when it comes to organizing a dynamic capitalist transformation (Khan 2002b). During this transition period, state success or failure is not related in any simple way to the state's neutrality in upholding preexisting property rights or its abstention from intervening in the economy or in social conflicts. If these were indeed important preconditions, a minimalist service delivery state tightly constrained by good governance reforms would begin to make sense as a policy goal.

In connection with the potential locations of state failure during the transformation, states have differed along four dimensions. First, transformation states have

FIGURE 3. Factors Determining State Success or Failure

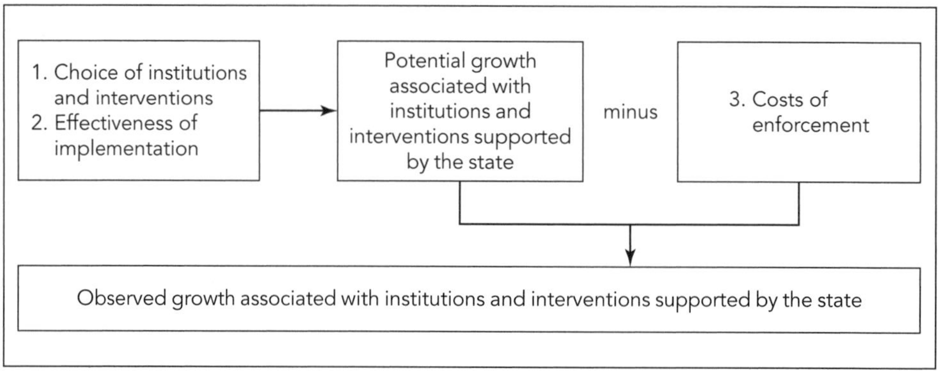

Source: Author.

differed in terms of their institutions and policies. Second, they have differed in terms of how effectively they enforced these institutions. Third, they have differed in relation to the costs of enforcement, defined as the costs of creating, operating, and enforcing institutions. Finally, they have differed in the processes driving institutional change. Institutions have changed in efficient directions in some cases, but not others. This relates back to the first dimension: if damaging institutions continue to exist, slowing down the transformation, why do they not change? In a dynamic setting, errors of omission do not really differ from errors of commission.

Figure 3 shows how a state's growth performance can be attributed to the first three dimensions. Growth requires not only that the state supports institutions that drive the capitalist transformation, but also requires effective enforcement of these institutions and relatively low costs of enforcement. If growth is systematically low, then the fourth factor, the process of institutional change, will have to be considered.

Institutions and Policies during Social Transformations

The liberal market consensus argues that the institutional structure for maximizing growth is one that ensures the absence of rents. The main task for the state is supposed to be the delivery of democratically agreed on public goods. While service delivery is important, evidence from developing countries casts doubt on its adequacy for ensuring rapid social transformation. Indeed, the state's ability to carry out relatively massive interventions in property rights systems and to create and manage growth-generating rents has been critical in high-growth economies. States have also carried out significant transfers that have contributed to political stability and thereby made the emerging institutional structure politically viable.

Dynamic States Can Alter Property Rights in the Interests of Growth

Consensus theorists have frequently pointed out the instability of property rights in poorly performing countries, but in dynamic countries, the rapid emergence of new classes of capitalists has typically also entailed relatively long periods of instability of preexisting rights. This is not surprising. All developing countries are characterized by large precapitalist sectors that have become unviable and that do not produce enough of a surplus to pay for the protection of their rights. Some of these rights begin to be transferred to more efficient users through the market, but in every developing country a significant part of these necessary transfers takes place through nonmarket mechanisms. These include politically mediated transfers of assets (land reform, transfers through the fiscal mechanism), indirect politically mediated transfers (licensing of land use, manipulation of relative prices), and illegal and quasi-legal activities (land grabbing, staking claims on common property). The scale of nonmarket transfers at this stage can be explained first by the absence of a preexisting and already efficient capitalist sector that can purchase these rights through the market mechanism. Second, the transaction costs of strictly legal exchanges are typically high at this stage, because constructing a generalized institutional structure that can ensure low transaction costs for all market participants is itself an expensive proposition that is difficult to implement until the economy collectively produces a sufficient surplus to pay for it. While nonmarket transfers play a necessary role at this stage, these transfers of assets can and do contribute to the perception that property rights are unstable and contested in developing countries.

If and when a dynamic capitalism emerges through these processes, the new property rights system can rapidly stabilize, because dynamic emerging capitalists can soon spend enough to control or influence the state to protect their rights. Thus a look at property rights stability in high-growth economies once their growth has stabilized can give the misleading impression that property rights stability was the cause of growth. This is where historical evidence is important. Even superficial historical observations show that virtually all high-growth countries undertook or allowed dramatic reallocations of property rights in the early stages of their takeoffs. The stability that distinguishes high-growth countries is not a stability of property rights, but rather a more subtle commitment to growth and to transfer and protect rights in ways that promote growth.

For instance, before the economic takeoff in Korea and Taiwan (China), their states carried out rapid and far-reaching land reforms, in Korea between 1949 and 1950 and in Taiwan (China) between 1949 and 1953. The state compulsorily acquired all agricultural land above a low landholding ceiling at a price well below the market price and distributed it to tenants at this artificially low price. By any account, such enforced transfers are not consistent with well-defined property rights. In Thailand, transfers of public and common property resources to emerging capitalists took place in a more decentralized way through "primitive accumulation" organized by emerging capitalists who controlled local money politics and the state (Pasuk and Baker 1997). Not surprisingly, in the 1980s Thailand was characterized as one of the most corrupt countries in the world, and yet managed to grow rapidly for decades. Failed transformation states are also characterized by regular seizures of land and resources by the politically connected from the weak and unconnected, but in these cases the grabbers are not operating under a broader institutional system that induces or forces them to become productive capitalists.

Lal and Myint (1996) point out that the most important role of the publicly-owned banking system in the context of Korea's industrial policy was to transfer massive amounts of wealth to an emerging capitalist class much more rapidly than might have happened in a market, while maintaining sufficient discipline to ensure that this process was not entirely captured by inefficient groups. Indeed, the ability of the Korean state to reallocate rights through nonmarket mechanisms contributed significantly to the effective implementation of its industrial policy regime. Its conditional subsidy scheme, which essentially subsidized technology acquisition by emerging capitalists, could have had high social costs if many subsidized plants failed to acquire new technologies rapidly, and became bankrupt. However, the Korean state demonstrated its ability to reallocate entire plants across industrial groups before failure had set in, using its financial muscle in the banking sector to get its way (Chang 1994; Lee 1991). By not having to respect the limitations of property rights, civil courts, and procedures, the Korean state could credibly threaten inefficient capitalists with the loss of their assets if they did not meet state export targets, and the state was able to implement these threats with little opposition from the courts or from the losers themselves. In other words, far from weakly defined rights holding back Korea's development, they allowed the implementation of a hothouse strategy for acquiring technology.

This power was often misused, for example, in 1985 when the Kukje group, the country's sixth largest conglomerate at the time, was brought down because it offered insufficient paybacks to the regime (*Far Eastern Economic Review* April 21, 1988; Fields 1995). The government's ability to push the *chaebol* (big conglomerates) around clearly reflected the latters' weak property rights. This political ability on the part of the state inevitably declined over time, so that in 1990, when President Roh Tae-Woo ordered 49 *chaebol* to sell real estate holdings that he believed were speculative, he found that obtaining compliance was extremely difficult (Fields 1995). The growing political independence of the *chaebol* and the increasing technological complexity of the Korean economy were clearly related to the decline of the Korean industrial policy system in the 1990s (Khan 2000b), but by then Korea was already an industrialized economy. The important observation is that when the Korean economy took off, the *chaebol* did not enjoy well-defined property rights in the conventional sense.

In contemporary China, property rights in many of the most dynamic sectors are also not well defined, and even though China's institutions are very different from those of Korea, they are once again assisting the capture of resources by emerging dynamic entrepreneurs (Qian 2002; Rodrik forthcoming). China's dynamic township and village enterprises account for at least 40 percent of industrial employment and exports, but observers have been puzzled about the vagueness of property rights in relation to these enterprises' assets (Bowles and Dong 1999). Although notionally owned by townships or villages, they are actually controlled by dynamic managers who own a small share of the residual. This is puzzling to those who believe that much clearer ownership of the residuals is required for dynamic management. The answer may be that the very vagueness of rights in China is allowing an effective transfer of rights over public assets to an emerging class of entrepreneurs, and that these proto-capitalists are confident that the state will formalize their de facto ownership in the long run provided they remain efficient. In the meantime, this arrangement keeps social contestation low and prevents the upheavals that straightforward privatization might have unleashed (Qian 2002). It is the political coalition backing growth that was new in China after the 1980s. The state's ability to restructure property rights in line with its changing objectives is not, and has been demonstrated time and again since 1949.

Contemporary China scores somewhat higher than the average developing country in rule of law indexes, but these are based primarily on risk perceptions by joint venture companies in export zones. These indexes are misleading, because while export-oriented companies in China are fairly safe from expropriation, other holders of rights are not. A more instructive approach would be to look at the state's ability to reallocate rights over land, and indeed its ability to control internal population movements that allowed it to set up massive export zones in the first place. Such a degree of power is, of course, not always desirable. As an example of a controversial, state-driven reallocation of rights, consider the Three Gorges Dam project. Nearly 2 million people are to receive compulsory compensation on a scale and at a time decided by the state, and many others who are displaced will probably never be compensated. Setting aside questions about the project's technical viability and cost-benefit ratio, it is an example of how the Chinese state can reallocate property rights if it believes that a project will further national development. In contrast, property rights are much better defined in many developing countries such as India, where projects much smaller than the Three Gorges Dam have been successfully blocked in the courts for years. Again, whether this is in the social interest or not depends on the specific projects, but arguing that property rights are well defined in China and that this has driven its growth would be wrong.

Dynamic States Can Manage Growth-Enhancing Rents and Destroy Growth-Reducing Rents

The mere emergence of proto-capitalists is not sufficient to ensure that they have the capacity to compete. Historically, developing and maintaining competitiveness has required interventionist and regulatory capacities on the part of the state to create, as well as to remove, different types of rents. In an important critique of the standard model of market competition, Stiglitz (1996) argues that a wide range of information rents are critical for the working of an efficient market system. These information rents create the incentives for information to be generated and properly used. A well-established and advanced market economy would need institutions to regulate these information rents, to ensure that information was not cornered in such a way that these rents became monopoly rents, and to make sure that markets continue to work efficiently. No less important are Schumpeterian rents that are essential for driving innovation in market economies. These too require regulation to ensure that Schumpeterian innovators do not become effective monopolists over time. In developing economies, the rent management problem is even more acute. Emerging capitalists often lack technological capacities, and even entrepreneurial capacities, to compete in world markets. Learning to use advanced technologies involves high risk, and the private return can be lower than the social return. At the same time, many types of unproductive activities can yield high returns. In such contexts, state-created "learning rents" have often accelerated the acquisition of technology and the development of entrepreneurial skills, thereby enabling capitalist market economies to develop. Thus analysis reveals the existence of a range of positive or growth-enhancing rents in developing countries, such as information rents, Schumpeterian rents, natural resource rents, and learning rents (for more on growth-enhancing and growth-reducing rents, see Amsden 1989; Aoki, Kim, and Okuno-Fujiwara 1997; Khan 2000a; Lall and Teubal 1998; Page 1994; Rodrik 1995; Wade 1990; World Bank 1993).

However, in the case of almost all growth-enhancing rents, effective regulation is essential for these rents to have a positive effect. Schumpeterian rents or learning rents can, in theory, have limited, or even negative, effects if they last for too long or for not long enough, suggesting an inverted U relationship between learning and the period of protection of learning rents (Khan 2000a). The optimal period of protection is not technically determined, and learning is most rapid when transformation states have the pragmatic capacity to observe performance and the much more difficult political capacity to reallocate rents when necessary. Incidentally, a similar inverted U relationship between innovation and the degree of competition is also found in advanced countries like the United Kingdom, suggesting that extremely competitive markets are not always desirable (Aghion and others 2002).

In contrast, the damaging effects of such growth-reducing rents as monopoly rents are well known. Growth-reducing rents also have to be removed through competition policy and regulation, but both theory and evidence suggest that the creation of dynamic capitalist economies requires much more than institutional structures and policies that ensure that no rents emerge. Because many rents are critical for rapid entrepreneurial growth and technology acquisition while other rents are extremely damaging, rapid growth requires a more demanding set of institutions with the regulatory capacity to distinguish between different kinds of rents and with the political capacity to create, destroy, or manage rents to generate growth and rapid transformation. The rents that need to be managed can vary widely across developing countries depending on their initial endowments, their level of development and the technologies being used or adapted, and their internal political settlements. As a result, the rent management institutions and the political arrangements that have allowed them to be effective have varied considerably across successful developers. Nevertheless, all successful developers had states that actively intervened in markets to create and manage rents and property rights (Aoki, Kim, and Okuno-Fujiwara 1997; Khan and Jomo 2000). In all successful countries, states manipulated changes in property rights to accelerate the emergence of proto-capitalists and managed rents to accelerate the acquisition of technology by these proto-capitalists while ensuring that inefficiency was not sustained or increased. At the same time, transformations in states that lacked these institutional and political capacities were blocked or took place much more slowly (Khan 2000b).

The World Bank and other agencies that support the good governance and service delivery agenda have often recognized the highly interventionist and rent-creating role of the state among the successful developers (for instance, World Bank 1993), but they have immediately followed this observation with the argument that these countries were few in number and had exceptional state capacities. In the absence of such state capacities, they argue, focusing the state on core service delivery and relying on good governance reforms is better. My response to this is twofold. First, while successful developers are indeed few in number and their state capacities were exceptional, however exceptional they were, no examples exist of failed or failing states that adopted good governance policies and then enjoyed a sustained and successful capitalist transformation to achieve prosperity. Second, it therefore follows that however exceptional the capacities of the successful developers, we have to learn the lessons of how best to develop state capacities in the direction of these countries if performance is to be improved in the less satisfactory cases. As no single model of interventions is common across all the high-growth countries, what we are learning are general principles that then have to be translated into specific institutions given the political realities and initial conditions of different countries.

Dynamic States Can Organize Ring-Fenced Transfers to Maintain Political Stability

In developing countries, no less than in advanced ones, maintaining political stability often requires significant state-organized transfers. Massive social dislocations also make social instability a much more serious problem in developing countries. Official budgetary transfers are a small fraction of the overall system of hidden patron-client transfers that are routinely deployed to maintain stability in these contexts. In theory, transfers that cannot be contested by further rent-seeking can have relatively low deadweight costs. In reality, transfers can actually cause serious economic damage if fragmented groups can capture resources by creating or capturing a large number of uncoordinated, value-reducing rents. When high-growth states like Malaysia needed to organize significant transfers to maintain political stability, they were able to centrally organize and ring-fence these transfers, which means that further rent-seeking over the type and allocation of transfers was virtually ruled out. Distributive coalitions were prevented from trying to capture additional rents by capturing public good provision systems or subsidies for industrial learners. To the extent that a state can achieve this, a system of significant transfers can be compatible with rapid growth (Jomo and Gomez 2000). Where it cannot, as in India, fragmented rent capture can contribute to the poor provision of public goods and the protection of inefficiency (Khan 2000a,b; Bardhan 1988).

These observations suggest that the creation of high-growth conditions is a much more demanding process than the standard model suggests. Even a cursory examination of the evidence suggests that takeoffs in high-growth countries were not preceded by the achievement of property rights stability and the removal of rents. Rather, as table 2 summarizes, high-growth transformation states intervened in property rights to accelerate the emergence of productive capitalist classes; created and managed rents to accelerate technology acquisition and promote entrepreneurial capacity; and maintained political stability through transfers, often on a large scale. They also delivered public goods efficiently as the standard theory demands, but that is not surprising, because with growing prosperity bureaucrats could be properly paid, and increasing fiscal resources meant that states could meet generalized, as opposed to particularistic, demands.

TABLE 2. Institutions and Interventions in Transformation States

Type of transformation	Property rights	Rent and competition policy	Service delivery
Dynamic transformation state	Protection, creation, and transfers of property rights for *productive* groups	Regulatory and industrial policy to manage *growth-enhancing* rents	Efficient provision of infrastructure by ring-fenced institutions
	Destruction or loss of property rights of *unproductive* groups	Regulatory and competition policy to remove *growth-reducing rents*	Ring-fenced transfers to maintain political stability
Stagnating or failed transformation state	Protection, creation, and transfers of property rights for *unproductive* groups	Protection of *growth-reducing* rents	Service delivery systems captured by privileged groups
	Destruction or loss of property rights of *productive* groups		Open-ended transfers to maintain political stability

Source: Author.

Even when they recognize many of these theoretical and historical observations, economists remain reluctant to trust the state, and with good reason, particularly in developing countries. Thus after developing some powerful critiques of the liberal market model, Stiglitz (1998b) argues that governments should be prevented from restricting competition or intervening in areas where there are special interests, or in other words, from creating rents. This policy caution is clearly based on a skepticism about the capacity of the state to create and manage growth-promoting rents, a skepticism that is entirely justified given the vast majority of poorly performing states. But as their own work on financial institutions points out (Hellman, Murdock, and Stiglitz 1997), state-created rents played an important role in explaining the success, and not just the vulnerability, of the Asian high-growth economies. Thus Stiglitz, like the World Bank, is implicitly saying that while high-growth economies had the capacity to create and manage vital rents, most states cannot be trusted to do this.

Saying that East Asian institutions and transformation strategies are not directly relevant to failing states that clearly lack critical capacities is entirely correct. However, the evidence of equally limited success in implementing good governance reforms and creating liberal market economies in countries with failing states suggests that the problem may be that even a competitive market economy may require substantial regulatory capacities. What is more, attempting to construct liberal market economies in countries where a viable capitalist class has not yet emerged or learned to use modern technologies is likely to fail anyway. However imperfect and partial the process of enhancing these interventionist capacities, directly tackling the weak transformation capacities of developing country states may be the only option.

Effectiveness of Institutional Enforcement

In advanced economies, the state's monopoly of legitimate violence has become a metaphor for describing the state's ability to enforce institutions. In developing countries, states often do not have this monopoly and find enforcing any institution difficult (Bates 2001). The effectiveness of enforcement is a measure of the degree to which agents with notional residual control rights in an institutional structure can actually enforce their decisions. Residual control rights are rights to determine resource allocations that are not otherwise controlled by law or assigned to others by contract. If the owner of a property right cannot actually sell the right or make hiring and firing decisions freely, or if an industrial policy planner with residual control rights over the allocation of subsidies cannot actually reallocate them, the extent to which they cannot do so is a measure of the ineffectiveness of enforcement. In the 1960s and 1970s, developing country states did not just fail to enforce dynamic transformation regimes effectively, they failed to enforce even the existing structure of rights (North 1990). How can this systematic failure be explained?

The conventional explanation is that this was a problem of credible commitment on the part of the state. Because the state has no higher enforcer, in principle it can subvert property rights ex post to appropriate the investments of others (Bardhan 2000; Bates 2001; Stiglitz 1998b). If this was the major source of enforcement failure in developing countries, having democratic or other constraints on the state that made it difficult for state leaders to change their ex ante commitments easily would be necessary. But as already noted in the context of both property rights transfers and rent management, growth during the capitalist transition has required a great deal of ex post flexibility (a term suggested by Okuno-Fujiwara 1997) on the state's part. Far from protecting the property rights inherited from the precapitalist past, dynamic transformation states in say China or Korea have been the agency through which massive property rights transfers were organized and the necessary rents created, maintained, and changed as required. As a result, history suggests a much more demanding commitment on the part of the high-growth states. Instead of committing ahead of time not to intervene in property rights and markets, high-growth states have to commit to disrupting property rights and creating rents, but in ways that promote growth. Of course, commitment here is another metaphor, because in reality the state is not an agent that can commit or not commit to do anything. Rather its ability to enforce critical rights and rents depends on the interests and organization of powerful groups in society and the balance of power between them.

Effective enforcement requires both institutional capacity and institutions compatible with the interests of powerful social groups. When the state is engaged in managing rents and intervening in property rights to promote a capitalist transformation, enforcement is more difficult than in an advanced capitalist economy, both from the perspective of institutional capacity (because the state has to have the capacity to do positive things), and because social resistance and rent-seeking are likely to be more intense. Obviously institutional capacity is important: enforcing or transforming a property rights system is impossible without the appropriate bureaucratic capacity. At the same time, however, institutional capacity is insufficient without effective political capacity to overcome the resistance of powerful social groups who are opposed to particular property rights transformations or the implications of particular rent-management strategies.

Institutional and political factors are closely intertwined, because the political failure to enforce productive rights and rents can often rapidly lead to a loss of morale and personnel in the bureaucracy and persuade the remaining public officials to share unproductive rents as a second-best strategy. One of the worrying trends in many developing countries has been the worsening institutional capacity of the state and the quality of public officials. By contrast, the achievement of better enforcement capacity can often make previously predatory leaders commit themselves to dynamic transformation strategies that can offer them higher personal payoffs if they can be enforced. Consider the case of Chiang Kai Shek before and after 1949. In pre-1949 China, the relative weakness of the Kuomintang and its failure to control competing warlords led the Chiang Kai Shek regime to follow highly predatory policies, but in post-1949 Taiwan (China), the same party and leader organized an exemplary developing state, largely because the balance of power between state and society in Taiwan (China) allowed the state to engage in effective enforcement of transformation strategies. Case studies of high-growth transformation states suggest that improving enforcement capacity has been based on a range of political strategies, including the neutralization of unproductive groups, the creation of political organizations of productive groups to counter the power of unproductive groups, or even the accommodation of some unproductive groups through less damaging transfers (Khan 2000b; Wade 1990; Woo-Cumings 1999).

In Korea, the enforcement of its industrial policy regime from above relied on the absence of well-organized factions that could protect inefficient industrial interests. The fragmentation of organized, middle-class political factions by Japanese colonialism and of traditional landed elites by far-reaching land reforms meant that recipients of subsidies could not easily buy protection from organized factional politics. This power structure ensured that the state could allocate rights and rents to whomever it liked, and this in turn ensured that the state had no interest in accepting payoffs from the inefficient, because it was better served by promoting the efficient and thereby captured even bigger payoffs (Amsden 1989; Chibber 1999; Kohli 1994; Woo-Cumings 1997).

In Thailand in the 1980s, industrial policy was less important, but the intense primitive accumulation organized by a more dispersed class of emerging capitalists drove growth. The latter aggressively captured valuable common property and public resources. They were able to enforce their captured rights effectively, because unlike in most developing countries, Thai capitalists directly controlled many of the factions involved in competitive politics and could buy themselves access to state power. At the same time, intense competition between capitalist factions prevented any potentially monopolistic faction from capturing the state for long. Thus the enforcement of emerging capitalist property rights from below reflected the capture of political factions by emerging capitalists (Doner and Ramsay 2000; Pasuk and Baker 1997; Rock 2000).

Yet another pattern is discernable in Malaysia, where the state's ability to attract multinational investors by credibly promising to protect their rights drove growth in the 1980s. Its ability to do this was based on a unique, internal, ethno-political arrangement that created massive, but ring-fenced, transfer rents that bought off those who would otherwise have contested the state's policies. Thus the compatibility between institutional enforcement and political forces was brought about by the state's organization of politics in a way that allowed it to buy off potential opposition through a form of highly centralized clientelism (Jomo and Gomez 2000). This assured investors, including multinationals, that internal distributive conflicts would not spill over to affect them.

Thus while the growth-promoting transformation interventions varied across countries, enforcement was effective in all the high-growth countries, because the institutions of social transformation enforced by the state were compatible with, or could not be opposed by, powerful, organized interests within these societies (Khan 2000b).

In contrast, an inability by the state to suppress or accommodate interests opposed to transformation is frequently observed in cases of ineffective enforcement. Pakistan's industrial policy regime of the 1960s failed, even though the quality of its planning personnel was moderately good and its military leadership was committed to export-led growth. Control over enforcement was, as in Korea, formally centralized in the president's office. Yet institutional enforcement failed, because unproductive subsidy recipients discovered that they could easily purchase protection in a society with many fragmented but powerful political organizations (Khan 1999). Centralized industrial policy was not compatible with this fragmented distribution of social power. While subsequent liberalization and privatization did attack some aspects of the rent capture that had become entrenched under statist strategies in South Asian countries (Bhaskar and Khan 1995), during the liberalization of the 1980s, these countries also discovered that their states could not properly enforce any property rights and were unable to make a significant dent in growth-reducing rent-seeking by unproductive groups (Bardhan 1988). Thus enforcement capacity of any variety has a political dimension, and in most developing countries this is the critical dimension where state failure is frequently located.

These observations suggest that policy to improve enforcement in developing countries is unlikely to succeed if it simply focuses on the institutional capacity of enforcement institutions, such as anticorruption bureaus or judiciaries. A compatible package of institutional reform and political restructuring of organized power is needed that may allow better enforcement of a dynamic transformation strategy in the future. Here the notion of feasibility is important, as Qian (2002) suggests in the case of China. Ambitious transformation strategies as used in Korea that promise high growth if properly enforced are only potential options; if compatible political arrangements are unfeasible, such strategies will fail. Fortunately, alternative transformation strategies do exist, as the cases of Malaysia, Thailand, and other high-growth developers show, but even these require specific internal political settlements to ensure their enforcement. No country is likely to be an exact replica of any of the high-growth economies of the past in terms of the mix of policies, institutions, and political settlements. Nevertheless, the lesson is that poorly performing countries have to take much more deliberate steps than conventional policy advice suggests to construct compatible packages of institutions and political settlements to achieve even second-best transformation success. A starting point must be a much better understanding of the experience of transformation in the dynamic transformation economies.

Costs of Enforcement

The effectiveness of enforcement should not be confused with the costs of enforcement. Enforcement costs include the costs of policing, regulating, and lobbying; the resources spent on economic and political corruption; and the costs of all types of political activity, from maintaining patron-client networks to contributions to political parties. Indeed, enforcement costs include all expenditures and activities, regardless of their legality or morality, that aim to protect or change rights or rents. Thus enforcement costs are nothing but rent-seeking costs defined in the broadest possible way. In theory, lower enforcement costs are obviously better for the economy, but in practice, enforcement costs are likely to be significant even in countries with effective enforcement of transformation strategies.

Clearly the elements of rent-seeking most relevant to a particular case will depend on the institution and on the country and its stage of development, but given that every right, rent, and intervention is valuable for someone, the overall costs of rent-seeking are likely to be high in every economy, regardless of its success or failure (Samuels and Mercuro 1984). Crude estimates of overall transaction costs in advanced economies confirm this (North and Wallis 1987), as do observations of widespread rent-seeking in all developing countries, including the high-growth ones (Khan 2000b). Every act of attempted enforcement has a cost regardless of the type of intervention, the right or the rent that is being enforced, and the success of the enforcement. Thus as a simplification, the intervention and the effectiveness of its enforcement can be viewed as determining the gross or potential output, with the deduction of the cost of enforcement giving the net or actual output (see figure 3). This is a simplification, because enforcement costs are not really a deduction from output, but represent costs that prevent economic activity in the first place. Nevertheless, this simplification helps us understand why the share of enforcement costs in gross domestic product is likely to be high even in efficient and dynamic transformation economies. If the degree of intervention and rent creation is high, then the aggregate enforcement costs as a share of gross domestic product will also be high. What is different about the successful transformation economy is simply the types of interventions and the effectiveness of enforcement.

The Location of State Failure

Figure 4 summarizes the discussion so far. Societies can differ both in terms of the rents and rights they effectively enforce and their enforcement costs. Nonperforming states score badly on both counts. The service delivery and good governance model assumes that the solution is to eliminate all rents as a way of reducing enforcement

FIGURE 4. Social Transformations and the Location of State Failure

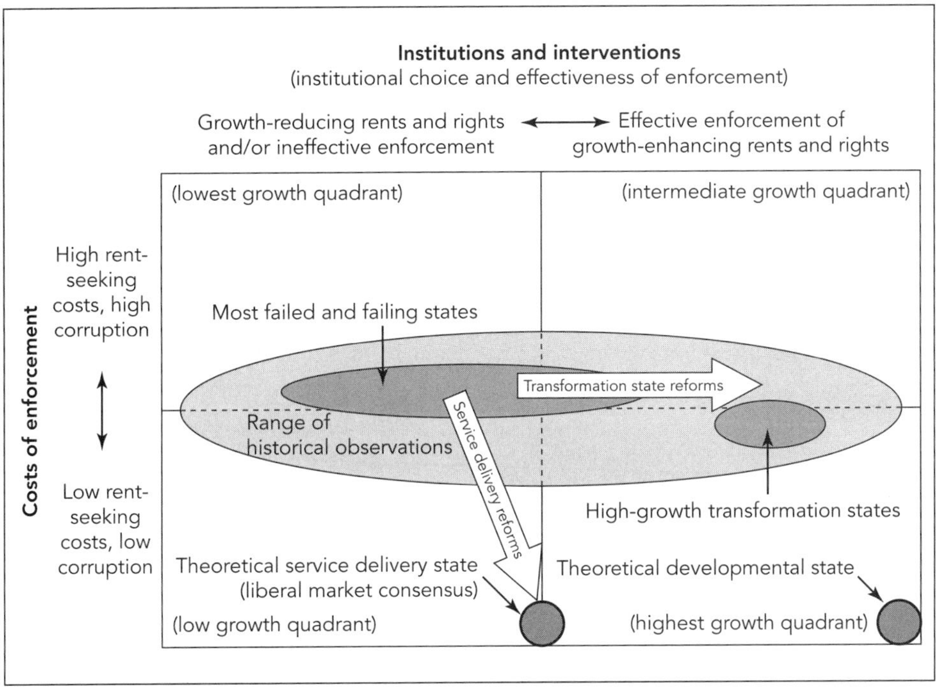

Source: Author.

costs, using strengthened property rights and anticorruption strategies as a way to reduce the state's capacity to create rents. Such reforms attempt to achieve an unattainable goal that has no convincing historical precedents. Instead successful transformation states have intervened heavily in property rights and rents, and while their aggregate rent-seeking and enforcement costs have been high, the internal disposition of political power has allowed them to effectively enforce critical changes in rights and rents essential for a capitalist transformation. If lessons from history are to be learnt, the reforms suggested (see figure 4) are entirely different. Instead of trying to reduce enforcement costs by stabilizing property rights and reducing rents, reformers should focus on identifying in each case the critical state capacities needed to enable the interventions in rights and rents necessary for accelerating a capitalist transformation. Enforcement costs are likely to remain high under such a strategy, including perhaps illegal enforcement costs such as corruption. In many cases progress along these lines will also require a discussion on how issues of political and organizational power need to be addressed, something that has received little attention so far.

The argument presented here explains why high-growth states do not score significantly better than the developing country average in terms of conventional governance indicators. Most indicators of good governance, such as corruption or expropriation risk, are primarily imperfect measures of perceived enforcement costs. The theoretical expectation in the liberal market model is that high enforcement costs and bad interventions or policies go together. In reality, because many rents and property rights interventions are growth enhancing, particularly during the transition to capitalism, and because such interventions are likely to provoke high enforcement costs, it is not surprising that we find at best a weak correlation between most governance indicators and developing country performance. The correlation that is picked up between governance and economic performance only reflects the fact that most developing countries lack dynamic transformation capacities, so that high enforcement costs and poor governance as defined in the service delivery sense appear to correlate with poor growth. The huge jump in growth in the high-growth economies with insignificantly better governance indicators (figure 2) suggests that the relationship between governance and growth in the consensus approach is mis-specified and that the missing variables are those that measure the state's dynamic transformation capacity.

From a policy point of view, this analysis suggests why an uncritical application of the good governance and service delivery framework may potentially do more harm than good. Everything else remaining the same, lower enforcement costs, in particular, lower levels of corruption, are always preferable to higher enforcement costs. This is simply arithmetic in terms of the logic outlined in figure 3. Hence it is not surprising that when countries with similar economic policies and levels of development are compared, or when these factors are fully controlled for, economic performance is better when corruption is lower (Rodrik 1997; Wei 2000).

Lowering any cost is always beneficial, and this result is important, but not particularly profound. Not only that, the result can be misleading, because enforcement costs can be associated with completely different state interventions in property rights and rents during the transformation period and beyond. If reformers attempt to reduce corruption by reducing the state's capacity to intervene in general (in the direction of the service delivery reforms shown in figure 4), they may reduce corruption marginally in the short run, but they may also fatally damage the possibility of creating a developmental transformation state. This is because destroying a state's capacity to create bad rents through downsizing, decentralizing, subcontracting to nongovernmental organizations, and attracting the best talents away from the state all rapidly add up to a state that is incapable of creating, maintaining, or regulating any growth-enhancing rents either. Without such a capacity, the possibility of dramatic growth, and therefore of a sustainable and lasting impact on corruption and democracy, is also fatally delayed. Thus while anticorruption and democracy are vital goals, a critical first step is to focus on developing state capacity for a capitalist transformation in the direction of the very different reform path shown as the dynamic transformation path in figure 4.

Transforming the State

Finally, if the state is not already a dynamic transformation state, the state itself has to be transformed. Are the critical variables here political will and political institutions or the organization of social power?

Political Will and Political Institutions

Political will is the least likely explanation of sustained differences in performance, not because it is not necessary, but rather because it is not as scarce as often thought.

Committed reformers with considerable political will have often failed in many countries because accommodating social conditions were absent. Nor do political institutions provide a sufficient explanation of transition success. North (1990) made the case for democracy as an institution that facilitates efficient transitions, arguing that democracy would best accelerate the creation of efficient institutions by providing an efficient way of organizing transfers to compensate losers. This is a theoretical possibility, but almost none of the significant path changes in high-growth developers over the last century took place through formally democratic institutions. Nor did countries with formal democracy, such as India, do well in organizing growth-enhancing institutional change. In contrast, Olson (1982) points out that special interest groups that have an advantage in organizing rent-seeking compared with the rest of society are likely to dominate democracies, a perspective developed in Bardhan's (1984) work on rent-seeking in India. Democracy is an end in itself, but historically it has been neither necessary nor sufficient for ensuring growth-enhancing institutional change.

Social Power

When developing countries become mired in low growth or in stagnant transformation processes, the failure is widely perceived and understood in these countries, not just by policymakers and politicians, but by society at large as well. Any investigation of why the state cannot introduce growth-enhancing strategies leads quickly to the identification of powerful interests opposed to change who can impose unacceptable costs on others or on the state. In this sense, the problem of transition is no different from that of enforcement, except that the former concerns the formal introduction of institutions and the latter concerns their real operation. Not surprisingly, the distribution of power between social factions and classes provides a good historical explanation of the pace and direction of institutional change in many countries (Bardhan 2000; Brenner 1976, 1985).

The service delivery approach to the state also recognizes the importance of building constituencies to support state reform processes (see, for instance, World Bank 1997). However, what is involved in the two approaches is quite different. In the liberal market consensus, state failure is related to rent capture by unproductive groups who play no role in the dynamism of the market economy. Society as a whole could potentially be mobilized against them if only democracy, civil society participation, and other desirable political institutions could be deepened. In contrast, the transformation perspective provides less comforting prescriptions. Both productive and unproductive groups are involved in rent and resource capture, and the enforcement of growth-enhancing changes can also be strongly contested and be of much greater benefit to minorities in the first instance.

The Challenge for Policy

The discussion presented here raises a number of policy issues and throws up new questions for research and policy discussion. To begin with, developing country reformers and their policy advisers need to question the claims being made for governance reforms of the types that follow from the service delivery model and the underlying liberal market good governance consensus. There is no historical evidence to indicate that these reforms were a precondition for growth or that they can be effectively implemented in transformation economies. But there is obviously support for this reform agenda in developing countries, where anticorruption and democracy are legitimately pursued as ends in themselves. However, competing political factions have also found anticorruption slogans useful, for instance, in factional political conflicts. What is worrying is the lack of evidence that emerging capitalist coalitions have coalesced around these reforms as genuine demands, except in the same opportunistic and factional way, but this should not be surprising given that the service delivery model does not address the key property rights, rent management, and accumulation issues facing emerging capitalists in their relationship with the state. Much more seriously, a real danger exists that disillusionment will grow even further in the developing countries if, as is likely, no significant economic progress is achieved in the end. A reasonable question is whether the multilateral agencies are spending public resources properly in pushing major reforms on the basis of dubious evidence linking these reforms to growth improvements.

In contrast, the transformation state perspective identifies critical state capacities for managing and regulating rents and for organizing changes in property rights systems. The experience of the high-growth economies suggests that if growth and sustained poverty reduction are the objectives, these capacities have to become the focus of institutional and political reform. Engagement in a political restructuring of the organization of power within countries is formally outside the remit of multilateral agencies, but they could begin by concentrating on the simplest and least contentious regulatory capacities. Central banks and securities markets have received much attention, but transformation capacities are broader regulatory capacities that states require during this period, and these have not, in general, been widely recognized. One problem for the transformation approach is that the critical capacities that need to be focused on will vary from country to country as discussed, but this is a reality that has to be accepted. At a general level, the transformation approach would focus on institutional and political capacities that would be required for creating capitalists, transforming property rights in their favor, providing them with conditional support for acquiring and learning the appropriate technology, negotiating trade and technology deals in international agreements to protect national capitalists, attracting multinationals and inducing them to transfer technology to domestic capitalists through subcontracting and licensing, and so on. To assume that all this will happen spontaneously through the market is making an enormous, theoretical leap of faith that the historical evidence does not justify. Most damaging of all, because of its concentration on reducing the costs of intervention, a focus on the service delivery model can actually weaken states' interventionist capacities, because the simplest way of reducing the cost of enforcing interventions is to reduce the scope of interventions.

Finally, the effectiveness of institutional capacities depends on their compatibility with the underlying distribution of power. In many cases of state failure in developing countries, institutional capacity building has to proceed in parallel with political interventions that aim to restructure the distribution of political and organizational power. The challenge is to suggest feasible reforms for particular countries, taking into account preexisting political settlements, prior capitalist development, and capitalists' technological capacities. Institutional reform is deeply political and should be explicitly recognized as such. The proper role of international agencies should be to transfer knowledge of the experiences of successful transformations, offer support in enhancing dynamic transformation capacities, and encourage the construction of productive coalitions to support these reforms, even if interventions in politics must remain an internal matter for developing countries. In turn the challenge for research is to proceed further with the analysis of how the distribution and disposition of organizational power has helped or hindered different transformation strategies and how this information can be used to suggest feasible institutional and political reform strategies for countries that have not done well.

References

The word "processed" describes informally reproduced works that may not be commonly available in libraries.

Aghion, Philippe, Nicholas Bloom, Richard Blundell, Rachel Griffith, and Peter Howitt. 2002. "Competition and Innovation: An Inverted U Relationship." Working Paper no. WP02/04. London: Institute for Fiscal Studies.

Amsden, Alice. 1989. *Asia's Next Giant: South Korea and Late Industrialization.* Oxford, U.K.: Oxford University Press.

Andvig, Jens, and Kalle Moene. 1990. "How Corruption May Corrupt." *Journal of Economic Behaviour and Organization* 3(1): 63–76.

Andvig, Jens, Odd-Helge Fjeldstad, Inge Amundsen, Tone Sissener, and Tina Søreide. 2000. *Research on Corruption: A Policy Oriented Survey.* Report commissioned by the Norwegian Agency for Development Cooperation. Bergen, Norway: Chr. Michelsen Institute and Norwegian Institute of International Affairs.

Aoki, Masahiko, Hyung-Ki Kim, and Masahiro Okuno-Fujiwara, eds. 1997. *The Role of Government in East Asian Economic Development: Comparative Institutional Analysis.* Oxford, U.K.: Clarendon Press.

Asian Development Bank. 2000. *Promoting Good Governance: ADB's Medium-Term Agenda and Action Plan.* Manila.

Bardhan, Pranab. 1984. *The Political Economy of Development in India.* Oxford, U.K.: Basil Blackwell.

_____. 1988. "Dominant Proprietary Classes and India's Democracy." In Atul Kohli, ed., *India's Democracy: An Analysis of Changing State-Society Relations.* Princeton, N.J.: Princeton University Press.

_____. 1997. "Corruption and Development: A Review of Issues" *Journal of Economic Literature* 35(3): 1320–46.

_____. 2000. "The Nature of Institutional Impediments to Economic Development." In Mancur Olson and Satu Kähkönen, eds., *A Not-so-Dismal Science: A Broader View of Economies and Societies.* Oxford, U.K.: Oxford University Press.

Barro, Robert. 1996. "Democracy and Growth." *Journal of Economic Growth* 1(1): 1–27.

Bates, Robert H. 2001. *Prosperity and Violence: The Political Economy of Development.* New York: W. W. Norton.

Bhaskar, V., and Mushtaq H. Khan. 1995. "Privatization and Employment: A Study of the Jute Industry in Bangladesh." *American Economic Review* 85(1): 267–72.

Bowles, Paul, and Xiao-Yuan Dong. 1999. "Enterprise Ownership, Enterprise Organization, and Worker Attitudes in Chinese Rural Industry: Some New Evidence." *Cambridge Journal of Economics* 23(1): 1–20.

Brenner, Robert. 1976. "Agrarian Class Structure and Economic Development in Pre-Industrial Europe." *Past and Present* 70(February): 30–75.

———. 1985. "The Agrarian Roots of European Capitalism." In T. H. Aston and C. H. E. Philpin, eds., *The Brenner Debate: Agrarian Class Structure and Economic Development in Pre-Industrial Europe.* Cambridge, U.K.: Cambridge University Press.

Burkhart, Ross, and Michael Lewis-Beck. 1994. "Comparative Democracy: The Economic Development Thesis." *American Political Science Review* 88(4): 903–10.

Chang, Ha-Joon. 1994. *The Political Economy of Industrial Policy.* London: Macmillan.

Chibber, Vivek. 1999. "Building a Developmental State: The Korean Case Reconsidered." *Politics and Society* 27(3): 309–46.

Clague, Christopher, Philip Keefer, Stephen Knack, and Mancur Olson. 1997. "Democracy, Autocracy, and the Institutions Supportive of Economic Growth." In Christopher Clague, ed., *Institutions and Economic Development: Growth and Governance in Less-Developed and Post-Socialist Countries.* Baltimore, Md.: The Johns Hopkins University Press.

Dollar, David, and Aart Kraay. 2001. "Growth Is Good for the Poor." World Bank, Washington, D.C. Processed. http://www.worldbank.org/research/growth/pdfiles/GIGFTP3.pdf.

Doner, Richard F., and Ansil Ramsay. 2000. "Rent-Seeking and Economic Development in Thailand." In Mushtaq H. Khan and K. S. Jomo, eds., *Rents, Rent-Seeking, and Economic Development: Theory and Evidence in Asia.* Cambridge, U.K.: Cambridge University Press.

Fields, Karl J. 1995. *Enterprise and the State in Korea and Taiwan.* Ithaca, N.Y.: Cornell University Press.

Hall, Robert, and Charles Jones. 1999. "Why Do Some Countries Produce So Much More Output Per Worker Than Others?" *Quarterly Journal of Economics* 114(1): 83–116.

Hellman, Thomas, Kevin Murdock, and Joseph Stiglitz. 1997. "Financial Restraints: Toward a New Paradigm." In Aoki Masahiko, Hyung-Ki Kim, and Masahiro Okuno-Fujiwara, eds., *The Role of Government in East Asian Economic Development: Comparative Institutional Analysis.* Oxford, U.K.: Clarendon Press.

Johnson, Simon, Daniel Kaufmann, and Pablo Zoido-Lobatón. 1998. "Regulatory Discretion and the Unofficial Economy." *American Economic Review* 88(2): 387–92.

Jomo, K. S., and Edmund T. Gomez. 2000. "The Malaysian Development Dilemma." In Mushtaq H. Khan and K. S. Jomo, eds., *Rents, Rent-Seeking, and Economic Development: Theory and Evidence in Asia.* Cambridge, U.K.: Cambridge University Press.

Kaufmann, Daniel, Aart Kraay, and Pablo Zoido-Lobatón. 1999. "Governance Matters." Policy Working Paper no. 2196. World Bank, Washington, D.C.

Khan, Mushtaq H. 1995. "State Failure in Weak States: A Critique of New Institutionalist Explanations." In John Harriss, Janet Hunter, and Colin M. Lewis, eds., *The New Institutional Economics and Third World Development.* London: Routledge.

———. 1999. "The Political Economy of Industrial Policy in Pakistan 1947–1971." Working Paper no. 98. University of London, Department of Economics, School of Oriental and African Studies, London.

_____. 2000a. "Rents, Efficiency, and Growth." In Mushtaq H. Khan and K. S. Jomo, eds., *Rents, Rent-Seeking, and Economic Development: Theory and Evidence in Asia*. Cambridge, U.K.: Cambridge University Press.

_____. 2000b. "Rent-Seeking as Process." In Mushtaq H. Khan and K. S. Jomo, eds., *Rents, Rent-Seeking, and Economic Development: Theory and Evidence in Asia*. Cambridge, U.K.: Cambridge University Press.

_____. 2002a. "Corruption and Governance in Early Capitalism: World Bank Strategies and Their Limitations." In J. Pincus and J. Winters, eds., *Reinventing the World Bank*. Ithaca, N.Y.: Cornell University Press.

_____. 2002b. "Fundamental Tensions in the Democratic Compromise." *New Political Economy* 7(2): 275–77.

Khan, Mushtaq H., and K. S. Jomo, eds. 2000. *Rents, Rent-Seeking, and Economic Development: Theory and Evidence in Asia*. Cambridge, U.K.: Cambridge University Press.

Knack, Stephen, and Philip Keefer. 1995. "Institutions and Economic Performance: Cross-Country Tests Using Alternative Institutional Measures." *Economics and Politics* 7(3): 207–27.

_____. 1997. "Why Don't Poor Countries Catch Up? A Cross-National Test of an Institutional Explanation." *Economic Inquiry* 35(3): 590–602.

Kohli, Atul. 1994. "Where Do High Growth Political Economies Come From? The Japanese Lineage of Korea's 'Developmental State'." *World Development* 22(9): 1269–93.

Krueger, Ann. 1974. "The Political Economy of the Rent-Seeking Society." *American Economic Review* 64(3): 291–303.

_____. 1990. "Government Failures in Development." *Journal of Economic Perspectives* 4(3): 9–23.

Lal, Deepak, and Hla Myint. 1996. *The Political Economy of Poverty, Equity, and Growth: A Comparative Study*. Oxford, U.K.: Clarendon Press.

Lall, Sanjaya, and Morris Teubal. 1998. "'Market-Stimulating' Technology Policies in Developing Countries: A Framework with Examples from East Asia." *World Development* 26(8): 1369–85.

Lee, Suk-Chae. 1991. "The Heavy and Chemical Industries Promotion Plan." In Lee-Jay Cho and Yoon Hyung Kim, eds., *Economic Development in the Republic of Korea: A Policy Perspective*. Honolulu, Hawaii: East West Center.

Mauro, Paolo. 1995. "Corruption and Growth." *Quarterly Journal of Economics* 110(3): 681–712.

Migdal, Joel S. 1988. *Strong Societies and Weak States: State-Society Relations and State Capabilities in the Third World*. Princeton, N.J.: Princeton University Press.

Murphy, Kevin M., Andrei Shleifer, and Robert W. Vishny. 1993. "Why Is Rent Seeking So Costly to Growth?" *American Economic Review Papers and Proceedings* 82(3): 409–14.

Myrdal, Gunnar. 1968. *Asian Drama*, 3 vols. New York: Pantheon.

North, Douglass C. 1981. *Structure and Change in Economic History*. New York: W. W. Norton.

_____. 1990. *Institutions, Institutional Change, and Economic Performance*. Cambridge, U.K.: Cambridge University Press.

North, Douglass C., and J. Wallis. 1987. "Measuring the Transaction Sector in the American Economy 1870–1970." In S. L. Engerman and R. E. Gallman, eds., *Long-Term Factors in American Economic Growth*. Chicago: Chicago University Press.

Okuno-Fujiwara, Masahiro. 1997. "Toward a Comparative Institutional Analysis of the Government-Business Relationship." In Aoki Masahiko, Hyung-Ki Kim, and Masahiro

Okuno-Fujiwara, eds., *The Role of Government in East Asian Economic Development: Comparative Institutional Analysis.* Oxford, U.K.: Clarendon Press.

Olson, Mancur. 1982. *The Rise and Decline of Nations.* London: Yale University Press.

———. 1997. "The New Institutional Economics: The Collective Choice Approach to Economic Development." In Christopher Clague, ed., *Institutions and Economic Development.* Baltimore, Md.: The Johns Hopkins University Press.

———. 2000. "Dictatorship, Democracy, and Development." In Olson Mancur and Satu Kähkönen, eds., *A Not-so-Dismal Science: A Broader View of Economies and Societies.* Oxford, U.K.: Oxford University Press.

Page, John. 1994. "The East Asian Miracle: Four Lessons for Development Policy." In Stanley Fischer and J. Rotemberg, eds., *NBER Macroeconomics Annual.* Cambridge, Mass.: National Bureau of Economic Research.

Pasuk, Phongpaichit, and Chris Baker. 1997. *Thailand: Economy and Polity.* Oxford, U.K.: Oxford University Press.

Posner, Richard A. 1975. "The Social Costs of Monopoly and Regulation." *Journal of Political Economy* 83(4): 807–27.

Qian, Yingyi. 2002. "How Reform Worked in China." Working Paper no. 473. University of Michigan Business School, William Davidson Institute, Ann Arbor, Mich. http://elsa. berkeley.edu/~yqian/how%20reform%20worked%20in%20china.pdf.

Rock, Michael T. 2000. "Thailand's Old Bureaucratic Polity and Its New Semi-Democracy." In Mushtaq H. Khan and K. S. Jomo, eds., *Rents, Rent-Seeking, and Economic Development: Theory and Evidence in Asia.* Cambridge, U.K.: Cambridge University Press.

Rodrik, Dani. 1995. "Getting Interventions Right: How South Korea and Taiwan Grew Rich." *Economic Policy* 20(April): 55–107.

———. 1997. "TFPG Controversies, Institutions, and Economic Performance in East Asia." Working Paper no. 5914. National Bureau of Economic Research, Cambridge, Mass.

———. Forthcoming. *Institutions, Integration, and Geography: In Search of the Deep Determinants of Economic Growth.* Princeton, N.J.: Princeton University Press. http://ksghome.harvard.edu/~.drodrik.academic.ksg/growthintro.pdf.

Samuels, Warren J., and Nicholas Mercuro. 1984. "A Critique of Rent-Seeking Theory." In David C. Colander, ed., *Neoclassical Political Economy: The Analysis of Rent-Seeking and DUP Activities.* Cambridge, Mass.: Ballinger.

Shleifer, Andrei, and Robert W. Vishny. 1998. *The Grabbing Hand: Government Pathologies and Their Cures.* Cambridge, Mass.: Harvard University Press.

Stiglitz, Joseph. 1996. *Whither Socialism?* Cambridge, Mass.: MIT Press.

———. 1998a. "More Instruments and Broader Goals: Moving Toward the Post Washington Consensus." World Institute for Development Economics Research Annual Lecture, January 7, Helsinki. Processed.

———. 1998b. "Redefining the Role of the State: *What* should it do? *How* should it do it? And *How* should these decisions be made?" Paper presented at the Tenth Anniversary of the Japanese Ministry of Trade and Industry Research Institute, March 17, Tokyo. http://web.worldbank.org/WBSITE/EXTERNAL/NEWS/0,,contentMDK:20024945~men uPK:34474~pagePK:34370~piPK:34424~theSitePK:4607,00.html.

Transparency International and Göttingen University. 2002. *Historical Comparisons.* Internet Center for Corruption Research. http://wwwuser.gwdg.de/~uwvw/corruption.index.html.

Treisman, Daniel. 2000. "The Causes of Corruption: A Cross National Study." *Journal of Public Economics* 76(3): 399–457.

Wade, Robert. 1990. *Governing the Market: Economic Theory and the Role of Government in East Asian Industrialization*. Princeton, N.J.: Princeton University Press.

Wei, Shang-Jin. 2000. "Why Does China Attract so Little Foreign Direct Investment?" In Ito Takatoshi and Anne Krueger, eds., *The Role of Foreign Direct Investment in East Asian Economic Development*. NBER East Asia Seminar on Economics, vol. 9. Chicago: University of Chicago Press.

Woo-Cumings, Meredith. 1997. "The Political Economy of Growth in East Asia: A Perspective on the State, Market, and Ideology." In Masahiko Aoki, Hyung-Ki Kim, and Masahiro Okuno-Fujiwara, eds., *The Role of Government in East Asian Economic Development: Comparative Institutional Analysis*. Oxford, U.K.: Clarendon Press.

_____, ed. 1999. *The Developmental State*. Ithaca, N.Y.: Cornell University Press.

World Bank 1993. *The East Asian Miracle: Economic Growth and Public Policy*. Oxford, U.K.: Oxford University Press.

_____. 1997. *World Development Report 1997: The State in a Changing World*. New York: Oxford University Press.

_____. 1999. *World Development Report 1998/99: Knowledge for Development*. New York: Oxford University Press.

States, Reforms, and Institutional Change: The Dynamics of Failure

DAVID DUNHAM

The results expected from economic policy reform in developing and transition economies—sustained economic growth, poverty reduction and widespread prosperity, democracy and social empowerment—have frequently proved, in practice, to be disturbingly elusive. A handful of countries have restructured their economies and done so relatively smoothly. Many more have become embroiled in political chaos; economic recession; ethnic, regional, or other forms of social conflict; almost endemic corruption; and authoritarianism. Reforms have generated new opportunities for personal gain and for patronage, exacerbating rent-seeking features they had been expected to eliminate. Indeed, the evidence suggests that, unless their interplay with political interests is better understood and anticipated at the outset, reforms will continue to be incomplete and to result in major problems (Dollar and Svensson 2000).

Over the last two decades, discussions of economic policy reform have nevertheless reflected growing awareness of its enormous complexity, and new dimensions have been added to offset the social costs of reform and to increase its effectiveness. The donor community recognized the need to underpin it with strong public sector organizations relatively early. The inability, or unwillingness, of government agencies to carry through prescribed reforms spotlighted problems of organization and policy management. International observers, and the World Bank in particular, viewed burdensome administrative requirements, corruption, lack of accountability and bureaucratic leadership, or lack of political will as having contributed heavily to earlier policy failures. Reducing the size and role of the state became a major plank of policy advice, and more emphasis was placed on process: on reduced corruption, on democratic good governance, and on the management capacity of government (World Bank 1992, 1994).

As awareness of the limitations imposed by the general lack of institutional context in the early reform agenda grew, policy analysts showed increasing concern for

David Dunham is associate professor of development geography at the Institute of Social Studies, The Hague.

Annual World Bank Conference on Development Economics—Europe 2003
© 2004 The International Bank for Reconstruction and Development/The World Bank

institutional capacity. They looked to the expanding economic literature on institutions, extending discussion to the micro-institutional arrangements affecting economic policy and, in the wake of experience in the former Soviet Union and later during the East Asian crisis, the importance of macro regulatory institutions and corporate governance. More recently, the debate has been broadened to nonmarket institutions that could affect the workings of an economy, namely, to social networks and participatory organizations that stimulate flows of information, promote competition, and speed up the adoption of norms and values pertinent to market development (World Bank 2002). Over time, development practitioners have steadily identified and incorporated additional dimensions, seeking management and institutional solutions to problems that often seemed, in practice, to be inherently political.

Policy discussions did not overlook political dimensions, but as the focus of attention shifted from policies to process, they tended to tackle them in much the same way as the institutional context. They sought new factors that could help explain why reforms went wrong and clarify the conditions under which they were more successful. As a result, we now know a great deal more about the influence of international financial institutions (IFIs) on domestic policy; about the conditions under which reforms are more likely to be implemented; and about what is needed and what is likely to happen during the process of adopting, implementing, and sustaining economic reform initiatives (Devarajan, Dollar, and Holmgren 2001; Dollar and Svensson 2000; Grindle and Thomas 1991; Haggard and Webb 1993; Liddle 1992; Mosley, Harrigan, and Toye 1991; Williamson 1994). However, the work was all reform oriented. Investigators tended to look at reform as a familiar, well-understood policy package that was derailed by politics rather than depicting it, much more realistically, as one element of the broader economic and political program of a particular government. The logic and internal dynamics of such a broader government program as it evolved in a specific national setting over the longer-term—the particular context, the motives and objectives of policymakers, the way their ideas and their overall program affected and were in turn affected by their social context, the institutional changes that resulted, and the influence of all this on the range and prioritization of future policy choices and eventual policy outcomes—tended to be restricted to a narrow concern with what was happening to reform, even when it was clearly not the overriding preoccupation of those in power.

Similarly, with growing interest in process and governance, policy discussions on institutional change tended to concentrate on upgrading or replacing "faulty" management systems so that they were more functional in relation to the reform process. The discussions paid less attention to the possibility that management systems might be functional as they were in serving other objectives or that new opportunities opened up by reform could provide a reason for political leaders to reinforce what existed, thereby pushing institutional change in what, for advocates of reform, was an adverse direction. However, both possibilities existed. Over time, government programs that promoted market-oriented reforms led to qualitative and structural changes in the socio-political and institutional environments. They redefined the scope of future policy choices, as they did to facilitate reform under Margaret

Thatcher in the United Kingdom or in post-Maoist China, and as they have to serve a range of different priorities in other countries. The iterative relationship between a government's broader and evolving policy package and its social setting and the possibility that economic reforms could be used for very different purposes from those intended has often seemed crucial for understanding policy failures.

This paper is concerned with the links between the broader policy package, macro institutional structures, and socio-political outcomes. It highlights how an evolving government program containing extensive reforms can result in the erosion of social and political institutions and a downward spiral into crisis. It explores this possibility using the case of Sri Lanka, a country that has implemented major policy reforms and undergone considerable growth over the last quarter of a century, but during the process has also experienced severe socio-political convulsions. Three statements underlie the argument:

- The overall program in which economic policy reforms are embedded matters.

- The initial conditions and societal context matter.

- The process of reform is an iterative and evolving one in which past decisions, commitments, and events delimit possibilities today and history, present decisions, agreements, and events delimit what can be done tomorrow.

The following section elaborates on the contextual framework, that is, on the way in which reform is approached and on the societal context. This is followed by a discussion of the Sri Lankan case. A final section is devoted to conclusions.

Understanding the Context

Though the paper will look at economic reform as part of a broader government program, some comment is required on the policy context in which it is located.

Unpacking Reform

Most economists agree that economic reform involves macroeconomic stability, economic liberalization, market-oriented institutional reforms, and redesign of the state's role in facilitating and regulating these developments. Though not particularly pro-poor, economic reform is also concerned with short-term social costs and the need for political stability. The range of policy areas is indeed so wide that this paper needs to be clear about how they are broached. It is not about specific reforms or the best combination or sequence of policies, and it is certainly not about reform experience measured against some ideal package of what is theoretically desirable. It is about the way particular governments view and use reforms.

In practice, government policies are always subject to external influence to some extent. The significance of international agencies, especially of the World Bank, as a major source of policy prescriptions and financial resources and as a catalyst in getting reforms adopted in developing and transition economies has long been explicitly recognized by policy analysts, and Mosley, Harrigan, and Toye (1991) show that this relationship can be complex. However, a growing body of opinion maintains that domestic politics, political institutions, and political commitment to reform are more important in accounting for success and failure (Dollar and Svensson 2000; Rodrik 1996; van de Walle 2001). Enormous amounts of advice and aid have fed reform programs that failed and have sustained corrupt and uncommitted governments.

This study therefore focuses on domestic political economy and the way it shapes reform, and in this context, changing perceptions of the reform process are a relevant starting point. When it began in the late 1970s, the IFIs saw structural adjustment as comprising a series of partial reforms (Williamson 1994). They were concerned with trade liberalization, complementary changes to the exchange rate, and some removal of subsidies, but rarely much more. Liberalization was new and it was contentious politically, and analysts feared massive popular unrest if the process went too fast and the social costs were too high. By the early 1990s, with the demise of the former Soviet Union and the adoption of pro-market policies in China, the credibility of a socialist (or state-led) alternative had effectively evaporated and liberalization had become mainstream. The IFIs increasingly saw reform as a fundamental transformation of the entire society (eventually as almost synonymous with a pro-development strategy). Embarking on a concerted liberalization program secured the blessing of the IFIs and the prospect of significant rewards in terms of foreign aid, and in Asia, Latin America, and some transition economies, of foreign capital inflows. Resistance no longer offered tangible benefits.

This shift from episodic to systemic reforms had far-reaching implications for the kinds of changes that were likely to appear on governments' policy agendas, their complexity, and the political commitment and state capacity required to pursue them effectively. In the early years, the central bank or ministry of finance could generally formulate and implement measures to achieve macroeconomic stability or partial or sectoral liberalization. Later institutional reforms—such as privatization, labor market liberalization, redesign of social security, health and education systems, or pro-poor growth initiatives—were to prove far more messy. They required broader consultation and negotiation, at the very least with line ministries, but often at the provincial level, with nongovernmental organizations, and with a range of stakeholders, a task for which most governments were ill-equipped (Devarajan, Dollar, and Holmgren 2001; Nelson 1996). The learning process behind the search for new dimensions that was alluded to earlier needs to be seen in this context.

However, the change did not necessarily mean that policies lacked coherence—at least not on paper. Various authors have pointed to the importance of technical groups within governments leading policy reform and to political leaders who were well aware of what was necessary and what constituted sound economic policy (Schamis 1999; Williamson 1994). Technocrats have been prominent in policy formulation and negotiations with donors, especially during times of economic crisis, but eventually governments need to come to grips with political realities, and once the crisis is over or the funds have been secured, slippage has often occurred. Policies proved open to adjustment or maneuver for political purposes and to the influence of an ill-equipped and all too often corrupt and disaffected bureaucracy. As the complexity of the reform effort increased, the leadership could also claim that some measures posed a potential threat to the sustainability of the longer-term reform agenda and concentrate on elements that were more in line with their interests. Hence the importance attached to the motives and commitment of the political leadership and to the specificities of the societal context in which it is operating.

Societal Context

Observers often depict policymaking in developing and transition economies as typically closed and concentrated (even personalized) in the hands of the country's political leadership and a small coterie of top administrators and key advisers. In this view, the principal preoccupation of national leaders is retaining power, and often getting rich, and in attempting to do so they are characterized as having little or no compunction in employing state resources for their personal benefit and to build and strengthen coalitions and reward loyal supporters (Grindle 1991; Manzetti and Blake 1996; Schamis 1999; van de Walle 2001). It is seen as no surprise when the media, the judiciary and the police serve the interests of the leadership (or the ruling party) or when state institutions and public policy are used as sources of patronage and funding for political purposes. This view sees policymaking as a process that is neither transparent nor accountable, and where neither parliament nor government politicians and officials outside the central clique (let alone the business community or the public) are likely to be aware of plans until the leadership announces them. Thus interest groups and civil society are always reacting, and are seen as either poorly organized, and therefore weak politically, or else as co-opted and unable to exert sufficient pressure to force a change in policy (Grindle 2001).

In such a view of the state, the Western pluralist notion of public policy shaped by the give and take of competition in a political marketplace is largely unhelpful. In the absence of political and institutional constraints, the leadership is effectively autonomous, with discretionary control over policy and the allocation of resources. Reforms may be a central part of the government's program: because they will please donors and secure funding, because they can be implemented in ways that yield financial benefits or are advantageous politically, or because the leaders are simply convinced that they are technically superior. If leaders can rationalize or disguise their own objectives in the prevailing policy discourse, they will see it as advantageous to do so, but that does not mean they are committed to reform or that it will be sustained. Retaining power and feeding support structures will always tend to take precedence over sound economic policy. Leaders are unlikely to embrace enthusiastically reforms that jeopardize their position, and they will be much more inclined to adapt them, implement them selectively, or simply put them off until they are more acceptable.

This model has been presented most starkly in literature on some of the countries of Sub-Saharan Africa. It portrays the state as being heavily dependent on aid, being presidential in style, and lacking political institutions that link state and society.

Instead, clientelism and rent distribution are institutionalized, papering over differences among the ruling elite to ensure political stability, and corruption is widely accepted as a tool used for political purposes (Gulhati 1990; Lewis 1996; van de Walle 2001). However, institutionalized patronage and corruption require resources. Observers see unprecedented flows of aid and reforms such as the privatization of state assets reinforcing personal accumulation, patronage structures, and government expenditures on consumption, thereby allowing the ruling elite to pursue their own economic and political program at the expense of the rest of the population. Developmental activities are then passed on to nongovernmental organizations and to donor agencies, which play a growing role in day-to-day decisionmaking through the creation of parallel institutions, further eroding the capacity of the state (van de Walle 2001). Links with foreign investors can also be an important basis for nepotism and patronage in the context of reform, as occurred in Indonesia under Soeharto or the Philippines under Ferdinand Marcos.

By contrast, where nonstate interests are stronger and far more organized, or where the constitution and the electoral system are such that shaky multiparty coalitions are highly probable, links between the state and society become much more relevant (Manzetti and Blake 1996; Moran 1999; Roberts 1995; Theobald 1999). In such cases, the building and sustaining of coalitions of support can be critical, the reform process is more sensitive to stakeholders' inputs and to political reactions, and the progress of reform is more iterative in nature. If the leadership is not strong, institutional relationships within the state itself can pose an obstacle to policy (Grindle and Thomas 1991; Williams 2002). However, when support has to be built by means of intimidation, argument, concessions, or the distribution of favors, the government's own support structures and the interests and social and political commitments that lie behind them can constrain its capacity to implement reforms (Hellman 1998). Schamis's (1999) conclusion that state-centered approaches overlook the extent to which support strategies shape policy choices and their implementation seems particularly pertinent in this context.

The increasingly debilitating effects of highly centralized control, the use of economic reform as a source of individual enrichment and patronage, the constraining influence of support structures, and the erosion of representative institutions are important dimensions of many instances of failure and seriously limit the scope for any pro-poor growth. To illustrate how these sources of failure can develop in practice, the paper now turns to an analysis of the Sri Lankan case.

Reform and Institutional Change: The Case of Sri Lanka

In 1977, when it embarked on reform, Sri Lanka was a relatively peaceful and stable democracy with an impressive record of human development by the standards of developing countries. The most significant changes since independence in 1948 had been a shift from a multiethnic to a Sinhalese-Buddhist state and a sharp increase in the state's involvement in the economy and in people's lives (Athukorala and

Jayasuriya 1994; de Silva 1993). A westernized landed and professional elite that led the two major parties, the United National Party (UNP) and the Sri Lanka Freedom Party, dominated politics and had traditionally competed for the elected right to distribute state patronage (Moore 1990). The majority Sinhalese community and the Tamil and Muslim minorities had a history of friction over access to jobs, land, and other resources. Friction also existed among the Sinhalese between the urban elite and educated youth in rural areas, which in 1971 went so far as an insurrection and an attempt by rural youth to seize power. By the mid-1970s, the country was also an almost classic case of an inward-looking, state-dominated economy.

A new government then came to power on a platform of economic change. The reform process has been sustained over the last quarter of a century, the average annual growth rate has been 5 percent, and the economy is the most liberal in South Asia. Thus at one level, Sri Lanka has been cited as an example of successful reform, but at the same time it has been in the grip of almost continuous social and political conflict that has torn apart its social fabric and placed a brake on growth, hence other references to it as a country of missed opportunities (Snodgrass 1998; World Bank 2000). The conventional view is that the conflict and the parallel deterioration in social and political institutions were quite unrelated to the shift in economic policy; they were unfortunate exogenous developments that prevented Sri Lanka from reaping the full benefits of its economic reform policies (World Bank 2000). On closer examination, however, a different picture emerges.

The significance of the changes that have taken place in Sri Lanka has to be seen cumulatively over the entire period since the start of reforms. Events also have to be understood against the history, ideology, and background of the country's party leadership and the preexisting class and ethnic tensions in Sri Lankan society.

The Jayawardene Government, 1977–89

The UNP, which was elected to office in 1977, was traditionally conservative and pro-business. It came to power by having correctly judged the public mood as being open to radical change to avoid any repetition of the economic crisis and widespread suffering of the mid-1970s. It promised an open economy and a just and righteous (*dharmista*) government, and it received an overwhelming majority. In 1977–78, support for dismantling domestic marketing restrictions, especially those on rice marketing, was widespread, and the initial response to components of trade liberalization was generally favorable: initial conditions and societal context clearly mattered.

The UNP's policy package was (and still is) commonly described as a major liberalization program, and visible changes were quickly apparent in the Sri Lankan economy. In reality, however, its program was considerably broader and included a range of economic and political elements of which the liberalization measures were just a part. While the package entailed significant trade and exchange rate reforms, it also contained a major donor-supported public sector investment program (PSIP)— including the accelerated development of a massive irrigation, resettlement, and power project; the construction of a new national capital; and large-scale public housing—that was not technically a liberalization measure and that soon became by far the most prominent aspect. The package also contained sharp cuts in food subsidies and incorporated a number of highly controversial political measures, such as the introduction of constitutional changes, the repression of opposition and dissent, and the muzzling of unions, that emerged over time as a central part of the UNP's strategy.

The program was therefore not a conventional liberalization package as laid out in the literature, but a distinctive political and economic program of J. R. Jayawardene's UNP government. Nor was it just about reform. It looked to revamp the country's economic and political landscape in line with the vision of its leader, Jayawardene, who was committed to lifting domestic market restrictions and introducing a more open international trade regime (de Silva and Wriggins 1994). Reform played a part in his program, but his more fundamental aim was to stimulate growth and alter patterns of resource allocation and benefits toward his own supporters, to reshape political institutions to ensure that his vision could not be derailed, and to entrench his own and his party's domination over the long term.

As a result, implementation revealed the program's advantages for its Sinhalese constituency, the need to create and preserve important sources of patronage, and a determination to marginalize an already weak opposition once and for all. The government applied trade liberalization in a manner that was highly discriminatory, with a significant pro-Sinhalese bias (Cuthbertson and Athukorala 1990). The government heralded the massive irrigation, resettlement, and power scheme, the centerpiece of the PSIP, as a revival of the ancient Sinhalese heartland in a way that appealed to deep-seated nationalist and religious sentiments in the Sinhalese-Buddhist community, and the PSIP in general provided state land and housing and generated contracts, employment, and other sources of political patronage. The UNP used cuts in food subsidies, which Jayawardene had forcefully advocated since the 1950s, to provoke and to crush opposition in the trade union movement and to bolster party support among the farming community, while particularly hurting urban workers, who traditionally supported his opponents.

In parallel, and just as much an integral part of the overall policy package, was the replacement of the Westminster-style parliamentary system with a Gaullist-type of constitution (led by an executive president with minimum accountability to parliament) and proportional representation rather than competition in constituencies. The result was a significant increase in centralization. It led to a steady erosion of civil and electoral rights, an increasingly high-handed treatment of ethnic minorities, a refusal to hold parliamentary elections, and an eventual extension of parliament's term by means of a referendum that observers perceived as seriously flawed (Manor 1984). The combination of selective liberalization, the PSIP, and growing authoritarianism (alongside decreasing transparency) provided a favorable environment for corruption to flourish, in large part boosted by the sheer scale of donor aid for the PSIP. Initially, Sri Lankans accepted the corruption and it was not a political issue because perceptible benefits had resulted, but as growth weakened and employment creation fell toward the mid-1980s, dissatisfaction mounted. The PSIP had an adverse effect on export industries by appreciating the exchange rate, and coming after two decades of mounting dissatisfaction with Sinhalese governments, the PSIP—together with the discriminatory trade liberalization—increased the sense of marginalization among minority communities. Cuts in consumer subsides and the urban middle-class dynamic of the early trade liberalization also created a growing perception among low-income youth that the government's package was pro-rich and therefore anti-poor. The view that normal legal and parliamentary protest was being stifled was also widespread.

There can be no doubt that the UNP package as a whole exacerbated preexisting divisions in Sri Lankan society and contributed both to the increasing ethnic tension that was to escalate into a war of secession in the north and east in the mid-1980s until February 2002 and to an insurrection by Sinhalese youth in the south from 1987 to 1989. In the context of clear, preexisting fault lines in Sri Lankan society, the discriminatory implementation of economic policies in combination with Jayawardene's political strategy had heightened social tensions to breaking point. With other avenues cut off, support for extraparliamentary forms of struggle began to widen, triggering an iterative cycle of responses. People increasingly resented the regime's authoritarian nature, requiring an even firmer hand to retain control, forcing the regime to arm its cadres, and in the process provoking further resentment and mounting violence. In turn, repression and authoritarianism fostered an environment where transparency could be eroded, enabling corruption to flourish.

So why did donors bankroll the PSIP with its opportunities for corruption? The main reason was because here was a government in a strategic location in South Asia that had clearly turned pro-Western, and that as early as 1977 supported pro-market policies. To some extent, the PSIP helped the donor countries' construction industries that were to build Sri Lanka's major dams during a period of recession at home, and perhaps there was also an implicit view that the country had suffered far too long from the prolonged inefficiency of populist democracy and that encouraging a determined government would help advance reform. At that time, in per capita terms, Sri Lanka was one of the largest recipients of aid, but it was fed through a state apparatus that reflected less and less transparency. The leadership was, as a result, able to direct that aid to its own political advantage. "Liberalization" provided Jayawardene with the chance to pursue his political interests.

Socially and politically, the country moved into a period of violent conflict, authoritarian political rule, escalation of defense expenditures, reduced investment, and slow growth. Liberalization stalled, but it was not reversed. By the late 1980s, the country faced a full-blown balance of payments crisis and a paralysis in domestic economic activity, forcing Jayawardene to relinquish the presidency and to hold fresh elections.

The Premadasa Government, 1989–93

After elections in 1989, held in an atmosphere of violence and alleged electoral fraud against a deliberately weakened and disorganized opposition, the new UNP president,

Ranasinghe Premadasa, faced the political challenge of dealing both with insurrection and a major economic crisis. His response was firm and effective, establishing a virtual dictatorship. The government negotiated an agreement with the International Monetary Fund, which at that time was in a strong position to wield influence, and implemented a second wave of liberalization reforms. For the first time, privatization and income transfers to the poor became major items on the agenda. The latter occurred largely because the new president did not come from the country's elite and building personal support structures and changing the social base of the party were his main priority.[1] Nevertheless, the agenda had a definite pro-poor dimension. The economy recovered strongly: liberalization enhanced the incentives for export-oriented production; foreign investment started to flow again; export industries, particularly in the garment sector, expanded rapidly; and a general sense of optimism emerged within the business and donor communities.

Premadasa was the first Sri Lankan leader to have come from a modest background, and the elite that had traditionally dominated his party had in the past treated him as an outsider. This he had bitterly resented, and when he came to power he turned to non-elite groups for support, particularly the poor and the newly created Sinhalese-speaking business class. Premadasa was also aware that unemployment and marginalization of the poor were at the root of Sinhalese extremism. As a result, the UNP election platform of 1989 accorded the highest priority to creating employment and giving the poor access to assets; however, in the context of such a highly politicized environment, the results were inevitably limited.[2] New garment factories were steered to rural areas, any move that could be construed to imply labor retrenchment was generally avoided, and when job creation failed to take off, Premadasa tried to force the pace by pressurizing the Sri Lankan business community to keep on investing.

Even though he never eliminated the opposition to the same extent, the Premadasa regime revealed parallels with that of Soeharto in Indonesia. Power and decision-making were centralized, the president's dictatorial practices became increasingly blatant, and corruption was institutionalized, but there was also policy clarity and predictability. Businesses became increasingly confident that they would not have to deal with labor problems or the disruption of economic activity anywhere outside the distant war zone. They were left with no doubt about the rewards they could secure by opening factories, creating jobs, and cooperating closely with the government—about the favors that could be granted, the almost immediate redress of grievances or administrative encumbrances, or indeed the unswerving support that would subsequently be expected of them (Dunham and Kelegama 1997). Political intervention to "get things done" was strong, as was partisan political control over public officers.

Such was Premadasa's personal power as president that institutions were created, used, or adapted to serve his political needs. However, this was only possible because he was able to build on the centralized political system he had inherited from Jayewardena, and that he could then use to push through further reforms and build his personal and party support base. Remodeled political institutions facilitated reform; institutions were adjusted to take charge of implementation; and a new trajectory took shape as cronyism, connections, and corruption became standard operating policy. When the funds that could be extracted from the PSIP dried up in the mid-1980s, the scope for large-scale corruption in direct state economic activities subsided temporarily, only to be revived by privatization in the early 1990s. The latter involved little transparency (Dunham and Kelegama 1997), although the potential gains were extremely high.[3] They provided resources that could finance support and enable Premadasa to maintain his hold on power, and they were a massive source of political advantage that had to be protected. Political violence, thuggery, and assassination increased, eliminating competitors within the party, intimidating opponents, and resulting in an increasing brutalization of Sri Lankan society. As protest and opposition mounted, first via a failed impeachment motion and then spilling over into extraparliamentary action, it was met with repression and more authoritarianism, generating even less transparency and allowing more corruption. Social tensions built up to breaking point, and the population at large began to see corruption and repression as major national problems.

The Kumaratunga Government, 1994–2001

Premadasa was assassinated in May 1993, and a year later a center-left coalition was elected to power on an anticorruption and pro-peace platform, with growing pressure to abolish the executive presidency. By this time, there was no question of any reversal of pro-market policies, and expectations were high that there would be a new start and a new kind of society in which the poor would benefit. At the time a real chance of a change of trajectory seemed possible, but it was not to be. The coalition of incoming President Chandrika Kumaratunga commanded a tenuous one-seat majority in parliament. The accommodations needed to hold it together led to a mushrooming of ministries, and such was the fragmentation in this arrangement that the executive presidency was retained as the central focus of power and national policymaking. Patronage and the resources to fund it were also crucial and, reversing its initial stand, the government surpassed the efforts of its predecessor in relation to privatization. The national airline, telecommunications companies, plantation management, and ports were all privatized, again with little transparency, and regulatory powers controlling competition in particular markets were used as a source of additional rents (Jayasuriya and Knight-John 2002). Again, the Premadasa regime had cleared the path and the new government exploited the opportunities that the situation presented. Path dependence was evident in every sense.

Other forces were also emerging that provided added weight to the culture of corruption and patronage. The escalation of military expenditures from the mid-1980s had introduced a new dimension. It had two principal strands. Large-scale military purchases from abroad provided opportunities for brokerage, yielding significant "commissions" for military personnel and for the politically-favored civilians who became involved, and domestically, the expansion of the military and security-related activities presented opportunities through the tendering and state purchase of necessary goods and services.

This continued throughout the Jayawardene and Premadasa years, but with the outbreak of virtually open war in the mid-1990s, the military, state security, and the private security business took on new dimensions, creating a pro-war lobby that put additional pressure on the government to push for a military solution or maintain the status quo. The situation provided considerable employment for the poor, though as the number of deaths increased it was one they were to appreciate less and less. It also saw an increasing availability of weapons throughout Sri Lankan society, with a consequent rise in political thuggery and armed crime. Police became an extension of the interests of politicians, election violence increased, and weaker groups in society faced a mounting problem of physical security.

As the war escalated and social stability became increasingly in question, the business community adopted a wait and see attitude, investment fell, and the economy slowed, requiring even greater levels of patronage to hold the coalition together. The interests of politicians and business people who were in a position to extract continuing rents from the privatization exercise gelled with those who could raise rents from the other major continuing source, the civil war. Shared economic incentives converged in shared political interests, and for both groups continued access to political power was essential. This created the economic basis for a coalition within the government's ranks (with some outside participants) to stifle any initiative to establish more transparency in government purchases, contracts, and other commercial dealings.

The wealth the situation yielded was a major source of finance for the clientelism that continues to provide the bases of political power and influence throughout the country. The antipoverty program continued in a revised form, although it became even more politicized. The state enterprise sector had shrunk, and with it many opportunities for exploiting the state apparatus to dispense employment and other benefits, but other possibilities had surfaced. The problem was circumvented to a considerable degree by the expansion of the ministerial posts and privileges that had ballooned with coalition politics and, more generally, by the extensive privileges of politicians. In combination, these processes entrenched a system of political corruption that subverted political democracy and judicial independence.

At the same time, the circumstances also created incentives for others to organize and to challenge them: teams and individuals, excluded from the game by adjustments to the rules, seek new games and new rules. After a quarter of a century of reform, the country's business community had expanded significantly, exploiting the opportunities presented by the more liberal economic environment, however much the machinations of government may have distorted it. It had a genuine interest in the political rules of the game and their implications for investment, reflected in its demands for negotiated peace as a solution to the ethnic problem. Wider Sri Lankan society had also clearly reached a point, as in 1994, when it had seen enough of corruption and, by the turn of the century, of civil war. In the 2001 parliamentary elections the UNP was once again returned to power as the coalition of its predecessor crumbled, heralding a difficult period of cohabitation with Kumaratunga, who had been re-elected as president. However, the undercurrent of discontent offered the possibility of a new trajectory: peace talks began the following year, only to stall when cohabitation led to political crisis in late 2003. The hope is that they will eventually lead to sustainable peace and the reconstruction of society, but serious problems of corruption and policy management will still remain to be resolved.

Concluding Remarks

This paper has explored interrelationships between a government program that contains major economic policy reforms, macro institutions, and socio-political outcomes. It has also stressed the crucial importance of politics, showing how leadership decisions and institutional change shape longer-term policy options, resulting in what North (1990) has referred to as path dependence. In such a context, any suggestion that economic reform can be seen as a linear process in which an aloof, public-minded government sequentially adopts, then implements, a required package of economic policies that succeeds or fails offers little guidance for understanding the complex dynamics that are observed in practice. A country's history, its societal context, the motives and commitment of its leadership, its broader economic and political program, and the state's management capacity all matter considerably. As a result, decisions are modified, elaborated, or reversed in the course of implementation and the reform process is iterative in nature (Grindle and Thomas 1991).

The paper has also shown that, far from being unreservedly beneficial, reforms can be a contributory factor in the breakdown of society. Economic reforms may stimulate growth and greater economic efficiency, but if they are applied selectively and discriminately, or are widely believed by powerful groups or by the population at large to have been applied as such, they can generate powerful political responses (Dunham and Jayasuriya 2000). If adequate checks and balances are not sufficiently rooted, reforms can also spark adverse changes in the country's political institutions. They can offer major new opportunities for rent extraction (Manzetti and Blake 1996; Schamis 1999) and, in the process, provide those in power with a massive source of political advantage over their competitors that they then feel they must be protected because of the largesse and influence it yields and because of the much increased political cost of being marginalized as losers. Insofar as they prefer "more power to less, survival in office to defeat, re-election to loss, and influence to irrelevance" (Grindle 2001, p. 349), those in power have every incentive to change the rules of the game to ensure their hold on power, and that is often bitterly resented.

In Sri Lanka, with its history of social tensions, not only between the different communities, but among the Sinhalese themselves, discriminatory policies heightened existing perceptions of inequality, fueled already simmering feelings of injustice and exclusion, and tore the social fabric apart. This set the stage for violent political conflict and authoritarianism, creating fertile ground for the entrenchment of corruption and political repression, weakening regulatory and representative institutions, and setting in motion a downward spiral to social and political instability. At the outset, an ethnically biased regime implemented liberalization measures to foster its own political purposes. They were implemented as part of a broader program (alongside other, highly charged, and at times more important policies that had nothing to do with economic reform), and extracting them from that wider setting made no real sense. In the second phase of liberalization in the early 1990s, the privatization of large state utilities and increasing war expenditures replaced the waning PSIP as a source of rents and, given the scale of the potential gains, there was every incentive for those in power to influence or bypass privatization commissions, minimize transparency, and weaken parliament and the judiciary.

As the process unfolded, politicians, state bureaucrats, and a new group, the military and police hierarchy, found fertile ground for rapid, large-scale self-advancement through the control of state power. However, as political freedoms, public scrutiny, and normal democratic processes threatened the opportunities that this created, the temptation to undermine legal and political institutions grew quickly. Once they were locked into this path, those in control of the state had little choice for their own political survival but to ensure that economic reforms were designed and implemented so that the flow of benefits continued. The country's leadership was increasingly prepared to subvert political institutions, processes, and movements that could threaten its grip on power. It suppressed public scrutiny and dissent, undermined the activities of political opponents, and eroded democratic freedoms. As a result, preexisting ethnic and other social divisions exploded into large-scale violence, dramatically redefining the country's political and institutional landscape.

In such a situation, the scope for implementing economic reforms or a pro-poor growth strategy has to be seen against the societal context, the broader program of the leadership, and the state's management capacity. In Sri Lanka, benefits from the growth of the economy were considerable. Real per capita income more than tripled over a quarter of a century, and its distribution did not change significantly: the new rich who amassed enormous wealth and pursued a conspicuous urban lifestyle were in practice relatively few (Dunham and Jayasuriya 2000). However, stark discrepancies that existed between the stated objectives of the political elite (of whatever party) and their failure to act impartially, tackle corruption, secure the much-awaited peace dividend, and stimulate the economy created a serious credibility gap in Sri Lankan society. It was not just the content of policy that mattered, but the social dynamics of the process.

Notes

1. The government also took steps to bring nongovernmental organization funding under its control to stifle opposition and to weaken competing signals at the local level that might undermine its support.

2. Dunham and Edwards (1997) estimate that between 1989 and 1993, remittances from temporary emigration to the Middle East and from military service together contributed more to poverty reduction than government transfers and garment factories.

3. Under earlier trade restrictions, the scale of rent extraction was of necessity limited. The volume of trade was small, and import-competing industries were few, small, and financially weak. Over time, the cumulative value of rents may not have been insignificant, but they could not be appropriated rapidly or as a lump sum, as with the privatization of large state utilities.

References

Athukorala P., and S. Jayasuriya. 1994. *Macroeconomic Policies, Crises, and Growth in Sri Lanka, 1969–90.* Washington, D.C.: World Bank.

Cuthbertson, A. G., and P. Athukorala. 1990. "Sri Lanka." In D. Papageorgiou, M. Michaely, and A. M. Choksi, eds., *Liberalising Foreign Trade: Indonesia, Pakistan, and Sri Lanka.* Oxford, U.K.: Basil Blackwell.

de Silva, K. M., ed. 1993. *Sri Lanka: Problems of Governance.* Kandy, Sri Lanka: International Centre for Ethnic Studies.

de Silva, K. M., and H. Wriggins. 1994. *J. R. Jayawardene of Sri Lanka—A Political Biography,* vol. II, *From 1956 to His Retirement (1989).* London: Leo Cooper/Pen and Sword Books.

Devarajan, S., D. R. Dollar, and T. Holmgren. 2001. *Aid and Reform in Africa: Lessons from Ten Case Studies.* Washington, D.C.: World Bank.

Dollar, D., and J. Svensson. 2000. "What Explains the Success or Failure of Structural Adjustment Programmes?" *Economic Journal* 110(October): 894–917.

Dunham, D., and C. Edwards. 1997. *Rural Poverty and an Agrarian Crisis in Sri Lanka, 1985–95: Making Sense of the Picture.* Colombo: Institute of Policy Studies.

Dunham, D., and S. Jayasuriya. 2000. "Equity, Growth, and Insurrection: Liberalisation and the Welfare Debate in Contemporary Sri Lanka." *Oxford Development Studies* 28(1): 97–110.

Dunham D., and S. Kelegama. 1997. "Does Leadership Matter in the Economic Reform Process? Liberalization and Governance in Sri Lanka, 1989–93." *World Development* 25(2): 179–90.

Grindle, M. S. 1991. "The New Political Economy: Positive Economics and Negative Politics." In G. M. Meier, ed., *Politics and Policy Making in Developing Countries: Perspectives on the New Political Economy.* San Francisco: ICS Press.

———. 2001. "In Quest of the Political: The Political Economy of Development Policy-Making." In G. M. Meier and J. Stiglitz, eds., *Frontiers of Development Economics: The Future Perspective.* New York: Oxford University Press.

Grindle, M. S., and J. W. Thomas. 1991. *The Political Economy of Reform in Developing Countries.* Baltimore, Md.: The Johns Hopkins University Press.

Gulhati, R. 1990. "Who Makes Economic Policy in Africa and How?" *World Development* 18(8): 1147–61.

Haggard, S., and S. Webb. 1993. "What Do We Know About the Political Economy of Economic Policy Reform?" *World Development* 18(2): 143–68.

Hellman, J. S. 1998. "Winners Take All: The Politics of Partial Reform in Postcommunist Transitions." *World Politics* 50(January): 203–34.

Jayasuriya, S., and M. Knight-John. Forthcoming. "Sri Lanka's Telecommunications Industry: From Privatisation to Anti-Competition?" In M. Hossain, A. Brown, and T. Nguyen, eds., *Telecommunications Reform in the Asia Pacific Region: Economic and Regulatory Experiences.* London: Edward Elgar.

Lewis, P. M. 1996. "Economic Reform and Political Transition in Africa: The Quest for a Politics of Development." *World Politics* 49(1): 92–129.

Liddle, R. W. 1992. "The Politics of Development Policy." *World Development* 20(6): 793–807.

Manor, J., ed. 1984. *Sri Lanka in Change and Crisis.* London: Croom Helm.

Manzetti, L., and C. H. Blake. 1996. "Market Reforms and Corruption in Latin America: New Means for Old Ways." *Review of International Political Economy* 3(4): 662–97.

Moore, M. 1990. "Economic Liberalisation Versus Political Liberalism in Sri Lanka?" *Journal of Modern Asian Studies* 24(2): 341–83.

Moran, J. 1999. "Patterns of Corruption and Development in East Asia." *Third World Quarterly* 20(3): 569–87.

Mosley, P., J. Harrigan, and J. Toye. 1991. *Aid and Power: The World Bank and Policy Based Lending.* London: Routledge.

Nelson, J. 1996. "Promoting Policy Reforms: The Twilight of Conditionality?" *World Development* 24(9): 1551–59.

North, D. C. 1990. *Institutions, Institutional Change, and Economic Performance.* Cambridge, U.K.: Cambridge University Press.

Roberts, K. M. 1995. "Neoliberalism and the Transformation of Populism in Latin America: The Peruvian Case." *World Politics* 48(1): 82–116.

Rodrik, D. 1996. "Understanding Economic Policy Reform." *Journal of Economic Literature* 34(1): 9–41.

Schamis, H. E. 1999. "Distributional Coalitions and the Politics of Economic Reform in Latin America." *World Politics* 51(2): 236–68.

Snodgrass, D. R. 1998. *The Economic Development of Sri Lanka: A Tale of Missed Opportunities.* Development Discussion Paper no. 637. Cambridge, Mass.: Harvard Institute of International Development.

Theobald, R. 1999. "So What Really Is the Problem About Corruption?" *Third World Quarterly* 20(3): 491–502.

van de Walle, N. 2001. *African Economies and the Politics of Permanent Crisis, 1979–99.* Cambridge, U.K.: Cambridge University Press.

Williams, M. E. 2002. "Market Reform, Technocrats, and Institutional Innovation." *World Development* 30(3): 395–412.

Williamson, J., ed. 1994. *The Political Economy of Policy Reform.* Washington, D.C.: Institute of International Economics.

World Bank. 1992. *Governance and Development.* Washington, D.C.

———. 1994. *Governance: The World Bank's Experience.* Washington, D.C.

———. 2000. *Sri Lanka: Recapturing Missed Opportunities.* Country Report. Washington, D.C.

———. 2002. *World Development Report 2002: Building Institutions for Markets.* New York: Oxford University Press.

Inequality before and under the Law: Paths of Long-Run Development in the Americas

STANLEY L. ENGERMAN AND KENNETH L. SOKOLOFF

Economists have long recognized geographic patterns in economic performance, but the question of where these empirical regularities come from has only recently attracted increased attention. One group of scholars has highlighted the significance of the direct effects on productivity of conditions closely associated with geography, such as climate, disease environment, soil quality, and access to markets (Diamond 1997; Hall and Jones 1999; Sachs and Warner 1997). Another set of studies, however, has focused on the possibility that geographic patterns in performance might stem from the effects of factor endowments (or of variables associated with geography more generally) on the way institutions evolve (Acemoglu, Johnson, and Robinson 2001, 2002; Engerman and Sokoloff 1997). Both approaches have long intellectual traditions, but the idea that systematic reasons may account for why in some societies institutions evolve that are more conducive to growth than the institutions that evolve in other places seems to have generated particular excitement. This is perhaps easy to understand. Despite an emerging consensus that institutions are important for growth, our knowledge of the processes of institutional change generally, and more specifically, of how institutions that are bad for growth persist over time, remains limited.

Our own research program on whether systematic patterns are apparent in the way institutions evolve, and whether and how those patterns are related to factor endowments or geography, has focused on how institutions evolved over the long run in a particular context: the societies of the New World. (For a fuller discussion of the research project and of many of the issues addressed here, see Engerman and Sokoloff 2002.) The experience of the limited number of European countries that ventured to the Americas to establish colonies in quite dissimilar environments within a relatively short span of time makes for an extremely interesting natural experiment.

Stanley Engerman is professor of economics and history at the University of Rochester in New York and research fellow at the National Bureau of Economics Research in Cambridge, Massachusetts. Kenneth Sokoloff is professor of economics at the University of California, Los Angeles, and research fellow at the National Bureau of Economics Research in Cambridge, Massachusetts.

Annual World Bank Conference on Development Economics—Europe 2003
© 2004 The International Bank for Reconstruction and Development/The World Bank

Differences in income levels across the economies of the Americas were quite small for the first quarter of a millennium after the Europeans arrived, and indeed, per capita incomes in at least parts of the Caribbean and South America exceeded those in the regions that were to comprise Canada and the United States. Looking back from the vantage point of the early 21st century, this record seems especially puzzling, because the areas that were first settled and the choices of the first Europeans as to which parts of the Americas to colonize were those that fell behind. Conversely, the societies that were established by Europeans who came late and had to settle for areas viewed less favorably in terms of prospects have proved more successful in economic terms over the long run.

The explanations for these differentials in growth rates or long-run economic performance have run the gamut from an emphasis on strictly economic factors to mainly cultural and religious factors. Those who have highlighted the role of institutions have traditionally credited the success of the North American economies to an alleged superiority of the English institutional heritage or a better fit of Protestant beliefs with market institutions (Coatsworth 1998; North 1981, 1988). Our examination of the basis for differential paths of development was originally inspired, however, by the observation that the British colonies in the New World, despite beginning with roughly the same legal and cultural background and drawing immigrants from similar places and economic classes, evolved quite distinct societies and sets of economic institutions. Only a few were able to realize sustained economic growth before the end of the 19th century. The majority that failed shared certain salient features with their neighboring societies, whether in the Caribbean or in Latin America. While all New World societies began with a relative abundance of land and other resources compared with Europe, other aspects of their factor endowments varied, contributing to extreme differences across them in the distributions of wealth, human capital, legal standing, and political influence.

Some, like the colonies established in Brazil or the Caribbean, had climates and soil conditions extremely well suited for growing crops such as sugar that were of high value on the market and could be produced at lowest cost on large slave-using plantations (Fogel 1989). Their populations came to be dominated by the many slaves obtained through the international slave market, and they quickly generated vastly unequal distributions of wealth, human capital, and political power. Early on, Spanish America was similarly characterized by extreme inequality, at least partially because of its factor endowments. The extensive populations of natives in the regions the Spanish colonization effort focused on (Mexico and Peru) and the Spanish practices (significantly influenced by preexisting Native American organizations in those areas) of awarding claims to land, native labor, and rich mineral resources to members of the elite were powerful factors leading to extreme inequality (Lockhart and Schwartz 1983). With inflows of Europeans constrained by Spain's extremely restrictive immigration policies, instituted at least partially at the behest of the early Spanish immigrants and their descendants and made feasible by the relative abundance of Native American labor, the population of Spanish America came to be composed

TABLE 1. The Distribution and Composition of Population in New World Economies, Selected Years, 1570–1935

(percent)

Location	Year	White	Black	Indian	Share in total New World population
Spanish America	1570	1.3	2.5	96.3	83.5
	1650	6.3	9.3	84.4	84.3
	1825	18.0	22.5	59.5	55.2
	1935	35.5	13.3	50.4	30.3
Brazil	1570	2.4	3.5	94.1	7.6
	1650	7.4	13.7	78.9	7.7
	1825	23.4	55.6	21.0	11.6
	1935	41.0	35.5	23.0	17.1
Canada and the United States	1570	0.2	0.2	99.6	8.9
	1650	12.0	2.2	85.8	8.1
	1825	79.6	16.7	3.7	33.2
	1935	89.4	8.9	1.4	52.6

Source: Engerman and Sokoloff (1997).

predominantly of Indians and *mestizos*. As late as 1825, less than 20 percent of the population of Spanish America was composed of whites (table 1).

In contrast, small family-size farms were the rule in the northern colonies of the North American mainland, where climatic conditions favored a regime of mixed farming centered on grains and livestock that exhibited relatively limited economies of scale in production and used few slaves. Moreover, relatively few Native Americans lived on the East Coast, where the English, French, and Dutch established their mainland colonies. Although these locations do not appear to have been particularly attractive to Europeans during the first quarter of a millennium after they began to colonize the New World, because only a small fraction of migrants opted to locate there, the circumstances did foster somewhat homogenous populations with relatively equal distributions of human capital and wealth (Galenson 1995; Greene 1988).

These initial differences in the degree of inequality—which can be attributed largely to factor endowments, broadly conceived—had profound and enduring effects on the development paths of the respective economies. Previous treatments of the impact of inequality on growth have typically focused on the impact of inequality on savings or investment rates. Our hypothesis, however, concerns the possibility that the extreme differences in the extent of inequality that arose early in the history of the New World economies led to systematic differences in the ways institutions evolved. More specifically, in societies that began with extreme inequality, elites were better able to establish a basic legal framework that ensured that they gained access to disproportionate shares of political power and could use that influence to establish rules, laws, and other government policies that greatly favored them relative to the rest of the population in terms of access to economic opportunities, thereby contributing to the persistence of the high degree of inequality. In societies that began with greater equality in wealth and human capital or more homogeneity among the population, however, elites were either less able or less inclined to institutionalize rules, laws, and other government policies that gave them disproportionate advantages, and thus the institutions that evolved tended to provide more equal treatment and opportunities, thereby contributing to the persistence of the relatively high degree of equality.

We contend that these sorts of mechanisms can not only help explain the long-term persistence of the differences in inequality between the respective societies, but may also play a role in accounting for the differences in the rates of increase of per capita income over the last two centuries. If the processes of early industrialization in the 19th century were based on broad participation in the commercial economy as the evidence from the three leaders (the Netherlands, the United Kingdom, and the United States) suggests, then societies with institutions that limited effective access to opportunities might have been less capable of realizing the potential of the new technologies and markets that developed during that crucial century when just a few New World economies pulled well ahead of their neighbors.

Elites, with their greater wealth, human capital, and other resources, are, of course, generally advantaged in securing selective enforcement of laws, exerting informal influence on policymakers, and procuring goods and services privately that could have been provided publicly. For this reason, the formal legal frameworks we rely on to gauge the differences in institutions across societies understate the extent of inequality under the law within any society, and especially in societies with extreme inequality. The implication of this social pattern is that our findings about the relationship between the way institutions evolved and initial inequality are probably quite conservative.

The Impact of Inequality on How Institutions Evolve

This section discusses three important institutions and how they are related to the degree of inequality in a society. These are suffrage, education, and land policy.

Suffrage Institutions and Voting

A natural starting point for an examination of whether inequality has a systematic effect on the way institutions evolve is to look at suffrage institutions: how broadly was the franchise extended and what fractions of respective populations actually voted in elections (for a more complete treatment of the evolution of suffrage institutions, see Engerman and Sokoloff 2001). As most societies in the Americas were nominally democracies by the middle of the 19th century, how their laws framed the right to vote and the conduct of elections bears directly on the extent to which elites based largely on wealth and human capital held disproportionate political power in their respective countries, and on whether and how initial differences in such power or influence persisted over time.

Table 2 summarizes information about differences across New World societies during the late 19th and early 20th centuries in how the right to vote was restricted. The table reveals that while restricting the right to vote to adult males was common until the 20th century, Canada and the United States were the clear leaders in doing away with restrictions based on wealth and literacy, and much higher fractions of their populations voted than anywhere else in the Americas, a pattern that persisted in the 20th century as Canada and the United States were the first nations in the Americas to introduce female suffrage. Not only did Canada and the United States introduce the secret ballot and extend the franchise to even the poor and illiterate (gains that were

TABLE 2. Laws Governing the Franchise and the Extent of Voting, Selected American Countries, 1840–1940

Country	Years	Lack of secrecy in balloting	Wealth requirement	Literacy requirement	Percentage of the population voting
	1840–80				
Chile	1869	No	Yes	Yes	1.6
	1878	No	No	No[a]	—
Costa Rica	1880	Yes	Yes	Yes	—
Ecuador	1848	Yes	Yes	Yes	0.0
	1856	Yes	Yes	Yes	0.1
Mexico	1840	Yes	Yes	Yes	—
Peru	1875	Yes	Yes	Yes	—
Uruguay	1840	Yes	Yes	Yes	—
	1880	Yes	Yes	Yes	—
Venezuela	1840	Yes	Yes	Yes	—
	1880	Yes	Yes	Yes	—
Canada	1867	Yes	Yes	No	7.7
	1878	No	Yes	No	12.9
United States	1850[b]	No	No	No	12.9
	1880	No	No	No	18.3
	1881–1920				
Argentina	1896	Yes	Yes	Yes	1.8[c]
	1916	No	No	No	9.0
Brazil	1894	Yes	Yes	Yes	2.2
	1914	Yes	Yes	Yes	2.4
Chile	1881	No	No	No	3.1
	1920	No	No	Yes	4.4
Colombia	1918[d]	No	No	No	6.9
Costa Rica	1912	Yes	Yes	Yes	—
	1919	Yes	No	No	10.6
Ecuador	1888	No	Yes	Yes	2.8
	1894	No	No	Yes	3.3

(Continues on next page)

TABLE 2. (Continued)

Country	Years	Lack of secrecy in balloting	Wealth requirement	Literacy requirement	Percentage of the population voting
Mexico	1920	No	No	No	8.6
Peru	1920	Yes	Yes	Yes	—
Uruguay	1900	Yes	Yes	Yes	—
	1920	No	No	No	13.8
Venezuela	1920	Yes	Yes	Yes	—
Canada	1911	No	No	No	18.1
	1917	No	No	No	20.5
United States	1900	No	No	Yes[e]	18.4
	1920	No	No	Yes	25.1
1921–51					
Argentina	1928	No	No	No	12.8
	1937	No	No	No	15.0
Bolivia	1951	—	Yes	Yes	4.1
Brazil	1930	Yes	Yes	Yes	5.7
Chile	1920	No	No	Yes	4.4
	1931	No	No	Yes	6.5
	1938	No	No	Yes	9.4
Colombia	1930	No	No	No	11.1
	1936	No	No	No	5.9
Costa Rica	1940	No	No	No	17.6
Ecuador	1940	No	No	Yes	3.3
Mexico	1940	No	No	No	11.8
Peru	1940	No	No	Yes	—
Uruguay	1940	No	No	No	19.7
Venezuela	1940	No	Yes	Yes	—
Canada	1940	No	No	No	41.1
United States	1940	No	No	Yes	37.8

— Not available.

a. After eliminating wealth and education requirements in 1878, Chile instituted a literacy requirement in 1885, which seems to have been responsible for a sharp decline in the proportion of the population who were registered to vote.

b. Three states, Connecticut, Louisiana, and New Jersey, still maintained wealth requirements in 1840, but eliminated them soon afterward. All states except for Illinois and Virginia had implemented the secret ballot by the end of the 1840s.

c. This figure is for the city of Buenos Aires and probably overstates the proportion who voted at the national level.

d. The information on restrictions refers to national laws. The 1863 Constitution empowered provincial state governments to regulate electoral affairs. Afterwards, elections became restricted (in terms of the franchise for adult males) and indirect in some states. It was not until 1948 that a national law established universal adult male suffrage throughout the country. This pattern was followed in other Latin American countries, as it was in Canada and the United States to a lesser extent.

e. Eighteen states, 7 southern and 11 others, introduced literacy requirements between 1890 and 1926. These restrictions were directed primarily at blacks and immigrants.

Source: Engerman and Sokoloff (2001); Engerman, Haber, and Sokoloff (2000).

removed in the United States at the expense of the southern black population in the 1890s) much earlier, but in terms of the proportions of the population voting, they were at least half a century ahead of even the most democratic countries of South America, namely, Argentina, Costa Rica, and Uruguay, which have generally been regarded as among the most egalitarian of Latin American societies and whose initial factor endowments most closely resembled those of Canada and the United States.

The contrast across the societies of the Americas was not as evident at the outset. In the late 18th century, restrictions based on wealth or other economic criteria were essentially universal. Despite the sentiments popularly attributed to the Founding Fathers, until the early 19th century, voting in the United States, for example, was largely a privilege reserved for white men with significant amounts of property. By 1815, only four states had adopted universal white male suffrage, but as the movement to do away with political inequality gained strength, they were joined by the rest of the country as virtually all new entrants to the Union extended voting rights to all white men (with explicit racial restrictions generally introduced in the same state constitutions that did away with economic requirements), while older states engaged in protracted political debates, but ultimately revised their laws as well (table 3). The key states of New York and Massachusetts made the break with wealth restrictions during the 1820s, and the shift to full white, male suffrage was largely complete by the late 1850s, with Rhode Island, Virginia, and North Carolina being the laggards. The relatively more egalitarian and labor-scarce states on the western frontier were the clear leaders in the movement, with their rapid extension of access to the franchise paralleling their liberal policies toward public schools and access to land and other policies that they expected would be attractive to potential migrants.

Similar political movements with comparable outcomes followed with only a short lag in the various Canadian provinces, but analogous developments were not to occur in Latin America until the 20th century. Despite brief episodes in a number of countries where suffrage was extended, such efforts invariably failed and the liberal measures were retracted or compromised.[1] Argentina, for example, had largely done away with restrictions that determined which men could qualify as citizens and vote by the second half of the 19th century, but oral voting and limits on the number of polling places helped elites maintain effective political control. As a result, through 1940 Canada and the United States routinely had proportions of the population voting that were 50 to 100 percent higher than those of their most progressive neighbors to the south, including 3 times higher than in Mexico and 5 to 10 times higher than in countries such as Bolivia, Brazil, Ecuador, and even Chile. Remarkably, as late as the beginning of the 20th century, none of the countries in Latin America had the secret ballot, and only Argentina had done away with wealth and literacy requirements for adult male suffrage. Although many factors may have contributed to the relatively low vote totals in the Caribbean and South America, wealth and literacy requirements were serious binding constraints well into the 20th century. Although some societies, such as Barbados, maintained suffrage restrictions based on wealth until the middle of the 20th century, most joined Canada and the United States in moving away from economic requirements during the 19th century. However, whereas the U.S. states

TABLE 3. Summary of Economic-Based Qualifications for Suffrage

State	Qualification in 1787 or year of entry	Year economic qualifications ended or qualifications in 1860
Original thirteen states		
New Hampshire	Tax	1792
Massachusetts	Property	1821 (property), tax requirement in 1860[a]
Rhode Island	Property	1842 (property), tax requirement in 1860[a]
Connecticut	Property	1818 (property), 1845 (tax)
New York	Property	1821 (property), 1826 (tax)
New Jersey	Property	1807 (property), 1844 (tax)
Pennsylvania	Tax	tax requirement in 1860
Delaware	Property	1792 (property), tax requirement in 1860[a]
Maryland	Property	1802
Virginia	Property	1850
North Carolina	Property	1856 (property), tax requirement in 1860[a]
South Carolina	Tax	1810 (tax)
Georgia	Property	1789 (property), 1798 (tax)
New states		
Vermont	None (1791)	
Kentucky	None (1792)	
Tennessee	None (1796)	
Ohio	Tax (1803)	1851 (tax)
Louisiana	Tax (1812)	1845 (tax)
Indiana	None (1816)	
Mississippi	Tax (1817)	1832 (tax)
Illinois	None (1818)	
Maine	None (1819)	
Alabama	None (1819)	
Missouri	None (1820)	

a. Tax requirement in 1860 means that a tax-based qualification for suffrage was still in effect that year.

Source: Engerman and Sokoloff (2001).

frequently adopted explicit racial limitations when they abandoned economic requirements, Latin American countries typically chose to screen by literacy.[2]

A fundamental question about the pattern of diffusion of universal male suffrage across New World economies is whether differences in the degrees of initial inequality in wealth, human capital, and political influence were related to the timing or likelihood of extending access to political influence in this way. More work needs to be done, but the cross-sectional patterns and the countries' histories, which indicate that the attainment of universal male suffrage and of the secret ballot were often the products of a long series of hard fought political battles, with the elites more likely to be opposed to liberalizing the franchise, are certainly consistent with this view. Another factor that may have been important, and not unrelated to inequality, was the desire to attract immigrants. A striking observation is that pioneers in extending suffrage, such as new U.S. states, Argentina, and Uruguay, were areas of labor scarcity and took steps during periods when they wanted to attract migrants. At the same time they extended suffrage they typically offered other inducements as well, such as easy terms for acquiring ownership of land or commitments to invest in providing such public goods as schools and infrastructure. This pattern shows that where elites, such as holders of land or other assets, want immigrants to locate in their polity, they may choose to extend access to privileges and opportunities even without effective political pressure from below or the threat of civil disorder. Indeed, a polity (or one set of elites) may find itself competing with another to attract labor or whatever else is desired.

Schooling Institutions and Literacy

Another fundamental question is whether differences in the distribution of political power had any feedback effects on the distribution of access to economic opportunities and on the prospects for economic growth through the impact of political power on the way institutions evolve. Schooling institutions seem appropriate for studying this issue, as increases in a society's levels of schooling and literacy have been related theoretically, as well as empirically, to many socioeconomic changes conducive to growth, including higher labor productivity, more rapid technological change, and higher rates of commercial and political participation. Moreover, in addition to promoting growth, they also have a major influence on the distribution of the benefits of growth.

Even though many New World societies arising out of European colonization were so prosperous that they clearly had the material resources to support the establishment of a widespread network of primary schools, before the 20th century only a relatively small number made such investments on a scale sufficient to serve the general population. The exceptional societies, in terms of leadership in investing in institutions of primary education, were again Canada and the United States (for a more comprehensive discussion of the evolution of schooling institutions in the Americas, see Engerman, Mariscal, and Sokoloff 2002). Virtually from the time of settlement, these North Americans seem generally to have been convinced of the value of providing their children with a basic education, including the ability to read and write. Especially in New England, schools were commonly organized and funded at the village or town level. By the beginning of the 19th century, the United States probably had the most literate population in the world, but the common school movement, which got under way in the 1820s (following closely after the movement for extending the franchise), put the country on an accelerated path of investment in education institutions. Between 1825 and 1850, nearly every northern state that had not already done so enacted a law strongly encouraging or requiring localities to establish free schools open to all children and supported by general taxes (Cubberley 1920). Although the movement made slower progress in the South, schooling had spread sufficiently by the middle of the 19th century such that more than 40 percent of the school-age population was enrolled and nearly 90 percent of white adults were literate (table 4). Schools were also widespread in early 19th century Canada, and even though this northern-most English colony lagged the United States by several decades in establishing tax-supported schools with universal access, its literacy rates were nearly as high.

TABLE 4. Literacy Rates in the Americas, Selected Years, 1850–1950

Country	Year	Age	Literacy rate (%)
Argentina	1869	+6	23.8
	1895	+6	45.6
	1900	+10	52.0
	1925	+10	73.0
Barbados	1946	+10	92.7
Bolivia	1900	+10	17.0
Brazil	1872	+7	15.8
	1890	+7	14.8
	1900	+7	25.6
	1920	+10	30.0
	1939	+10	57.0
British Honduras	1911	+10	59.6
(Belize)	1931	+10	71.8
Chile	1865	+7	18.0
	1875	+7	25.7
	1885	+7	30.3
	1900	+10	43.0
	1925	+10	66.0
	1945	+10	76.0
Colombia	1918	+15	32.0
	1938	+15	56.0
	1951	+15	62.0
Costa Rica	1892	+7	23.6
	1900	+10	33.0
	1925	+10	64.0
Cuba	1861	+7	23.8
			(38.5, 5.3)[a]
	1899	+10	40.5
	1925	+10	67.0
	1946	+10	77.9
Guatemala	1893	+7	11.3
	1925	+10	15.0
	1945	+10	20.0
Honduras	1887	+7	15.2
	1925	+10	29.0
Jamaica	1871	+5	16.3
	1891	+5	32.0
	1911	+5	47.2
	1943	+5	67.9
	1943	+10	76.1
Mexico	1900	+10	22.2
	1925	+10	36.0
	1946	+10	48.4

(Continues on next page)

Country	Year	Age	Literacy rate (%)
Paraguay	1886	+7	19.3
	1900	+10	30.0
Peru	1925	+10	38.0
Puerto Rico	1860	+7	11.8
			(19.8, 3.1)[a]
Uruguay	1900	+10	54.0
	1925	+10	70.0
Venezuela	1925	+10	34.0
Canada	1861	All	82.5
English-majority counties	1861	All	93.0
French-majority counties	1861	All	81.2
United States			
North, whites	1860	+10	96.9
South, whites	1860	+10	91.5
All	1870	+10	80.0
			(88.5, 21.1)[a]
	1890	+10	86.7
			(92.3, 43.2)[a]
	1910	+10	92.3
			(95.0, 69.5)[a]

a. The figures in parentheses are those for whites and non-whites, respectively.

Source: Engerman, Mariscal, and Sokoloff (2002).

The rest of the hemisphere trailed far behind Canada and the United States in providing primary schooling and attaining literacy. Despite enormous wealth, the British West Indian colonies were slow to organize schooling institutions that would serve broad segments of the population. Indeed, significant steps were not taken in this direction until the British Colonial Office began promoting schooling during the 1870s. Similarly, even the most progressive Latin American countries (as with suffrage, Argentina, Costa Rica, and Uruguay) were more than 75 years behind Canada and the United States. Major investments in primary schooling were not widespread in any Latin American country, with the possible exception of Costa Rica, until national governments provided the funds. In contrast to the pattern in North America, local and state governments in Latin America were generally not willing or able to take on this responsibility on their own. The exceptions were most often large cities, where the presence of significant middle-class populations likely altered political debates about public schools, as well as provinces undergoing resource-based booms. This pattern may have been due to resistance of local elites to property taxes, which were the major revenue source for local governments in Canada and the United States, and probably the most straightforward tax for a local government to levy in the absence of a resource such as gold, guano, or phosphates to tax. National governments typically relied more on trade taxes, which had quite different distributional implications. However, relatively generous support was always available for universities and other institutions of higher learning that were more oriented toward the children of the elite.

Argentina and Uruguay were the clear leaders among the subset of Latin American countries in realizing substantial increases in literacy that paralleled major extensions of public schooling during the late 1800s, with more than half their populations aged 10 and older being literate by 1900. Chile and Cuba trailed somewhat behind, with roughly 40 percent literacy, and Costa Rica was still further behind at 33 percent. These five countries, which varied considerably in many important respects, had attained literacy rates greater than 66 percent by 1925. In contrast, a broad range of other Latin American countries, including Bolivia, Brazil, Colombia, Guatemala, Honduras, Mexico, Peru, and Venezuela, were unable to move much beyond 30 percent literacy until after 1925. Note that the association between initial inequality and the timing of the decision to invest in an extensive system of public schools holds across Latin America, and not just across a comparison of North and South American nations.

Although differences in per capita income and in the support for and timing of efforts to attract and assimilate immigrants from Europe play important roles in this pattern of differential investments in primary education, a detailed examination of specific cases and pooled multivariate regressions indicate that differences in the degree of inequality or population heterogeneity also account for the differences (Engerman, Mariscal, and Sokoloff 2002). Several mechanisms could help explain why extreme levels of inequality depressed investments in schooling. First, in settings where private schooling predominated or where parents paid user fees for their children to attend school, greater wealth or income inequality would generally reduce the fraction of the school-age population enrolled, holding per capita income constant. Second, greater inequality probably exacerbated the collective action problems associated with the establishment and funding of universal public schools, because the distribution of benefits across the population was quite different from the incidence of taxes and other costs, or simply because population heterogeneity made reaching consensus on public projects more difficult for communities. Where the wealthy enjoyed disproportionate political power, elites were able to procure schooling services for their own children and to resist being taxed to subsidize services to others. This, as well as the differences in income levels across geographic districts within countries, may account for the substantial disparities in schooling and literacy between urban and rural areas in virtually all the New World societies except Canada and the United States.

Public Land Policies

Another prime example of how institutions were shaped in ways that contributed to the persistence of inequality over the long run is public land policy. Virtually all economies of the Americas had ample supplies of public lands well into the 19th century and beyond; and because the respective governments of each colony, province, or nation were regarded as the owners of this resource, they set those policies that would influence the distribution of wealth, as well as the pace of settlement for effective production, by controlling its availability, setting prices, establishing minimum or maximum acreages, granting credit, and designing tax systems. With agriculture being the dominant sector throughout the Americas, questions of how best to employ this public resource for the national interest and how to make land available for private use were widely recognized as extremely important. Land policy could, and was, also used to influence the labor force, either by encouraging immigration by making land more available or by increasing the pool of wage labor by limiting access and raising land prices.

In the United States, which never had major obstacles to land ownership (despite some contentious debates), the terms of land acquisition became easier over the course of 19th century (Gates 1968). The well-known Homestead Act of 1862, which essentially made land available for free in plots suitable for family farms to all those who settled and worked the land for a specified period, was perhaps the culmination of this policy of promoting broad access to land. Canada pursued similar policies, and the Dominion Lands Act of 1872 closely resembled the Homestead Act in both spirit and substance. Both Argentina and Brazil sought similar changes during the second half of the 19th century as a way to encourage immigration, but they were much less successful than in Canada and the United States in getting land to smallholders. Taking Argentina as an example, a number of factors may help to explain the contrast in outcomes (Adelman 1994; Castro 1971). First, policies that granted large concessions to land developers and that turned over public lands to "occupants" who were already using the land, including those who used it for grazing livestock, served to convey public lands to private owners in much larger and concentrated holdings than did Canadian or U.S. policies. Second, once the land was in private hands, the potential value of land in grazing may have set too high a floor for land prices for immigrants to be able to afford land, especially given the underdevelopment of mortgage and financial institutions.

Argentina, Canada, and the United States are examples of countries that had an extraordinary abundance of sparsely populated public lands to transfer to private hands so as to best bring this public resource into production, while perhaps serving other general interests at the same time. In societies such as Mexico, however, the issues at stake in land policy were completely different. Here good land was relatively scarce and labor was relatively abundant. The public lands in question were primarily lands that had traditionally been controlled by villages of Native Americans, but without individual private property rights. Mexico was far from unique in pursuing policies over time, and especially during the final decades of the 19th century and the first decade of the 20th, that had the effect of transferring much of this land to large non–Native American landholders (McBride 1923; Tannebaum 1929). In Mexico, the 1856 Lerdo Law and the 1857 Constitution had set down methods for privatizing these public lands in a manner that was clearly originally intended to help Native American farmers enter a national land market and commercial economy. These laws became the basis, however, for a series of new statutes and policies that between 1878 and 1908 effected a massive transfer of such lands (more than 10.7 percent of the

TABLE 5. Landholding in Rural Regions of Argentina, Mexico, Canada, and the United States, Early 1900s

Country, year, and region	Proportion of household heads who owned land[a]
Argentina, 1895	
Chaco	27.8
Formosa	18.5
Missiones	26.7
La Pampa	9.7
Neuquén	12.3
Río Negro	15.4
Chubut	35.2
Santa Cruz	20.2
Tierra del Fuego	6.6
Mexico, 1910	
North Pacific	5.6
North	3.4
Central	2.0
Gulf	2.1
South Pacific	1.5
Total rural Mexico	2.4
Canada, 1901	
British Columbia	87.1
Alberta	95.8
Saskatchewan	96.2
Manitoba	88.9
Ontario	80.2
Quebec	90.1
Maritime[b]	95.0
Total Canada	87.1
United States, 1900	
North Atlantic	79.2
South Atlantic	55.8
North Central	72.1
South Central	51.4
Western	83.4
Alaska/Hawaii	42.1
Total United States	74.5

a. Landownership is defined as follows: in Argentina, the ratio of landowners to the number of men between the ages of 18 and 50; in Mexico, household heads who own land; in Canada, total occupiers of farm lands who are owners; and in the United States, farms that are owner operated.

b. The Maritime region includes Nova Scotia, New Brunswick, and Prince Edward Island.

Source: Engerman and Sokoloff (2002).

national territory) to large landowners such as survey companies, either in the form of outright grants for services rendered by the companies or for prices set by decree.

We are currently constructing estimates of the fractions of household heads, or the nearest equivalents, in agricultural areas who owned land in a number of economies of the Americas during the late 19th and early 20th centuries. The proportion that owned land is far from an ideal measure of the extent of inequality and it will be sensitive to the mix of products produced in the respective areas. Nevertheless, the number does provide useful insight into the impact or effectiveness of the land policies pursued, and a set of estimates that are comparable across a broad range of economies can be assembled. Table 5 presents the figures for Argentina, Canada, Mexico, and the United States, and they reveal enormous differences in the prevalence of land ownership among the adult male population in rural areas. On the eve of the Mexican Revolution, the figures from the 1910 census suggest that only 2.4 percent of household heads in rural Mexico owned land. This number is astoundingly low, but confidence in the basic qualitative result of extreme inequality comes not only from this low figure, but also from the observation that it varied across states in the way one would expect, that is, inversely with the proportion of the population that were Native American. The dramatic land policy measures in Mexico at the end of the 19th century may have succeeded in privatizing most public lands, but appear to have left most of the population without any land at all.

The proportion of adult males in rural areas who owned land was much higher in the United States, ranging between 70 and 75 percent during 1880–1900. Even though the prevalence of land ownership was markedly lower in the South, where blacks were disproportionately concentrated, the overall picture was one of land policies providing broad access to this fundamental type of economic opportunity. Canada has an even better record, with nearly 90 percent of household heads owning land in virtually all provinces during 1881–1911. For now, the estimates for Argentina pertain only to a number of frontier provinces, but the figures suggest a much more limited prevalence of land ownership in that country in 1895 compared with Canada and the United States, but a much greater prevalence than in Mexico.

Conclusions

While more study is obviously needed, the records of how countries' policies and institutions related to suffrage, schooling, and land policy developed over time across the Americas seem consistent with the hypothesis that the initial extent of inequality in society had profound and lingering effects on how strategic economic institutions evolved over time. In countries with relative equality and population homogeneity, the institutions that evolved were more likely to provide the population with broad access to opportunities. We believe that this served both to preserve a relatively greater degree of equality in wealth, human capital, and political influence within the society in question and to promote growth by stimulating broad participation in commercial or other growth-enhancing activities, such as human capital accumulation.[3] In contrast, where inequality was high, institutions tended to evolve in such a way as to restrict access to opportunities, thereby benefiting members of the elite and preserving relative inequality. What was good for elites, however, may have reduced the countries' prospects for sustained economic growth.

Researchers have long wondered how and why Canada and the United States have followed such different paths of development than other New World economies since the era of European colonization. Virtually all the societies enjoyed high levels of product per capita early in their histories, and indeed, an overwhelming share of European migrants voted with their feet to pursue the economic opportunities in the Caribbean or South America for the first 250 years of settlement. The divergence can be traced back to the achievement of sustained economic growth by Canada and the United States during the late 18th and early 19th centuries, while the other countries did not manage to attain this goal until late in the 19th century or in the 20th century.

Although traditional explanations have generally pointed to the significance of national heritage or religion, we have highlighted the relevance of substantial differences in the degree of inequality in wealth, human capital, and political power in accounting for the contrasts in the records of development. Inspired by the observation that many former British colonies in the Americas, such as Belize, Guyana, and Jamaica, have done much less well than Canada and the United States, just as Costa Rica and the countries of the southern cone have developed along quite different paths than other parts of Spanish America, our research suggests that the roots of these disparities lay in the extreme differences in inequality that arose from variations in the initial factor endowments of the respective colonies. Of particular significance for generating extreme inequality were the countries' suitability for cultivating sugar and other highly valued commodities in which the use of slaves resulted in economies of production, as well as the presence of large concentrations of Native Americans. Both these conditions encouraged the evolution of societies where relatively small elites of European descent could hold highly disproportionate shares of the wealth, human capital, and political power and could establish economic and political dominance over the bulk of the population. The systematic differences in the sorts of laws and institutions that developed in these countries, and the common element among them of limiting access to economic opportunity, are consistent with the view that institutions have been a powerful force behind Latin America and the Caribbean basin long remaining as the part of the world with the most extreme inequality (Deininger and Squire 1996).

Notes

1. Jeremy Bentham, who devoted considerable energies to providing Latin Americans with advice about how to design their institutions in the early 19th century, was one of many who underestimated the difficulty of implanting liberal designs from England in a radically different environment (see Williford 1980).

2. Clearly the elites in nearly all the countries were intent on excluding groups that stood out as being different. In the United States they did so primarily through racial restrictions

until constitutional amendments after the Civil War put an end to the practice. In Latin America they used restrictions based on literacy, perhaps because racial distinctions were not as easily drawn. This may have had the unfortunate effect of further eroding support for public schools among the elite.

3. Early industrialization in the United States was characterized by broad participation in the commercial economy and responsiveness to economic opportunities throughout the population (see Khan and Sokoloff 1993; Sokoloff 1988; Sokoloff and Khan 1990).

References

Acemoglu, Daron, Simon Johnson, and James A. Robinson. 2001. "The Colonial Origins of Comparative Development: An Empirical Investigation." *American Economic Review* 91(December): 1369–1401.

———. 2002. "Reversal of Fortune: Geography and Institutions in the Making of the Modern World Income Distribution." *Quarterly Journal of Economics* 117(November): 1231–94.

Adelman, Jeremy. 1994. *Frontier Development: Land, Labour, and Capital on the Wheatlands of Argentina and Canada, 1890–1914.* Oxford, U.K.: Oxford University Press.

Castro, Donald. 1971. *The Development of Argentine Immigration Policy, 1852–1914.* Ann Arbor, Mich.: University of Michigan Press.

Coatsworth, John H. 1998. "Economic and Institutional Trajectories in Nineteenth-Century Latin America." In John H. Coatsworth and Alan M. Taylor, eds., *Latin America and the World Economy Since 1800.* Cambridge, Mass.: Harvard University Press.

Cubberley, Ellwood P. 1920. *The History of Education.* Boston: Houghton and Mifflin.

Deininger, Klaus, and Lyn Squire. 1996. "A New Data Set and Measure of Income Inequality." *World Bank Economic Review* 10(September): 565–91.

Diamond, Jared. 1997. *Guns, Germs, and Steel: The Fate of Human Societies.* New York: Norton.

Engerman, Stanley L., and Kenneth L. Sokoloff. 1997. "Factor Endowments, Institutions, and Differential Paths of Growth among New World Economies: A View from Economic Historians of the United States." In Stephen Haber, ed., *How Latin America Fell Behind.* Stanford, Calif.: Stanford University Press.

———. 2001. "The Evolution of Suffrage Institutions in the New World." Working Paper no. 8512. National Bureau of Economic Research, Cambridge, Mass.

———. 2002. "Factor Endowments, Inequality, and Paths of Development among New World Economics." *Economia* 3(Fall): 41–109.

Engerman, Stanley L., Stephen Haber, and Kenneth L. Sokoloff. 2000. "Inequality, Institutions, and Differential Paths of Growth among New World Economies." In Claude Menard, ed., *Institutions, Contracts, and Organizations.* Cheltenham, U.K.: Edward Elgar.

Engerman, Stanley L., Elisa V. Mariscal, and Kenneth L. Sokoloff. 2002. "The Evolution of Schooling Institutions in the Americas, 1800–1925." Working paper. University of California, Los Angeles.

Fogel, Robert William. 1989. *Without Consent or Contract.* New York: Norton.

Galenson, David W. 1995. "The Settlement and Growth of the Colonies: Population, Labor, and Economic Development." In S. L. Engerman and R. E. Gallman, eds., *The Cambridge Economic History of the United States,* vol. I, *The Colonial Period.* Cambridge, U.K.: Cambridge University Press.

Gates, Paul W. 1968. *History of Public Land Law Development*. Washington, D.C.: Government Printing Office.

Greene, Jack P. 1988. *Pursuits of Happiness*. Chapel Hill, N.C.: University of North Carolina Press.

Hall, Robert, and Charles Jones. 1999. "Why Do Some Countries Produce So Much More Output Than Others." *Quarterly Journal of Economics* 114(February): 83–116.

Khan, B. Zorina, and Kenneth L. Sokoloff. 1993. "Schemes of Practical Utility: Entrepreneurship and Innovation among 'Great Inventors' in the United States, 1790–1865." *Journal of Economic History* 53(June): 289–307.

Lockhart, James, and Stuart B. Schwartz. 1983. *Early Latin America: A History of Colonial Spanish America and Brazil*. Cambridge, U.K.: Cambridge University Press.

McBride, George McCutchen. 1923. *The Land Systems of Mexico*. New York: American Geographical Society.

North, Douglass C. 1981. *Structure and Change in Economic History*. New York: Norton.

———. 1988. "Institutions, Economic Growth, and Freedom: A Historical Introduction." In Michael A. Walker, ed., *Freedom, Democracy, and Economic Welfare*. Vancouver: Fraser Institute.

Sachs, Jeffrey, and Andrew Warner. 1997. "Fundamental Sources of Long-Run Growth." *American Economic Review* 87(May): 184–88.

Sokoloff, Kenneth L. 1988. "Inventive Activity in Early Industrial America: Evidence from Patent Records, 1790–1846." *Journal of Economic History* 48(December): 813–50.

Sokoloff, Kenneth L., and B. Zorina Khan. 1990. "The Democratization of Invention during Early Industrialization: Evidence from the United States, 1790–1846." *Journal of Economic History* 50(June): 363–78.

Tannebaum, Frank. 1929. *The Mexican Agrarian Revolution*. New York: Macmillan.

Williford, Miriam. 1980. *Jeremy Bentham on Spanish America: An Account of His Letters and Proposals to the New World*. Baton Rouge, La.: Louisiana State University Press.

The Transition Process in Postcommunist Societies: Toward a Political Economy of Property Rights

KARLA HOFF AND JOSEPH E. STIGLITZ

Economists have long recognized that institutions shape incentives and therefore have an enormous influence on economic growth, but economists have only recently been concerned with understanding the forces that may hinder the emergence of efficient institutions. Because of a lack of secure property rights—the rule of law—many countries remain poor. This paper addresses one issue pertinent to institutional change: the obstacles to the demand for the rule of law in the transition economies.[1]

After the collapse of communism and the mass privatization in 1992–94 of state assets in Russia (the so-called big bang), the market in Russia could fairly be characterized as a " 'wild' market outside the law" (Rose 1993, p. 430). Many argued that out of this wild market, a political constituency for the rule of law would emerge (for example, Boycko, Shleifer, and Vishny 1995), that is, those to whom state assets had been transferred would become that political constituency. Mass privatization would initiate a demand-driven evolution of institutions toward the rule of law.

This did not happen. Despite the eventual passage of a blizzard of laws, most observers agree that a strong constituency for their enforcement, or for the rule of law, has not yet emerged in Russia and many other transition economies (see, for example, Black, Kraakman, and Tarassova 2000; Gray and Hendley 1997; Pistor 1999). In Russia, the last 10 years have witnessed not the hoped-for burst of entrepreneurship, but a massive stripping of assets. Russia has become a net capital exporter. Capital flight from Russia averaged, depending on the measure used, more than US$15 billion to US$20 billion per year during 1995–2001, or 5 percent of gross domestic product (Loungani and Mauro 2001; Reuters February 20, 2002).

What explains the gap between what emerged in the 1990s and what the reformers hoped would emerge? In earlier work (Hoff and Stiglitz 2003, forthcoming), we provided an explanation based on simple models in which individuals make both

Karla Hoff is a senior research economist at the World Bank in Washington, D.C. Joseph Stiglitz is professor of economics at Columbia University in New York. This paper is a revised version of the paper presented at the conference.

Annual World Bank Conference on Development Economics—Europe 2003
© 2004 The International Bank for Reconstruction and Development/The World Bank

economic choices (to build value or strip assets) and political choices (for example, by voting over policies that would establish the rule of law). Individuals' choices are interdependent, and therefore considering the circumstances in which the equilibrium does or does not lead to the establishment of the rule of law is appropriate. This paper provides a diagrammatic exposition of a simple model to highlight the reasons why the self-interested demands of each person may not lead to a strong demand for a broadly beneficial legal regime.

Traditionally, questions about the emergence of property rights institutions were viewed as prior to, and thus outside, the domain of economics. Neoclassical economics assumed that the rule of law prevailed and "gained the title of queen of the social sciences by choosing *solved* political problems" (Lerner 1972, p. 259).[2] When neoclassical economists, for example, Demsetz (1967), North and Thomas (1970), and Barzel (1989), began to study the formation of property rights, they adopted a functionalist position. In this view, the choice of institutions is dictated by efficiency considerations. In Barzel (1989, pp. 65, 74), the implicit assumption was that property rights could be treated like a private consumption good:

> [By taking] actions directly in the private sector and indirectly, through the state, in the public sector . . . individuals are able to control and to affect the delineation of their rights over "their" property. Individuals will exercise such control as part of their maximizing process. Whenever individuals find the existing level of delineation to be unsatisfactory, they will alter it until they are satisfied.

However, this statement is true only if the private and social benefits of an individual's actions to influence property rights institutions are the same. In general, they are not the same. An obvious reason is that property rights institutions can reinforce inequalities in power; political insiders may be able to establish a legal regime that privileges their own interests. In this paper, we abstract from this problem. We analyze the interdependence between economic and political choices under conditions that we would interpret as highly favorable to the emergence of the rule of law: individuals are too weak individually to obtain privileged property rights protection from the state, but are strong enough collectively to secure the rule of law.

The problem on which we focus is unintended spillovers from individual actions.[3] In the past, economists believed that the implication of spillovers (externalities) was that the economy would be slightly distorted, but we now understand that the interaction of these slightly distorted behaviors may produce extremely large distortions.[4] This paper focuses on externalities mediated by the political environment. As a result of these spillovers, the political positions of a set of mutually interacting individuals can be quite different from what one would have predicted by looking at the preferences of each individual in isolation. In the model, individuals are rational, risk neutral, and forward looking, but in some political environments individuals will correctly believe that the rule of law will not be, or is unlikely to be, established. Given that belief, many individuals with control rights over assets will choose to strip assets. In turn, stripping gives some of these individuals an interest in prolonging the absence of the rule of law so that they can enjoy the fruits of stripping without the constraint of government enforcement of property rights. The interaction between individuals' choices about whether to build value or strip assets, on the one hand, and individuals' political demands, on the other, can lead to an equilibrium in which the demand for the rule of law is weak. Each individual, in attempting to influence society's choice of the environment, focuses on the impact on himself, not the impact on others. He takes the political positions of others as given, independent of his own vote. The political environment, in that sense, is a public good (or public bad).

In our analysis, we try to parse out the role of various market failures. We show that how agents vote influences others' economic actions (a spillover effect) and how each individual acts in the economic sphere influences how he votes (an intertemporal incentive effect). The first section presents a model in the standard form of a coordination game. The second section explains why the implications of that model extend to a dynamic setting with forward-looking individuals. The third section argues that because individuals' economic and political choices are interdependent, demand for and opposition to the rule of law cannot be separated from macroeconomic policy. A too stringent macroeconomic policy can lower the returns to building value relative to stripping assets and thereby weaken the equilibrium demand for the rule of law. The model suggests why a narrow focus on stabilization policy can lead to policy errors.

A Static Model of the Demand for the Rule of Law

The agents in the model are individuals who have control rights over assets. (This was the hoped-for natural constituency for the rule of law.) We consider the case where many such individuals exist and where each is small in the sense that no single individual can dictate the legal regime. Instead, the legal regime that is established reflects the demands of the group, for example, by majority voting.

We assume that the establishment of the rule of law raises the return to building value for every agent. This assumption captures the idea that to build value, individuals must interact with others in the economy. They benefit from the rule of law because it enforces property rights and contracts and expands their access to markets. Without the rule of law, they risk not even being able to capture the return on their investments. As an alternative to building value, individuals can strip the assets they control by whisking capital to a safe place, tunneling value out through self-dealing at the expense of minority shareholders who do not have control rights over assets, and letting the capital stock wear out.[5] Russia implemented mass privatization on the basis of a government decree that stipulated only the most basic shareholders' rights and rules of corporate governance. This left ample scope for those with control rights over firms to tunnel value out at the expense of other shareholders and to harvest public resources. Privatization expanded the ability of firm managers to do that, because it granted them greater independence from the state.

We assume that individuals differ in their ability to strip assets. In the real world, many factors would give rise to such differences. The ability to strip is larger the greater (a) the equity of minority shareholders, (b) the firm's debt, and (c) the ability

FIGURE 1. Distribution of Payoffs to Asset Stripping

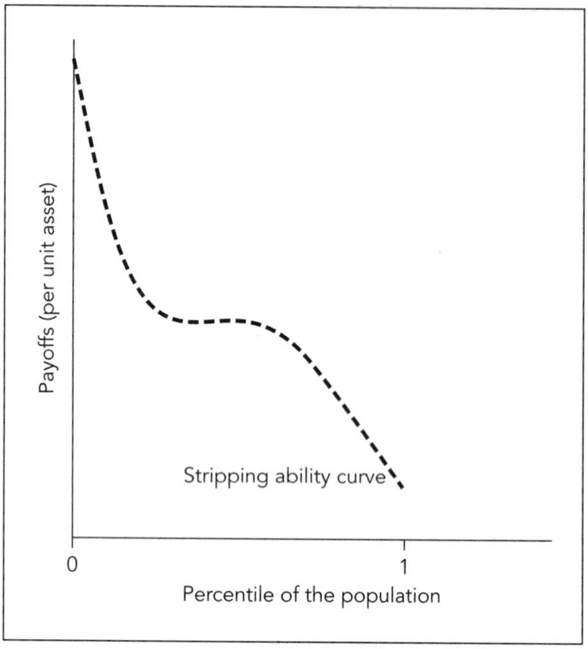

Source: Authors.

to harvest commodities that require little or no processing and that can be sold on thick international markets where they are hard to trace (for an earlier paper that emphasized this factor, see Stephan 1996). If the ability to strip assets is normally distributed, then the distribution of stripping returns will have the shape depicted in figure 1.

The horizontal axis in the figure plots the percentile of the population and the vertical axis plots the payoff to stripping (per unit asset) for each percentile, beginning with the top percentile. The figure depicts the case where a few individuals have a great ability to strip assets, a few individuals have a small ability to strip assets, and most individuals have a moderate ability to do so. (That shape, however, is not necessary for our results).

Figure 2 adds two horizontal lines to figure 1 to represent the returns to building value under the rule of law, denoted by v^L, and under no rule of law, denoted by v^N. We assume, as depicted in the figure, that most individuals are better off building value than stripping assets if the rule of law is established, but worse off otherwise. This is a central aspect of the situation that interests us: the relative ranking of an individual's alternatives may depend on the political environment.

Those who build value make up the constituency for the rule of law. They demand reform—the rule of law—because it is the only legal regime that allows them to earn a high return on investment. In contrast, asset-strippers, who follow a strategy of "take the money and run" and can illegitimately profit from their control rights, do

FIGURE 2. Dependence on the Legal Regime of Payoffs to Building Value

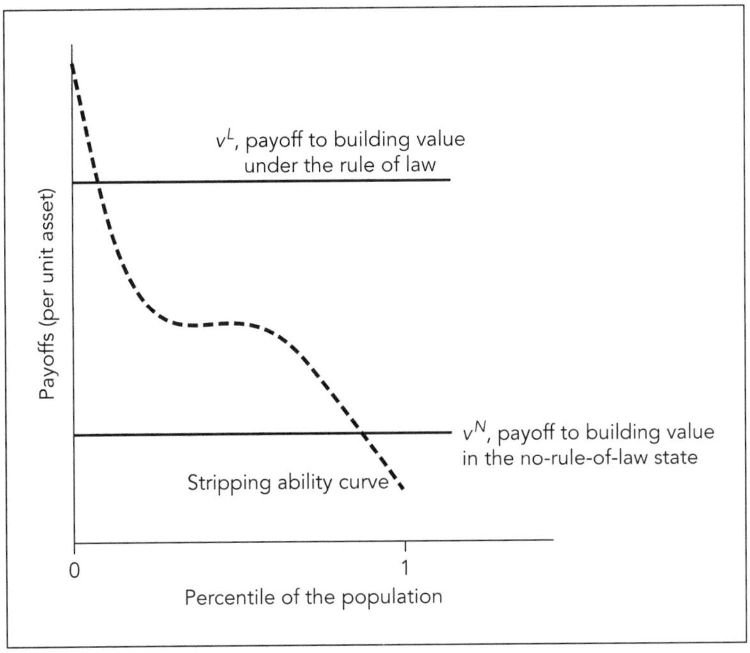

Source: Authors.

not gain from the rule of law. The economic strategy of an individual therefore determines his political position.[6]

In a slightly more general model, presented formally in Hoff and Stiglitz (forthcoming), the establishment of the rule of law would hurt asset-strippers by constraining their ability to strip assets. By abstracting from this effect here, we leave out an influence on behavior that will be important in our dynamic model, which we discuss later, while we gain a simpler way to exposit the coordination game diagrammatically, with one curve representing the payoff to the marginal asset-stripper and the other representing the expected payoff to building value.

Let x denote the fraction of individuals who do not support the rule of law; thus $1 - x$ denotes the constituency for the rule of law. We capture the idea that government is responsive to political interests by assuming that the probability, π, of the establishment of the rule of law is a decreasing function of x. Associated with any value of x, there is thus an expected payoff to building value, denoted by $\bar{v}(x)$, where

$$\bar{v}(x) = \pi(x)v^L + [1 - \pi(x)]v^N.$$

Each individual is assumed to know not how any other single individual votes, but rather to have beliefs about those votes that, in the equilibrium explored here, are fulfilled.

Figure 3 depicts a typical expected payoff function. As the political environment becomes less favorable to the establishment of the rule of law, the expected payoff to

FIGURE 3. The Expected Payoff to Building Value

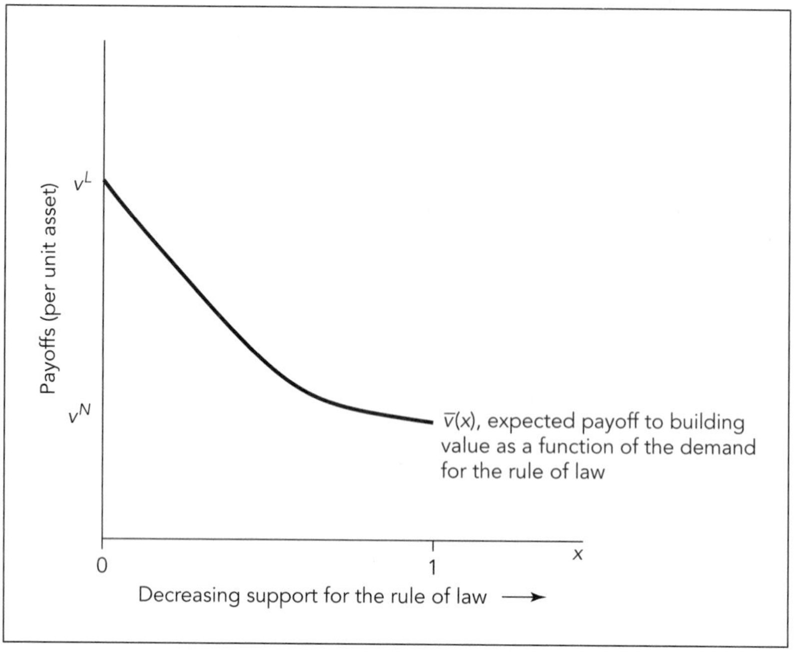

Source: Authors.

building value decreases. The curve in figure 3 indicates all the possible values of the expected payoff to building value ($\bar{v}$) as x varies from 0 to 1 (and the constituency for the rule of law varies from 1 to 0). The equilibrium is now easy to describe: it is a fraction of individuals, x^*, whose return to stripping exceeds the expected payoff to building value, $\bar{v}$, evaluated at x^*.

An interior equilibrium (where x lies between 0 and 1) occurs at any point where the expected payoff to building value equals the payoff to stripping assets for the marginal asset-stripper. Hence an interior equilibrium is any point where the curve $\bar{v}(x)$ intersects the stripping ability curve.

Figures 4–6 illustrate the possibilities. The figures capture both relationships described earlier: the fact that the expected return to building value depends on the constituency for the rule of law and the fact that individuals differ in their ability to strip.

The figures depict three cases. Figure 4 depicts the case where the expected return—the curve $\bar{v}(x)$—cuts the stripping ability curve in three places. All agents except a fraction x_0 are strictly better off building value under the rule of law than stripping assets under no rule of law. However, the constituency for the rule of law has three equilibrium values. The "good equilibrium" occurs at x_1^*, where the demand for the rule of law is strong, and the "bad equilibrium" occurs at x_3^*, where the demand for the rule of law is weak. The equilibrium at x_2^* is unstable, because at that point there are increasing relative returns to stripping assets (relative to building value). The expected return to building value falls more steeply than the stripping

FIGURE 4. Two Stable Equilibrium Levels of Demand for the Rule of Law

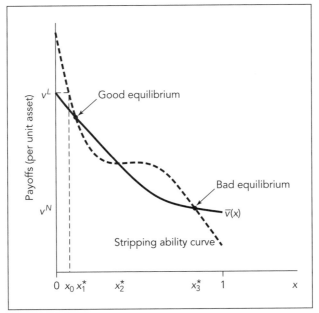

Source: Authors.

FIGURE 5. A Case Where Equilibrium Is Unique

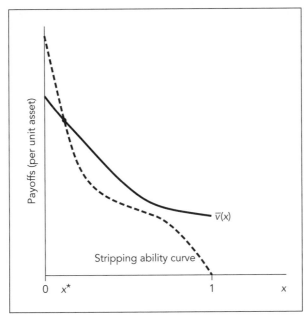

Source: Authors.

FIGURE 6. Two Stable Equilibrium Levels of Demand
for the Rule of Law under Majority Rule

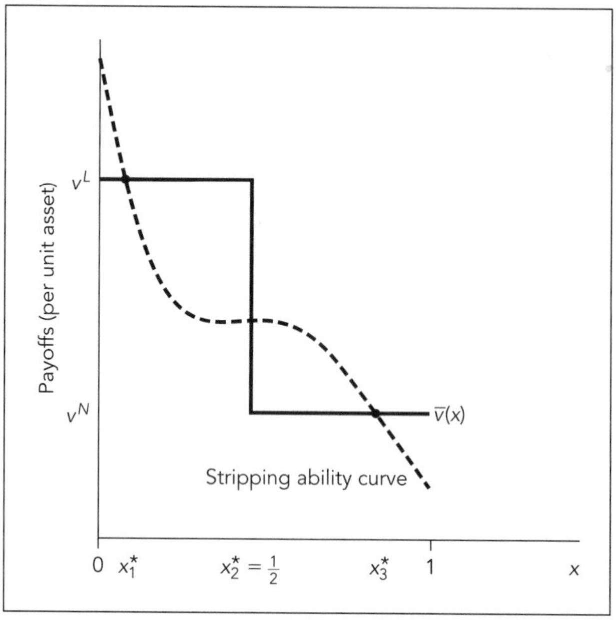

Source: Authors.

ability curve. Starting from such a point, the slightest disturbance that increases the
number of those who strip lowers the return to building value by so much that the
fraction of individuals who choose to strip increases further until it comes to rest at
x_3^*. By the same token, a slight disturbance that lowers the number of agents who
strip assets raises the return to building value by so much that the fraction of individuals who choose to strip decreases further. Thus, in practice, an unstable equilibrium would not occur.[7]

Figure 5 depicts the case where a unique equilibrium exists. There is a unique
intersection of the returns to building value and the returns to stripping assets. To the
left of the intersection, the return to stripping assets exceeds the return to building
value, hence $x = 0$ cannot be an equilibrium. To the right of the intersection, the
return to stripping assets is less than the return to building value, hence $x = 1$ cannot be an equilibrium.

Figure 6 depicts the case of majority rule, where the curve that describes the
expected return to building value is a step function. It equals v^L for $x < \frac{1}{2}$, and otherwise it equals v^N.

The simple relationships captured in the model illustrate a paradox: even if most
individuals are better off building value under the rule of law than stripping assets
under no rule of law,[8] an equilibrium can exist in which the demand for the rule of
law is weak. The paradox is due to social interactions mediated by the political environment. Society has no equivalent to the physicists' vacuum: there is always an environment in which individuals make their decisions. One of the most important
aspects of that environment is the behavior of others. When other individuals exploit

their opportunities for stripping, they will not demand the rule of law, because they do not need it and do not benefit from it. If the demand for the rule of law is weak, it is unlikely to be established. In that political environment, many individuals will have an interest in taking what they can quickly rather than waiting for the establishment of property rights protection that would permit them to build more valuable assets. Therefore many individuals will strip, which can make that set of behaviors an equilibrium.

The model sheds light on the highly charged debate in the 1990s between Russian studies scholars and the Western economists who advised the Russian government on transition policy. Russian studies scholars generally argued that the Soviet inheritance would make it extremely difficult for Russia to quickly undertake real reform. They emphasized that the former Soviet Union lacked experience with the market, responsive institutions such as distribution and marketing infrastructure, an independent judiciary, and a history of the rule of law (see, for example, Braguinsky and Yavlinsky 2000; Goldman 1994). They pointed out that during the long period of Soviet rule, a parallel, informal structure had grown up alongside the official party structure in which people engaged in illegal trade, often at the expense of the state.[9] The parallel structure survived the collapse of Soviet rule and made stripping public assets easier (Anderson 1995).

On the other side of this debate, many Western economists argued that the Soviet legacy did not matter. In their view, the rapid privatization of state enterprises both solved the problem of committing the government to the market—because a mass privatization would be difficult to reverse—and ensured a political constituency for institutions that would support the market. They argued that there was no "Soviet man," only "economic man," and given democracy and privatization, those "economic men" who benefited from privatization would create an automatic and irresistible lobbying force for the rule of law.

The model sheds light on this debate. In the model individuals are "economic men." Moreover, the model makes the seemingly favorable assumption that no individual has sufficient power to buy rules à la carte from the state or to simply impose them. Nonetheless, spillovers mediated through the political environment can block the demand for the rule of law. An individual's political position both depends on the political environment and is a constituent part of the political environment. The diffuse spillovers may mean that, in effect, no one demands what he might have been expected to want (in a setting that abstracted from those spillovers).

The Soviet legacy can have several effects in the model. First, if there are multiple equilibria, then history helps to select the equilibrium that will exist. What people see has happened in the past affects what they believe will happen in the future; expectations can be self-confirming.

Second, an aspect of the Soviet legacy was the absence of civil society institutions, such as churches, the press, and political clubs, with countervailing power to hold the state to account. In contrast, Poland, for example, had powerful social networks, including the Catholic church and the Solidarity trade union. The former Soviet Union had few institutions on which individuals could build to try to coordinate their interests in legal reform. This legacy would tend to depress the probability of the near-term establishment of the rule of law, shifting down, at any level of x, the functions $\pi(x)$, and hence $\bar{v}(x)$. The institutions inherited from the Soviet period also tend to enhance the ability to strip (shifting up the stripping ability curve). Both kinds of shifts increase the likelihood that an equilibrium exists with only a weak constituency for the rule of law.

Forward-Looking Individuals

The preceding section presented a chicken and egg problem, whereby the political environment could lead individuals to adopt certain economic strategies and, given those economic strategies, they would not support the rule of law. However, do the implications of this simple model extend to a dynamic framework? Should not forward-looking behavior affect voting, so that an individual can strip assets today and also demand the rule of law for the sake of the benefits it would provide in the future? If so, even an asset-stripper might vote for the rule of law.

To explore this argument, we have extended the model to a dynamic framework (Hoff and Stiglitz 2003). Two variables play a key role in this extension. First, a current decision to strip assets reduces the stake that an individual has in the future legal regime. Second, a current decision to strip assets reduces the individual's current return from the rule of law (relative to the absence of the rule of law) if the establishment of the rule of law at the end of any period constrains his ability to strip during that period. The basis for the rule of law cannot be only power; the rules must have some legitimacy. The perceived justice of a system is important in gaining the cooperation of those involved in the process of producing the rule of law, namely, judges, regulators, jurors, potential offenders, and so on (Robinson and Darley 1995). Accordingly, state protection of past asset-strippers may be infeasible under the rule of law. Knowing this, they will be less supportive of the rule of law.

Given the link between present and future, stripping may give individuals an interest in prolonging the no rule of law state. We can therefore demonstrate that the qualitative results of the static model carry over to a dynamic framework with forward-looking, rational individuals.

The intuition for this result can be put another way. If the expected probability of transition to the rule of law is low, then the relative return to building value is low, because both current income and the expected return to increasing the asset base are reduced. Thus some individuals will rationally strip. If they strip, the asset base that will remain to invest in the future shrinks, which reduces the future benefit of the rule of law. Furthermore, the immediate establishment of the rule of law would lower asset-strippers' current income by constraining their ability to tunnel; to harvest public assets; to withhold payments on debt, taxes, and wages; and so on. Thus the immediate establishment of the rule of law imposes a cost on asset-strippers and some individuals will rationally vote to postpone the establishment of the rule of law state. This can make the no rule of law regime persist, period after period.

In choosing their economic actions, individuals ignore the effect of their economic decisions on how they themselves vote, how other people believe the system will

**FIGURE 7. Interdependence between
Economic Actions and Political Positions**

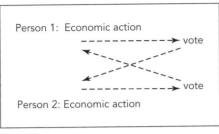

Person 1: Economic action

vote

vote

Person 2: Economic action

Source: Authors.

evolve, and thus how others invest and vote. Therefore two distortions of individual behavior are associated with the public good nature of votes.

Figure 7 illustrates this idea. Consider two individuals, person 1 and person 2. Each person's action influences his political position (an intertemporal incentive effect), as indicated by the horizontal arrows. How each person votes influences the political environment, and thus the other person's action (a spillover effect), as indicated by the diagonal arrows. In attempting to influence society's choice of legal regime, each individual focuses on the impact on himself, not on others. Economic choices that affect political outcomes beget spillovers that affect economic choices.

A deeper point is that if capital markets were perfect (with nongovernmental enforcement), then the prospect of the establishment of the rule of law in the future would make it in individuals' interests to take actions that would maximize the social value of the assets they control because they could "capture" that value. In that case, all individuals would build value and all would support the rule of law. The imperfections in capital markets cause the inefficient behaviors that, in turn, cause the opposition to the establishment of the rule of law. An economy with perfect capital markets may have been the economic model in the minds of those who implicitly made the functionalist argument for the emergence of a strong demand for the rule of law, but privatization occurred prior to the creation of effective capital markets.

Macroeconomic Policy

As noted earlier, until the recent past, questions about the emergence of property rights institutions were viewed as prior to, and thus outside the domain of, neoclassical economics. Economists still view macroeconomic policies and the emergence of property rights institutions as two separate issues. This section argues that this view is incorrect and that it can lead to policy errors. To make this argument, we present a highly stylized example.

Suppose that the establishment of the rule of law depends on a simple majority voting rule, thus $\pi = 0$ if $x > \frac{1}{2}$, and otherwise $\pi = 1$. The tipping point at which the rule of law will be established is a population fraction $x = \frac{1}{2}$.

Associated with the tipping point is a critical value of stripping ability. Let $\hat{\theta}$ denote the critical value. Half of the population has a stripping ability above the critical value and half has a stripping ability below the critical value. To make things interesting, assume that $\hat{\theta}$ is sufficiently high that if an individual of type $\hat{\theta}$ strips, then that individual will have an interest in voting against the establishment of the rule of law in the current period.

The establishment of the rule of law now depends completely on the incentives of the individual of type $\hat{\theta}$. If the individual prefers to strip rather than build value, then so will at least half the population (those with the ability to strip above $\hat{\theta}$), and the rule of law will surely not be established. The discounted sum of the individual's lifetime payoffs from stripping assets is denoted by $S^N(\hat{\theta}, r)$, where $\hat{\theta}$ denotes the individual's stripping ability and r denotes the interest rate.

If, however, the individual prefers to build value rather than strip, then again so will at least half the population (those with the ability to strip less than $\hat{\theta}$), and the rule of law will be established with certainty. Thus, as an individual of type $\hat{\theta}$ votes, so votes a majority. The discounted sum of lifetime payoffs from building value is denoted by $V^L(r)$.

The government chooses a level of public spending (G), and through monetary policy influences the level of the interest rate. Under plausible circumstances, raising r lowers the relative return to building value: at a higher value of r, the cost of capital is higher, the likelihood of credit rationing is greater, and future profits obtained from current investments are more heavily discounted. For simplicity, suppose that the level of G does not affect the relative return to stripping and to building value. In that case, the rule of law will be established if, and only if,

$$S^N(\hat{\theta}, r) \leq V^L(r).$$

Equating the two sides of this inequality defines a critical value of the interest rate, $\hat{r}$. Only if the interest rate is below the critical value will the rule of law be established. We call this the rule of law constraint.

As in standard macroeconomics, suppose that social welfare can be viewed as a function of the levels of economic growth, social expenditures, and inflation, and that these three variables in turn depend on r and G. This means that social welfare is an indirect function of these two government policies. A possible shape for iso-welfare curves is depicted in figure 8. The social optimum is depicted at point P.

This paper poses a fundamental objection to this standard approach: namely, that the structural equations relating growth, social expenditures, and inflation to the policy instruments $\{r, G\}$ depend on the institutional structure, which itself is endogenous. Macroeconomic policies and institutional evolution are not independent issues.

Suppose that social welfare under the rule of law is so much higher than under no rule of law that we need only focus on the rule of law state. However, we must then recognize that $\{r, G\}$ must be chosen so that the rule of law emerges as part of the political equilibrium. This requires $r \leq \hat{r}$. In figure 8, the iso-welfare curves are dashed in the policy region where the rule of law is unattainable, and maximum social welfare is obtained at point P', not P.

FIGURE 8. A Rule of Law Constraint on Macroeconomic Policy

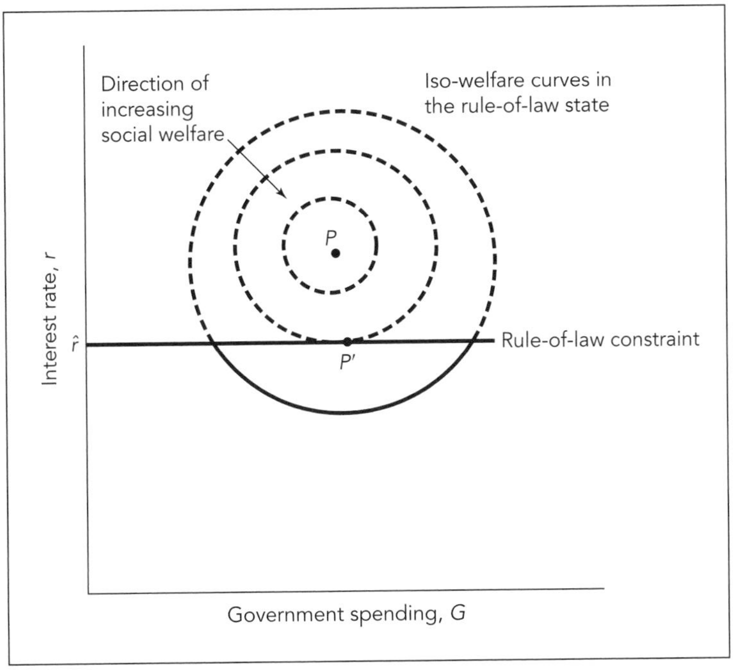

Source: Authors.

In this case, the defenders of tight monetary policies in Russia who said that the problem was not the policies, but the weak Russian institutions, are missing the mark. If our analysis is correct, the institutions themselves are affected by the macroeconomic policies and in a way that can be adverse to the creation of the rule of law.

Conclusion

We have used a simple diagrammatic approach to argue that mass privatization without institutions to limit asset stripping is a perilous path to take in building a constituency for the rule of law. The political environment created by asset-strippers can give many individuals an interest in taking what they can quickly, rather than waiting for the establishment of property rights protection that would permit them to build more valuable assets. Asset-strippers neither need nor want the rule of law, and so they will not be part of a constituency for the rule of law. The functionalist argument that if the rule of law is good for the group, then it will always be good for each individual, is wrong, because the argument abstracts from spillovers mediated by the political environment.

Notes

1. The idea developed here is briefly described in Hoff (2001). Here we provide a diagrammatic exposition. For a mathematical treatment see Hoff and Stiglitz (2003, forthcoming). Berglof and Bolton (2002) and Sonin (2003) have developed related models.

2. More formally, the traditional model assumes that only endowments, preferences, and technology determine the allocation of resources, and that economic outcomes are the same as those that would emerge as the equilibrium allocation under a competitive market system with the rule of law.

3. In this respect, this paper is related to de Meza and Gould (1992). In their work, the private and social benefits of the enforcement of private property rights differ because of spillovers mediated through the labor market, whereas in this paper, private and social benefits from the establishment of a broadly beneficial legal regime differ because of spillovers mediated through the political environment.

4. This interaction gives rise to coordination failures. See Hoff (2001) for a survey of the literature on coordination failures in economic development.

5. For a firm with multiple shareholders, the controlling shareholder might want to pursue both the value-creating and the tunneling strategies, but that would not be sustainable, because investors would ultimately refuse to do business with a firm that defrauds them.

6. This will not be true in the case of long-lived individuals. In that case, some individuals who strip assets will at the same time support the establishment of the rule of law because of the future benefits that the rule of law would provide them. In the dynamic model, an individual's economic action influences, but does not alone determine his political position.

7. The role of increasing relative returns (over some range) is a feature of all models with multiple equilibria. This idea is emphasized, for example, in the diagrammatic exposition of rent-seeking equilibria in Murphy, Shleifer, and Vishny (1993). They analyze a case of direct externalities in a setting where agents prey on productive entrepreneurs. We abstract from such externalities in order to highlight the role of spillovers mediated through the political environment.

8. This is true for all but a fraction of the individuals equal to x_0 in figure 4. The paradox can occur even if the stripping ability of every individual is less than the return to building value under the rule of law. In that case, one equilibrium will be at $x = 0$ (unanimous demand for the rule of law), but other equilibria may exist where the demand is weak. Hoff and Stiglitz (forthcoming) provide a numerical example.

9. This idea is also captured in the following humorous exchange (quoted in Kotkin 2001, p. 113):

> "I think," says Ivan to Volodya, "that we have the richest country in the world."
> "Why" asks Volodya.
> "Because for nearly 60 years everyone has been stealing from the state and still there is something left to steal."

References

The word "processed" describes informally reproduced works that may not be commonly available in libraries.

Anderson, Annelise. 1995. "The Red Mafia: A Legacy of Communism." In Edward P. Lazear, ed., *Economic Transition in Eastern Europe and Russia*. Stanford, Calif.: Hoover Institution.

Barzel, Yoram. 1989. *Economic Analysis of Property Rights*. Cambridge, U.K.: Cambridge University Press.

Berglof, Erik, and Patrick Bolton. 2002. "Law Enforcement, Fiscal Responsibility, and Economic Development." Princeton University, N.J. Processed.

Black, Bernard, Reinier Kraakman, and Anna Tarassova. 2000. "Russian Privatization and Corporate Governance: What Went Wrong?" *Stanford Law Review* 52: 1731–1801.

Boycko, Maxim, Andrei Shleifer, and Robert W. Vishny. 1995. *Privatizing Russia.* Cambridge, Mass.: MIT Press.

Braguinsky, Serguey, and Grigory Yavlinsky. 2000. *Incentives and Institutions: The Transition to a Market Economy in Russia.* Princeton, N.J.: Princeton University Press.

de Meza, David, and J. R. Gould. 1992. "The Social Efficiency of Private Decisions to Enforce Property Rights." *Journal of Political Economy* 100(3): 561–80.

Demsetz, Harold. 1967. "Toward a Theory of Property Rights." *American Economic Review* 57(2): 347–59.

Goldman, Marshall I. 1994. *Lost Opportunity: What Has Made Economic Reform in Russia so Difficult?* New York: W. W. Norton.

Gray, Cheryl, and Kathryn Hendley. 1997. "Developing Commercial Law in Transition Economies: Examples from Hungary and Russia." In Jeffrey Sachs and Katharina Pistor, eds., *The Rule of Law and Economic Reform in Russia.* Boulder, Colo., and Oxford, U.K.: HarperCollins and Westview Press.

Hoff, Karla. 2001. "Beyond Rosenstein-Rodan: The Modern Theory of Coordination Problems in Development." In *Proceedings of the Annual World Bank Conference on Development Economics 2000.* Washington, D.C.: World Bank.

Hoff, Karla, and Joseph. E. Stiglitz. 2003. "A Dynamic Model of the Demand for the Rule of Law, with Applications to Post-Communist Transition." World Bank, Washington, D.C. Processed.

———. Forthcoming. "After the Big Bang? Obstacles to the Emergence of the Rule of Law in Post-Communist Societies." *American Economic Review.*

Kotkin, Stephen. 2001. *Armageddon Averted: The Soviet Collapse 1970–2000.* Oxford, U.K.: Oxford University Press.

Lerner, Abba P. 1972. "The Economics and Politics of Consumer Sovereignty." *American Economic Review* 62(2): 258–66.

Loungani, Prakash, and Paolo Mauro. 2001. "Capital Flight from Russia." *World Economy* 24(5): 689–706.

Murphy, Kevin M., Andrei Shleifer, and Robert W. Vishny. 1993. "Why Is Rent-Seeking so Costly to Growth?" *American Economic Review* 83(May): 409–14.

North, Douglass C., and Robert Paul Thomas. 1970. "An Economic Theory of the Growth of the Western World." *Economic History Review* 23(second series): 1–17.

Pistor, Katharina. 1999. "Supply and Demand for Law in Russia." *East European Constitutional Review* 8(4): 105–08.

Robinson, Paul H., and John M. Darley. 1995. *Justice, Liability, and Blame: Community Views and the Criminal Law.* Boulder, Colo.: Westview Press.

Rose, Richard. 1993. "Contradictions between Micro- and Macroeconomic Goals in Postcommunist Societies." *Europe-Asia Studies* 45(3): 419–44.

Sonin, Konstantin. 2003 "Why the Rich May Favor Poor Protection of Property Rights." *Journal of Comparative Economics* 31(4): 715–31.

Stephan, Paul. 1996. "Toward a Positive Theory of Privatization—Lessons from Soviet-Type Economies." *International Review of Law and Economics* 16: 173–93.

Part III. Globalization

Lessons from the 1997–98 East Asian Crises

JOMO KWAME SUNDARAM

The East Asian crises of 1997–98 gave rise to two major responses from mainstream or orthodox economists. The first was an attempt to explain the unexpected events from mid-1997 in terms of several aspects of the orthodoxy, especially theories of currency crisis. Proponents of this explanation made much of current account or fiscal deficits, real as well as imagined. When this line of reasoning clearly proved to be wrong, inadequate, or unpersuasive, the second line of defense was to turn the preceding celebration of the East Asian miracle on its head by suggesting that key elements of East Asian exceptionalism, for example, government intervention and social capital, were responsible for the crises. Those promoting this explanation emphasized cronyism (government favoritism for particular business interests) and poor corporate governance—both genuine problems, but irrelevant in this context—with some grudging acknowledgment of the poor or wrong sequencing of financial liberalization, rather than the implications of liberalization itself with its open capital accounts.

Two consequences of this failure to deal with the full implications of the East Asian debacle require revisiting the crises to try to ensure that their most important lessons are not lost. Subsequent currency and financial crises elsewhere suggest that many important lessons have not been appreciated or translated into appropriate policy. First, erroneous lessons drawn by orthodox economists, financial analysts, and the media have obscured the important policy-relevant analysis that has emerged. Second, the policies and policymakers responsible for creating the conditions that culminated in the crises need to be identified. Perhaps more important, the wrong lessons have diverted attention away from the intellectual and ideological bases of the erroneous thinking, analyses, and policies responsible for the crises.

Jomo Kwame Sundaram is a professor in the Applied Economics Department of the University of Malaya. This chapter draws heavily on earlier work, especially Jomo (1998, 2001a,b).

Annual World Bank Conference on Development Economics—Europe 2003

Suggesting that such ideas are associated with the so-called Washington consensus's advocacy of economic liberalization at both the national and global levels would not be an exaggeration. Needless to say, drawing the right lessons would likely undermine the intellectual, analytical, and policy authority of the interests and institutions upholding this consensus.

This paper considers various views of the origins of the crisis and its development and spread through the region (referred to as contagion). This is then set against the larger drama of the transformation of the East Asian miracle into a debacle. All this is placed against the larger context of policy advocacy for financial liberalization, especially since the late 1980s. It focuses on the consequences of financial liberalization in the region. It also argues that the crises were of a new type and were somewhat different from earlier currency and financial crises. In particular, it emphasizes the implications of easily reversible capital flows. While much of the literature emphasizes the problems associated with foreign bank borrowing, this paper also draws attention to the dangers of portfolio capital flows. It considers whether the work of Hyman Minsky anticipated the crises and looks at the role of the International Monetary Fund (IMF) in exacerbating the crises. Finally, it suggests six urgent areas for international financial system reform from a development perspective that go beyond crisis avoidance and management.

Even though considerable work was critical of East Asia's record and potential, none actually anticipated the East Asian debacle of 1997–98 (Krugman 1994). While certain aspects of the crises were common to all four East Asian economies— Indonesia, the Republic of Korea, Malaysia, and Thailand—most adversely affected, others were unique to a particular country or common only to the more open economies of Southeast Asia, namely, Indonesia, Malaysia, and Thailand. Of course, some of the weaknesses identified in the literature did imply that the region was economically vulnerable. The dominance of manufacturing activities, especially the most technologically sophisticated and dynamic ones, by foreign transnationals subordinated domestic industrial capital in the region, allowing finance capital, both domestic and foreign, to become more influential (Jomo 1998). None of the critical writing seriously addressed the crucial implications of the greater role and fluidity of foreign capital in Southeast Asia, particularly with regard to international financial liberalization, which had become more pronounced in the 1990s.

Indeed, financial capital developed a complex symbiotic relationship with politically influential *rentiers,* now dubbed cronies, in the aftermath of 1997–98. Although threatened by the full implications of international financial liberalization, Southeast Asian financial interests were quick to identify and secure new possibilities for capturing rents from arbitrage, as well as other opportunities offered by gradual international financial integration. In these and other ways (Gomez and Jomo 1999; Khan and Jomo 2000), transnational dominance of Southeast Asian industrialization facilitated the ascendance and consolidation of financial interests and politically influential *rentiers.* This increasingly powerful alliance was primarily responsible for promoting financial liberalization in the region, both externally and internally. However, insofar as the interests of domestic financial capital did not entirely coincide with those of international finance capital, the processes of international financial liberalization were partial and uneven. The varying policy influence of domestic financial interests in different parts of the region also played a part.

History too was relevant. For example, the banking crisis in Malaysia in the late 1980s led to the introduction of a prudential regulatory framework unlike those anywhere else in the region, and caution was thrown to the winds as early external liberalization measures succeeded in securing capital inflows. Both Malaysia and Thailand wanted such flows to finance current account deficits caused primarily by service account deficits (mainly for imported financial services and investment income payments abroad) and growing imports for consumption; speculative activity in regional stock markets; and output of nontradables, mainly in the real estate sector. There is little evidence that such capital inflows contributed significantly to accelerating the pace of economic growth, especially of the tradable sectors. Instead, they probably contributed greatly to the asset price bubbles, whose inevitable deflation was accelerated by the advent of the crises, with their devastating economic, social, and political consequences.

After months of international speculative attacks on the Thai baht, the Bank of Thailand let its currency float from July 2, 1997, allowing it to drop suddenly. By mid-July 1997, the currencies of Indonesia, Malaysia, and the Philippines had also fallen precipitously after being floated, with their stock market price indexes following suit. In the following months, currencies and stock markets throughout the region came under pressure as easily reversible short-term capital inflows took flight in herd-like fashion. In November 1997, despite Korea's somewhat different economic structure, the won too had collapsed following the withdrawal of official support. Most other economies in East Asia were also under considerable pressure, either directly (for example, the attack on the Hong Kong dollar) or indirectly (for instance, because of the desire to maintain a competitive cost advantage against the devalued currencies of Southeast Asian exporters).

Contrary to the impression conveyed mainly by the business media, as well as by the IMF, consensus on how to understand and characterize the crises is still lacking. One manifestation of this has been the debates between the IMF and its various critics about the appropriateness of its negotiated programs in Indonesia, Korea, and Thailand. While policy debates have understandably captured the most attention, especially among the public at large, the East Asian crises have also challenged previously accepted international economic theories. However, contrary to the popular impression promoted by the Western-dominated financial media of crony capitalism as the main culprit, most serious analysts now agree that the crises essentially began as currency crises of a new type, different from those previously identified with either fiscal profligacy or macroeconomic indiscipline. A growing number of observers also seem to agree that the crises started off as currency crises and quickly became more generalized financial crises, before affecting the real economy, because of reduced liquidity in the financial system and the consequences of inappropriate official policy and ill-informed, herd-like market responses.

From Miracle to Debacle

Rapid economic growth and structural change, mainly associated with export-led industrialization in the region, can generally be traced back to the mid-1980s. Then devaluation of the currencies of Indonesia, Malaysia, and Thailand, as well as selective deregulation of onerous rules, helped to create attractive conditions for the relocation of production facilities in these countries and elsewhere in Southeast Asia and in China. This was especially attractive for Japan, and the first-tier or first-generation newly industrializing economies, that is, Hong Kong (China), Korea, Singapore, and Taiwan (China), most of which experienced currency appreciation, tight labor markets, and higher production costs. This sustained export-oriented industrialization well into the 1990s and was accompanied by the growth of other manufacturing, services, and construction activities.

High growth was sustained for about a decade, during much of which fiscal surpluses were maintained, monetary expansion was not excessive, and inflation was generally under control. Table 1 shows various summary macroeconomic indicators for the 1990s, paying greater attention to the period from 1996. Prior to 1997, savings and investment rates were high and rising in all three Southeast Asian economies. Foreign savings supplemented high domestic savings in all four East Asian crisis economies, especially in Malaysia and Thailand. Unemployment was low, while fiscal balances generally remained positive until 1997–98.

This is not to suggest, however, that fundamentals in East Asia were not experiencing any problems (Rasiah 2001). As table 1 shows, the incremental capital-output ratio rose in all three Southeast Asian economies during the 1990s before 1997, with the increase being the largest in Thailand and the smallest in Indonesia. The rising incremental capital-output ratios suggest declining returns to new investments before the crises. Export-led growth had been followed by a construction and property boom, fueled by financial systems favoring such "short-termist" investments—which involved loans with collateral, that is, the kind that bankers like—over more productive, but also seemingly more risky, investments in manufacturing and agriculture. The exaggerated expansion of investment in such nontradables exacerbated the economies' current account deficits. Although widespread in East Asia, the property-finance nexus was particularly strong in Thailand, which made it especially vulnerable to the inevitable bursting of the bubble (Jomo 1998; Pasuk and Baker 2000).

Financial liberalization from the 1980s had major ramifications in the region, as foreign savings supplemented the already high domestic savings rates to further accelerate the rate of capital accumulation, albeit in increasingly unproductive activities, because of the foreign domination of most internationally competitive industries. The rapid growth of the previous decade gave rise to several related macroeconomic concerns that had emerged by the mid-1990s.

First, the savings-investment gap had historically been financed by heavy reliance on foreign direct investment (FDI), as well as by public sector foreign borrowing, with the latter declining rapidly from the mid-1980s. Both FDI and foreign debt, in turn, caused investment income outflows abroad.[1] In the 1990s, the current account deficit was increasingly being financed by short-term capital inflows, as in 1993 and

TABLE 1. Macroeconomic Indicators, East Asian Four, Selected Years

Country	1990	1996	1997	1998	1999
Unemployment rate					
Indonesia	—	4.1	4.6	5.5	6.3
Korea, Rep. of	2.4	3.0	2.6	6.8	6.3
Malaysia	6.0	2.5	2.4	3.2	3.0
Thailand	4.9	1.1	0.9	3.5	4.1
	1990–95	**1996**	**1997**	**1998**	**1999**
Savings/GDP					
Indonesia	31.0	26.2	26.4	26.1	23.7
Korea, Rep. of	35.6	33.7	33.3	33.8	33.5
Malaysia	36.6	37.1	37.3	39.6	38.0
Thailand	34.4	33.0	32.5	34.9	31.0
	1990–95	**1996**	**1997**	**1998**	**1999**
Investment/GDP					
Indonesia	31.3	29.6	28.7	22.1	19.3
Korea, Rep. of	36.8	36.8	35.1	29.8	28.0
Malaysia	37.5	42.5	43.1	26.8	22.3
Thailand	41.0	41.1	33.3	22.2	21.0
	1990–95	**1996**	**1997**	**1998**	**1999**
Savings-Investment/GDP					
Indonesia	−0.3	−3.4	−2.3	4.0	4.4
Korea, Rep. of	−1.2	−3.1	−1.8	4.1	5.5
Malaysia	−0.9	−5.4	−5.8	12.8	15.7
Thailand	−5.6	−8.1	−0.9	12.8	10.0

	1987–89	**1990–92**	**1993–95**	**1997**	**1998**	**1999**
Incremental capital-output ratios						
Indonesia	4.0	3.9	4.4	1.7	0.4	1.8
Korea, Rep. of	3.5	5.1	5.1	4.2	−15.1	3.2
Malaysia	3.6	4.4	5.0	3.9	28.2	4.3
Thailand	2.9	4.6	5.2	12.9	−11.5	14.5

	1990–95	**1996**	**1997**	**1998**	**1999**
Fiscal balance/GDP					
Indonesia	0.2	1.4	1.3	−2.6	−3.4
Korea, Rep. of	0.2	0.5	−1.4	−4.2	−2.9
Malaysia	−0.4	0.7	2.4	−1.8	−3.2
Thailand	3.2	2.4	−0.9	−3.4	−3.0

— Not available.

Sources: ADB (1999); Radelet and Sachs (1998, table 11); Bank of Thailand, Bank Indonesia, Bank of Korea, and Bank Negara Malaysia data.

1995–96, with disastrous consequences later when such flows reversed.[2] Many recent confidence restoration measures seek to induce such short-term inflows once again, but they cannot be relied upon to address the underlying problem in the medium to long term. Although always in the minority, foreign portfolio investments increasingly influenced stock markets in the region in the 1990s. With incomplete information exacerbated by limited transparency, the presence of foreign portfolio investment, the biased nature of fund managers' incentives and remuneration, and the short-termism of fund managers' investment horizons, foreign financial institutions were much more prone to herd behavior than they might otherwise have been, and thus contributed decisively to regional contagion.

Second, private sector debt exploded in the 1990s, especially from abroad, not least because of the efforts of debt-pushers keen to secure higher returns from the fast-growing region.[3] Commercial banks' foreign liabilities also increased quickly, as the ratio of loans to gross national product rose rapidly during the period. Overinvestment of investible funds, especially from abroad, in nontradables only made things worse, especially in relation to the current account. Only a small proportion of commercial banks and other lending agencies were involved with manufacturing and other productive activities. This share is likely to have been even smaller with foreign borrowing, most of which was collateralized with such assets as real property and stock.[4]

Thus much of the inflow of foreign savings actually contributed to asset price inflation, mainly involving real estate and share prices. Insofar as such investments did not increase the production of tradables, they actually exacerbated the current account deficit rather than alleviated it as they were thought to be doing. This, in turn, worsened the problem of currency mismatch, with borrowing in U.S. dollars invested in activities that did not generate foreign exchange. As a high proportion of this foreign borrowing was short-term in nature and deployed to finance medium- to long-term projects, a term mismatch problem also arose. According to the Bank for International Settlements (BIS) (*Asian Wall Street Journal* January 6, 1998), well over half of the foreign borrowing by commercial banks was short-term in nature: 56 percent in Malaysia, 59 percent in Indonesia, 66 percent in Thailand, and 68 percent in Korea.

More generally, the foreign exchange risks of investment generally rose, increasing the vulnerability of these economies to the maintenance of currency pegs to the U.S. dollar.[5] The pegs encouraged a great deal of unhedged borrowing by an influential constituency with a strong stake in defending the pegs regardless of their adverse consequences for the economy. Because of the foreign domination of export-oriented industries in Southeast Asia, unlike in Northeast Asia, no politically influential industrial community that was oriented toward national exports was available to lobby for floating or depreciating the Southeast Asian currencies, despite the obvious adverse consequences of the pegs for international cost competitiveness. Instead, after pegging their currencies to the U.S. dollar from the early 1990s, and especially from the mid-1990s, most Southeast Asian central banks resisted downward adjustments to their exchange rates, which would have reduced, if not averted, some of the more disruptive consequences of the 1997–98 currency collapses.[6] Yet economists now generally agree that the 1997–98 East Asian crises saw tremendous "overshooting" in exchange rate adjustments well in excess of expected corrections.

The economic literature before the crises tended to characterize the affected Southeast Asian economies in terms of the following key fundamentals:

- Viability of domestic financial systems[7]

- Responsiveness of domestic output and exports to nominal devaluations[8]

- Sustainability of current account deficits[9]

- Prevalence of high savings rates and robust public finances.

Financial Liberalization and the East Asian Crises

Montes (1998) attributes the Southeast Asian currency crises to the "twin liberalizations" of domestic financial systems and opening of the capital account. Financial liberalization induced new behavior in financial systems, notably:

- Domestic financial institutions had greater flexibility in offering interest rates to secure funds domestically and in bidding for foreign funds.

- Domestic financial institutions became less reliant on lending to the government.

- Regulations, such as credit allocation rules and ceilings, were reduced.

- Greater domestic competition meant that ascendance depended on expanding lending portfolios, often at the expense of prudence.

Kaminsky and Reinhart's (1996) study of 71 balance of payments crises and 25 banking crises during 1970–95 finds that only 3 banking crises were associated with the 25 balance of payments crises during 1970–79. However, during 1980–95, 22 banking crises coincided with 46 balance of payments crises, which the authors attribute to the financial liberalization of the 1980s, with a private lending boom culminating in a banking crisis and then a currency crisis.

In their review of 57 countries during 1970–96, Carleton, Rosario, and Woo (2000) find that inflationary macroeconomic policies and small foreign reserves stocks reliably predicted currency collapses. They argue that as the probability of Indonesia, Malaysia, Korea, and Thailand experiencing a currency collapse in 1997 was about 20 percent, and all four currencies (and economies) collapsed—rather than just one, as expected—financial contagion is a better explanation than weak domestic fundamentals.

One of the most cited crises explanations (Montes 1998) suggests that they stemmed from the banking sector because of imprudent expansion and diversification of domestic financial markets, fueled by short-term private borrowing. While this may have been true of Thailand, it was certainly less true for Indonesia, Malaysia, the Philippines, and Korea (in order of decreasing relevance). Instead, the significance of contagion cannot be exaggerated, as "the differences raise questions about how sensitive the currency knockdowns (and the associated divestment from these economies) are to economic fundamentals" (Montes 1998, p. 3).

Even though East Asia's financial systems were quite varied and were hardly clones of the Japanese main bank system (as often wrongly alleged), they had nevertheless become prone to similar asset price bubbles, albeit for somewhat different reasons. Arguably, the more bank-based systems of Indonesia, Korea and Thailand had a stronger nexus of this kind compared with, say, Malaysia's much more market-oriented financial system. Rapid growth based on export-oriented industrialization from the late 1980s gave rise to accelerated financial expansion, which contributed to asset price bubbles, including property booms, both in more market-oriented or Anglo-American Malaysia, as well as in the other more bank-oriented economies badly hit by the crises.[10]

Little was achieved by insisting that the crises should not have happened because East Asia's economic fundamentals were fine, even if that were true. In some instances, such official denials exacerbated the problem, because the authorities did not seem to be responding to ostensible problems in ways deemed appropriate by market opinion makers. Unfortunately, as East Asia has painfully learnt, financial markets are driven by sentiments as much as by fundamentals. Hence, even though much more serious current account deficits in 1995, for instance, did not result in crises, this does not mean that an economy can maintain such deficits indefinitely without being vulnerable to speculative attack or loss of confidence.

Governments cannot, for example, liberalize the capital account and then complain when short-term portfolio investors suddenly withdraw following their whims and fancies. Capital controls can make rapidly withdrawing capital from an economy difficult, costly, or both. Many governments treat FDI quite differently from portfolio investments. Some authorities try to distinguish between speculative investments by hedge funds that are clearly short-termist from, say, pension funds with more medium-term orientations. In the early and mid-1990s, some Southeast Asian economies had become excessively reliant on short-term capital inflows to finance their current account deficits. This problem was exacerbated by excessive imports to manufacture more items that could not be exported, such as buildings, infrastructure, and heavily protected import substitutes. Ostensibly, prudent financial institutions often preferred to lend for real property and stock purchases, and thereby secure assets with rising values as collateral, rather than to provide credit for more productive uses.

While foreign banks were more than happy to lend U.S. dollars at higher interest rates than were available in their home economies, East Asian businesses were keen to borrow at lower interest rates than were available domestically. The sustained dollar pegs of the Southeast Asian currencies may have induced some moral hazard by discouraging borrowers from hedging their loans, but little systematic evidence of the extent of this problem is available. In any case, the existence of well-developed swap markets allowed Southeast Asian companies to tap into foreign capital markets, at low cost, by swapping away the currency risk.

Hence many such loans remained unhedged as Southeast Asian currencies had been pegged to the U.S. dollar since the 1970s, despite the official fictions of exchange rates moving with the baskets of the currencies of countries' major foreign trading partners. The growth in foreign banking in the region in the 1990s led to lending competition reminiscent of the loans to developing country governments in the late 1970s (which led to the debt crises of the 1980s). However, the new belief in international policymaking circles before the crises was that such accumulation of private sector debt did not matter as long as public sector debt was reined in.

Meanwhile, portfolio investors moved into newly emerging stock markets in East Asia with encouragement from the International Finance Corporation, an arm of the World Bank. In Malaysia, for example, they came in a big way in 1993, only to withdraw even more suddenly in early 1994, leaving most retail stockholders in the lurch. The government introduced some capital control measures, only to withdraw them later in 1994. Unfortunately, policymakers did not learn the lessons from that experience, as the new, unsustainable stock market buildup from 1995 sent stock prices soaring once again despite declining price-earnings ratios.

Clearly investor panic was the principal cause of the Asian financial crises (McKibbin 1998; Montes 1998). The tightening of macroeconomic policies in response to the panic served to exacerbate rather than to check the crises. Economic disasters are not necessarily punishment for economic sins, and while cronyism is wrong, it was not the cause of the East Asian crises, and as the crises demonstrated, even sound macroeconomic fundamentals cannot guarantee immunity from contagion and crisis.

With the currency collapses, the assets acquired by portfolio and other investors in the region depreciated correspondingly in value from their perspectives, precipitating an even greater sell-off and panic, causing herd behavior and contagion to spread across national borders to the rest of the region. Meanwhile, liberalizing the capital account essentially guaranteed residents and nonresidents ease of exit and placed fewer limitations on nationals holding foreign assets, thereby inadvertently facilitating capital flight. Thus financial liberalization allowed lucrative opportunities for taking advantage of falling currencies, accelerating and exacerbating the volatility of regional currency and share markets. All this, together with injudicious official responses, transformed the inevitable correction of overvalued currencies in the region into a collapse of the currencies and the stock markets aggravated by herd behavior and contagion.

Crises of a New Type

Many economists were obliged to reconsider their earlier assessments of the causes of the Asian crises, most notably Krugman. In the immediate aftermath of its outbreak, some saw the crises as vindication of Krugman's earlier popularization of a critique of the East Asian miracle as primarily due to massive factor inputs subject to diminishing returns (Krugman 1994). In March 1998, Krugman dissented from the view—associated with Radelet and Sachs (1998)—of the East Asian crises as being due to a "good old-fashioned financial panic . . . a panic need not be a punishment for your sins . . . an economy can be 'fundamentally sound' . . . and yet be subjected to a devastating run started by nothing more than a self-fulfilling rumor." Instead Krugman (1998c) argued that

> [T]he preconditions for that panic were created by bad policies in the years running up to the crisis. The crisis, in short, was a punishment for Asian crimes, even if the punishment was disproportionate to the crime . . . The specific spirit that pushed Asia to the brink was the problem of moral hazard in lending – mainly domestic lending.

Krugman associated the crises with crony capitalism. Attributing the crises to cronyism turned on its head one of the main arguments about how intimate business-government relations in East Asian economies had helped to create the conditions for the regional miracle. However, by October 1998, Krugman (1998a) had completely changed his view:

> When the Asian crisis struck . . . countries were told to raise interest rates, not cut them, in order to persuade some foreign investors to keep their money in place and thereby limit the exchange-rate plunge . . . In effect, countries were told to forget about macroeconomic policy; instead of trying to prevent or even alleviate the looming slumps in their economies, they were told to follow policies that would actually deepen those slumps . . . But, because crises can be self-fulfilling, sound economic policy is not sufficient to gain market confidence; one must cater to the perceptions, the prejudices, and the whims of the market. Or, rather, one must cater to what one hopes will be the perceptions of the market . . . The perceived need to play the confidence game supersedes the normal concerns of economic policy.

Later, Krugman (1999) added:

> The scope of global "contagion"—the rapid spread of the crisis to countries with no real economic links to the original victim—convinced me that IMF critics such as Jeffrey Sachs were right in insisting that this was less a matter of economic fundamentals than it was a case of self-fulfilling prophecy, of market panic that, by causing a collapse of the real economy, ends up validating itself.

Clearly no one fully anticipated the crises in East Asia, mainly because they were crises of a new type. Some observers argued that the crises had important parallels with the Mexican tequila crisis of 1995, while others emphasized the differences (Kregel 1998). There were, of course, skeptics who regarded the claims of an East Asian economic miracle as somewhat exaggerated in the first place (for example, Krugman 1994). However, these were different criticisms of the East Asian miracle and certainly did not anticipate, let alone predict, the East Asian debacle of 1997–98.

The East Asian crises differed from conventional currency crisis scenarios in at least several important ways (Krugman 1998a), namely:[11]

- The absence of the usual sources of currency stress, whether fiscal deficits or macroeconomic indiscipline[12]

- The governments' lack of any incentive to abandon their pegged exchange rates, for instance, to reduce unemployment

- The pronounced boom and bust cycles in asset prices (real estate and stock markets) preceded the currency crises, especially in Thailand, where the crises began

- The fact that financial intermediaries were key players in all the economies involved

- The severity of the crises in the absence of strong, adverse shocks

- The rapid spread of the initial crisis from Thailand even to economies with few links or similarities to the first victims.

Thus the traditional indexes of vulnerability did not signal crises, because the source of the problem was not to be found in government fiscal balances, or even in national income accounts. The liabilities of the mainly private financial intermediaries were not part of the governments' liabilities until after the crises, after foreign lenders and the international financial institutions "persuaded" them to nationalize much of the private foreign debt. Other issues also need to be taken into account for an adequate analysis of the East Asian crises, namely:

- The crises had severe adverse effects on growth by disrupting the productive contribution of financial intermediation.

- The crises involved not only excessive investment, but also unwise investment.

- The huge real currency depreciations caused large output declines and seemed to do little to promote exports.

Other kinds of market failure also need to be taken into account.

Furman and Stiglitz (1998) emphasize that economic downturns caused by financial crises are far more severe and have longer-lasting effects than those caused by inventory cycles. High leveraging by companies and high lending for asset price (stock or property market) booms enhance financial fragility and increased insolvencies disrupt the credit mechanism. Large unanticipated interest rate increases may not only precipitate financial crises, but are also likely to cause economic downturns as the value of bank assets and highly indebted firms collapse. Such adverse effects are likely to persist well after the interest rate has returned to more normal levels. In addition to asset price bubbles, excessive investments, and other problems caused by moral hazard resulting from implicit government guarantees for weakly regulated financial intermediaries, as well as the exchange rate peg, a more comprehensive analysis must also consider the following phenomena:

- The implications of the growth in currency trading and speculation for the post–Bretton Woods international monetary system

- The reasons why the Southeast Asian monetary authorities defended their quasi pegs against the strengthening U.S. dollar, despite the obvious adverse consequences for export competitiveness, and hence for growth

- The consequences of financial liberalization, including the creation of conditions that contributed to the magnitude of the crises

- The role of herd behavior in exacerbating the crises

- The factors accounting for the contagion effects.

Reversible Capital Inflows

Analysts have increasingly acknowledged the role of easily reversible capital flows into the East Asian region as the principal cause of the 1997–98 crises. They now generally accept that the national financial systems in the region did not adapt well to international financial liberalization (Jomo 1998). The bank-based financial systems of most of the East Asian economies affected by the crises were especially vulnerable to the sudden drop in the availability of short-term loans as international confidence in the region dropped suddenly during 1997. Available foreign exchange reserves were exposed as inadequate to meet financial obligations abroad, requiring governments to seek temporary credit facilities to meet such obligations that had been incurred mainly by their private sectors.

Data from the BIS show that the banks were responsible for much of this short-term debt, though some of it did consist of trade credit and other short-term debt deemed essential for ensuring liquidity in an economy. However, the rapid growth of short-term bank debt during stock market and property boom periods suggests that much short-term debt is due to factors other than trade credit expansion. In Malaysia, the temporary capital controls the central bank introduced in early 1994 momentarily dampened the growth of such debt, but by 1996 and early 1997, a new short-term borrowing frenzy was evident that involved not only the banks, but also other large, private companies with enough political influence to circumvent the central bank's guidelines.

As table 2 shows, in Indonesia, Malaysia, and Thailand, the nonbank private sector was the major recipient of international bank loans, accounting for more than half of total foreign borrowing by the end of June 1997, that is, well above the developing country average of slightly under half. In contrast, 65 percent of borrowing in Korea was by banks, with only 31 percent by the nonbank private sector. Government borrowing was low, and was lowest in Korea and Malaysia, although the data do not permit differentiating between state-owned public companies or partially private, but corporatized previously fully state-owned enterprises.

TABLE 2. Lending by Banks Reporting to the BIS by Sector, East Asian Four, and Developing Countries, End of June 1997
(US$ billions)

Sector	Indonesia	Korea, Rep. of	Malaysia	Thailand	Developing countries
Total borrowing, of which	58.7	103.4	28.8	79.4	743.8
Bank	12.4	67.3	10.5	26.1	275.3
	(21.1)	(65.1)	(36.5)	(32.9)	(37.0)
Private nonbank	39.7	31.7	16.5	41.3	352.9
	(67.6)	(30.6)	(57.3)	(52.0)	(47.4)
Government	6.5	4.4	1.9	12.0	115.6
	(11.1)	(4.3)	(6.6)	(15.1)	(15.5)

Note: Figures in parentheses are percentages.

Source: BIS data.

Jomo (2001b, appendix tables 2a–2d) shows the remarkable growth of mainly private foreign debt in the early and mid-1990s, especially in the three most externally indebted economies of Indonesia, Korea, and Thailand. While FDI grew in all four economies in the 1990s, it grew the least in Korea. Profit remittances on FDI were least from Korea and Thailand and highest from Malaysia, reflecting its historically greater role, although FDI in Indonesia was actually higher in 1995–96. Portfolio equity flows into all four economies grew strongly in the mid-1990s.

External debt as a share of export earnings rose from 112 percent in 1995 to 120 percent in 1996 in Thailand and from 57 to 74 percent over the same period in Korea, but declined in Indonesia and grew more modestly in Malaysia. By 1996, foreign exchange reserves as a share of external debt were 15 percent in Indonesia, 30 percent in Korea, 43 percent in Thailand, and 70 percent in Malaysia. By 1997, this ratio had dropped further to 15 percent in Korea, 29 percent in Thailand, and 46 percent in Malaysia, reflecting the reserves lost in futile currency defense efforts. Despite recessions in 1998, reserves picked up in all four economies, mainly because of the effects of currency devaluations on exports and imports. The short-term debt share of total external debt in 1996 stood at 58 percent in Korea, 41 percent in Thailand, 28 percent in Malaysia, and 25 percent in Indonesia.

Table 3 shows that French, German, Japanese, U.K., and U.S. banks that reported to the BIS accounted for much of the lending to developing countries, with the share of U.K. and U.S. banks being far less significant than lending to other emerging markets. This pattern was quite different from that of lending before the 1980s debt crises, and suggests that Anglo-American banks were generally far more reluctant to lend in the 1990s following their experiences in the 1980s. Little evidence suggests that such banks were more averse to lending either to governments or to developing economies. Indeed, the pattern of lending in the late 1970s and early 1980s suggests the contrary.

From the beginning of the 1990s, Malaysia sustained a current account deficit. Overinvestment of investible funds in non-tradables only made things worse. Insofar as such investments did not contribute to export earnings, for example, in power generation and telecommunications, they aggravated the problem of currency mismatch, with foreign borrowing invested in activities that did not generate foreign exchange.

TABLE 3. Exposure of Banks Reporting to the BIS to Non-BIS Borrowers, End of June 1997

(US$ billions)

Banks' location	Amount
Total	1,054.9
France	100.2
Germany	178.2
Japan	172.7
United Kingdom	77.8
United States	131.0
Percentage of private nonbank borrowers	45

Source: BIS data.

TABLE 4. Maturity Distribution of Lending by Banks Reporting to the BIS to the East Asian Four, 1996 and 1997

(US$ millions)

Country	All loans			Loans under 1 year			Loans of 1–2 years		
	June 1996	December 1996	June 1997	June 1996	December 1996	June 1997	June 1996	December 1996	June 1997
Indonesia	49,306	55,523	58,726	29,587	34,248	34,661	3,473	3,589	3,541
Korea, Rep. of	88,027	99,953	103,432	62,332	67,506	70,182	3,438	4,107	4,139
Malaysia	20,100	22,234	28,820	9,991	11,178	16,268	834	721	615
Thailand	69,409	70,147	69,382	47,834	45,702	45,567	4,083	4,829	4,592

Source: BIS data.

An additional problem of term mismatch also arose, as a high proportion of the foreign borrowing was short-term in nature (table 4), but was deployed to finance medium- to long-term projects.

Foreign capital inflows into East Asia augmented the high domestic savings rate to boost the domestic investment rate and East Asian investments abroad in the 1990s. Thus, even though some evidence suggests that foreign capital inflows may have had an indirect adverse effect on the domestic savings rate, they generally supplemented, rather than substituted for, domestic savings (Wong with Jomo 2001). Being conclusive on this point is difficult, because the nature of foreign capital inflows has changed significantly over time. Hence even if earlier foreign capital inflows may have adversely affected domestic savings, one possibility is that the changed composition of foreign capital inflows just before the crises no longer adversely affected domestic savings.

International financial liberalization undoubtedly succeeded in temporarily generating massive net capital inflows into East Asia, unlike into many other developing and transition economies, some of which experienced net outflows. However, it also exacerbated systemic instability and reduced the scope for the government interventions responsible for the region's economic miracle. Increased foreign capital inflows reduced foreign exchange constraints, allowing the financing of additional imports, but thereby also inadvertently encouraging current account deficits. Finally, foreign capital inflows adversely affected factor payment outflows, export and import propensities, terms of trade, and capital flight, and thus the balance of payments. These consequences suggest that governments should be cautious when determining the extent to which they should encourage foreign capital inflows. Furthermore, the Southeast Asian trio's heavy dependence on FDI in relation to gross domestic capital formation, especially for manufacturing investments, probably also limited the development of domestic entrepreneurship, as well as many other indigenous economic capabilities, by the increased reliance on foreign capabilities usually associated with some types of FDI (Jomo with others 1997).

As noted earlier, starting in the mid-1990s, three major indicators began to cause concern. The current account of the balance of payments and the savings-investment gap were recording large imbalances in the Southeast Asian economies, especially

TABLE 5. Debt Service and Short-Term Debt, East Asian Four, Selected Years

Country	Debt service as a percentage of exports			Short-term debt (US$ billions)[a]				Current account deficit plus short-term debt as a percentage of international reserves			
	1980	1992	1995	1992	1994	1995	1996	1992	1994	1995	1996
Indonesia	13.9	32.1	30.9	18.2	14.0	16.2	17.9	191	139	169	138
Korea, Rep. of	14.5	6.9	5.8	11.9	31.6	46.6	66.6	133	125	131	127
Malaysia	6.3	6.6	7.8	3.6	7.6	7.5	8.5	29	46	60	55
Thailand	18.9	14.1	10.2	14.7	29.2	41.1	44.0	101	127	152	153

a. Year end figures.

Sources: UNCTAD (1997, table 14); World Bank (1994, tables 20, 23; 1997, table 17).

Malaysia and Thailand. However, as table 5 shows, the short-term foreign debt and current account deficits as proportions of international reserves were better in Malaysia than in Indonesia, Korea, and Thailand, thereby averting the need for IMF emergency credit. Domestic credit expansion had also soared in all four countries by the mid-1990s. Prior to the crises, since the mid-1980s East Asia had moved steadily toward financial liberation, including bank liberalization, promotion of the region's newly emerging stock markets, and greater capital account convertibility. Thus East Asia succeeded in attracting a great deal of capital inflow.

Whereas the other three crisis-affected East Asian economies succeeded in attracting considerable, mainly short-term, U.S. dollar bank loans into their more bank-based financed systems, Malaysia's vulnerability was mainly due to the volatility of international portfolio capital flows into its stock market. As a consequence, the nature of Malaysia's external liabilities at the beginning of the crisis was quite different from that of the other crisis-stricken East Asian economies. A greater proportion of Malaysia's external liabilities consisted of equity rather than debt. Compared with Malaysia's exposure in the mid-1980s, many of the liabilities, including the debt, were private rather than public. In addition, much of Malaysia's debt in the late 1990s was long-term rather than short-term in nature, again in contrast to the other crisis-affected economies.

Monetary policy and banking supervision had generally been much more prudent in Malaysia than in the other victims of the crises, for example, Malaysian banks had not been allowed to borrow heavily from abroad to lend on the domestic market. Such practices involved currency and term mismatches, which increased the vulnerability of countries' financial systems to foreign bankers' confidence and exerted pressure on the exchange rate pegs. These differences have lent support to the claim that Malaysia was an innocent bystander that fell victim to regional contagion by being in the wrong part of the world at the wrong time. Such a view takes a benign perspective of portfolio investment inflows and does not recognize that such inflows are even more easily reversible and volatile than bank loan inflows (Jomo 2001a). Contrary to the innocent bystander hypothesis, Malaysia's experience actually suggests greater vulnerability because of its greater reliance on the capital market. As a consequence, the Malaysian economy became hostage to international portfolio investors' confidence. Hence when government leaders engaged in rhetoric and policy initiatives that upset such investors' confidence, Malaysia paid a heavy price when portfolio divestment accelerated.

International Financial Liberalization

An explosion of international financial flows followed the substitution of the Bretton Woods system of fixed exchange rates with the prevailing system of flexible exchange rates. Analysts have ascribed strong speculative motives to most of the international capital flows not associated with FDI. Much recent FDI, especially into East Asia in the wake of the crises, has been for mergers and acquisitions rather than to add new economic capacity through greenfield investments.

The demise of fixed exchange rate regimes also encouraged capital account liberalization. Recent financial developments have resulted in a proliferation of financial instruments, enabling investors to diversify their holdings of financial assets. These trends gathered steam with international financial liberalization in the wake of the international debt crises of the 1980s and picked up further momentum in the 1990s. By 1995, the volume of foreign exchange spot transactions had grown to well over a trillion U.S. dollars per day, or more than 67 times the total value of the international trade in goods by 1995, or more than 40 times the value of all international trade (including services). Estimates put the daily foreign exchange market in 1997 at US$1,250 billion. In a world economy where foreign exchange spot transactions are now worth more than 70 times the total value of international commodity trade transactions, the financial sector has become increasingly divorced from the real economy.

Viewed from a historical perspective, such currency trading is hardly natural, inevitable, or even desirable. For most of human history it has not been "integral to global trade in goods and services," as then U.S. Treasury Secretary Robert Rubin (1998) claimed. Indeed, critics have offered various alternatives to the current system. With the recent proliferation of new financial instruments and markets, the financial sector has an even greater capacity to inflict damage on the real economy. Ever since Keynes (1936) advocated "throwing sand" into the financial system to halt the potentially disastrous consequences of unfettered liberalization, Keynesians and others have been wary of the financial liberalization advocated by ideological neoliberals and their often naïve allies.

Furthermore, many of the promised benefits of international financial liberalization have not been realized (Eatwell 1997), namely:

- Liberalization was expected to move financial resources from capital-rich to capital-poor countries.[13] Instead, such net flows of finance—and of real resources—over time have been modest and have tended to go to the capital-rich economies.[14] Of course, most net flows to the capital-poor states were mainly to the most attractive emerging markets, especially in East Asia before 1998. The rush to convertibility and capital control deregulation in most transition economies has resulted in many becoming significant net capital exporters, for example, the Russian Federation.[15] Such flows arguably contributed to asset price bubbles and, eventually, to financial panic, and thus to currency and stock market collapses.

- Liberalization was expected to enhance options and returns for savers and to lower the cost of funds to borrowers; however, savers have benefited most from higher real interest rates. Some have claimed that the lower cost of funds in the late 1970s was attributable to the exceptional circumstances caused by financial repression, enhanced liquidity brought about by the availability of petroleum revenues, and high inflation.

- New financial derivatives, which were expected to improve risk management and have undoubtedly reduced some of the older sources of volatility and instability, also generated new systemic risks especially vulnerable to sudden changes in sentiment.

- Improved macroeconomic performance resulting in greater investment and growth that was expected from better allocative efficiency has not been realized. Instead, overall macroeconomic performance has been worse than during the postwar "golden age" before financial liberalization.

- Financial liberalization has introduced a persistent deflationary bias in economic policy as governments try to gain credibility in financial markets to avert destabilizing capital outflows, instead of exerting the healthy discipline on governments that was expected to improve macroeconomic stability.

More generally, financial liberalization has further constrained the role of the state and governments face reduced options in both monetary and fiscal policies. In addition to such macroeconomic policy limitations, the room for discretionary state interventions has been much reduced, for example, in the form of selective industrial promotion, which was so crucial to late industrialization. Thus financial liberalization has greatly weakened governments' capacity in relation to development. Given the desirability of preserving the limited, but still significant, scope for monetary independence, liberalization should not be allowed to frustrate the sound development of a country's financial system and its effective deployment for development purposes. The scope for monetary independence depends partly on the soundness of macroeconomic management, as well as on political will.

Financial markets seem to function in such a way as to impose their own expectations on the real economy, thereby defining their own fundamentals and logic, and in turn become self-fulfilling prophecies. In other words, financial markets do not simply process information in order to allocate resources efficiently.

The threat of instability in the now massive capital market forces both governments and private investors to pursue risk-averse strategies, resulting in low growth and employment creation. A deflationary bias in government policy and the private sector emerges in response to the costly risks of violating the rules of the game. This is exacerbated by the high costs of debt caused by high real interest rates that result from efforts to maintain financial stability in a potentially volatile world. Thus long-term price stability supersedes a high and stable level of employment as the macro-economic policy priority.

A successfully liberalized financial system that gives high priority to flexibility or the possibility of easy exit necessarily tends to become fragile, as reflected in

- Liquidity crises that reduce real output

- Private sector risk aversion that encourages short-termism

- Public sector risk aversion that results in a deflationary policy bias

- Persistent pressure for ever greater flexibility that increases the ease of exit.

The benefits of reduced financial controls to emerging markets must be weighed against the increased instability resulting from enhanced ease and speed of exit. While increased (real) FDI flows generally require countries to agree to unrestricted repatriation of profits, this is quite different from the instant exit conditions financial markets demand.

Considerable evidence indicates that in the longer term, economic development has been associated with developmental states effectively promoting selected new economic activities by the use of industrial or selective investment policy. The postwar golden age—which saw high levels of output and employment and short-run efficiency—was based on the premise of active macroeconomic management under the Bretton Woods system. Postwar European reconstruction was achieved with tight capital controls. Similarly, Japan, Korea, and Taiwan (China) all began their industrialization and achieved rapid capital accumulation with the aid of capital controls.

The adverse consequences for economic development of financial disintermediation and of grossly undervalued currencies also deserve attention, particularly as the crises threatened the future of growth and structural change in the region, not only directly, but also as a consequence of policy responses. The typically deflationary policies the international financial community and others favor may well throw out the baby of economic development with the bathwater of financial crisis.

Some dangers associated with financial liberalization have now become evident, but most have not been sufficiently recognized, let alone debated and addressed. Most initiatives in this regard cannot be undertaken unilaterally without great cost, as market reactions to Malaysian Prime Minister Mahathir's critical remarks in the second half of 1997 showed (see Jomo 2001b). The few options available for unilateral initiatives need to be carefully considered and only implemented if deemed desirable. Selectively invoking instances of bad or incompetent policymaking or implementation does not justify leaving matters to liberalized markets that render systematic policymaking impossible. Instead, the experience of financial crisis emphasizes the importance of creating an environment and developing the capability such that good and competent policy is effective.

Many policies need to be actively pursued through multilateral initiatives, for which governments need the support of neighboring countries and others. Given the power of the dominant ideology that infuses the prevailing international system, asserting control over the financial system is virtually impossible without a fundamental change in priorities and thinking by the governments of the major economic powers. The currencies of a small number of countries—Germany, Japan, the United Kingdom, and the United States—were involved in more than three-quarters of currency transactions in 1995; thus such countries have the capacity and capability to monitor and control transborder capital flows by acting in concert.

Minskyian Crises?

Minsky's theory of financial crisis is instructive for understanding the recent East Asian financial crises. In particular, his financial instability hypothesis "does not rely upon exogenous shocks to generate business cycles of varying severity" (Minsky 1993). His theory maintains that business cycles can be explained by a combination of the "internal dynamics of capitalist economy" and the "system of interventions and regulations" intended to "keep the economy operating within reasonable bounds" (Minsky 1992).

According to Minsky, financial instability and the likelihood of crisis are compounded by systemic fragility, meaning the "development of a fragile financial structure" resulting from the "normal functioning" of the capitalist economy. "Financial fragility and thus the susceptibility of our economy to disruption is not due to either accidents or policy errors," thus Minsky's theory of systemic fragility explains why the economy "endogenously develops fragile or crisis prone financial structures" (Minsky 1986). He argues that the "structural characteristics of the financial system change during periods of prolonged expansion and economic boom" and that these changes cumulate to reduce the "stability of the system" (Minsky 1972). Euphoria during the boom undoubtedly contributes to the growing vulnerability of the situation: "No clearer expression of economic euphoria can be imagined than the words 'Asian miracle'" (Mayer 1998).

"Thus, after an expansion has been in progress for some time, an event that is not of unusual size or duration can trigger a sharp financial reaction" (Minsky 1972). "Once fragile financial structures exist, the *incoherent behavior* characteristic of a financial crisis can develop. *Incoherent behavior* occurs when the reaction to a disturbance amplifies—rather than dampens—the initial disturbance" (Minsky 1986). Clearly, the procyclical policy responses of market pundits, most orthodox economists, and the IMF insisted on had such consequences. Whereas the IMF has urged industrial economies to adopt countercyclical reflationary policies during their recent downturns, it has a different policy prescription for developing economies, thereby compounding rather than ameliorating their problems. The financial crises can thus be said to have been "compounded out of initial displacement or shocks, structural characteristics of the system, and human error" (Minsky 1972).

In the wake of the crises, pointing to other seemingly more compelling and immediate explanatory factors was easy. Observers have made much of exchange rate misalignments, emphasizing the overvalued Southeast Asian currencies, but careful examination of the real effective exchange rates suggests that the misalignment has been grossly exaggerated. After the crises, many of the East Asian institutions previously credited with the region's miracle came to be maligned as responsible for the crises, but again, little strong evidence suggests that it was an outcome of crony-ism or poor corporate governance. As Minsky (1972) notes:

> Once the sharp financial reaction occurs, institutional deficiencies will be evident. Thus, after a crisis, it will always be possible to construct plausible arguments—by emphasizing the triggering events or institutional flaws—that accidents, mistakes, or easily corrected shortcomings were responsible for the disaster.

Wade (1998) agrees that the "whipsaw movement of capital inflows and outflows is the main proximate cause of the crisis," but asks, "Could it have happened without serious vulnerabilities in the real economy?" His answer too is, "Almost certainly, yes."

Considerable work has drawn attention to various weaknesses of East Asian growth, development, and industrialization (Krugman 1994; Jomo 2001b, 2002; Jomo with others 1997; Rasiah 2001). While Malaysia and Thailand had run current account deficits financed by net capital inflows for many years, these weaknesses of the real economy do not offer plausible, comprehensive explanations for the region's crises.

Minsky developed his theory principally with reference to the U.S. economy, and he does not seem to have carefully considered the possibly different nature of systemic fragility in developing economies with open capital accounts. The East Asian crises were new and different in several regards from a Minsky-type crisis as envisaged for the United States or other industrial economies, but they were also dif-ferent from other earlier currency and financial crises, including the Mexican tequila crisis of 1995 (Kregel 1998). Nevertheless, insofar as many familiar elements of a Minsky-type crisis were apparent in East Asia, the crises could be characterized as "post-Minskyian."

The Role of the IMF

Critical consideration of the causes and consequences of the East Asian crisis requires paying close and careful attention to the nature and implications of IMF rescue pro-grams and conditionalities, as well as policies favored by international, as distinct from domestic, financial communities. IMF prescriptions and conventional policy-making wisdom urged bank closures, government spending cuts, and higher interest rates in the wake of the crises. Such contractionary measures transformed what had started as currency crises, and then become full-blown financial crises, into crises of the real economy. Thus Indonesia, Korea, and Malaysia, which had previously enjoyed massive capital inflows in the form of short-term bank loans or portfolio investments, went into recession during 1998, following Thailand, which went into recession in 1997.

Not only did the IMF underestimate the severity of the collapse in all the East Asian economies, it also underestimated the speed and strength of recovery (IMF 1997, 1998; Lane and others 1999). This suggests that the IMF not only did not understand the causes of the crises, but was also incapable of designing optimal policies in response to it. Critics still doubt whether the IMF recognized the novel elements of the crises and their implications, especially at the outset. The IMF's apparent failure to anticipate the crises in its generally glowing reports on the region prior to the crises and its role in exacerbating the downturns in Indonesia, Korea, and Thailand certainly did not inspire much confidence. In addition, even though the Philippines had long been involved in IMF programs and supervision, it was not spared the contagion.[16] International skepticism about the IMF's role in and prescriptions for the East Asian crises is considerable. Most economists now agree that the early IMF programs for Indonesia, Korea, and Thailand were ill-conceived, although they do not seem able to agree on why the IMF made such mistakes. Perhaps partly out of force of habit from dealing with situations in Africa, Eastern Europe, Latin America, and elsewhere where fiscal deficits had been part of the problem, the IMF insisted on the same prescription of deflationary policies in its early policy responses to the East Asian crises. Thus many of its programs were effectively contractionary, though this was sometimes disguised by poorly conceived measures to provide social safety nets for the poor. Hence what started off as currency and financial crises led—partly because of policy responses recommended or imposed by the IMF—to economic recessions in much of the region in 1998. The accounts vary with the different countries involved (Jomo 1998; *Cambridge Journal of Economics* November 1998; see Jomo 2001a, chapter 1, for an account of the Malaysian experience).

The early IMF policy prescription to raise domestic interest rates not only failed to stem capital flight, but instead exacerbated the impact of the crises, causing financial pain through currency depreciation, stock market collapses, and rising interest rates. Even if higher interest rates had succeeded in preventing capital flight, it can only be halted temporarily, and even then at great and permanent costs to productive investments in the real economy. When inflows are eventually reversed in the precipitous manner East Asia experienced from the second half of 1997, a large amount of collateral damage is inevitable.

Furman and Stiglitz (1998) provide a critical review of the literature and argue against raising interest rates to protect the exchange rate. In particular, where leveraging is high, as in East Asia, high interest rates will take a huge toll by weakening aggregate demand and increasing the likelihood and frequency of insolvencies. Unexpected interest rate hikes tend to weaken financial institutions, lower investment, and thereby reduce output. Furman and Stiglitz (1998) offer the following three main reasons why keeping interest rates low while letting the exchange rate depreciate may be a preferable option in light of the trade-off involved:

- To avoid crisis, policymakers should be more concerned about interest rate increases than about exchange rate declines (Demirguc-Kunt and Detragiache 1998; Furman and Stiglitz 1998).

- Any government intervention to stabilize the exchange rate is likely to encourage economic agents to take positions they would otherwise not take, later compelling the government to support the exchange rate to avoid the now larger adverse effects. This point is based on a moral hazard argument.

- When a government defends its currency, it is often making a one-way bet, where the expected loss is speculators' expected gain. In contrast, if the government does not wager any reserves, the gains of some speculators are simply the losses of others. Thus invoking an equity argument, they ask why borrowers, workers, firms, and others adversely affected by higher interest rates should be compelled to pay for speculators' profits.

Despite their sound fiscal balances before the crises, the IMF also asked the East Asian economies to cut government spending to restore confidence in their currencies, despite the ominous implications for economic recovery. Even though all the affected East Asian economies had been running fiscal surpluses in the years preceding the crises (except Indonesia, which had a small deficit in 1996), the IMF expected the governments to slash public expenditure. With the possible exception of Indonesia, which could not raise the financing required, the other crises-affected economies eventually ignored this advice and began to undertake Keynesian-style reflationary, countercyclical measures starting in the second half of 1998, which have been primarily responsible for their economic recovery.

Incredibly, the IMF did not seem to be cognizant of the subjective elements that had contributed to the crises and seemed to approach the situation as if it was solely due to weaknesses in the countries' macroeconomic or financial systems. Examining the changing risk premiums on Eurobonds issued by East Asia, Woo (2000) finds evidence of "irrational exuberance," implying that the potential for investor panic also existed. Moreover, even though the risk premiums on Thai Eurobonds increased by 10 basis points following the July 1997 devaluation, they jumped by four times as much with the acceptance of the IMF program for Thailand in August 1997. This suggests that the latter's deflationary macroeconomic policies and abrupt closure of financial institutions had undermined, rather than restored, investor confidence.

Insolvent financial institutions should have been restructured so as to avoid the possibility of triggering bank runs and consequent social instability. By insisting on closing down banks and other financial institutions in Indonesia, Korea, and Thailand, the IMF undermined much of the remaining confidence, inducing further panic in the process. Nasution (2000) points out that the IMF's way of taking insolvent banks out of Indonesia's financial system in late 1997 exacerbated the country's economic crisis. He argues that the Indonesian government should have temporarily taken over the insolvent banks rather than closing them down suddenly to sustain credit to solvent borrowers and to retain depositors' confidence. Also, even though the IMF insisted on greater transparency by the crises-affected governments and those under their jurisdiction, it continued to operate under considerable secrecy.

Such double standards on the part of the IMF, reflected by the priority it gave to protecting the interests of foreign banks and governments, also compromised its ostensible role as an impartial agent working in the interests of affected economies. The burden of IMF programs invariably fell on countries' domestic financial sectors and, eventually, on the public at large, which has borne most of the costs of adjustment and reform. The social costs of the public policy responses have been considerable, usually involving bailouts of much of the financial sector and of the corporate sector more generally.

Unhappiness in East Asia about how differently the IMF responded to the East Asian crises compared with the earlier Mexican one is widespread. People generally believe that the IMF was far more generous in helping Mexico because of the interest of the United States in ensuring that the tequila crisis was not seen as an adverse consequence of Mexico joining the North American Free Trade Agreement. In contrast, East Asians saw the IMF as far less generous and more demanding with all three countries, which had long seen themselves as allies of the United States and of the West in general.

The IMF has invariably given priority to liabilities and other commitments to foreign banks, even though both foreign and domestic banks may have been equally irresponsible or imprudent in their lending practices. As the BIS noted: "In spite of growing strains in Southeast Asia, overall bank lending to Asian developing countries showed no evidence of abating in the first half of 1997" (Raghavan 1998). From mid-1996 to mid-1997, Korea received US$15 billion in new loans while Indonesia received US$9 billion from the banks. Short-term lending continued to dominate, with 70 percent due within one year, while the share of lending to private nonbank borrowers rose to 45 percent by the end of June 1997. The banks were also actively acquiring nontraditional assets in the region, for instance, in higher-yielding local money markets and other debt securities. Most of this lending was by Japanese and European banks.

Thus Japanese and Western banks have emerged from the crises relatively unscathed and stronger than the domestic financial sectors of the crises-affected economies, which have taken the brunt of the cost of adjustment. Some merchant banks and other financial institutions were also able to make lucrative commissions from marketing sovereign debt, as the short-term private borrowing that precipitated the crises is converted into longer-term, government-guaranteed bonds under the terms of IMF programs.

Conclusion: Priorities for International Financial System Reform

The experiences of the 1997–98 East Asian crises give rise to six major lessons for international financial reform. First, existing mechanisms and institutions for preventing financial crises are grossly inadequate. As recent experiences suggest, current trends in financial liberalization are likely to increase rather than decrease the likelihood, frequency, and severity of currency and financial crises. Too little was done by the national authorities and their foreign advisers to discourage short-term capital flows and too much emphasis has been placed on the expected protection provided by international adherence to codes and standards (Rodrik 1999).[17] Financial liberalization has also reduced the macroeconomic instruments available to governments for crisis aversion, and has instead left governments with little choice but to react procyclically, which tends to exacerbate economic downturns. Governments need to be assured of their autonomy in relation to national macroeconomic policy to enable them to intervene countercyclically to avoid crises, which have had much more devastating consequences in developing countries than elsewhere. Recognition of the exaggerated effects of currency movements at the international level should also lead to greater surveillance and coordination among the three major international currency issuers: Japan, the United States, and Europe.

Second, existing mechanisms and institutions for financial crisis management are also grossly inadequate. The greater likelihood, frequency, and severity of currency and financial crises in middle-income developing countries in recent times—with devastating consequences for the real economy and for innocent bystanders "in the neighborhood," as in the East Asian crises—makes speedy crisis resolution imperative. There is an urgent need to increase emergency financing during crises and to establish adequate new procedures for timely and orderly debt standstills and workouts.[18] International financial institutions, including regional institutions, should be able to provide adequate countercyclical financing, for instance, for social safety nets during crises (Ocampo 2000).[19] Instead of current arrangements, which tend to benefit foreign creditors, new procedures and mechanisms are needed to ensure that they too share responsibility for the consequences of their lending practices.

Third, the agenda for international financial reform needs to go beyond the recent preoccupation with crisis prevention and resolution to address the declining availability and provision of development finance, especially to small and poor countries (Ocampo 2000) that have limited and expensive access to capital markets. The IMF, in particular, is facing growing pressure to return to its supposedly core function of providing emergency credit and core competencies of crisis prevention and mitigation.[20] Furthermore, the World Bank and other multilateral development banks have either abandoned or sharply reduced industrial financing, further limiting the likelihood that developing countries will be able to secure funding to develop new manufacturing capacities and capabilities. The United Nations Conference on Financing for Development, held in Mexico in March 2002, clearly did not address this challenge adequately despite the promise of the Monterrey consensus after the modest proposals of the Zedillo group report commissioned by the UN's secretary-general.

Fourth, inertia and vested interests stand in the way of urgently needed international institutional reforms. The international financial institutions need to reform their governance to ensure greater and more equitable participation and decision-making—and hence ownership—by developing countries at all levels and in various tasks that the new international financial system must begin to address more adequately. A related need concerns reducing the concentration of power in and the power of some apex institutions, such as the IMF, by delegating authority to other agencies, for example, the proposed World Financial Organization or World Financial Authority, as well as by encouraging decentralization, devolution, complementarity, and competition with other international financial institutions, including regional ones.[21] The Group of Seven must engage in more serious consultations with developing countries in relation to international economic issues to avoid insensitive and potentially disastrous oversights and further loss of policy legitimacy (Rodrik 1999).

Fifth, the reforms should restore and ensure national economic authority and autonomy, which have been greatly undermined by international liberalization and regulation, and which are essential for more effective macroeconomic management and initiatives pertaining to development. Policy conditionalities accompanying IMF financing must be minimized, if not eliminated altogether.[22] One size clearly does not fit all, and imposed policies have not contributed much to either economic recovery or growth (Weisbrot and others 2000), let alone sustainable development. Such ownership will ensure greater legitimacy for public policies and must include regulation of the capital account and choice of exchange rate regime.[23] Because international financial reforms in the foreseeable future are unlikely to adequately provide the global public goods and other international financial services most developing countries need, it is imperative that reforms of the international system assure national policy independence so that governments are better able to address regulatory and interventionist functions beyond a global and regional purview.

Finally, appreciation is growing of the desirability of regional monetary cooperation in the face of growing capital mobility and the increasing frequency of currency and related financial crises, often with devastating consequences for the real economy. Some observers argue, for instance, that growing European monetary integration in recent decades arose out of governments' recognition of their declining sovereignty in the face of growing capital mobility, especially as their capital accounts were liberalized (Baines 2002). Instead of trying to assert greater national control with probably limited efficacy, cooperation among governments in a region is more likely to be effective in the face of the larger magnitude and velocity of capital flows. However, no single formula or trajectory for fostering such cooperation is available, and it probably cannot be promoted successfully independently of economic cooperation on other fronts. The existence of such regional arrangements also offers an intermediate alternative between national and global levels of action and intervention and reduces the possibly monopolistic powers of global authorities. To be successful and effective, such regional arrangements must be flexible, but credible, and must be capable of both effective countercyclical initiatives for crisis prevention and management. In East Asia, the Japanese proposal for an Asian monetary facility soon after the outbreak of the Asian crises could have made a major difference in checking and managing the crises, but Western opposition blocked the proposal. With the growing reluctance in the West—especially the United States—to allow the IMF to serve as a lender of last resort (as in the recent Argentinean crisis), it should at least be more tolerant of regional cooperative arrangements as alternatives.

Notes

1. Of course, the availability of cheap foreign funds, for example, because of a low real interest rate, can help to temporarily close both domestic savings-investments and foreign exchange gaps, especially if well invested or deployed.

2. Financial analysts had become fixated with the current account deficit, especially since the Mexican meltdown of early 1995. In earlier times, some economies sustained similar deficits for much longer without comparable consequences. In the immediate aftermath of the Mexican crisis, several Southeast Asian economies already had comparable current account deficits, despite, or rather because of, rapid economic growth.

3. In some countries, government-owned, nonfinancial, public enterprises were very much part of the growth of supposedly private sector debt.

4. There is also no evidence that the stock market boom of the mid-1990s raised funds for productive investment more effectively. Indeed, the converse was true, with financial disintermediation from commercial banks to the stock market.

5. Even though the U.S. economy was strengthening, the Southeast Asian economies were growing even faster.

6. In the mid-1990s, as the U.S. dollar strengthened along with the U.S. economy, both the Germans and the Japanese allowed their currencies to depreciate against the U.S. dollar, with relatively little disruption, in an effort to regain international competitiveness.

7. Sentiments can influence fundamentals and the health of financial systems either favorably or unfavorably (Montes 1998). In particular, the collapse of the Southeast Asian currencies because of sentiments adversely affected the viability of investments made at different exchange rates, which in turn exacerbated the domestic banking crises.

8. Montes (1998) argues that the more rural-based Southeast Asian economies were better able to carry out real devaluations from nominal changes in currency value, because their export sectors were not too tied down by supply-side inflexibilities to respond to real devaluations. After asserting that stock markets served to share risks among asset owners rather than to raise financing, he notes that, except for financial system weaknesses, Southeast Asian real sectors were relatively immune from the 1997–98 asset market frenzy.

9. Equity and portfolio investments had overtaken direct investment, loans, and trade credit in providing external financing by the 1990s. Montes (1998, p. 34) cites Reisen's warning that offers of foreign financing should be resisted if they would "cause unsustainable currency appreciation, excessive risk-taking in the banking system, and a sharp drop in private savings." Hence, in a sentiment-driven market, currencies become too strong with the prospect of strong external financing and too weak when capital withdraws or threatens to.

10. Woo (2000) argues that occasional excessive price movements in financial markets should not be too readily attributed to the rational anticipation of changes in government policies that were not eventually realized, the main argument usually invoked to reject claims of speculative bubbles.

11. Krugman's (1998c) attempt at theoretical catching-up is particularly worthy of consideration in light of his own previous attempts to understand related international economic phenomena as well as East Asian economic growth. As the crises were still unfolding, such an attempt was hardly definitive, especially without the benefit of hindsight. Yet, as policy was very much being made on the hoof, his attempt to highlight certain relationships were illuminating. Hence Krugman (1998c) argues that:

> It is necessary to adopt an approach quite different from that of traditional currency crisis theory. Of course Asian economies did experience currency crises, and the usual channels of speculation were operative here as always. However, the currency crises were only part of a broader financial crisis, which had very little to do with currencies or even monetary issues per se. Nor did the crisis have much to do with traditional fiscal issues. Instead, to make sense of what went wrong, we need to focus on two issues normally neglected in currency crisis analysis. These are the role of financial intermediaries (and of the moral hazard associated with such intermediaries when they are poorly regulated), and the prices of real assets such as capital and land.

12. None of the fundamentals usually emphasized seemed to have been important in the affected economies: all the governments had fiscal surpluses and none were involved in excessive monetary expansion, while inflation rates were generally low.

13. Recent findings suggest that national savings tend to equal national investment, indicating that flows of capital to the best possible use are far from universal and much smaller than simple theories predict. Lack of information or other risks and uncertainties tend to reduce cross-border capital flows.

14. Eatwell (1997) suggests a negative correlation between dependence on foreign savings and economic performance. This is true if foreign savings are not broken down into their components. The numbers are strongly biased by the inclusion of short-term money market flows, which may include efforts by governments to prop up their currencies with high interest rates, which temporarily suck in money from overseas. Brazil, Mexico, and especially Venezuela typified this a few years ago. If only long-term direct (or equity) investment was considered, many poorly performing Latin American economies would not be considered to be heavily dependent on foreign savings any more. Southeast Asian countries, especially Malaysia and Singapore, would then rank high in both foreign savings (measured "appropriately") and economic performance.

15. Of course, capital flight is not an inevitable consequence of financial liberalization, but may reflect locals' fears and hedging behavior.

16. Arguably, the Philippines currency did not take quite as hard a hit as those of the other crises-affected economies, in part because its banking and accounting standards were relatively better, but also because its short-term capital inflows before the crises were relatively low.

17. Pistor (2000) demonstrates that international legal standards are unlikely to have the desired outcomes because of the significance of historical original conditions and varied path dependence.

18. Consensus is growing on the need to set up standstill and other procedures for international debt workouts akin to U.S. bankruptcy provisions for corporations and municipal authorities, although IMF Deputy Managing Director Anne Krueger's (2002) proposals have not been well received by those governments most likely to be affected by them because of their adverse selection consequences for such governments.

19. Social safety nets should not be seen as a substitute for social policy, which should be adequate to ensure a decent standard of living within a government's means in addition to enhancing human resources for development.

20. Then U.S. Treasury Secretary and former World Bank Vice President and Chief Economist Lawrence Summers is a prominent proponent of this view. See, for example, Summers (1999).

21. As Ocampo (2000) puts it:

    The required financial architecture should in some cases have the nature of a network of institutions that provide the services required in a complementary fashion (in the areas of emergency financing, surveillance of macroeconomic policies, prudential regulation and supervision of domestic financial systems, etc.), and in others (particularly in development finance) should exhibit the characteristics of a system of competitive organizations.

22. They have been shown to be ill-informed, erroneous, and irrelevant to the problems at hand, and as noted, also exacerbated the East Asian crises.

23. Then IMF Senior Deputy Managing Director Stanley Fischer (2001) admitted that *"willingly or otherwise,* a growing number of countries have come to accept [the belief that intermediate regimes between hard pegs and free floating are unsustainable] . . . Proponents of the bipolar view—myself included—have perhaps exaggerated their argument for dramatic effect."

References

The word "processed" describes informally reproduced works that may not be commonly available in libraries.

ADB (Asian Development Bank). 1999. *Asian Development Outlook.* Hong Kong, China: Oxford University Press.

Baines, Adam. 2002. "Capital Mobility and European Financial and Monetary Integration: A Structural Analysis." *Review of International Studies* 28: 337–57.

Carleton, P. D., B. P. Rosario, and W. T. Woo. 2000. "The Unorthodox Origins of the Asian Financial Crisis: Evidence from Logit Estimations. *ASEAN Economic Bulletin* Special Issue (April).

Demirguc-Kunt, A., and E. Detragiache. 1998. "The Determinants of Banking Crises in Developing and Developed Countries." *IMF Staff Paper,* 45(1): 81–109.

Eatwell, John. 1997. *International Financial Liberalization: The Impact on World Development.* Discussion Paper Series. New York: United Nations Development Programme, Office of Development Studies.

Fischer, Stanley. 2001. "Exchange Rate Regimes: Is the Bipolar View Correct?" *Finance and Development* 38(2): 18–21.

Furman, Jason, and J. E. Stiglitz. 1998. "Economic Crises: Evidence and Insights from East Asia." In *Brookings Papers on Economic Activity no. 2.* Washington, D.C.: Brookings Institution.

Gomez, E. T., and K.S. Jomo. 1999. *Malaysia's Political Economy: Politics, Patronage, and Profits.* New York: Cambridge University Press.

IMF (International Monetary Fund). 1997. *World Economic Outlook: Interim Assessment.* Washington, D.C.

———. 1998. *World Economic Outlook and International Financial Markets: Interim Assessment.* Washington, D.C.

Jomo, K. S., ed. 1998. *Tigers in Trouble: Financial Governance, Liberalisation and Crises in East Asia.* London: Zed Books.

———. 2001a. *Growth After the Asian Crisis: What Remains of the East Asian Model?* Group of 24 Discussion Paper no. 10., Geneva and Cambridge, Mass.: United Nations Conference on Trade and Development and Harvard University, Kennedy School of Government.

———, ed. 2001b. *Malaysian Eclipse: Economic Crisis and Recovery.* London: Zed Books.

———, ed. 2002. *Paper Tigers in Southeast Asia? Behind Miracle and Debacle.* London: Routledge.

Jomo, K. S., with Chen Yun Chung, Brian C. Folk, Irfan ul-Haque, Pasuk Phongpaichit, Batara Simatupang, and Mayuri Tateishi. 1997. *Southeast Asia's Misunderstood Miracle: Industrial Policy and Economic Development in Thailand, Malaysia, and Indonesia.* Boulder, Colo.: Westview.

Kaminsky, Gabriela, and C. M. Reinhart. 1996. "The Twin Crises: The Causes of Banking and Balance-of-Payments Problems." Working Paper no. 17. University of Maryland, Centre for International Economics, Baltimore, MD.

Keynes, J. M. 1936. *The General Theory of Employment, Interest, and Money.* New York: Harcourt Brace.

Khan, Mushtaq, and K. S. Jomo. eds 2000. *Rents, Rent-Seeking, and Economic Development: Theory and Evidence in Asia.* Cambridge, U.K.: Cambridge University Press.

Kregel, Jan. 1998. "East Asia Is Not Mexico: The Differences between Balance of Payments Crises and Debt Deflation." In K. S. Jomo, ed., *Tigers in Trouble: Financial Governance, Liberalisation, and Crises in East Asia*. London: Zed Books.

Krueger, Anne. 2002. Speech on a sovereign debt restructuring mechanism. International Monetary Fund, Washington, DC.

Krugman, Paul 1994. "The Myth of the Asian Miracle." *Foreign Affairs* (November–December).

———. 1998a. "The Confidence Game: How Washington Worsened Asia's Crash." *The New Republic*, October 5.

———. 1998b. "What Happened to Asia?" Paper prepared for a conference in Japan, January. http://www.mit.edu/krugman/www/DISINTER/html.

———. 1998c. "Will Asia Bounce Back?" Speech for Credit Suisse First Boston, Hong Kong (China). http://web.mit.edu/krugman/www.

———. 1999. *The Return of Depression Economics*. London: Allen Lane.

Lane, Timothy, A. Ghrosh, J. Hamann, S. Phillips, M. Schulze-Ghattas, and T. Tsikata. 1999. *IMF-Supported Programs in Indonesia, Korea, and Thailand: A Preliminary Assessment*. International Monetary Fund, Washington, D.C.

Mayer, Martin. 1998. "The Asian Disease: Plausible Diagnoses, Possible Remedies." Working Paper no. 232. Jerome Levy Economics Institute, Bard College, New York.

McKibbin, Warwick. 1998. "Modelling the Crisis in Asia." *ASEAN Economic Bulletin* (December).

Minsky, Hyman P. 1972. *Financial Instability Revisited: The Economics of Disaster: Reappraisal of the Federal Reserve Discount Mechanism*. Washington, D.C.: Board of Governors of the Federal Reserve System.

———. 1986. "A Theory of Systemic Fragility." In Edward Altman and Arnold Sametz, eds. *Financial Crises in a Fragile Environment*. London: John Wiley.

———. 1993. "The Financial Instability Hypothesis." In Philip Arestis and Malcolm Sawyer, eds., *Handbook of Radical Political Economy*. Aldershot, U.K.: Edward Elgar.

Montes, M. F. 1998. *The Currency Crisis in Southeast Asia*. Singapore: Institute of Southeast Asian Studies.

Nasution, A. 2000. "The Meltdown of the Indonesian Economy: Causes, Responses, and Lessons." *ASEAN Economic Bulletin* Special Issue (April).

Ocampo, Jose A. 2000. "A Broad Agenda for International Financial Reform." In *Financial Globalization and the Emerging Economies*. Santiago: United Nations Economic Commission for Latin America and the Caribbean.

Pasuk, P., and C. Baker. 2000. *Thailand's Crisis*. Chiang Mai, Thailand: Silkworm Books.

Pistor, Katarina. 2000. "The Standardization of Law and Its Effect on Developing Economies." Group of 24 Discussion Paper series no. 4. Geneva and Cambridge, Mass.: United Nations Conference on Trade and Development and Harvard University, Center for International Development.

Radelet, Steve, and Jeffrey Sachs. 1998. "The East Asian Financial Crisis: Diagnosis, Remedies, Prospects." *Brookings Papers on Economic Activity* 1: 1–90.

Raghavan, Chakravarthi. 1998. "BIS Banks Kept Shovelling Funds to Asia Despite Warnings." *Third World Economics* (January): 16–31.

Rasiah, Rajah. 2001. "Pre-Crisis Economic Weaknesses and Vulnerabilities." In K. S. Jomo, ed., *Malaysian Eclipse: Economic Crisis and Recovery*. London: Zed Books.

Rodrik, Dani, 1999. "Governing the Global Economy: Does One Architectural Style Fit All?" Paper prepared for the Brookings Institution Trade Policy Forum Conference on Governing in a Global Economy, April 14–16, Washington, D.C.

Rubin, Robert, 1998. "Strengthening the Architecture of the International Financial System." Public statement delivered at the Brookings Institution, April 14, Washington, D.C.

Summers, Lawrence. 1999. Speech at the London Business School, December 14. *Financial Times,* December 15. http://www.lbs.ac.uk/news-events/scripts/summers.

UNCTAD (United Nations Conference on Trade and Development). 1997. *Trade and Development Report, 1997.* Geneva.

Wade, Robert. 1998. "From 'Miracle to 'Cronyism': Explaining the Great Asian Slump." *Cambridge Journal of Economics* 22: 693–706.

Weisbrot, Mark, and others. 2000. "The Emperor Has No Growth: Declining Economic Growth Rates in the Era of Globalization." Center for Economic Policy Research, Washington, D.C.

Wong, Hwa Kiong, with K. S. Jomo. 2001. "The Impact of Foreign Capital Inflows on the Malaysian Economy, 1966–1996." University of Malaya, Faculty of Economics and Administration, Kuala Lumpur. Processed.

Woo, W. T. 2000. "Coping with Accelerated Capital Flows from the Globalization of Financial Markets." *ASEAN Economic Bulletin* Special Issue (April).

World Bank. 1994. *World Development Report, 1994: Infrastructure for Development.* New York: Oxford University Press.

_____. 1997. *World Development Report, 1997: The State in a Changing World.* New York: Oxford University Press.

Determinants of Foreign Direct Investment: Globalization-Induced Changes and the Role of Policies

JOHN H. DUNNING

One of the most remarkable features of the last decade has been the rapidly growing trans-nationalization of most economies in the world. As set out in table 1, and expressed as a percentage of the global gross domestic product (GDP), the share of combined inward and outward foreign direct investment (FDI) stocks for the world as a whole rose from 14.2 percent in 1985 to an estimated 38.9 percent in 2000. Even following a 46 percent fall in world FDI outflows in 2001 and 2002, the FDI to GDP ratio had risen to 43.9 percent. As table 1 shows, the increase in this share was particularly notable for Central and Eastern European countries. These figures demonstrate that FDI flows still remain one of the most dynamic constituents of the global economy, and expectations were that in 2002, as in 2001, they would considerably outpace the growth of both trade and world GDP.

This paper is primarily concerned with the impact of recent economic and political events and the likely course of future events on the geographic distribution of FDI, in particular, the role of FDI policies in influencing the location of the value added activities of multinational enterprises (MNEs). To what extent has the recent slowdown in economic growth, the growth of regional integration schemes, and the aftermath of the terrorist attacks of September 11, 2001, caused international firms to retrench or realign their locational strategies and which parts of the value chain are now being relocated? What about the role of e-commerce and the setting up of multiple regional headquarters? How do the characteristics and determinants of industrial country-industrial country FDI differ from those of industrial country-developing country or developing country-developing country FDI?

John Dunning is emeritus professor of international business at the Centre for International Business History at Reading University, Reading, United Kingdom, and at Rutgers University, New Brunswick, New Jersey. This paper is an updated version of the one presented at the conference. Some material contained in this paper was first published in Economist Intelligence Unit, *World Investment Prospects, 2002* (London: Economist Intelligence Unit, 2002), and permission to reprint this version has been granted.

Annual World Bank Conference on Development Economics—Europe 2003
© 2004 The International Bank for Reconstruction and Development/The World Bank

TABLE 1. Combined Inward and Outward FDI Stocks, Selected Years
(percentage of global GDP)

Region	1985	1990	1995	1997	1998	1999	2000	2001	2002
World	14.2	19.2	20.5	23.6	27.8	34.0	38.9	41.6	43.9
Industrial countries	13.6	18.2	21.0	24.4	28.5	33.5	37.9	40.9	43.1
Developing countries	15.7	16.0	20.4	22.4	26.7	38.1	44.0	46.2	49.5
Central and Eastern Europe	. . .	1.8	6.0	9.5	13.8	15.1	21.1	22.2	24.1

. . . Negligible.

Source: UNCTAD (1998, 2001, 2003).

Factors Influencing Recent Trends in FDI

The data in table 2 suggest that the late 1990s and early 2000s saw a redirection of global FDI inflows away from the industrial regions, and especially from North America and Western Europe. Three main reasons accounted for this. First, a huge cross-border merger and acquisition (M&A) boom overwhelmingly involved MNEs from one part of the "triad" (Japan, North America, and Western Europe) buying firms in another part of the triad. Between 1995 and 2000, M&As accounted for almost 70 percent of all new FDI.[1] Most of these M&As were geared toward augmenting the technological, managerial, or entrepreneurial assets of the acquiring firms or accessing new markets. In 2000, the service sector accounted for at least 73 percent of all cross-border sales and mergers, with four-fifths of these in transport, communications, finance, and business services. In manufacturing, deals in the electrical; electronic equipment; and food, drink, and tobacco sectors headed the list. The slowdown in economic growth, particularly among the triad countries, dramatically reduced the number of cross-border M&As in 2001. Nevertheless, in the first nine months of that year, even though they amounted to only about half of the value for the same period of the previous year, cross-border M&A sales were still higher than the average for the preceding six years. Again, most of these involved European or trans-Atlantic corporations.

The second reason for the redirection of global FDI flows was the growth of regional integration schemes, especially the completion of the internal market in Europe and the maturation of the North America Free Trade Agreement (NAFTA). Table 3 shows a steadily rising share of FDI inflows into these two regions in the latter half of the 1990s. However, data for 2001 and 2002 suggest a considerable decline of that share to around 67.4 percent. The fall was particularly marked in the case of NAFTA. This mainly reflected a dramatic decline (namely, of 43.5 percent in 2001 and 60.5 percent in 2002) of cross-border sales of North American companies (UNCTAD 2003).

The third reason for the redirection of global FDI flows was the slowdown in the economic growth of mainland China and the East Asian economic crises of the mid- and later 1990s, which considerably reduced Asia's earlier attractiveness to foreign investors. Indeed, between 1996 and 1999, the share of new South, East, and Southeast Asian FDI inflows, as a percentage of world inflows, fell from 23.2 percent to

TABLE 2. Share of FDI Inflows, Selected Regions and Countries, Selected Years

(percentage of total FDI)

Region and country	1995	1998	1999	2000	2001	2002
Industrial countries, of which:	61.4	69.7	77.0	82.2	68.4	70.7
North America	20.5	28.4	28.3	24.6	20.7	7.8
Western Europe	35.4	37.8	46.6	55.8	45.7	57.5
Japan	0.1	0.5	1.2	0.6	8.4	14.3
Developing countries, of which:	34.2	27.0	20.7	15.9	27.9	24.9
Africa	1.4	1.2	1.2	0.6	2.3	1.7
Asia and the Pacific, of which:	22.9	13.8	9.5	9.0	13.9	14.6
China, including Hong Kong	12.7	9.4	6.0	6.9	9.5	10.2
Latin America and the Caribbean	9.8	11.8	10.1	6.4	11.6	8.6
Central and Eastern Europe[a]	4.3	3.3	2.3	1.8	3.7	4.4
World	100.0	100.0	100.0	100.0	100.0	100.0

a. Including countries comprising the former Yugoslavia.

Source: UNCTAD (2001, 2002, 2003).

TABLE 3. Shares of FDI Flows Directed toward Two Areas of Regional Economic Integration, 1989–2002

(percentage of total FDI)

Area	1989–94	1995–98	1999	2000	2001	2002
European Union	38.3	32.4	43.5	48.6	38.0	57.5
NAFTA	27.4	27.5	30.9	28.1	24.5	9.9
Total	65.7	59.9	74.4	76.7	62.5	67.4

Source: UNCTAD (2001, 2003).

9.8 percent. Since then, mainly because of the Republic of Korea's restructuring of its economic policy and the depreciation of the won, together with foreign investors' renewed optimism about the Chinese, and particularly the Hong Kong economy, FDI inflows recovered to 10.0 percent in 2000, 11.8 percent in 2001, and 13.6 percent in 2002.[2]

What, however, of the specific effect of September 11?[3] Certainly the immediate impact was to accentuate the economic downturn of the previous nine months, to create a higher level of corporate uncertainty, and to encourage more firms to adopt a wait and see attitude in relation to their FDI plans.

In the medium term, the new global economic environment is likely to have two major effects on the geographical distribution of FDI. First, by placing a higher premium on environmental risk, it is likely to steer MNE activity toward locations perceived to be friendly toward their home country regimes and to be the least subject to terrorist attacks or political instability. Second, it is likely to add to the competitive pressures in many industries and force companies to enhance their cost efficiency. Faced by more price-driven competition, some MNEs may choose to relocate some of their production facilities to low-cost developing and/or transition countries. At the same time, because of their increased economic vulnerability, other MNEs may choose to reduce their foreign equity stakes, particularly in advanced technology sectors, and conclude more strategic alliances and subcontracting arrangements with foreign firms.

The Changing Locational Determinants of FDI

Most empirical studies of the locational determinants of FDI (as, for example, summarized in UNCTAD 1998) recognize that these are strongly dependent on

- The motivation for the FDI, for example, natural resource-seeking versus market-seeking, efficiency-seeking versus asset-augmenting objectives

- The economic and business environment of host, or potential host, countries and the FDI-related policies pursued by their governments

- The mode of entry or expansion of the FDI, for instance, greenfield FDI as opposed to M&As.

Figure 1 sets out these locational determinants of FDI. In recent years, much scholarly research and a plethora of business surveys on the host country determinants of FDI have been concerned with evaluating the significance of the variables presented in this figure (see UNCTAD 1998 for more details), especially policy, tax and investment incentives, labor costs, market size, and the policy framework for FDI (in this connection see Siebert 2000 on locational competition and appropriate policy instruments for attracting appropriate FDI).

However, the focus of this paper is on the changes in the significance of some of these variables during the last decade or so. Note the four types of FDI set out in table 4 and how both the principal economic determinants and the responses of host country governments to these determinants have affected, and are affecting, the locational strategies of mobile investors (which may include both foreign-owned and domestically-owned MNEs). While the table is largely self-explanatory, a couple of points related to the first two kinds of MNE activity should be emphasized.

In relation to industrial country-industrial country FDI, in addition to the traditional market resource-seeking FDI, recent MNE activity has been dominated by two kinds of FDI, each of which responds differently to host country determinants. The first is by means of M&As. In 2000, intra-industrial country cross-border M&A purchases accounted for 93.2 percent of all cross-border M&A purchases. The corresponding figure for cross-border sales was 88.3 percent. Cross-border M&As are essentially motivated by the expectation that the acquired firms will help the acquiring firms to upgrade their competitive advantage, to gain access to new markets or supply capabilities, or both. In this respect, the host country's business environment and its government regulations, for example, as they pertain to competition, financing, research and development (R&D), and cross-border M&As, are proving to be an increasingly influential determinant of location.

FIGURE 1. Host Country Determinants of FDI

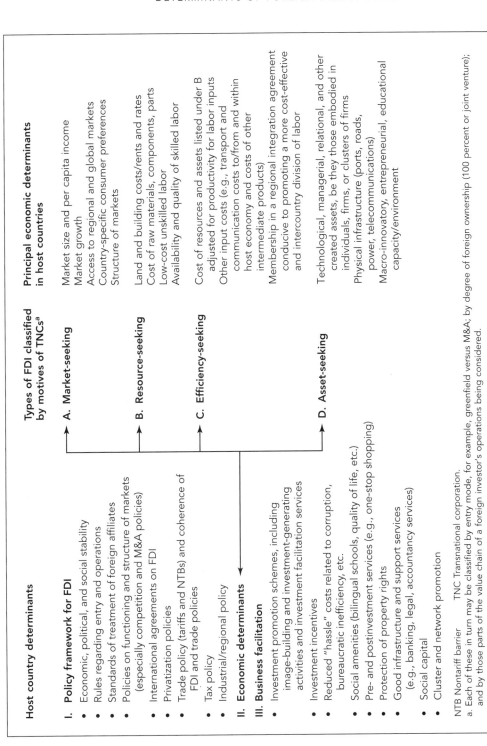

Host country determinants

I. Policy framework for FDI

- Economic, political, and social stability
- Rules regarding entry and operations
- Standards of treatment of foreign affiliates
- Policies on functioning and structure of markets (especially competition and M&A policies)
- International agreements on FDI
- Privatization policies
- Trade policy (tariffs and NTBs) and coherence of FDI and trade policies
- Tax policy
- Industrial/regional policy

II. Economic determinants

III. Business facilitation

- Investment promotion schemes, including image-building and investment-generating activities and investment facilitation services
- Investment incentives
- Reduced "hassle" costs related to corruption, bureaucratic inefficiency, etc.
- Social amenities (bilingual schools, quality of life, etc.)
- Pre- and postinvestment services (e.g., one-stop shopping)
- Protection of property rights
- Good infrastructure and support services (e.g., banking, legal, accountancy services)
- Social capital
- Cluster and network promotion

NTB Nontariff barrier   TNC Transnational corporation.
a. Each of these in turn may be classified by entry mode, for example, greenfield versus M&A; by degree of foreign ownership (100 percent or joint venture); and by those parts of the value chain of a foreign investor's operations being considered.

Types of FDI classified by motives of TNCs[a]

A. Market-seeking

B. Resource-seeking

C. Efficiency-seeking

D. Asset-seeking

Principal economic determinants in host countries

Market size and per capita income
Market growth
Access to regional and global markets
Country-specific consumer preferences
Structure of markets

Land and building costs/rents and rates
Cost of raw materials, components, parts
Low-cost unskilled labor
Availability and quality of skilled labor

Cost of resources and assets listed under B adjusted for productivity for labor inputs
Other input costs (e.g., transport and communication costs to/from and within host economy and costs of other intermediate products)
Membership in a regional integration agreement conducive to promoting a more cost-effective and intercountry division of labor

Technological, managerial, relational, and other created assets, be they those embodied in individuals, firms, or clusters of firms
Physical infrastructure (ports, roads, power, telecommunications)
Macro-innovatory, entrepreneurial, educational capacity/environment

Source: Adapted from UNCTAD (1998, p. 91, table IV.1).

TABLE 4. Changing Locational Variables Affecting FDI, 1970–80 and 1990–2000

	1970–80	1990–2000
1. Industrial country–industrial country		
Firms' motives and strategies	• Mainly market-seeking and horizontal efficiency-seeking FDI • Mixture of greenfield FDI (or expansion of same) and M&As	• More asset-augmenting and horizontal efficiency-seeking FDI • More M&As and strategic alliances • Integrated MNE operations
Host country determinants	• Many domestic MNE operations • Predominantly FDI policy and economic determinants affecting market efficiency-seeking FDI	• Emphasis on business facilitating variables • Availability of creative assets • Agglomerative economies
2. Industrial country–developing country		
Firms' motives and strategies	• Mainly market resource-seeking • Greenfield and joint ventures • Many domestic MNE operations	• More vertical efficiency-seeking FDI and subcontracting
Host country determinants	• Predominantly FDI policy and economic determinants, especially regulation of incentives in relation to FDI	• Emphasis switched to using FDI to upgrade domestic competitive advantages • More attention given to economic policies and business facilitation
3. Developing country–industrial country		
Firms' motives and strategies	• Little FDI	• Some market-seeking and asset-seeking FDI
Host country determinants	• As for (1) above	• Market size and growth • Availability of technology, organizational capacity
4. Developing country–developing country		
Firms' motives and strategies	• Almost entirely market resource-seeking	• As for 1970–80, but an increasing amount of efficiency-seeking and some asset-augmenting FDI.
Host country determinants	• Many domestic MNE operations • As for (2) above	• As for (2) above

Source: Author.

The second kind of FDI is horizontal efficiency-seeking FDI, which is being encouraged by market liberalization and regional integration schemes. Here the critical locational determinants are increasingly those identified under C and III rather than A, B, D, and I in figure 1.

In relation to industrial country-developing country FDI, again two forms of FDI are predominant. The first is the traditional market-seeking or resource-seeking FDI, which, excluding FDI related to tax havens, still accounts for the majority of industrial country-developing country FDI, probably around 70 percent, especially in the larger countries, such as Brazil, China, and India.[4] Here the critical variables are those identified by A, B, 1, and 2 in figure 1. Such FDI tends to be fairly location-bound, although the policy and business-facilitating framework may be critical in determining whether FDI takes place at all.

The second type of FDI is vertical efficiency-seeking FDI, in which foreign companies seek to produce intermediate and/or final products in the cheapest locations, primarily for exports to third markets. Here the variables identified by C, II, and III in figure 1 are the critical ones, given a satisfactory general policy framework for FDI (and indeed, for domestic investment). Currently such investment is largely concentrated in South, East, and Southeast Asia and Mexico.

Impact of the Value Chain on the Location of FDI

So far this paper has considered the location of all foreign activities of MNEs financed by FDI; however, choices about location and host governments' policies are likely to vary not only between industrial sectors, but also according to the justification for the activities and the particular parts of the value chain that MNEs choose to locate outside their home countries. Given that a good deal of intra-triad FDI is now being made to protect or augment the existing competitive advantages of the investing firms rather than to exploit such advantages suggests a different distribution of MNE activity both between industrial countries and within them. By contrast, by far the greater part of FDI in developing countries, notably in the larger and faster-growing economies, is directed toward accessing local natural resources and/or national or regional markets. Thus MNEs' future locational strategies and the impact of host governments' FDI-related policies are likely to rest on the relative significance and growth of the two types of FDI. This, in turn, will reflect the opportunities offered by local markets and supply capabilities on the one hand, and the need to tap into the global panorama of resources and capabilities, particularly of all kinds of knowledge, on the other.

On the question of which functions MNEs are most likely to locate outside their home countries, the literature is fairly clear. In a survey conducted in the 1990s, Dunning (1996) found that even though 40 percent of the global assets of 150 of the world's leading industrial companies were located outside their home countries, only 23.3 percent of their R&D activities were located elsewhere. Data on the extent to which patents registered in the United States by the world's largest firms are attributable to research undertaken by their foreign affiliates confirm MNEs' tendency to concentrate their innovatory activities in their home countries—usually for good economic reasons. However, as Cantwell and Janne (2000) show, this proportion has gradually risen over the years, averaging some 11.5 percent in the first half of the 1990s, compared with 11.0 percent in the 1980s and 10.5 percent in the 1970s. It is now highest in the case of European firms (35.0 percent) and lowest in the case of Japanese and U.S. firms (1.1 and 8.6 percent, respectively).

Furthermore, whereas 70.2 percent of MNEs' stock of FDI was located in the industrial countries in 2002, between 80 and 85 percent of their innovatory activities were so located. Despite the increasing tendency for MNEs to site some of their R&D activities (mostly development activities) in the larger or higher-income developing countries, notably Brazil, China, India, Korea, and Singapore, the bulk continue to be performed within the triad. Indeed, a growing number of the more knowledge- or information-intensive MNEs are obtaining an active R&D presence in each of the main triad regions (Kuemmerle 1999). Research has also shown that such a presence is offering handsome benefits to the investing companies, both in terms of the access it gives them to new sources of technological, organizational, and marketing expertise and to foreign innovatory systems and in terms of the R&D actually undertaken by the MNEs' local affiliates. The situation is also causing host governments to reappraise their technology policies in light of the increasing presence of innovatory activities by MNEs (for an exploration of these issues, see Archibugi, Howells, and Michie 1999).

Other Factors Affecting the Location of FDI

Three other observations are pertinent in relation to the recent and likely future locational pattern of MNE activity. The first concerns the likely impact of the Internet, in particular, business to business electronic commerce. While a few examples exist of tangible goods (which need to be produced in a particular location) being replaced by services downloaded from the computer, the main effect of the Internet is currently on the mode of delivery of the goods and services in question (Dunning and Wymbs 2001). If nothing else, the Internet is a market-facilitating instrument, because it reduces information asymmetries in firms and spatial transaction costs, both along and across value chains. In so doing, it has enormously widened the locational options open to firms in seeking out their suppliers, customers, and possible collaborators. This is particularly the case where reasonably standardized commodities are being produced and sold, and where the necessary information and knowledge, for example, in the form of designs, blueprints, and specifications, can be transferred and used across national boundaries without difficulty. Supply chains in such sectors as automobiles, garments, and electronic goods are not only becoming dis-internalized by firms, but are becoming more spatially dispersed, particularly in developing Asian countries and the transition economies of Eastern Europe. Indeed, the Internet is a major force for globalization and for widening MNEs' locational choices (Zaheer and Manrakhan 2001). Moreover, in the case of the more labor-intensive activities, the

Internet has significantly favored the economies of lower- and middle-income developing countries that pursue the right policies toward, or in light of, inbound FDI.

At the same time, the advent of e-commerce is having much less impact on the location of the higher-value and more idiosyncratic activities of firms, as these tend to involve market failures or distortions that the Internet is unable to correct. As a result, the geographical dispersion of MNEs' innovatory activities in the years to come is likely to be modest. These are likely to remain concentrated in the industrial world and in a relatively few developing countries, notably China and India, whose resource capabilities and infrastructure are congenial to such activity.

The second, and related, new element affecting the location of international business is the trend toward a subnational agglomeration of related activities by firms (for a recent review of the extensive literature developing on this subject, see Dunning 2000). Sometimes this clustering is among firms that produce similar products, and sometimes between firms and their suppliers and customers. While the principle of comparative advantage has long since helped explain the allocation of production between countries, economists now recognize that, at least in the world's larger economies, the principle is no less relevant in explaining the spatial distribution of some kinds of activities within countries. Examples include the agglomeration of high-technology activities in Silicon Valley and Route 128 in the United States; of software activities in Bangalore, India; of the port wine industry in Oporto, Portugal; of the cutlery industry in Solingen, Germany; and of the financial services sector in the City of London and in Hong Kong (China). Moreover, the advantages of spatial agglomeration, for instance, access to common learning facilities, information, infrastructure, and factor and product markets, are no less applicable to services as to manufacturing activities, and can be realized in both developing and industrial countries. MNEs will likely be increasingly drawn to such subnational groupings in the next decade and beyond.

The third observation is the growing trend among MNEs toward setting up, diversifying, and expanding their regional headquarters (RHQs). This trend is again evident both in the case of industrial and developing countries, and is lending support to Rugman's (2000) assertion that MNE activity is becoming increasingly regionalized (within the Americas, Asia, and Europe) rather than globalized. This is certainly being encouraged by the growing number of regional integration schemes and the extent to which MNEs engage in intraregional versus inter-regional trade. For example, according to the annual surveys conducted by the U.S. Department of Commerce and published in the *Survey of Current Business,* in the late 1990s, some 75 percent of the exports of U.S. industrial affiliates located in the European Union were intra-European Union, and 80 percent of those in Mexico and Canada were intra-NAFTA.

RHQs are by no means confined to the advanced industrial countries or to firms engaged in manufacturing. Both Hong Kong (China) and Singapore house the RHQs of Asian-based trade, shipping, and financial and business service firms, most of whose value-added activities are conducted within the region (Enright 2000).[5]

The RHQ trend once again demonstrates not only a tendency toward more geographical diversification, but also to increased specialization within regions to take advantage of economies of scale, access to high-quality skills and services, and strategic locations.

Conclusions

The evidence strongly suggests that both short- and long-term forces are compelling MNEs to rethink their locational strategies and national and subnational governments to reappraise their microeconomic management policies designed to attract and retain the "right" kind of FDI. In relation to the former, spatially-related decisions, especially in respect of what and how much to subcontract, what and how much to produce, and to whom and where to sell end products, are clearly becoming a more important component of competitive advantage. While corporations must still generate their core competences internally, they must also efficiently use these— many of which are geographically mobile—jointly with other resources and capabilities in different parts of the world that are spatially less mobile.

However, the locational strategies firms actually choose are likely to be highly contextual and to vary according to a variety of industry-specific characteristics, the motives for FDI, and the functions being performed by MNEs' subsidiaries. Quite apart from the impact of the current economic slowdown and the events of September 11, the Internet, the widening scope of the knowledge-based economy, and the increasing number of regional integration schemes are also affecting the location of FDI.

As concerns the role of governments as they seek to attract MNE activity, they need to recognize that the location-specific advantages mobile investors seek are changing. While in some countries, for example, the larger developing countries, such traditional economic variables as the availability of cheap labor, natural resources, and market size remain important, in others, such as the more advanced industrial countries, MNEs are increasingly seeking a range of complementary, knowledge-intensive resources and capabilities; a supportive and transparent commercial, legal, and communications infrastructure; and a gamut of institutions and government policies favorable to globalization, innovation, and entrepreneurship.

Field surveys of business executives' rankings of various countries (Economist Intelligence Unit 2002) show that business executives are increasingly ranking countries' political stability, quality of institutional infrastructure and social capital, and government policies toward private enterprise and competition, along with the macroeconomic environment, as the critical variables likely to affect the future location of FDI in the early years of the 21st century. The propensity to terrorist attacks or other destabilizing events could be added to this list. These results, which are broadly confirmed by econometric studies and surveys on firms' investment intentions, are useful pointers to governments wishing to attract such investment (for an excellent survey of the determinants of FDI in Central and Eastern Europe, see Holland and others 2000). The results also suggest that these same governments need to pay constant attention to upgrading and reconfiguring their own unique, location-bound advantages (both actual and potential) and to targeting the kinds of FDI that might help them best accomplish this objective.

Notes

1. Of course, no automatic one-to-one coincidence exists between FDI flows and cross-border M&A deals, as the latter may be financed by other means than FDI. For further details see UNCTAD (2000).

2. Observers suggest that the dramatic increase in FDI flows into Hong Kong, China, was due to (a) a general improvement in the local business environment; (b) the imminent succession of China to the World Trade Organization; (c) a US$23 billion merger deal involving China Mobile, but financed from new shares issued in the British Virgin Islands; and (d) the emergence of Hong Kong, China, as a funding hub for new business in the region (UNCTAD 2001).

3. Three separate field surveys undertaken in the latter part of 2001 found that around two-thirds of the MNEs questioned did not expect to change their investment plans in the light of the terrorist attacks. However, about half of the Japanese companies participating in a Japan Trade Center survey indicated that they intended to postpone their FDI plans until a clearer picture of global economic developments had emerged (Economist Intelligence Unit 2002; UNCTAD 2002).

4. This figure depends on whether or not (for statistical purposes) one treats Hong Kong as part of China. If one does not, then the 70 percent figure drops to around 50 percent.

5. In Hong Kong (China) alone, some 700 firms established RHQs in the services sector in 2001 (UNCTAD 2002).

References

Archibugi, D., J. Howells, and J. Michie. 1999. *Innovation Policy on a Global Economy.* Cambridge, U.K.: Cambridge University Press.

Cantwell, J., and O. Janne. 2000. "The Role of Multinational Corporations and Nation States in the Globalization of Innovatory Capacity: The European Perspective." *Technology Analysis and Strategic Management* 12(2): 243–62.

Dunning, J. H. 1996. "The Geographical Sources of Competitiveness." *Transnational Corporations* 5(3): 1–30.

_____, ed. 2000. *Regions, Globalization, and the Knowledge Based Economy.* Oxford, U.K.: Oxford University Press.

Dunning, J. H., and C. Wymbs. 2001. "The Challenge of Electronic Commerce for International Business Theory." *International Journal of the Economics of Business* 8(2): 273–302.

Economist Intelligence Unit. 2001. *World Investment Prospects.* London.

_____. 2002. *World Investment Prospects.* London.

Enright, M. J. 2000. "Globalization, Regionalization, and the Knowledge Based Economy in Hong Kong." In J. H. Dunning, ed., *Regions, Globalization, and the Knowledge Based Economy.* Oxford, U.K.: Oxford University Press.

Holland, D., M. Sass, V. Benacek, and M. Gronicki. 2000. "The Determinants and Impact of FDI in Central and Eastern Europe: A Comparison of Survey and Econometric Evidence." *Transnational Corporations* 9(3): 163–212.

Kuemmerle, W. 1999. "The Drivers of Foreign Direct Investment into Research and Development: An Empirical Investigation." *Journal of International Business Studies* 30(1): 1–24.

Rugman, A. M. 2000. *The End of Globalization.* London: Random House Business Books.

Siebert, H. 2000. *The Paradigm of Locational Competition*. Kiel Discussion Papers no. 367. Kiel, Germany: Institute of Global Economics.

UNCTAD (United Nations Conference on Trade and Development). 1998. *World Investment Report: Trends and Determinants*. New York and Geneva.

_____. 2000. *World Investment Report: Cross-Border Mergers and Acquisitions and Development*. New York and Geneva.

_____. 2001. *World Investment Report: Promoting Linkages*. New York and Geneva.

_____. 2002. *World Investment Report: Transnational Corporations and Export Competitiveness*. New York and Geneva.

_____. 2003. *World Investment Report: FDI Policies for Development: National and International Perspective*. New York and Geneva.

Zaheer, S., and S. Manrakhan. 2001. "Concentration and Dispersion in Global Industries: Remote Electronic Access and the Location of Economic Activities." *Journal of International Business Studies* 32(4): 667–86.

Income Distribution, Factor Endowments, and Trade Openness

ANTONIO SPILIMBERGO, JUAN LUIS LONDOÑO,
AND MIGUEL SZÉKELY

This paper studies the empirical links among factor endowments, trade, and personal income distribution. The motivation is that many developing countries have implemented radical trade reforms in recent years that have changed relative prices, have induced a reallocation of resources, and may have led to the introduction of new production techniques. These changes are relatively complex, and their final effect on income distribution is theoretically unclear.

Even though the links between personal income distribution and trade are important, only a few empirical papers on the topic have been written. Bourguignon and Morrison (1990) present a neoclassical model in which income distribution depends on factor endowments and the degree of openness. They estimate their model by using a cross-country analysis of 36 observations in 1970 and find that factor endowments can explain 60 percent of the difference in income shares of the bottom decile across countries, but they do not measure the effects of trade, pointing out the problems of defining openness. In addition, Edwards (1997) examines the relationship between trade and the distribution of income by using a larger sample of countries with time-series observations, which allows him to utilize a different estimation technique. Even though he uses more observations and several measures of openness, he does not find any significant effect of trade on income distribution by looking at the effects of changes in trade openness on changes in inequality.

In addition to these two papers directly related to our topic, a growing literature deals with the effects of trade on wage inequality (see, for instance, Borjas and Ramey 1995; Freeman and Katz 1995; Robbins 1996; Wood 1994, 1996). Most empirical studies have consistently found that wage dispersion has increased in recent years

At the time of writing this paper, all the authors were on the staff of the Inter-American Development Bank's Office of the Chief Economist in Washington, D.C. Antonio Spilimbergo is currently with the Fiscal Department of the International Monetary Fund and a research fellow with the Centre for Economic Policy Research and The William Davidson Institute. Due to the tragic death of Juan Luis Londoño, a previously published paper appears in this volume. An earlier version of this paper was published in the *Journal of Development Economics* 59 (June 1999): 77–101 and permission to reprint this version has been granted.

Annual World Bank Conference on Development Economics—Europe 2003
© 2004 The International Bank for Reconstruction and Development/The World Bank

in the developing countries that opened up to trade, and Katz, Loveman, and Blanchflower (1995), for instance, find that the shift in relative factor supplies can explain a fair amount of cross-time and cross-country differences in relative wages. While this literature analyzes the wage component of income quite thoroughly, we cannot deduce that an increase in wage inequality leads to an increase in income inequality, because official labor income represents only a fraction of total income.

The empirical analysis presented here differs from the aforementioned studies in that it uses panel data on factor endowments and the distribution of total income during 1965–92. The central idea is that income distribution and the impact of trade openness on inequality depend on a country's relative endowments of production factors with respect to the rest of the world.

The paper starts by describing a simple theoretical framework that constitutes the basis for the empirical analysis. The next section tests the hypothesis that relative factor endowments explain inequality. The following section uses a measure of openness, which is developed in appendix 1, to assess the effects of trade on income distribution and performs several tests to check the robustness of the main results. The paper finishes by drawing conclusions.

A Simple Framework

This section focuses on the theoretical relationship among the distribution of income, the prices of the factors of production, and the distribution of ownership. It starts by describing a model of a single closed economy. It then generalizes the framework to a world composed of several economies that share the same production function and preferences, but have different endowments. Finally, it discusses the implications of trade on personal income distribution. The framework draws on the model by Bourguignon and Morrisson (1990).

Closed Economy

Our closed economy has M different factors of production and N individuals. The vector E represents the total endowment of factors of the economy and the vector Q^c represents the total output. The production factors are used to produce Q^c goods through the production function F:

$$Q^c = F(E), \tag{1}$$

where F represents the vector of the production functions.[1] If there is perfect competition in the factor and in the final good markets, the price of every factor is equal to its marginal product in every sector where the factor is used as follows:

$$P^c F'(E) = W^c, \tag{2}$$

where P^c is the vector of prices of the final goods in the closed economy, $F'(E)$ is the vector of the marginal products of factors E, and W^c is the vector of factor prices. In addition, we assume full employment for all the factors.

The full employment conditions and equation (2) define the factor prices, $\mathbf{W}^c$, given the final good prices, $\mathbf{P}^c$, and the relative endowment of the economy, $\mathbf{E}$:

$$\mathbf{W}^c = \mathbf{W}(\mathbf{E}, \mathbf{P}^c). \tag{3}$$

The system is closed by the demands for final goods:

$$\mathbf{P}^c = \mathbf{P}(\mathbf{Q}^c). \tag{4}$$

Plugging equations (4) and (1) into equation (3), we obtain the factor prices as a function of the endowments:

$$\mathbf{W}^c = \mathbf{W}(\mathbf{E}). \tag{5}$$

Factor endowments fully determine the prices of the production factors in the closed economy. Note that the size of the economy does not determine the relative price of the production factors if the production functions $\mathbf{F}$ have constant returns to scale. Moreover, the relative price of a factor is negatively correlated with its abundance under the hypothesis of decreasing returns and no (or low) complementarity between factors.[2]

Small, Open Economy

In a small, open economy, the vector of international prices, $\mathbf{P}^*$, determines the internal prices of the tradable goods. International trade can also determine the factor prices under the following conditions: (a) the economy is sufficiently similar to that in the rest of the world in terms of endowments, (b) the economy has the same technology as that in the rest of the world, (c) the economy does not have any nontraded goods, (d) the economy has at least as many goods as factors, (e) the production functions are homogeneous of degree one, and (f) the economy has no factor intensity reversal. If the foregoing conditions are all satisfied, there is factor price equalization and the internal factor prices are determined by the international good prices as follows:

$$\mathbf{W}^o = \mathbf{W}(\mathbf{P}^*). \tag{6}$$

If any of the conditions fails to hold, factor price equalization is not assured and both international good prices and internal factor endowments determine internal factor prices:

$$\mathbf{W}^o = \mathbf{W}(\mathbf{P}^*, \mathbf{E}). \tag{7}$$

In an integrated world economy where the endowments of single countries do not differ too much, international prices are determined by the world's relative endowments in the same way as in the closed economy (see Dixit and Norman 1980):

$$\mathbf{P}^* = \mathbf{P}^*(\mathbf{E}^*). \tag{8}$$

Substituting equation (8) in equations (6) and (7) yields

$$\mathbf{W}^o = \mathbf{W}^o(\mathbf{E}^*) \qquad \text{and} \qquad \mathbf{W}^o = \mathbf{W}^o(\mathbf{E}^*, \mathbf{E}). \tag{9}$$

Equations (9) indicate that the factor prices are determined by international endowments under the foregoing conditions, and also by internal endowments under more general conditions.

The case illustrated above is just a benchmark and is not realistic, because almost no economy in the world has no tariffs. When governments intervene and impose tariffs and other barriers, factor price equalization does not take place. T is the distortion to the international factor prices. Therefore equation (9) becomes

$$\mathbf{W}^o = \mathbf{W}^o(T, \mathbf{E}^*, \mathbf{E}). \tag{10}$$

Income Distribution

The previous section makes explicit the determinants of the factor prices, the factor income distribution, and the openness of an economy. The link between factor income distribution and personal income distribution is the ownership structure. Each individual may get his or her income from several production factors so that the total income of individual i, y_i is the sum of income from all sources, namely:

$$y_i = w_1(\mathbf{E}, \mathbf{E}^*, T)E_1\omega_{i1} + \cdots + w_J(\mathbf{E}, \mathbf{E}^*, T)E_J\omega_{iJ} \quad \text{with } i = 1, \ldots, I, \tag{11}$$

where E_j is the endowment of the economy of factor j and ω_{i1} is the share of factor 1 owned by individual i. By construction,

$$\sum_{i=1}^{I} \omega_{ij} = 1 \qquad \text{for } j = 1, \ldots, J.$$

w_j represents the payment to factor j. The matrix of coefficients ω_{ij} that describes the ownership structure is referred to as $\mathbf{\Omega}$.

A synthetic indicator of income distribution, such as the Gini coefficient, is a function of the income of the single individuals:

$$gini \equiv g(\mathbf{Y}) = g(\mathbf{E}, \mathbf{E}^*, T, \mathbf{\Omega}). \tag{12}$$

Equation (12) is the basis for our empirical investigation. It indicates that personal income distribution depends on the same variables that determine the factor income distribution and on the structure of ownership $\mathbf{\Omega}$.[3]

The matrix $\mathbf{\Omega}$ is determined by historic conditions and may differ dramatically from country to country. Even though $\mathbf{\Omega}$ presents variation across time and countries, one general observation is possible, namely, some factors of production, such as land or capital, can be concentrated in the hands of a few people because no natural upward limit to their accumulation exists, while other factors of production, such as skills, cannot be concentrated to the same extent because a natural upward limit to the amount of education that an individual can accumulate does exist. This observation limits the variation of $\omega_{ij}E_j$ if the resource j is human capital. Consequently, if an economy is endowed mostly with land and capital, the concentration of wealth is unlimited; however, if an economy is endowed mostly with education, the distribution of income is expected to be more egalitarian, keeping the other factors constant.

Evidence on Endowments and Income Distribution

This section tests the empirical evidence for the arguments presented earlier, that is, that income distribution can be explained by factor endowments and the degree of openness.

We start by estimating a specification of equation (12) that ignores the structure of protection T and the structure of ownership Ω:

$$gini = g(\mathbf{E}, \mathbf{E}^*). \qquad (13)$$

The simplifications implicit in equation (13) are justified in the two polar cases of a completely closed or a completely open economy.[4]

For our dependent variable, the Gini coefficient, we use the database on income distribution compiled by Deininger and Squire (1996a). The data set consists of Gini coefficients and quintile shares for 108 countries for 1947–94. All the observations satisfy three criteria, namely, the observations (a) are taken directly from household surveys, (b) are at the national level, and (c) include all sources of income. The last requirement is extremely important for our empirical analysis, because we want to examine the whole personal distribution of income and not just the wage component.[5]

For our main exogenous variables we consider three endowments: arable land per capita, skill intensity, and capital per worker. The data on arable land and the stock of capital per worker per country come from the *1995 World Tables* (World Bank 1995). The endowment of skilled labor is defined as the proportion of the population over the age of 25 with higher education and the data are taken from the Barro and Lee (1996) data set.[6] We construct indicators of relative scarcity in the following manner:

$$A_{ift} = \ln\left(\frac{E_{ift}}{E_{ft}^*}\right), \qquad (14)$$

where f can be arable land, capital, or skill intensity; i stands for the country; t is the year; E_{ift} represents the per capita endowment of factor f of country i in year t; and E_{ft}^* represents the world's per capita effective endowment of factor f at time t, which is computed by weighting every country's endowment by the population and by the degree of openness. Given that this measure can be constructed in several ways, we explore other possibilities in the fifth test of robustness in the next section.[7] We take the logarithm of the ratio between E_{ft}^* and E_{ift}, because we want the variable A_{ift} to be unbounded in our estimations, and because this definition allows us an easy interpretation of the regression coefficients as semi-elasticity. We weight by the degree of openness to take into account that the endowments of closed countries do not compete in the world markets with other factors. So if a country is totally closed, its endowments will not affect the world average.

Figure 1 shows the evolution of the world's effective endowments from 1965 to 1992. Under our definition, the relative endowment of a country can vary significantly over time depending on other countries' trade policies, and so its comparative advantage can shift significantly simply because the world's effective endowments

FIGURE 1. Effective World Factor Endowments, 1965–1992

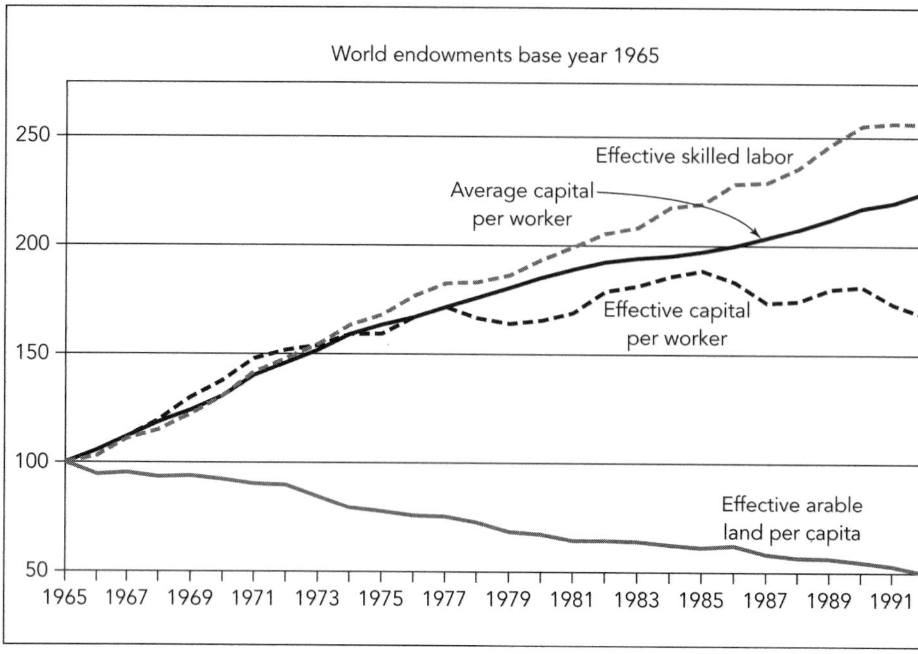

Source: Authors.

change. For instance, if instead of considering the world effective endowment of capital per worker we simply plot the population weighed average of this factor, it would seem that capital per worker in the world increased steadily (see figure 1). However, we find that the effective endowment of this factor remained fairly stable after 1978. The reason is that even though the rate of accumulation did not decline, five large, low-income countries (Bangladesh, China, India, Indonesia, and Pakistan) entered into the world economy around that year, and this increased the effective supply of labor in the world (see Wood 1996 for a similar argument).

In addition to factor endowments, other variables also explain income distribution. Ideally, we would like to have a satisfactory model explaining inequality to which we could add the effects of trade. Unfortunately, as Atkinson (1997) notes, such a model is not available and there is no clear indication of which variables should be used.

For many years, empirical studies on inequality have focused on the Kuznets hypothesis of an inverted *U*-shaped relationship between economic growth and income distribution. Following the Kuznets tradition, we add income per capita and its squared value as control variables in our base specification.[8]

So the testable equation derived from equation (13) is

$$Gini_{it} = c + \alpha_1 A_{ilt} + \alpha_2 A_{ikt} + \alpha_3 A_{ist} + \alpha_4 Gdppc_{it} + \alpha_5 Gdppc_{it}^2 + e_{it}, \quad (15)$$

where *l* stands for arable land per capita, *k* for capital per worker, *s* for the percentage of the population with higher education, and *Gdppc* for the gross domestic product

(GDP) per capita adjusted for purchasing power parity taken from the *Penn World Table* (Center for International Comparisons 1995).

By including the latter variables, the size of our sample is reduced to 320 observations for 34 countries for which information on income distribution and factor endowments is available (see appendix 2 for the summary statistics of the variables).[9] We do not use fixed effects, because many countries have few observations and change in relative endowments is relatively slow, therefore the major part of cross-country variation would be absorbed by the fixed effects. However, we calculate the residuals by using the Huber correction to take into account that the exogenous variables are not independently drawn.

The results of table 1 are in line with the previously stated qualitative hypotheses: the level of inequality increases when land and physical capital are relatively abundant, but declines when skilled labor is relatively abundant.[10] The proportion of income distribution explained (the R^2 is 0.27) is quite high, given that we use only factor endowments and level of income as explanatory variables. These results are robust to the inclusion of year dummies and to changes in the definition of A_{ilt}, A_{ikt}, and A_{ist}.[11] In an unreported regression, we use directly the absolute endowment E_{ft}^* and E_{ift} instead of our relative endowment indicator A_{ift}. In this case, all the coefficients on land remain significant while all the others lose significance, indicating that only the relative endowments are relevant while the absolute endowments are not important by themselves.

As mentioned before, equation (15) is a simplification that does not include variables on the structure of ownership Ω or the degree of openness T. The main reason why we do not include variables about Ω is that no systematic database on the structure of ownership is available. However, in an unreported regression we include measures of land and education inequality and of the level of financial depth as a proxy for the distribution of capital in the regression in table 1.[12] The three coefficients on factor endowments remain statistically significant at the 90 percent level, the coefficients on land and education distribution are positive and significant, while the coefficient on financial depth is negative but not significant.

TABLE 1. Factor Endowment and Income Distribution

(dependent variable: Gini)

Variable	Coefficient
A_{ilt}	1.29**
A_{ikt}	4.70**
A_{ist}	−1.20*
Gdppc	−0.003**
Gdppc^2	1.31**
Constant	52.26**
R^2	0.27

*Statistically significant at the 95 percent level.

**Statistically significant at the 99 percent level.

Note: The coefficient for Gdppc^2 is multiplied by 1,000,000.

Source: Unless otherwise stated, the authors are the source for all the tables.

Endowments, Income Distribution, and Openness

In this section we estimate equation (12) under the hypothesis that the level of trade distortion T enters in the determination of factor prices.

Even though the concept of trade openness is conceptually simple, controversy exists about how to measure it properly. No satisfactory direct measure of trade policy is available, because trade protection can take several forms, such as tariffs, nontariff barriers, and requirements on standards. For this reason, the empirical literature has used mostly outcome-based indexes, such as the intensity of trade. The main drawback of these indexes is that trade intensity, for example, is influenced by many other variables, such as geography, economic cycles, and resource endowments. Different authors have corrected the measures of trade openness for these factors, which are independent of trade policy. Appendix 2 reviews some commonly used indexes.

In addition to the foregoing issues, an additional problem is specific to our exercise. For instance, a country that is well endowed in land with respect to the world typically has a high volume of trade, therefore a measure of trade openness that does not control for endowments shows that this country is quite open. Given that relative intensity of land is associated with higher income inequality, as the analysis in the previous section shows, we could erroneously attribute the high inequality to the openness of the economy. To solve this problem, we have constructed an index of trade openness that controls for factor endowments (*Open*). We discuss the construction and properties of our index in appendix 2. We add our measures of trade distortion directly and interacting with every indicator of resource intensity. The testable specification derived from equation (12) is

$$Gini_{it} = c + \alpha_1 A_{ilt} + \alpha_2 A_{ikt} + \alpha_3 A_{ist} + \alpha_4 A_{ilt} Open_{it} + \alpha_5 A_{ikt} Open_{it}$$
$$+ \alpha_6 A_{ist} Open_{it} + \alpha_7 Open_{it} + \alpha_8 Gdppc_{it} + \alpha_9 Gdppc_{it}^2 + e_{it}. \qquad (16)$$

Three conclusions can be drawn from table 2. The first is that the signs and the significance of the resource endowments remain robust to the inclusion of the openness index.

The second conclusion is that the index of trade openness (*Open*) is positive and significant. This suggests that trade openness is associated with higher inequality keeping the factor endowments constant. This could be because more liberal governments have more liberal trade policy and fewer redistributional policies, so that we observe a positive correlation between inequality and trade openness.

The third and most important conclusion is that openness seems to undo the effect of factor endowments on inequality, because the coefficients on the interaction between a specific endowment and openness have opposite signs than the coefficient on the endowment itself. This result is opposite to what the simple Hecksher-Ohlin framework would predict. Take the example of a country relatively well endowed with land. Following the Hecksher-Ohlin framework, we should expect that this country, which as a closed economy already has a bad income distribution, would worsen its income distribution as it opens up because the price of internal land, which

TABLE 2. Income Distribution and Trade Openness
(dependent variable: Gini)

Variable	Coefficient
A_{ilt}	1.71**
A_{ikt}	17.26**
A_{ist}	−3.63**
$A_{ilt} * Open_{it}$	−1.71
$A_{ikt} * Open_{it}$	−52.40**
$A_{ist} * Open_{it}$	14.95*
$Open_{it}$	42.69**
$Gdppc_{it}$	−0.004**
$Gdppc_{it}^2$	1.50**
Constant	45.05
R^2	0.40

*Statistically significant at the 95 percent level.

**Statistically significant at the 99 percent level.

Note: The coefficient for $Gdppc^2$ is multiplied by 1,000,000.

is a scarce resource for the world, would go up. Our results indicate that the opposite happens.

Several theoretical and empirical reasons explain why this can happen. Theoretically, in a world with more factors of production and specialization one cannot extend the conclusions of the stylized two-factor Heckscher-Ohlin model; therefore our results cannot be read as a test against the Heckscher-Ohlin model. Empirically our results confirm what other studies have found from a different perspective. We find that inequality increases in countries that are relatively well endowed with skills when the economy opens, a result that confirms the findings of the empirical literature on wage inequality that trade openness increases the premium for skilled workers. In contrast, inequality decreases in countries that are relatively well endowed with capital when the economy opens, a result that is consistent with the trade literature on political economy, which argues that rents deriving from the ownership of capital reduce when the economy opens up (see Krueger 1974).

Robustness Tests

We perform six tests to check for the robustness of the latter conclusions.

First, our regressions have a potential problem of endogeneity. Factor endowments determine income distribution in the way discussed in the theoretical section, but income distribution also determines factor accumulation. Indeed, the recent literature on income distribution assumes that inequality determines investment in education and capital accumulation, which are flow variables (see Flug, Spilimbergo, and Wachtenheim 1997). Nevertheless, our regressions should not suffer from this endogeneity, because the A_{ift} variables are stock variables, which do not depend on present income distribution. To pursue the issue further, we have run our regression

TABLE 3. Income Distribution and Trade Openness

Variable	Poorest 20 percent	Quintile 2	Quintile 3	Quintile 4	Richest 20 percent
A_{ilt}	−0.002**	−0.001	−0.003	−0.001	0.006*
A_{ikt}	−0.041**	−0.419**	−0.030**	−0.014**	0.120**
A_{ist}	0.008	0.003	0.006*	0.008**	−0.029**
A_{ilt} * Open	−.001	−0.005*	0.003	−0.001	0.031**
A_{ikt} * Open	0.106**	0.136**	0.124**	0.062**	−0.441**
A_{ist} * Open	0.013	−0.011	−0.034*	−0.032**	0.078*
Open	−0.139**	−0.182**	−0.127**	0.062**	0.636**
Gdppc	0.001**	0.098**	0.063**	0.034**	−0.001**
$Gdppc^2$	−4.37**	−3.56**	−2.060**	−9.500**	1.110**
Constant	0.052**	0.115**	0.161**	0.222**	0.393**
R^2	0.36	0.30	0.42	0.47	0.40

*Statistically significant at the 95 percent level.

**Statistically significant at the 99 percent level.

Note: The coefficient for $Gdppc^2$ is multiplied by 1,000,000,000.

instrumenting for the stock of capital and education with financial depth (which is well correlated with these variables), and also with lagged variables. The unreported results confirm that our assumptions about the lack of endogeneity are valid.

Second, we check whether the results are robust to other inequality indexes given that different inequality measures place greater weight on different sections of the distribution, for instance, the Gini gives more weight to the center. Rather than choosing another index, we proceed in a more general way and estimate equation (16) using the income share of each quintile of the population instead of the Gini index to determine exactly where the changes take place.

Table 3 presents results that provide a clearer view of the relationships.[13] For instance, the negative effect of land is determined by the fact that the income share of the poorest 20 percent of the population declines with land abundance. In contrast, capital intensity is regressive, because it has a significant negative effect on the first four quintiles while raising the incomes of the richest 20 percent. Greater skill intensity increases the share of quintiles 3 and 4 (which could roughly be considered the middle classes), while reducing the relative incomes of quintile 5 and leaving the lowest quintiles unchanged.

With regard to the interaction terms, we obtain similar results. The interaction with land is not significant across quintiles, while the interaction of openness with capital reduces the share of the top 20 percent and improves the position of the other four quintiles. When a skilled, labor-intensive economy opens to trade, income inequality rises because the shares of quintiles 3 and 4 fall significantly, the income share of the richest 20 percent increases, while the poorest 40 percent are unaffected. The trade openness measure used independently has regressive effects, because it

TABLE 4. Subsample of Developing Countries

(dependent variable: Gini)

Variable	Coefficient
A_{ilt}	6.42**
A_{ikt}	14.14**
A_{ist}	−5.05*
A_{ilt} * Open	−12.82**
A_{ikt} * Open	−43.79**
A_{ist} * Open	24.46**
Open	−4.03
Gdppc	0.01
$Gdppc^2$	2.89**
Constant	−50.16**
R^2	0.54

*Statistically significant at the 95 percent level.

**Statistically significant at the 99 percent level.

Note: The coefficient for $Gdppc^2$ is multiplied by 1,000,000.

reduces the incomes of the poorest 60 percent of the population while raising the share of the top quintiles.

The third robustness test is about sample heterogeneity. To check whether factor endowments pick up unobservable differences between developing and industrial countries, we split our sample. Table 4 presents the results for the subsample of developing countries. The coefficients for the restricted sample are not very different from those of the complete sample. An interesting result is that the coefficient for the openness measure itself is negative, but not significant, indicating that trade openness has no influence on the distribution of income of developing economies apart from its effect on factor prices. This last result is in line with the finding by Edwards (1997).

The fourth set of robustness tests consists of the inclusion of different regressors. We introduce year dummies and the inflation rate as variables to account for other macroeconomic fluctuations. We also try different definitions of A_{ilt}, A_{ikt}, and A_{ist} as explained earlier. In all cases, the sign and significance of the coefficients do not change. In addition to structural changes, short-term fluctuations of macroeconomic activity could also affect inequality, for instance, if the most income-elastic sectors use a specific factor more intensively, the demand for such a factor may increase more than proportionally along the cycle. In an unreported regression, we introduced the deviation from the long-term income growth trend to control for cycle-related changes in income distribution. Our conclusions do not change.

As already mentioned, some controversy exists about which measure of trade openness is more appropriate, so the fifth robustness test concerns sensitivity to the index of trade openness. Table 5 contains the results of estimating the same regression with six different indexes of openness. The definitions of the indexes are

TABLE 5. Inequality and Trade with Alternative Measures of Trade Openness
(dependent variable: Gini)

Variable	Measure of openness					
	XM	Lee1	Lee2	SATI	PDI	BME
A_{ilt}	2.0**	1.9**	0.7*	1.2**	−216.9**	74.1
A_{ikt}	11.1**	11.9**	15.1**	4.5**	93.0	593.4*
A_{ist}	−3.1**	−3.0**	−2.4*	−1.7**	−5.5	−23.9
A_{ilt} * Open	−7.1**	−7.1**	4.8	110.5**	497.7**	−80.1
A_{ikt} * Open	−49.8**	−58.1**	−49.3**	−76.4**	−208.8	−647.1*
A_{ist} * Open	18.1*	23.7**	13.4	53.8**	15.2	25.3
Open	12.0	13.3	22.1**	−1.5	−148.1**	906.8**
Gdppc	−0.04**	−0.04**	−0.04**	−0.04**	−0.02**	−0.03**
Gdppc^2	1.5**	1.8**	1.8**	1.8**	8.9*	1.3**
Constant	54.1**	53.6**	52.8**	57.6**	−415.2**	−772.7**
R^2	0.44	0.47	0.44	0.47	0.32	0.28
Number of observations	320	280	247	286	75	320

*Statistically significant at the 95 percent level.

**Statistically significant at the 99 percent level.

Note: The coefficient for Gdppc^2 is multiplied by 1,000,000.

explained in appendix 1. To make the coefficients comparable, we normalize each index so that it ranges within the interval [0,1].

Even though the correlation matrix of table A1.3 in appendix 1 indicates that the measures of openness are loosely correlated, our conclusions about the relationship between income distribution and factor endowments are quite robust to the choice of index. In most cases, skill intensity is found to be progressive (although the coefficient is not significant when *PDI* and *BME* are used), while land and capital intensity worsen the distribution of income (the only exception is found with *PDI* in the case of land). Regarding the openness measure taken independently, the results vary. When we use *XM*, *Lee*1, *Lee*2, and the black market exchange rate, we find a positive relationship, but when the *SATI* and *PDI* indexes are introduced, the sign of the coefficient changes to negative, indicating that trade openness has a progressive effect on inequality. Thus our conclusion about the effect of openness independent of the influence on factor prices is not robust to the choice of openness indicator.

Among the interaction terms, the combination of trade openness and factor abundance is fairly robust in the case of skill and extremely robust for capital intensity, while the results for land vary considerably across indexes. The macroeconomic variables are also highly robust to the choice of openness indicator.

The last robustness test concerns the construction of the world's effective endowments, E_{ft}^*. Our primary concern in constructing this variable is to exclude autarchic countries. For this reason, we compute E_{ft}^* by weighting every country's endowment by the population and by the degree of openness as follows:

$$E_{ft}^* \equiv \frac{\text{adjusted endowment}}{\text{adjusted population}} = \frac{\sum_i \left(E_{ift} * \text{pop}_i * \left(\frac{X+M}{Gdp} \right)_i \right)}{\sum_i \left(\text{pop}_i * \left(\frac{X+M}{Gdp} \right)_i \right)} \qquad (17)$$

where pop_i refers to the population of country i, X are exports, and M are imports. The use of the openness ratio $X + M/Gdp$ as relative weights has the potential problem that countries that have the same relative endowment as the rest of the world should have very little weight, because they should trade relatively little. This fact could potentially bias our measure of the world's effective endowments. Theoretically, the proper way to correct this bias would be to have an accepted measure of openness and to use it as a relative weight, but unfortunately, as noted earlier, such a measure is not available. To check the empirical evidence of the problem, we use several different measures of trade openness to construct the relative weights. The results do not change significantly, showing that the potential bias does not determine our conclusions.

Significance of the Results and Regional Variations

To check for the economic significance of our results, we calculate the average value of each of the independent variables used in equation (16) and multiply them by the corresponding regression coefficients from our base regressions. Table 6 presents the results, and the variable means are found in appendix 1. All the variables with a line above are averages over all the time periods.

The results in table 6 and the average endowments presented in appendix 2 allow us to characterize regions according to the type of factors with which they are endowed. Industrial countries have more capital and skills than developing countries, but they have relatively less land. Latin America has less land, less capital per worker, and less skills than the world average, but factor endowments are close to the world's effective endowments.[14] As expected, Africa, followed by the Asian countries, has the lowest endowments of capital and skills. The main difference between these two regions is that Africa is well endowed with land, while this factor is scarce in Asia. Finally, East Asia has more capital and skills than the world average, but it is not well endowed with land.

With regard to the effect of trade on income distribution, we estimate the points of the Gini coefficient that are associated with the openness measure by adding up the interaction terms in table 6 and the openness measure taken independently. Then we simulate the impact of increasing the measure of openness by 10 percent in each region. The main result is that openness has a regressive impact through skills in the countries with the highest skill levels (namely, the industrial and East Asian countries), while it seems to be progressive in regions with abundant unskilled labor.

We find that trade has practically no impact on personal income distribution in the industrial countries. The reason is that even though openness worsens the distribution

TABLE 6. Effect of Factor Endowments and Trade Openness on Income Distribution by Country Group and Region

(points of the Gini coefficient)

Variable	Industrial countries	Latin America	Africa	East Asia	Asia[a]
$1.71 * \overline{A_{il}}$	−1.36	−0.94	0.78	−5.97	−2.22
$17.26 * \overline{A_{ik}}$	21.56	−1.95	−32.21	2.79	−15.53
$-3.63 * \overline{A_{is}}$	−3.12	0.53	7.88	−1.26	2.95
$-1.71 * \overline{A_{il}} * \overline{Open_i}$	0.35	0.08	−0.61	2.48	0.73
$-52.40 * \overline{A_{ik}} * \overline{Open_i}$	−13.20	−1.73	12.52	−2.52	9.80
$14.95 * \overline{A_{is}} * \overline{Open_i}$	2.87	−0.19	−6.56	1.76	−1.76
$42.69 * \overline{Open_i}$	9.01	8.15	9.22	14.26	9.35
$-0.004 * \overline{Gdppc_i}$	−40.96	−14.24	−4.54	−19.16	−8.02
$1.50 * \overline{Gdppc_i^2}$	15.90	2.37	0.27	5.31	2.63
Constant	45.05	45.05	45.05	45.05	45.05
Predicted Gini	36.09	37.12	31.81	42.75	42.97
Observed average Gini	34.20	49.01	45.11	34.82	36.81
Points of Gini due to trade[b]	−0.98	6.31	14.57	15.99	18.12
Impact of 10 percent rise in Open[c]	−0.10	0.63	1.46	1.60	1.81

a. Excludes East Asia.

b. Estimated by $(-1.71 * \overline{A_{il}} - 52.4 * \overline{A_{ik}} + 14.95 * \overline{A_{is}} + 42.69) * \overline{Open_i}$

c. Expressed as points of the Gini coefficient. Estimated by simulating an increase in the openness measure by 10 percent and recalculating the points of the Gini due to trade.

through its effect on skills, this is totally offset by the progressive impact over capital. In this case, land does not appear to play an important role.

Trade openness also has a negligible effect on income distribution in Latin America. This is in line with the argument that when factor endowments are similar to the world average, only small changes in relative prices will take place with openness because of the absence of a comparative advantage.

The impact of trade through skills and capital is similar in Africa and Asia. In both regions, trade has an equalizing effect because of the low levels of skills, but by contrast, it has a regressive impact because of the scarcity of capital. The main difference between these two regions is that openness is regressive in Asia but progressive through its effect on land in land-abundant Africa. In East Asia, trade openness has a progressive effect through the capital endowment, but this is totally offset by the regressive effect on skills and because land is scarce.

Conclusions

The objective of this paper is to explore the relationship between the distribution of income and trade openness. Our analysis differs from related works in that it uses panel data for a long period (28 years) and focuses on the personal distribution of income rather than solely on wage inequality.

We analyze theoretically the links among income distribution and factor endowments, structure of ownership, and the price of factors. We argue that some factors, such as land and capital, can be accumulated by a few individuals with no limit, while other factors, such as education, have limits to how much an individual can accumulate. This introduces natural bounds to the structure of ownership. The factor prices depend on their relative scarcity and on the degree of openness, as the neoclassical theory of trade suggests.

We test whether factor endowments and trade openness can explain income distribution and find that countries endowed with factors that do not have limits to their accumulation, for example, land and capital, are more unequal. In contrast, countries in which the average skill level is higher than the world's effective endowment have lower inequality. We show that this specification is theoretically valid if there is no impediment to trade.

We then drop the assumption of no impediments to free trade and introduce an index of trade distortion that is based on factor endowments. By using this index, we show that (a) after controlling for the effect of trade, income distribution remains well explained by relative factor endowments; (b) trade openness reduces inequality in capital-abundant countries; and (c) trade openness increases inequality in skill-abundant countries. Our conclusions are robust to endogeneity tests, to the use of different regressors, to seven different openness measures, and to the division of countries by income.

Finally, we argue that our results are compatible and confirm the findings of several country-specific studies; however, a simple version of the Hecksher-Ohlin framework cannot account for our conclusions.

Appendix 1. Measures of Openness

Even though the concept of trade openness is simple in theory, there is no widely accepted way of measuring it. In the literature, two types of measures of openness have been used: incidence and outcome-based measures.[15]

Incidence-based measures are direct indicators of trade policy, such as the level or dispersion of tariffs. While these indicators are about the closest one can get to inferring the trade policy of a country, they still have two shortcomings: first, they are imperfect because they cannot capture other types of interventions, such as nontariff barriers; and second, consistent data on tariffs are not available for many countries and for a sufficient number of years.

Outcome-based measures are widely used because they implicitly cover all the sources of distortion and are based on data that are more readily available. The most common of these measures is the trade openness of a country measured as the ratio of exports plus imports over gross domestic product (GDP). Other outcome-based measures are obtained from the deviations between actual trade and predicted trade, with the predicted values estimated according to some kind of theoretical framework, such as the Hecksher-Ohlin model or gravity equations. Therefore these types of indicators are subject to arbitrariness in the choice of relevant trade theory, and Pritchett (1996) shows that several outcome-based indexes of trade openness are weakly correlated.

For the purposes of this work, we use seven different indexes to test whether our results are sensitive to the use of a particular indicator. Six of them have been used previously in the literature, and we innovate by introducing a new index that is closer to the spirit of our exercise. The following are the six indexes from the previous literature:

- *Trade flows,* measured by (Exports + Imports)/GDP at constant prices (denoted *XM*), obtained directly from the *Penn World Table 1995* (Center for International Comparisons 1995).

- Inverse of the *black market exchange rate (BME)* obtained from Barro and Lee (1996). This is an indirect measure of trade distortion based on the fact that distorted trade regimes often induce distortions in the exchange rate, which are reflected in the black market premium. Therefore the inverse of the black market premium is a measure of trade distortions.

- *Price distortion index (PDI)* suggested by Dollar (1992) and obtained through the following regression:

$$rprice = a + \beta_1 Gdppc + \beta_2 Gdppc^2 + u, \tag{A1.1}$$

where *rprice* is the relative price level (real exchange rate adjusted for purchasing power parity [PPP]) and *Gdppc* is the PPP-adjusted GDP per capita, both obtained from the *World Penn Tables 1995*. The measure of trade openness is the residual in the regression. It is based on the idea that deviations from PPP indicate distortion in the trade flow.

- *Measure of structure adjusted trade (SATI),* suggested by Chenery and Syrquin (1986). This indicator measures the deviation of the observed trade composition from the predicted trade composition. It is obtained through the following formula:

$$TO = TB - \widehat{TB} = \frac{E_p - E_m}{E} - \frac{\widehat{E}_p - \widehat{E}_m}{\widehat{E}}, \tag{A1.2}$$

where *TB* measures trade composition, which is the share of manufacturing exports (E_m) over total merchandise exports (E). $\widehat{TB}$ is the expected trade composition, which is obtained from the predicted values of E_p (primary sector exports) and E_m based on the following regression:

$$
\begin{aligned}
E_i = \alpha + \beta_1 \ln Gdppc + \beta_2 (\ln Gdppc)^2 + \gamma_1 \ln Population \\
+ \gamma_2 (\ln Population)^2 + TD + u,
\end{aligned}
\tag{A1.3}
$$

where TD is a time dummy that indicates if the year of observation i is before or after the 1973 oil shock. As Pritchett (1996) argues, one of the drawbacks of this measure is that it does not have a strong theoretical foundation.

- *Lee's measure 1 (Lee1)*. Following the tradition of outcome-based indexes of trade openness, Lee (1993) proposes two measures that draw on the idea that trade orientation is determined by a country's geographic characteristics. The first of the measures is based on the following regression:[16]

$$\frac{X+M}{Gdp} = c + \alpha \ln(area) + \beta \ln(dist) + \gamma \ln(1 + bmexch) + u, \qquad \text{(A1.4)}$$

where *area* is the size of the country in square miles, *dist* measures the distance of each country to the major world exporters weighted by bilateral import values in 1985, and *bmexch* is the black market exchange rate. The source for these three variables is the Barro and Lee (1996) data set. A country's openness is determined by structural features, such as the natural resource endowment proxied by geographical size and the presence of natural trade barriers measured by the distance variable, and by trade distortions, which are proxied by the black market exchange rate. The measure of trade openness is the residual.

- *Lee's measure 2 (Lee2)*. This is a variation of the previous measure that does not include the black market premium as an argument:

$$\frac{X+M}{Gdp} = c + \alpha \ln(area) + \beta \ln(dist) + u. \qquad \text{(A1.5)}$$

As already mentioned, both of the variables included in the latter regression are proxies for the natural resource endowment and natural barriers to trade, respectively. We add the share of the primary sector's GDP as indirect measures of natural resource endowment, and we also add the GDP per capita to control for income effects such as intra-industry trade. Thus we have estimated to the following specification:

$$\frac{X+M}{Gdp} = c + \alpha \ln(area) + \beta \ln(dist) + \gamma \ln(agdp) + \delta \ln(Gdppc) + u, \qquad \text{(A1.6)}$$

where *agdp* is the share of the primary sector's *Gdp*. As usual, we take the residuals as an indicator of openness.

We now develop a new index of trade openness that is in line with our theoretical framework. The prior indexes are based on the deviations of actual trade from predicted trade. The equations used to predict trade have geographical variables, such as distance or area, and structural variables, such as percentage of income coming from agriculture. The measure that we construct is based on factor endowments.

Our exercise is similar in spirit to Leamer (1988). Leamer uses several endowments (capital, labor, land, oil, coal, and minerals) and 182 commodity classes in his cross-section analysis to compute expected trade. He interprets the residuals from this regression as an index of trade intervention. We construct our equation based on the idea that the coefficient of trade openness $(X + M/Gdp)$ is positively correlated with the difference in the endowments between a country and the rest of the world.

Trade openness is not only a function of factor endowments, but also of the geographic distance of a country from potential trading partners, as well as of the economic size of the country. Therefore we estimate the following regression:

$$\left(\frac{X+M}{Gdp}\right)_{it} = c + a_1 \ln(area_i) + a_2 \ln(Gdppc_{it}) + a_3 \ln(dist_{it})$$
$$+ \beta_1 \Delta^2_{ikt} + \beta_2 \Delta^2_{ilt} + \beta_3 \Delta^2_{ist} + \gamma_1(trend_t) + u_{it}, \qquad (A1.7)$$

where $\ln(area_i)$ is the logarithm of the size of country i in terms of square miles, $\ln(dist_i)$ is the average of the distance between country i and its 20 most important trading partners from Lee (1993), and Δ^2_{ift} (with $f = k, l, s$) is the discrepancy between country i's endowment of factor f and world effective endowments. The latter is defined as $\Delta^2_{ift} \equiv [(E_{ift} - E^*_{ft})/E^*_{ft}]^2$, where E_{ift} is the endowment of factor f of country i at time t, and E^*_{ft} (with $f = k, l, s$) is the world effective endowment of factor f at time t. Several options are available for specifying the difference in factor endowments. We opted for the square of the percentage difference because (a) the percentage ensures that endowments are trended and does not introduce econometric problems, and (b) the square magnifies the difference at the extreme.[17] We include a time trend to account for the change in transportation costs over time.

Table A1.1 presents the results from the panel regression for 1965–92. We use the Huber correction to obtain robust standard errors, which account for the fact that the exogenous variables are grouped by country. All the variables have the expected sign and significance, indicating that the volume of trade is inversely correlated to the size and distance of the country and positively correlated to the difference between the country's and the world's endowment. We use the residuals from this regression as an indicator of trade openness corrected for the endowments (*Open*). This measure has the advantage of being directly derived from our theory and of being available for a considerable time period and for a reasonable number of countries. The main disadvantage of the proposed measure is that it is derived from a regression, therefore if the regression is mis-specified or if there are errors in variables, the residuals cannot be taken as a measure of trade openness. Because we could have both problems, we check our results with other measures of openness.[18]

Tables A1.2 and A1.3 present summary statistics and the correlation matrix of the indexes of trade openness we have discussed so far. Given the significant differences in the way each measure is constructed and in the number of observations available in each case, the low correlation among some of the measures is not surprising (see

TABLE A1.1. Trade Openness and Factor Endowments

(dependent variable: trade openness)

Variable	Coefficient
ln(*dist*)	−12.52**
ln(*area*)	−6.85**
ln(*GDP*)	−5.99**
Δ_k^2	0.52**
Δ_l^2	1.47**
Δ_s^2	0.30**
trend	0.79**
Constant	−1346.24**
R^2	0.70

*Statistically significant at the 95 percent level.

**Statistically significant at the 99 percent level.

TABLE A1.2. Summary Statistics for Seven Trade Indexes

Variable	Number of observations	Mean	Standard deviation	Minimum	Maximum
XM	4,349	64.70	43.5	4.9	423.4
Lee1	2,551	−2.89e-08	39.8	−48.5	361.6
Lee2	2,334	−1.60e-08	37.2	−68.1	332.6
Open	896	3.90	23.3	−44.6	177.2
SATI	3,415	0.43	1.2	0.000	14.0
BME	562	1.34	9.7	−92.5	120.6
PDI	4,317	−0.07	2.6	−130.0	12.9

TABLE A1.3. Correlation Matrix between Openness Measures

Variable	XM	Lee1	Lee2	Open	SATI	PDI	BME
XM	1.00						
Lee1	0.80	1.00					
Lee2	0.67	0.90	1.00				
Open	0.58	0.64	0.60	1.00			
SATI	−0.11	0.06	−0.07	−0.22	1.00		
PDI	0.04	0.09	0.03	−0.17	0.25	1.00	
BME	0.04	0.02	−0.02	0.07	0.04	0.02	1.00

table A1.3). Pritchett (1996) reaches a similar conclusion with some of these indexes. Note that even though our measure *Open* is based on endowment differences, it is well correlated with *Lee*1 and *Lee*2, which are constructed without reference to the factor endowments.

Appendix 2. Data Description

TABLE A2.1. Summary Statistics

Variable	Mean	Standard deviation	Minimum	Maximum
Gini	35.76	9.25	17.83	63.18
A_{ilt}	−0.46	1.64	−7.85	4.85
A_{ikt}	0.05	1.33	−4.20	2.31
A_{ist}	0.13	1.01	−3.99	2.07
A_{ilt} * Open	−0.27	0.75	−6.48	0.50
A_{ikt} * Open	0.09	0.20	−0.41	0.70
A_{ist} * Open	0.09	0.20	−0.57	0.51
Open	0.22	0.10	0	1.00
Gdppc	3,842	3,971	257	33,946
$Gdppc^2$	3.05	6.27	66,049	1.15

Note: The coefficient for $Gdppc^2$ is divided by 1,000,000.

TABLE A2.2. Variable Means by Country Group and Region

Variable	Industrial countries	Latin America	Africa	East Asia	Asia[a]
A_{ilt}	−0.79	−0.55	0.46	−3.49	−1.30
A_{ikt}	1.25	−0.11	−1.87	0.16	−0.90
A_{ist}	0.86	−0.15	−2.17	0.35	−0.81
A_{ilt} * Open	−0.20	−0.05	0.36	−1.45	−0.43
A_{ikt} * Open	0.25	0.03	−0.24	0.05	−0.19
A_{ist} * Open	0.19	−0.01	−0.44	0.12	−0.12
Open	0.21	0.19	0.22	0.33	0.22
Gdppc	9,706	3.375	1,076	4,540	1,900
$Gdppc^2$	10.60	1.58	0.18	3.54	1.75

a. Excludes East Asia.

Note: The coefficient for $Gdppc^2$ is divided by 1,000,000.

Notes

1. We assume that the production functions **F** and the utility functions satisfy the general regularity conditions as described in Varian (1978).

2. Within the context of the recent income distribution literature, Stokey (1996) presents a model in which the complementarity between capital and unskilled labor breaks the positive relationship between the relative scarcity of a factor and its price.

3. Note that the computation of the Gini coefficient requires information on the complete structure of ownership **Ω**. Other synthetic indicators, such as the variance-covariance matrix of the factor distribution, are theoretically insufficient to calculate the Gini coefficient.

4. Bourguignon and Morrisson (1990) adopt a similar specification that allows them to avoid the problem of defining an index of trade openness.

5. We drop 10 observations from the original data set of 670 Gini coefficients to ensure that within any given country, inequality is measured consistently by using either expenditure or income.

6. The Barro and Lee (1994) data set contains four different educational categories: no schooling, some primary school education, some secondary school education, and some higher education. We chose to use just the last category, because we want to measure only the most skilled proportion of the population, and because the last category is measured with less error. If we try different categories in the same regression, our results do not change significantly. Putting more categories in the same regression can create problems of multicollinearity because they are highly correlated.

7. The formula used to calculate the per capita world effective endowment is

$$E_{ft}^* \equiv \frac{\text{adjusted endowment}}{\text{adjusted population}} = \frac{\sum_i \left(E_{ift} * \text{pop}_i * \left(\frac{X+M}{Gdp} \right)_i \right)}{\sum_i \left(\text{pop}_i * \left(\frac{X+M}{Gdp} \right)_i \right)},$$

where pop_i refers to the population of country i, X are exports, and M are imports. The original sources do not always provide information for all the years of the 1965–92 period for these four variables, which imposes problems for calculating world averages. To calculate consistent world averages, we interpolate the variables for the years for which no information was available.

8. For recent empirical evidence, or the lack thereof, on the Kuznets curve, see Bruno, Ravallion, and Squire (1995) and Deininger and Squire (1996b). Anand and Kanbur (1993) show that income can enter by means of other possible functional forms that are different from the one used here. Specifically, they suggest using the inverse of the level of income instead of the squared term to study the relationship between the Gini coefficient and the stage of development in the absence of other regressors. We have estimated our regressions with alternative specifications, including the one suggested by those authors, but none of the conclusions on the relationship between factor endowments and income distribution changes.

9. The reason why the sample is reduced is that the Barro and Lee data set—from which we obtain the education indicators—does not include information for all the economies for which we have data on inequality. The distribution of the observations by economy is as follows: Belgium 4, Canada 20, Chile 4, Colombia 7, Denmark 4, Finland 11, France 5, Germany 6, Greece 3, Guatemala 3, Hong Kong (China) 7, India 17, Islamic Republic of Iran 5, Ireland 3, Italy 15, Jamaica 5, Japan 20, Republic of Korea 11, Mauritius 3, Mexico 4, Netherlands 12, New Zealand 12, Norway 8, Peru 1, Philippines 5, Portugal 3, Spain 8, Sri Lanka 6, Thailand 7, Turkey 3, United Kingdom 26, United States 27, Republica Bolivariana de Venezúela 9, and Republic of Zambia 2. Overall we have 187 observations for industrial countries and 133 for developing countries.

10. In this specification, the relationship between income distribution and income per capita follows a U-shaped trend rather than the inverted U suggested by the Kuznets hypothesis. However, when we substitute GDP per capita and the squared value for their logarithms, we obtain the inverted U. So the coefficients on income are not robust to different specifications, but this does not affect our results on the coefficients on factor endowments.

11. Instead of taking the logarithm of the ratio of the endowment of the country to the world's effective endowment, we have used the absolute difference between them, the logarithmic absolute difference, the absolute difference squared, and the absolute difference divided by the world's effective endowments, respectively. In addition, we have changed the definition of world average by not weighting each country's factors by the share of international trade and used all the definitions mentioned before.

12. The results from this regression are not reported because the sample size was reduced to only 70 observations because of data limitations. The measure of the distribution of education is the ratio of the labor force over 25 years of age with no education to the proportion of the labor force with secondary schooling and higher education; the measure of financial depth is M2 over GDP from *International Financial Statistics* (International Monetary Fund 1995); and the data on the land Gini index are taken from Li, Squire, and Zoun (1996).

13. Not all the observations that have a Gini index contain the quintile shares, so the sample is reduced to 260 observations.

14. In line with the argument by Wood (1996), Latin America does not seem to have a comparative advantage in unskilled labor, as is normally thought, because the skill level and the amount of capital per worker are higher than the average registered in Africa and Asia.

15. Harrison (1996) and Pritchett (1996) have surveyed the literature on the measurement of trade orientation.

16. Lee's original regression also includes the logarithm of tariffs, but we were unable to include it in our estimations because we do not have information about this variable for a sufficient number of countries.

17. We tried different specifications of country i's distance from the effective world endowment: the simple difference between E_{ift} and E_{ft}^* and the absolute difference between E_{ift} and E_{ft}^*. Our conclusions about the relationship between trade flows and factor endowments are not sensitive to the different definitions.

18. Future research could extend our measure to include other endowments.

References

The word "processed" describes informally reproduced works that may not be commonly available in libraries.

Anand, S., and S. M. R. Kanbur. 1993. "The Kuznets Process and the Inequality-Development Relationship." *Journal of Development Economics* 40(1): 25–52.

Atkinson, A. B. 1997. "Bringing Income Distribution in from the Cold." *Economic Journal* 107(March): 297–321.

Barro, Robert J., and Jong-Wha Lee. 1996. "International Measures of Schooling Years and Schooling Quality." *American Economic Review* 86(2): 218–23.

Borjas, G. J., and V. A. Ramey. 1995. "Foreign Competition, Market Power, and Wage Inequality." *Quarterly Journal of Economics* CX(4): 1075–1110.

Bourguignon, François, and Christian Morrisson, eds. 1990. "Income Distribution, Development, and Foreign Trade." *European Economic Review* 34: 1113–32.

Bruno, Michael, Martin Ravallion, and Lyn Squire. 1995. "Equity and Growth in Developing Countries: Old and New Perspectives on the Policy Issues." World Bank, Washington, D.C.

Center for International Comparisons. 1995. *Penn World Table* (version 5). Philadelphia: University of Pennsylvania.

Chenery, Hollis, and Moshe Syrquin. 1986. "The Semi-Industrial Countries." In Hollis Chenery, Sherman Robinson, and Moshe Syrquin, eds., *Industrialization and Growth. A Comparative Study*. New York: Oxford University Press.

Deininger, Klaus, and Lyn Squire. 1996a. "Measuring Income Inequality: A New Database." *World Bank Economic Review* 10(3): 565–91.

_____. 1996b. "New Ways of Looking at Old Issues: Inequality and Growth." World Bank, Washington, D.C. Processed.

Dixit, Avinash, and Victor Norman. 1980. *Theory of International Trade*. Cambridge, U.K.: Cambridge University Press.

Dollar, David. 1992. "Outward-Oriented Developing Economies Really Do Grow More Rapidly: Evidence from 95 LDCs, 1976–1985." *Economic Development and Cultural Change* 40(3): 523–45.

———. 1997. "Trade Policy, Growth, and Income Inequality." *American Economic Review Papers and Proceedings* 87(2): 43–48.

Flug, Karnit, Antonio Spilimbergo, and Erik Wachtenheim. 1997. "Investment in Education: Do Economic Volatility and Credit Constraints Matter?" *Journal of Development Economics* 55(2): 465–81.

Freeman, R. B., and L. F. Katz, eds. 1995. "*Differences and Changes in Wage Structure.*" Chicago: University of Chicago Press.

Harrison, Ann. 1996. "Openness and Growth: A Time-Series, Cross-Country Analysis for Developing Countries." *Journal of Development Economics* 48(2): 419–47.

International Monetary Fund. 1995. *International Financial Statistics 1995*. Washington, D.C.

Katz, Lawrence, Gary Loveman, and David Blanchflower. 1995. "A Comparison of Changes in the Structures of Wages in Four OECD Countries." In *Differences and Changes in Wage Structure*. Chicago: University of Chicago Press.

Krueger, Ann. 1974. "The Political Economy of the Rent-Seeking Society." *American Economic Review* 4(3): 291–303.

Leamer, Edward E. 1988. "Measures of Openness." In Robert Baldwin, ed., *Trade Policy Issues and Empirical Analysis*. Chicago: University of Chicago Press.

Lee, Jong-Wha. 1993. "International Trade, Distortions, and Long Run Economic Growth." *IMF Staff Papers* 40(2): 299–328.

Li, Honggyi, Lyn Squire, and Heng-Fu Zoun. 1996. "Explaining International and Intertemporal Variations in Income Inequality." World Bank, Washington, D.C. Processed.

Pritchett, Lant. 1996. "Measuring Outward Orientation in LDCs: Can It Be Done?" *Journal of Development Economics* 49(2): 307–55.

Robbins, Donald. 1996. "HOS Hits Facts: Facts Win. Evidence on Trade and Wage in the Developing World." Harvard University, Cambridge, Mass.

Stokey, Nancy. 1996. "Free Trade, Factor Returns, and Factor Accumulation." *Journal of Economic Growth* 1(December): 421–47.

Varian, Hal. 1978. *Microeconomic Analysis*. Norton. New York.

Wood, Adrian. 1994. *North-South Trade Employment and Inequality. Changing Fortunes in a Skill-Driven World*. Oxford, U.K.: Oxford University Press.

———. 1996. "Openness and Wage Inequality in Developing Countries: The Latin American Challenge to East Asia Conventional Wisdom." *World Bank Economic Review* 11(1).

World Bank. 1995. *World Tables*. Washington, D.C.

Globalizing Talent and Human Capital: Implications for Developing Countries

ANDRÉS SOLIMANO

The new era of globalization of the late 20th and early 21st centuries has seen an increase in the international mobility of highly skilled, talented individuals (that is, human capital) and of entrepreneurs as globalization has made new job and business opportunities available. After being actively debated in the 1960s and 1970s, the topic of human capital mobility and the brain drain has remained somewhat dormant in the academic and policy literature in the last two to three decades. Two views dominated during that time: one was the internationalist view championed by Johnson (1964) and the other was the nationalist view put forward by Patinkin (1964) and others. The internationalists favored unrestricted international migration of highly skilled individuals as a vehicle for enhancing global efficiency, while the nationalists were concerned with the adverse impact on national development of human capital outflows to the industrial economies. In the global economy of the early 21st century, the debate is perhaps better framed in terms of the contribution of the international mobility of human capital to the creation of global knowledge and the development of technology in a world with significant inequalities across countries in terms of their capacity to generate and access knowledge and technology.

The international movement of human capital consists of the movement of scientists, engineers, executives, and other professionals across frontiers. These are people with special talents; high-level skills; and specialized knowledge in the scientific, technological, and cultural areas. Another dimension of the international mobility of talent is entrepreneurial migration, that is, people with a talent for business creation and resource mobilization, who are not necessarily individuals with a high level of formal education.

Developing countries and transition economies have viewed the international mobility of human capital with a mix of concern and consideration of the possibilities.

Andrés Solimano is regional adviser with the United Nations Economic Commission for Latin America and the Caribbean in Santiago. This is a revised version of the paper prepared for conference.

Annual World Bank Conference on Development Economics—Europe 2003
© 2004 The International Bank for Reconstruction and Development/The World Bank

On the one hand, developing countries encourage their students to earn graduate degrees abroad (typically in the United States and Europe) in science, technology, and other disciplines as a way to upgrade their countries' knowledge and human resource base. On the other hand, when outstanding scientists and professionals leave their home country and stay abroad, the concern arises of a brain drain caused by the flight of scarce human capital and talent whose contribution is needed for economic development at home.

This paper deals with several conceptual topics and policy issues related to the international flows of human capital, talent, and entrepreneurs mainly from developing countries' perspective. It discusses the main facts and trends in the international mobility of human capital; assesses the world distribution of science and technology (S&T) resources; deals with issues of definition and statistical measurement of migration by the highly skilled; examines the determinants of human capital migration and the peculiarities of increasing returns and factor complementarities that characterize the activities of knowledge generation; overviews issues pertaining to the brain drain and brain circulation, scientific diasporas, and entrepreneurial migration; discusses the impact of human capital migration on global inequality and national development; and highlights policies to induce human capital repatriation and greater sharing by developing countries in the benefits of global knowledge creation before concluding.

Facts and Trends in the International Mobility of Human Capital

The global demand for skilled individuals has been on the rise in the last decade or so, with most being attracted to the United States. Some 40 percent of the foreign-born population in the United States has completed tertiary education. Since the early 1990s, some 900,000 skilled professionals, mainly information technology (IT) specialists, have emigrated to the United States primarily from China; India; Russia; and some countries of the Organisation for Economic Co-operation and Development (OECD), notably, Canada, Germany, and the United Kingdom. These immigrants often come under the H1-B visa program for highly skilled professionals.

The United States is also one of the main recruiters of foreign students in higher education: it accounts for 32 percent of all foreign students in higher education in the OECD countries (*OECD Observer* 2002). Higher education is an important channel for attracting highly skilled personnel. Estimates indicate that in 1999, 25 percent of H1-B visa holders were students previously enrolled in U.S. universities (OECD 2002).

The United States is not the only net importer of foreign talent. In 2000, Germany launched a scheme to recruit some 20,000 foreign IT specialists. The main recruits come from Poland, Russia, and other Eastern European nations that have a sizable pool of scientific and technical specialists. Australia, New Zealand, and the United Kingdom have launched recruiting initiatives similar to that of Germany (box 1). In the developing world, Singapore has been meeting shortages of IT specialists with immigrants from China, Malaysia, and other neighboring countries.

BOX 1. Recent Policy Initiatives by OECD Countries to Attract Foreign Talent

Canada (Quebec Province)

The provincial government of Quebec is offering five-year income tax holidays (credits) to attract foreign academics in IT, engineering, health science, and finance to take employment in the provinces' universities.

European Union

As a follow-up to the Bologna Charter on education, efforts are under way to harmonize educational certification and qualification systems among member states in order to encourage greater student mobility within the EU.

Finland

The government has taken steps to encourage foreign students, including from Asia, to enroll in Finnish institutions of higher education.

France

France has recently taken several measures to facilitate the temporary migration of foreign scientists and researchers. In 1998, the government established an agency, EduFrance, to attract more students to France, particularly from Asia and Latin America.

Germany

The government seeks to increase inflows of foreign students through grants and fellowships schemes. In addition, it launched a program to issue 20,000 immigration visas to fill IT job vacancies. Around one-third of the visas have been granted, mainly to people from India and Eastern Europe who have been hired by small firms.

Ireland

The shortage of skilled workers, especially in IT, led to government campaigns in 2000 and 2001 to attract foreign workers and former Irish emigrants. Government-sponsored job fairs have been held in Canada, the Czech Republic, India, South Africa, and the United States. In addition, work visas were introduced in 2000 specifically to allow the entry of highly skilled workers into areas where shortages exist (MacEinri 2001).

Japan

The government seeks to double the number of foreign students through the use of scholarships.

United Kingdom

In 1999, the government launched a major campaign to increase the number of international students in higher education from 198,000 to 248,000. The strategy is based on a promotional and marketing campaign, the streamlining of visa procedures and rules on employment for foreign students, and the provision of special scholarships for top achievers.

United States

The U.S. Congress temporarily increased the annual cap on the number of temporary visas granted to professional immigrants under the H1-B visa program until 2003.

Source: OECD (2002).

The magnitude and impact of the outflow of human capital on developing countries varies from region to region. In Africa, the International Organization for Migration estimates that around 300,000 African professionals live and work in Europe and North America. Sending countries include Ethiopia, Ghana, Nigeria, and South Africa. Anecdotal evidence indicates that as a consequence of the large-scale emigration of doctors from Africa, the poor are forced to seek medical treatment from traditional healers, while the rich elite fly to London for their routine checkups (Africa Journal 2002). A recent study (Aedo 2002) shows that Africa may be losing as much as US$4 billion a year because of the annual emigration of about 20,000 top professionals seeking better jobs abroad. This emigration of professionals from Africa has several adverse effects, such as reducing the stock of scarce human capital at home; eroding the domestic tax base; and preventing the formation of a middle class of educated people, a stabilizing factor in most societies.

In developing countries with higher per capita incomes, the consequences of the outflow of human capital could be less dramatic. In China, the Ministry of Science and Technology estimates that Chinese returnees from the United States have started most Internet-based ventures. Returnees to Taiwan (China) from the United States have started nearly half of all the companies in the largest scientific park, the Hsinchu. In India, estimates for 2000 indicated that while some 1,500 highly qualified Indians had returned from the United States, more than 30 times that number depart each year (OECD 2002).

The outflow of human capital is led not only by better opportunities for study and work in the industrial countries (pulling factors), but also by economic and political conditions at home (pushing factors). In Latin America, a massive exodus of professionals, scientists, and intellectuals took place in the late 1960s and the 1970s. During those years, military regimes in Argentina, Brazil, Chile, Uruguay, and elsewhere targeted universities and other academic centers for ideological cleansing and to eliminate sources of internal opposition and criticism. This experience suggests that the emigration of scientists and intellectuals increases when authoritarian regimes suppress civil liberties and curtail academic freedom. The restoration of democracy in Latin America in the 1980s and 1990s led to the return of some scientists and intellectuals, although this flow would have been probably larger if the economic conditions in universities and research centers—that is, the salaries and resources available for research—had been better (see Hansen and others 2002; Pellegrino and Martinez 2001).

No clear relationship seems to exist between democracy and the amount of resources devoted to universities and research activity. Consider the recent experiences of such postsocialist countries as Poland and Russia. In these countries, particularly Russia, the end of communism and the transition to markets and democracy in the 1990s coincided with a net outflow of skilled professionals, scientists, and IT specialists.[1] For example, estimates indicate that around 1,000 to 2,000 people employed in science and scientific services have left Russia since the early 1990s. Germany and Israel accounted for 86 percent of the Russian emigrants in this category in 2000 (Gokhberg and Nekipelova 2002). The outflow of scientists from newly democratic Russia is largely attributable to a squeeze in the budget of the S&T sector that cut salaries and research budgets and resulted in deteriorated working conditions. This, along with changes in legislation that recognized a Russian's right to take employment abroad (a right restricted under communism), seems to be an important variable in explaining the outflow of scientists and professionals from Russia since the early 1990s (Gokhberg and Nekipelova 2002).

The World Distribution of Science and Technology Resources

An important determinant of the international migration of scientists and technology experts is the availability of resources to conduct research, including higher salaries for researchers, in destination countries compared with those available at home. Assessing the volume of resources devoted to S&T presents various statistical and definition problems ranging from the definition of science, which sometimes means only natural sciences (physics, biology, and so on), to the nonreporting or underestimation of research and development (R&D) expenditures in developing countries, all of which make international comparisons difficult.[2] Intertemporal and international comparisons of resources devoted to S&T in former socialist countries and Western economies are also difficult because of the different definitions of S&T activities (and national output) used during the socialist period.

With these caveats in mind, the available information shows large disparities in the world distribution of resources devoted to S&T between the industrial economies and developing and transition economies. Indeed, according to the United Nations Educational, Scientific, and Cultural Organization (UNESCO) (2001), the developing countries, which account for 78 percent of the world's population and 39 percent of world gross domestic product (GDP), only contributed 16 percent of global R&D expenditure in 1996–97 (table 1).

As table 1 shows, the United States has the largest share of world R&D expenditure: 36.4 percent in 1996–97. Particularly low shares of global R&D spending are apparent in Russia (1 percent) and Sub-Saharan Africa (0.5 percent).

Another indicator of the domestic effort in S&T is the share of GDP devoted to R&D. This ranges from 2.9 percent in Japan and 2.6 percent in the United States to 0.9 in Russia, 0.5 percent in Latin America and the Caribbean, and 0.3 percent in Sub-Saharan Africa.

The developing and transition economies also have significantly fewer resources (that is, salaries, research budgets, and equipment) per researcher than the industrial countries.[3] For instance, while the average R&D expenditure per researcher was US$10,100 (in purchasing power parity dollars) in Russia in 1996–97, that figure amounted to US$167,200 in the European Union and US$203,700 in the United States.

These indicators point to an extremely unequal distribution of world resources in S&T that mimics the large disparities in per capita income across nations. Rich countries spend more (as a share of GDP) on S&T than middle-income and poor countries. However, there are some significant outliers, such as China and India, whose ratios of spending on S&T to GDP are significantly higher than the international average corresponding to their per capita income levels. These international differentials in resources devoted to S&T must be correlated with the observed outflows of

TABLE 1. Key Indicators of World GDP, Population, and R&D, 1996–97

Regions and countries	GDP PPP US$ billions	GDP Percentage of world GDP	Population Millions	Population Percentage of world population	GERD PPP US$ billions	GERD Percentage of world GERD	GERD Percentage of GDP	GERD per inhabitant (PPP US$)	Researchers (thousands)	Percentage of world researchers total	Researchers per million inhabitants	GERD per researcher (PPP US$ thousands)
World	34,381.9	100.0	5,483.3	100.0	546.7	100.0	1.6	100.0	5,189.4	100.0	946.0	105.4
Developing countries	13,366.8	38.9	4,258.9	77.7	85.5	15.6	0.6	20.0	1,476.2	28.4	347.0	57.9
Industrial countries	21,015.1	61.1	1,224.4	22.3	461.3	84.4	2.2	377.0	3,713.3	71.6	3,033.0	124.2
Africa	1,246.5	3.6	626.5	11.4	3.8	0.7	0.3	6.0	132.0	2.5	211.0	28.5
Arab states	487.6	1.4	162.5	3.0	1.2	0.2	0.2	7.0	79.5	1.5	489.0	14.9
Sub-Saharan Africa (excluding Arab states)	759.0	2.2	464.0	8.5	2.6	0.5	0.3	6.0	52.5	1.0	113.0	49.1
Americas	11,333.8	33.0	782.2	14.3	225.8	41.3	2.0	289.0	1,410.5	27.2	1,803.0	160.1
Latin America and the Caribbean	3,164.8	9.2	487.1	8.9	16.8	3.1	0.5	34.0	348.3	6.7	715.0	48.2
North America	8,169.0	23.8	295.1	5.4	209.0	38.2	2.6	708.0	1,062.2	20.5	3,599.0	196.8
Asia	12,172.8	35.4	3,331.6	60.8	152.3	27.9	1.3	46.0	1,790.6	34.5	537.0	85.1
Arab states	398.2	1.2	71.2	1.3	0.8	0.1	0.2	11.0	3.7	0.1	52.0	211.4
China	3,542.8	10.3	1,215.4	22.2	21.1	3.9	0.6	17.0	551.8	10.6	454.0	38.3
Commonwealth of Independent States	168.1	0.5	71.0	1.3	0.6	0.1	0.3	8.0	97.1	1.9	1,368.0	6.0
India	1,529.5	4.4	945.6	17.2	10.8	2.0	0.7	11.0	142.8	2.8	151.0	75.8

Japan	3,000.3	8.7	125.8	2.3	83.1	15.2	2.9	661.0	617.4	11.9	4,909.0	134.6
Newly industrialized economies	2,322.5	6.8	405.1	7.4	26.7	4.9	1.1	66.0	240.9	4.6	595.0	110.7
Other	1,211.3	3.5	497.5	9.1	9.3	1.7	0.8	19.0	137.0	2.6	275.0	67.6
Europe	**9,186.0**	**26.7**	**714.2**	**13.0**	**157.7**	**28.8**	**1.7**	**221.0**	**1,768.2**	**34.1**	**2,476.0**	**89.2**
Central and Eastern Europe	679.2	2.0	115.4	2.1	5.6	1.0	0.8	49.0	167.5	3.2	1,451.0	33.5
Commonwealth of Independent States	810.4	2.4	213.5	3.9	7.6	1.4	0.9	35.0	733.1	14.1	3,434.0	10.3
European Union	7,404.4	21.5	373.1	6.8	137.9	25.2	1.8	370.0	824.9	15.9	2,211.0	167.2
Other	292.0	0.8	12.2	0.2	6.6	1.2	2.3	539.0	42.7	0.8	3,499.0	154.2
Oceania	**442.8**	**1.3**	**28.7**	**0.5**	**7.2**	**1.3**	**1.6**	**251.0**	**88.3**	**1.7**	**3,071.0**	**81.7**
Selected countries/regions												
Arab States (All)	885.8	2.6	233.8	4.3	2.0	0.4	0.2	8.0	83.2	1.6	356.0	23.6
Commonwealth of Independent States (All)	978.5	2.8	284.5	5.2	8.2	1.5	0.8	29.0	850.8	16.4	2,991.0	9.6
OECD countries	21,601.0	62.8	1,096.8	20.0	463.0	84.7	2.2	422.0	2,822.3	54.4	2,573.0	164.0
Russian Federation	643.7	1.9	147.7	2.7	5.7	1.0	0.9	38.0	561.6	10.8	3,801.0	10.1
South Africa	297.0	0.9	39.9	0.7	2.0	0.4	0.7	50.0	41.1	0.8	1,031.0	49.0
United States	7,511.3	21.8	265.2	4.8	198.8	36.4	2.6	749.0	980.5	18.9	3,697.0	202.7

PPP Purchasing power parity.

Source: UNESCO (2001).

scientists and technology experts from developing and transition economies to the United States and other OECD countries, where they have access to more resources (and better pay) to carry out their scientific research and technology work.

Definitional and Statistical Issues

A basic issue highlighted in the previous section is the definition of highly skilled and talented individuals. Although no consensus on such a definition exists, a generally accepted definition is to assume that such individuals have a tertiary educational qualification.[4] This definition is not free of problems either, as people can also acquire skills through experience.[5] In general, skill levels can be defined by education level or by occupation level. The main international standard classifications are the International Standard Classification of Education and the International Classification of Occupation. The education approach focuses on the supply of human resources in terms of their skills and qualifications. The occupations approach looks at the demand for highly skilled people. The most recent effort to develop a conceptual framework was undertaken by the OECD and Eurostat, the Statistical Office of the European Communities. Their attempt to measure human resources devoted to S&T is known as the *Canberra Manual*.

The *Canberra Manual* defines human resources devoted to S&T as people who have successfully completed tertiary education or who are employed in an S&T occupation where such qualifications are normally required. The *Canberra Manual* combines concepts pertaining to educational attainment and occupation. The S&T definition used is broad and includes engineering and technology, medical sciences, social sciences, and humanities as well as natural sciences.

For purposes of assessing the international mobility of human resources devoted to S&T, considering some definitions of migration is also useful. According to the United Nations, long-term migrants are people who move to a country other than their usual residence for periods of at least one year. By contrast, short-term migrants are those who move to another country for at least three months, but for less than a year. People who move internationally but are nonmigrants include tourists, short-term business travelers, frontier workers, pilgrims, and so on.

The main sources of migration statistics are (a) national administrative systems for regulating and monitoring immigration, including those issuing work visas and work permits for foreigners; (b) population registers and population censuses; (c) regular labor force surveys; and (d) special surveys.[6]

Determinants of Migration

The determinants of international migration, such as relative income differentials, immigration policies in destination countries, state of the business cycle, and network effects, are, in principle, applicable to individuals with different skills, although some factors, including the costs of migrating and cultural barriers, are probably more relevant for unskilled migrants than for highly skilled individuals.

Several types of human capital and talented individuals move across countries. Students go to the industrial countries to pursue graduate studies.[7] Some of these students return home after completing their studies, while others remain in the host country and find jobs in the private sector, universities, research centers, industry, government, and international organizations. Researchers and scientists may leave their home countries attracted not only by better pay abroad, but also by the allure of interacting with internationally recognized peers and with the aim of pursuing a successful career abroad. In contrast, the talented individuals who stay at home may find that they lack recognition, have poor career prospects and modest salaries, and suffer from the absence of a critical mass of professional peers.

Multinational corporations and international banks are other vehicles for the international transfer of talent. International investment often involves intracompany transfers of employees (managers, engineers, professionals, and so on) to overseas locations. Multinational corporations require that managers and international investors move internationally to establish contacts in foreign markets, make business deals, and set up offices and production units abroad. In addition, multinational corporations and firms that have an international scope hire highly skilled personnel in the countries in which they locate. Foreign personnel bring foreign competences, such as other languages, specialized knowledge, international corporate practices, and so on to the host country.

Individual researchers benefit from interacting with a critical mass of other researchers and scientists working in the same field, as intellectual creation is rarely a purely individual endeavor. Therefore the productivity of human capital depends, positively, on the availability of human capital. In other words, knowledge creation generates increasing returns. Complementarities and increasing returns are thus an essential part of the story of emigration of human capital.

As the literature on growth and development emphasizes, the emigration of highly skilled individuals can lead to virtuous circles in receiving countries. Receiving countries can set in motion a cycle of vigorous knowledge creation and application by attracting the most talented individuals from abroad in combination with an often strong knowledge base in the host country. Conversely, sending countries can stagnate in relation to the development of science, technology, and knowledge following the outflows of talent as a critical mass of scientists and technical experts disappear, resulting in a deterioration of the environment for knowledge generation and assimilation at home (Easterly 2001).

Brain Drain or Brain Cycle?

The economic effects of the emigration of human capital depend on the nature and dynamics of the emigration and return process. To understand these effects better, we need to move beyond simple characterization of the emigration of talent as a brain drain phenomenon.[8] Empirical evidence on foreign students studying and working after graduation in the United States (National Science Foundation 1998) indicates a pattern that combines a brain cycle with a brain drain.

The brain cycle would be roughly as follows. Foreign students go abroad to study, perhaps to an industrial country, to earn a graduate degree. After graduation, talented students with graduate degrees often receive good job offers in the host country and therefore choose to remain abroad on completing their higher education. The duration of their stay abroad can range from a few years to their entire working lives. If after a few years of work abroad individuals return home, the emigration of human capital can be understood more as a brain cycle and not as an irreversible loss. If emigrants decide to stay abroad for their entire productive life, the loss for the sending country is larger and the situation is more of a brain drain.

A relevant question here is whether the home country incurs a net loss if part of its qualified human resource base lives and works abroad. In a world of lower transport costs and almost instantaneous communications through the Internet, talented individuals living abroad can maintain permanent contact and develop professional exchanges with their peers. This may include periodic visits to their home countries, thereby contributing, indirectly or directly, to national development in their area of expertise. More generally, in a world of instant communication, accessing ideas and knowledge may not require the physical presence of the person who generates or is a specialist in that knowledge. Of course, this is, ultimately, a matter of degree, and the benefits of ideas are still likely to be greater when people interact directly with each other. In addition, income remittances sent by highly skilled emigrants are a benefit for the home country that should be taken into account when assessing the costs and benefits of the emigration of human capital.

The National Science Foundation (1998) study also shows that about 47 percent of the foreign students on temporary visas who earned doctorates in 1990 and 1991 were working in the United States in 1995. The figure includes 79 percent of Indian doctoral students and 88 percent of Chinese doctoral students. In contrast, only 11 percent of students from the Republic of Korea who completed science and engineering doctorates at U.S. universities in 1990–91 were working in the United States in 1995 (tables 2 and 3). The National Science Foundation study reports that foreign doctoral recipients in science and engineering who were working in the United States after 10 or 20 years tended to remain in the country. The apparent pattern that emerges is a that of a human capital emigration–return cycle (brain cycle) whose shape (duration of stay rates) varies according to country of origin and skill levels. Gaining a better understanding of the determinants of stay and return rates is an important subject for future research. Nevertheless, a reasonable assumption is that the decision to stay abroad versus returning home depends on such variables as (a) the expected earnings differentials between the host and home countries, (b) the cross-country differences in the possibilities for career advancement, and (c) the age of migrants.

Scientific Diasporas

The term diaspora is often associated with people and communities dispersed from their home countries for various reasons, including war; political and/or ethnic persecution; natural disasters; and economic disasters, such as famine (Shuval 2000).

TABLE 2. Percentage of 1990–91 Foreign S&E Doctoral Recipients from U.S. Universities working in the United States in 1995, by Country of Origin

Country	No. of students receiving S&E doctorates in 1990–91	Percentage working in the United States in 1995
Total	13,878	47
Canada	417	46
China[a]	2,779	88
Germany	177	35
Greece	240	41
India	1,235	79
Japan	227	13
Korea, Rep. of	1,912	11
Mexico	194	30
Taiwan (China)	1,824	42
United Kingdom	142	59

a. The high stay rate of Chinese students is attributable to a one-time granting of permanent residence status in the United States (Chinese Students Protection Act) following China's response to student demonstrations.

Note: Includes foreign doctoral recipients with temporary visa status at the time of receipt of degrees.

Source: National Science Foundation (1998).

TABLE 3. Chinese Students Studying Abroad and Returning Home, 1978–99

Year	No. of students studying abroad	No. of students returning
1978	860	248
1980	2,124	162
1985	4,888	1,424
1986	4,676	1,388
1987	4,703	1,605
1988	3,786	3,000
1989	3,329	1,753
1990	2,950	1,593
1991	2,900	2,069
1992	6,540	3,611
1993	10,742	5,128
1994	19,071	4,230
1995	20,381	5,750
1996	20,905	6,570
1997	22,410	7,130
1998	17,622	7,379
1999	23,749	7,748

Source: OECD (2002).

Diasporas often tend to maintain emotional, historical, and family attachments with their homeland.

Recent literature (see, for example, Meyer and Brown 1999) has identified the existence of scientific diasporas. These diasporas have created knowledge networks of nationals belonging to a certain scientific field who work or study abroad. A main purpose of these networks is to connect professionals and scientists scattered around the globe who are interested in maintaining contact and in helping to promote the scientific and economic development of their home countries. These networks may be linked to and supported by national governments or may be fully independent. Examples of such networks are Chinese Scholars Abroad, the Colombian Network of Engineers Abroad, the Global Korean Network, the Silicon Valley Indian Professionals Association, the Polish Scientists Abroad Network, the Reverse Brain Drain Project of Thailand, the Tunisian Scientific Consortium, the South African Network of Skills Abroad, and the Program of Venezuelan Talent Abroad.

Scientific knowledge generation taking place across the world can be transmitted through networks, thereby enabling, to some extent, the de-linking of the contribution of scientists from their physical place of residence. This can help transfer knowledge to developing countries.

Entrepreneurial Migration

An important feature of migration, relatively neglected in the discussions of brain drain, is the international mobility of entrepreneurship. This refers to people who settle in other countries and have a talent for business creation and job generation. Historically, internationally successful entrepreneurs and bankers in the late 19th and early 20th century in the United States and Europe—such as Andrew Carnegie, Andrew M. Mellon, John D. Rockefeller, Cornelius Vanderbilt, and the famous banking dynasty of the Rothschilds with operations in London, Zurich, and other financial centers—were foreign born or their parents were immigrants (Ferguson 1999). Note that the Mellons, Rockefellers, and others, in addition to accumulating wealth, had an interest in creating centers of education and learning. Indeed, they helped to establish universities and created private foundations devoted to education purposes. Carnegie, in particular, was one of the pioneers of the system of public libraries in the United States at the turn of the 20th century. A later example is George Soros, an immigrant from Central Europe who escaped from Nazi persecution in the 1930s and became a successful financier in his adopted country. Soros is also another example of a talented entrepreneur with a philanthropic bent manifested in his creation of the Soros Foundation and the network of Open Society Institutes throughout the world.

Some studies (for example, Kloosterman and Rath 2001) have observed a connection between ethnic diasporas and entrepreneurship (see box 2 for a detailed example). Classic examples of this are the Jewish emigration to the United States. Estimates suggest that the contribution of the Jewish community to business creation and banking is far larger than their share in the total population of the United States. In the context of developing countries, Chinese emigration has played an important role in building a business community of Chinese origin in several dynamic economies of Southeast Asia. Similarly, immigration from Germany, Italy, Palestine,

---

BOX 2. Asian Venture Capital in California

According to estimates from industry sources, Silicon Valley has several dozen Asian venture capital firms, 31 from Taiwan (China) alone and others from Hong Kong (China), Japan, Korea, Malaysia, and Singapore. Most of their money goes to start-ups that specialize in the Internet or semiconductors. A handful of venture funds, such as InveStar Capital, Inc., founded in 1996 and based in Taiwan (China), invest more heavily in Silicon Valley than in Asia. In 1998, 80 percent of InveStar Capital's investments (more than US$100 million) went to Silicon Valley firms. While there are no venture funds and few private financiers from India, the community is overflowing with local Indian investors who provide enough early funding to give companies the momentum to attract the attention of mainstream venture capital firms.

Since Asian ethic communities in the San Francisco Bay area reached critical mass in the 1990s, their networks and associations have expanded. Among the largest Chinese and Indian associations are the Monte Jade Science and Technology Association (1,000 members), formed in 1990 by wealthy individuals from Taiwan (China), and the Indus Entrepreneurs (600 members), founded in 1993 by South Asian entrepreneurs. These Chinese and Indian investors have mobilized resources from the venture capital industry.

Source: OECD (2002).

Lebanon, and Syria to Argentina, Brazil, and Chile at the turn of the 20th century played an important role in building the textile, banking, agriculture, and mining sectors in these Latin American countries (Solberg 1970).

The scale of business activity created by the entrepreneurship of foreign migrants varies significantly. Not all entrepreneurial immigrants operate at the economic scale of the Rockefellers and Rothschilds, or a Soros. Indeed, large numbers operate at the level of family businesses and small firms. A typical example is the ethnic restaurants in the large cities of the industrial countries. Another example is carpet and furniture businesses in these cities, where Indian, Moroccan, Pakistani, and Turkish owners predominate. Such patterns of immigrant entrepreneurship do not mobilize large amounts of financial resources, but they can be relatively labor intensive and their businesses add to the variety of services available in the host countries. The sociological profile of these endeavors is interesting: the businesses are usually owned and run by members of a specific ethnic group and their employees, who are often family members, also tend to be of the same ethnicity (Kloosterman and Rath 2001; Ndoen and others 2000).

The connections between ethnicity, entrepreneurship, and migration and migrants' patterns of integration into or exclusion from the local economy and society are themes that deserve further investigation. For example, migrants from certain ethnic groups who form entrepreneurial groups among themselves may have a more difficult time integrating into the local society than immigrants who develop entrepreneurial activities across a more diverse ethnic spectrum.

The relationship between human capital endowments and entrepreneurship is also an interesting subject. Entrepreneurs are not necessarily people with a high stock of formal education, and in addition, the psychology of the entrepreneur differs from that of the scientist, the expert, or the intellectual, those usually identified with human capital. Typically the entrepreneur is not averse to risk taking and has a talent for combining capital and labor and for envisaging opportunities and prospects for profits (Schumpeter 1954). In contrast, professionals, scientists, and engineers are often employees rather than business owners and tend to be more risk averse.

An important issue regarding entrepreneurial emigration is the extent to which this type of emigration has a negative effect on the development of the home country. Entrepreneurs are important agents of resource mobilization, investment, and innovation. This is a scarce trait in developing countries, thus their departure is likely to retard development. However, entrepreneurs often do return home, bringing with them new capital and contacts developed abroad, with an ensuing positive effect on development. An option in this context would be to distinguish between entrepreneurial drain and entrepreneurial circulation.

Impact on Global Output, Global Inequality, and National Development

What are the economic consequences of the international mobility of human capital, talent, and entrepreneurship? Who gains? Who loses?

In a world without barriers to the movement of people across nations, individuals would be expected to migrate from places where their productivity and income were lower to places where their productivity and income were higher, regardless of national borders.[9] As a result, human capital would flow from places with lower net returns to places with higher net returns, having discounted the costs of moving (including the psychological and emotional costs of leaving home). Unless significant negative externalities are present, world income should be higher with more mobile human capital, because at the margin, the marginal productivity of human capital will tend to be equalized around the world. As a result, increased mobility of human capital, talent, and entrepreneurship has global efficiency gains. This analysis does not, however, consider the international distribution impact of such migration flows between nations sending and receiving migrants.

Globalization is unfolding in a world of large inequalities across (and within) nations (Solimano 1999, 2001a), and the movement of human capital from low-income countries to rich nations may accentuate these differentials. Indeed, the emigration of the highly skilled increases the stock of human capital in advanced receiving countries and reduces it in sending countries with lower per capita incomes. If there are increasing returns to human capital and it tends to concentrate in places where the availability of human and physical capital is already high, the result may be to exacerbate inequalities in income and knowledge concentration across countries that tend to persist over time. Under increasing returns, the international mobility of talent and human capital from poor to rich countries may exacerbate global inequalities of income and wealth (see Krugman and Venables 1995 for a center-periphery model with increasing returns). Sending countries can also incur other losses from the migration of the highly skilled, namely: (a) the sending country might lose fiscal revenues; (b) the sending country government loses its initial investment in the education of highly skilled emigrants; (c) the science sector of the sending country might become weaker; and (d) the middle class, often a stabilizing force in developing countries, can weaken with the massive emigration of highly skilled individuals.

In the medium and long run, however, migration can bring about improvements. The human capital that emigrated might eventually return home, bringing with it accumulated knowledge and skills, and fresh capital, with the ensuing contribution to investment, productivity, and growth for the home economy. In addition, as mentioned earlier, during their absence, emigrants may transfer some of their knowledge and experience to their home country through periodic visits and participation in the knowledge networks that scientific diasporas set up abroad. Further positive effects for sending countries are associated with the fact that returnees have often developed contacts with foreign scientific communities and universities and have greater exposure to international best practices in their fields. Finally, emigrants' remittances are another benefit of the international circulation of people. Remittances ease foreign exchange constraints, complement national savings, help finance investment projects, and are a transfer to lower- and middle-income families (Solimano 2003).

Policy Issues

What can developing countries do to increase the contribution to the sending countries of their human capital that has emigrated? How can they stimulate the return of human capital and entrepreneurs residing abroad in order to boost national development? How can developing countries' share of the benefits derived from the global generation of knowledge and the development of new technologies be increased? How can the world distribution of resources for S&T be improved? These are important policy questions.

Seemingly "simple" solutions, such as enacting legal impediments to the international migration of human capital and/or imposing stiff taxes on such flows, are unlikely to succeed in dampening the outflow of qualified people and can ultimately be counterproductive. Such measures stifle mobility and are at odds with basic principles of individual freedom in an increasingly integrated global economy (Solimano 2001b). In an era of globalization and rapid technical change, the international mobility of human capital is needed to transfer knowledge across national boundaries. The issue, however, is how to increase developing countries' share of the benefits of knowledge generation and new technologies that mobile human capital, part of it coming from the developing countries, helps to generate.

The data show that the share of GDP devoted to R&D in many developing countries is well below world averages. This reflects the existence of other public policy priorities for resource allocation, such as physical infrastructure and social spending, over the development of S&T. However, this is shortsighted. In the medium to long run, neglect of the S&T sector will be reflected in lower productivity growth and competitiveness, thereby hampering the development potential of these countries.

Foreign aid also has a role to play in supporting the development of S&T in developing countries. Such aid can take several forms. One option is to provide support for universities and high-quality research centers to enhance developing countries' research capabilities and induce the repatriation of scientists and professionals. Another mechanism is to foster the development of international exchanges of scientists and highly qualified professionals whereby technical experts from industrial countries can spend time in developing countries interacting with local researchers, thereby contributing to the local development of the S&T sector. Foreign aid can also be used to promote use of the Internet and provide support for libraries to upgrade their collections of books, databases, specialized journals, and the like. Foreign aid can be channeled bilaterally or through international organizations such as UNESCO, the World Bank, and the OECD. Currently, the World Bank has a lending program for supporting the development of science in developing countries through the Millennium Science Initiative. The loans go to national governments that then provide matching funds and give financial support—often by means of grants—to the formation and maintenance of centers of excellence in science in their countries.

International private support of S&T in developing nations also has a role through private foundations with an international scope, such as the Ford Foundation, the Rockefeller Foundation, and the Bill and Melinda Gates Foundation. Such foundations can support programs in pure and applied science for development. The Gates Foundation's support for the development of vaccines and cost-efficient drugs for Africa seems to be an excellent precedent in this regard.

Another policy goal is to foster entrepreneurs as agents of innovation and economic progress. As many developing country entrepreneurs reside and invest abroad, such a policy requires an environment in which emigrant investors are encouraged to repatriate capital and launch investment projects at home.

Concluding Remarks

The increased international mobility of human capital, including highly skilled individuals and entrepreneurs, is a consequence of the globalization and technological change that now characterize the world economy. This paper shows that mobility does have global efficiency gains, but that the distribution of these gains is unequal among countries. Global inequalities in per capita income levels between nations are also reflected in the large disparities in the distribution of resources for S&T among industrial, developing, and transition economies. Indeed, the OECD accounts for nearly 85 percent of world expenditure on R&D. This concentration of S&T resources in the industrial economies attracts scientists and professionals from developing and transition economies, raising concerns about a brain drain, though in many cases such emigrants do eventually return home.

The evidence shows that the traditional brain drain, that is, a permanent and irreversible outflow of human capital, co-exists alongside cycles of emigration and return of national talent (brain circulation). Thus the emigration of domestic talent need not be always a permanent loss for developing countries. However, return rates vary from country to country, and poor regions such as Africa suffer particularly hard from the almost always permanent emigration of domestic talent.

Current imbalances in the international distribution of resources for S&T call for more resources and better incentives for the S&T sectors of developing and transition economies. This requires action on several fronts. To begin with, national governments of developing countries need to give greater priority to science, technology, and knowledge generation at home by recognizing its payoff in enhanced productivity, competitiveness, and long-run development. In turn, the industrial countries can increase the transfer of knowledge to developing countries and redefine foreign aid priorities toward S&T in developing countries. Public policy efforts in relation to S&T can be complemented by grants from international foundations to support S&T in developing countries by, for instance, creating centers of excellence. All such steps would be powerful signals to stimulate the return of talented emigrants to the developing world.

The emigration of entrepreneurs reveals the existence of broader business opportunities from globalization; however, this type of emigration may also reflect the limitations that investors face in realizing their potential for business creation and resource mobilization in the developing world. This requires a fresh look at the obstacles to business creation in different developing countries. These obstacles may range from lack of credit, poor enforcement of property rights, and bureaucratic red tape to macroeconomic uncertainty and political instability. More research is needed to gain a further understanding of why entrepreneurs emigrate.

Thus overall, imaginative policies are needed to harmonize the need for the international mobility of scarce human talent in an era of globalization with the aspirations for national development and more equitable distribution of the fruits of knowledge and technology among all nations.

Notes

1. For a dramatic account of how the emigration of the most talented individuals of the former German Democratic Republic severely debilitated the country, contributing to its unexpectedly rapid demise after the end of the communist regime in 1990, see Hirschman (1995).

2. The United Nations Educational, Scientific, and Cultural Organization and the OECD have developed a broad concept of S&T activities that includes R&D; scientific and technical services, which covers activities in museums, libraries, translation and editing of science and technology literature, surveying and prospecting, testing and quality control, and so on; and scientific and technical education and training, which refers to S&T education and training, notably tertiary education (UNESCO 2001).

3. The number of researchers in the developing countries as a share of the world total, 28 percent, is greater than their corresponding share of world R&D expenditure, 16 percent (table 1).

4. Empirical studies of human resources in science and technology also use broad categories of the International Classification of Occupation levels 1, 2, and 3 (see Auriol and Sexton 2002).

5. The lack of a generally accepted definition is reflected in the problems regarding the recognition of qualifications across countries. As the market for the highly skilled becomes even

more global, the issue of international recognition of professional qualifications will become more pressing.

6. An example of a special survey is the U.S. scientists and engineers statistical data system created by the National Science Foundation.

7. Another factor that encourages the emigration of students is the availability of financial support for foreign students to pursue graduate degrees abroad.

8. The academic literature presents various concepts of "brain mobility." For example brain exchange implies a two-way flow of expertise between a sending country and a receiving country, but when the net flow is heavily biased in one direction, the literature uses the terms brain gain or brain drain. Another term, brain waste, describes the waste of skills that occurs when highly skilled workers migrate into forms of employment that do not require the application of the skills and experience they applied in their former jobs. Finally, brain circulation refers to the cycle of moving abroad to study, then taking a job abroad, and later returning home.

9. This is a simplification, because individual attachments to family, language, traditions, and culture in the home country also influence the decision to emigrate.

References

The word "processed" describes informally reproduced works that may not be commonly available in libraries.

Aedo, D. 2002. "Brain Drain in Africa." Organization for Social Research in East Africa. Addis Ababa.

Africa Journal (Voice of America Radio). 2002. "Education in Africa: The Brain Drain."

Auriol, L., and J. Sexton. 2002. "Human Resources in Science and Technology: Measurement Issues and International Mobility." In OECD, ed., *International Mobility of the Highly Skilled*. Paris.

Easterly, W. 2001. *The Elusive Quest for Growth*. Cambridge, Mass.: MIT Press.

Ferguson, N. 1999. *The House of Rothschild. The World's Banker 1849–1999*. New York and London: Viking.

Gokhberg, L., and E. Nekipelova. 2002. "International Migration of Scientists and Engineers in Russia." In OECD, ed., *International Mobility of the Highly Skilled*. Paris.

Hansen, T., N. Agapitova, L. Holm-Nielsen, and O. Vukmirovic. 2002. "The Evolution of Science and Technology: Latin America and the Caribbean in Comparative Perspective." World Bank, Washington, D.C. Processed.

Hirschman, A., ed. 1995. "Exit, Voice, and the Fate of the German Democratic Republic." In *A Propensity to Self-Subversion*. Cambridge, Mass.: Harvard University Press.

Johnson, H. 1964. "An 'Internationalist' Model." In W. Adams, ed., *The Brain Drain*. London and New York: Macmillan.

Kloosterman, R., and J. Rath. 2001. "Immigrant Entrepreneurs in Advanced Economies: Mixed Embeddedness Further Explored." *Journal of Ethnic and Migration Studies* (special issue on immigrant entrepreneurship) 27(2): 1–14.

Krugman, P., and A. Venables. 1995. "Globalization and the Inequality of Nations." Working Paper no. 5098. National Bureau of Economic Research, Cambridge, Mass.

MacEinri, P. 2001. "Immigration into Ireland: Trends, Policy Responses, and Outlook." National University of Ireland, Irish Centre of Migration Studies, Cork, Ireland. Processed.

Meyer, J-B., and M. Brown. 1999. *Scientific Diasporas: A New Approach to the Brain Drain.* Management of Social Transformations Programme Discussion Paper no. 41. Paris: United Nations Educational, Scientific, and Cultural Organization.

National Science Foundation. 1998. "International Mobility of Scientists and Engineers to the United States: Brain Drain or Brain Circulation?" NSF no. 98-316, Issue Brief. National Science Foundation, Division of Science Resources Studies, Arlington, Va.

Ndoen, M., C. Gorter, P. Nijkamp, and P. Rietveld. 2000. *Entrepreneurial Migration and Regional Opportunities in Developing Countries.* Discussion Paper no. 2000-086/3. Amsterdam and Rotterdam: Tinbergen Institute.

OECD (Organisation for Economic Co-operation and Development), ed. 2002. *International Mobility of the Highly Skilled.* Paris.

OECD Observer. 2002. "The Brain Drain: Old Myths, New Realities." http://www.oecdobsever.org.

OECD (Organisation for Economic Co-operation and Development) and Eurostat. 1995. *Canberra Manual, 1995.* Paris.

Patinkin, D. 1964. "A 'Nationalist' Model." In W. Adams, ed., *The Brain Drain.* London and New York: Macmillan.

Pellegrino, A., and J. Martinez. 2001. *Una Aproximación al Diseño de Políticas sobre la Migración Internacional Calificada en América Latina.* Population and Development Series. Santiago: Latin American Center for Demography and United Nations Economic Commission for Latin America and the Caribbean.

Schumpeter, J. 1954. *A History of Economic Analysis.* New York: Oxford University Press.

Shuval, J. 2000. "Diaspora Migration: Definitional Ambiguities and Theoretical Paradigm." *International Migration* 38(5).

Solberg, C. E. 1970. *Immigration and Nationalism: Argentina and Chile 1890–1910.* Austin, Tex., and London: University of Texas Press.

Solimano, A. 1999. "Globalization and National Development at the End of the 20th Century." Policy Research Working Paper no. 2137. World Bank, Washington, D.C.

———. 2001a. *The Evolution of World Income Inequality: Assessing the Impact of Globalization.* Macroeconomics of Development Series no. 14. Santiago: United Nations Economic Commission for Latin America and the Caribbean.

———. 2001b. "International Migration and the Global Economic Order: An Overview." Policy Research Working Paper no. 2137. World Bank, Washington, D.C.

———. 2003. *Remittances by Emigrants: Issues and Evidence.* Macroeconomics of Development Series no. 26. Santiago: United Nations Economic Commission for Latin America and the Caribbean.

UNESCO (United Nations Educational, Scientific, and Cultural Organization). 2001. *The State of Science and Technology in the World.* Montreal: Institute for Statistics.

The Economics of the Brain Drain Turned on its Head

ODED STARK

Consensus is strong that deficiency in human capital is a major reason why poor countries remain poor. Much of the human capital in a country is a result of decisions made by individuals, but individual choices seldom add up to the social optimum. In particular, individuals do not consider the positive externalities that human capital confers in production. The result is that they acquire less human capital than is desirable. If individuals could be persuaded to form more human capital, then the human capital in an economy could rise to the socially optimal level.

What makes an unfortunate state of affairs worse is that whatever quantities of human capital are formed, some—and often more than a mere some—are lost through migration leakage. It comes as little surprise then that the concern heretofore has been to contain this leakage. In the words of a *World Development Report:* "Can something be done to stop the exodus of trained workers from poorer countries?" (World Bank 1995, p. 64). This concern follows, and is in congruence with, the large "brain drain" literature (for a systematic review see Bhagwati and Wilson 1989). The informed press also regularly echoes this concern. In a lead article that addresses the issue of migration to the European Union, *The Economist* (May 6, 2000) states: "[A]ny regime that concentrated on luring the highly skilled would run the risk of robbing poor countries of the people they are least able to do without." In a lead article a year later, while advocating the entry of migrants into Europe, *The Economist* (May 31, 2001) hastens to add: "There is a risk, especially when immigration policies target only the highly skilled, that the best talent will be drained from poor countries to rich ones." Students of migration voice similar expressions of alarm.

Oded Stark is professor of economics at the University of Bonn and at the University of Vienna, and is the research director of ESCE Economic and Social Research Center, Cologne and Eisenstadt. This paper draws on University of Bonn, Discussion Papers on Development Policy no. 11 (Bonn: Center for Development Research 1999) and on Institute for Advanced Studies, Economics Series no. 100 (Vienna: Institute for Advanced Studies, 2001). Partial financial support from the Humboldt Foundation, the Sohmen Foundation, and the School of Economics and Finance at the University of Hong Kong (China) is gratefully acknowledged.

Annual World Bank Conference on Development Economics—Europe 2003
© 2004 The International Bank for Reconstruction and Development/The World Bank

Shkolnikov (1995) writes: "If able younger scientists leave Russia, their older colleagues would have fewer talented people to whom they can pass their knowledge. This could lead to a decline in the quality of research in those scientific disciplines where Russia is currently ranked high internationally." Although expressed more cautiously, Carrington and Detragiache (1999) take a similar stance: "Another important issue is the extent to which the benefits of education acquired by citizens of developing countries are externalities that individuals cannot be expected to take into account when making their private decisions. If such externalities are substantial, as is emphasized by the 'new growth theory,' then policies to curb the brain drain may be warranted."

This paper turns this concern on its head. It argues that the prospect of migration can well be harnessed to induce individuals to form a socially desirable level of human capital. The point is that compared with a closed economy, an economy open to migration differs not only in the opportunities that workers face, but also in the structure of the incentives they confront: higher prospective returns to human capital in a foreign country impinge on human capital formation decisions at home. The paper considers a setting in which an individual's productivity is fostered by his or her own human capital as well as by the economy-wide average level of human capital. It examines the relationship between the actual formation of human capital in an economy and the socially optimal formation of human capital in the economy. It identifies conditions under which, from a social point of view, too little human capital formation takes place in the economy, and examines the relationship between the actual formation of human capital and the optimal formation of human capital in the presence of the possibility of migration. The paper then identifies conditions under which per capita output and the level of welfare of all workers are higher with migration than in its absence, and it shows that a controlled and restrictive migration policy can enhance welfare and nudge the economy toward the social optimum. It derives this result first when all workers are alike and are equally capable of responding to the migration prospect, and second when workers differ both in their skills and in their ability to respond. The paper concludes that migration is conducive to the formation of human capital, and thus casts migration as a harbinger of human capital gain, not as the culprit of human capital drain. An interesting implication is that the gains from migration that accrue to the home country are derived neither from migrants' remittances nor from migrants' return home with enhanced skills acquired abroad.[1]

Human Capital Formation in an Economy without Migration

Consider a closed economy or a small open economy without migration. The economy produces a single commodity and has N identical workers. The single production input is labor. The worker's cost function of forming human capital is linear in θ, where θ is the worker's human capital (the sum total of his or her efficiency units of labor). The economy-wide level of output is N times the per worker concave production function. This production function is a weighted sum of θ and of $\bar{\theta}$, the economy-wide average level of human capital. The reason for the dependence of the worker's output on $\bar{\theta}$ is the prevalence of externalities that accrue from the average level of human capital. Externalities in production arise when, as a result of individuals acquiring human capital, they not only make themselves more productive, but also make each other more productive. Conversely, when individuals fail to form human capital, they not only make themselves less productive, but also make each other less productive. A simple way of conditioning a worker's output not only on his or her own human capital, but also on the human capital of others, is to have the worker's output depend on the average level of human capital. Workers supply their human capital inelastically, having acquired it instantly, though not costlessly, at the beginning of their single-period life. Workers borrow the requisite funds to support the human capital formation at a zero rate of interest.

Because labor is the only production input, the gross earnings per worker are simply equal to the output per worker. The worker seeks to maximize his or her net earnings, that is, his or her output minus the cost of forming human capital. Let us refer to the solution to the worker's optimization problem as θ^*. It turns out that θ^* is fully specified by the parameters of the cost function of forming human capital and of the production function. (A formal derivation of this and subsequent results is in the appendix.) As the economy has N identical workers, the average level of human capital in the economy is also θ^*. Therefore the net earnings per worker are fully specified by the model's parameters. Let us refer to these earnings as $W(\theta^*)$. Because the social returns to human capital are not internalized by the individual worker, θ^* is not the socially optimal level of human capital. Net earnings per worker are maximized when the externalities from the economy-wide average level of human capital are taken into account. The $\bar{\theta}$ that appears in the worker's maximand is substituted by θ in the social planner's maximand. Let us refer to the solution of the social planner's optimization problem as θ^{**}.

Two results emerge. First, $\theta^{**} > \theta^*$. Second, if workers choose to form the socially optimal level of human capital, θ^{**}, the net earnings per worker will become $W(\theta^{**})$. It is easily shown that $W(\theta^{**}) > W(\theta^*)$: net earnings per worker attained under the social planner's choice of θ are higher than those achieved when workers choose how much human capital to form without taking into consideration the human capital externality. By construction, $W(\theta^{**})$ represents the highest net earnings per worker achievable, given the production technology. Unfortunately, when choosing how much human capital to form, an individual worker will not pay heed to the economy-wide average level of human capital, except as a parameter. In a large economy, no individual can influence the economy's average level of human capital. Thus the prevailing level of human capital will be θ^*.

Human Capital Formation in an Economy with Migration

This section considers migration policy as a tool for mitigating the inefficiency arising from human capital externalities. Assume that an opportunity to migrate to another, superior-technology country, D, presents itself. Assume further that human capital neither depreciates nor appreciates across countries, and that the human capital of individual migrant workers is deciphered in D fully and immediately upon the migrants' arrival. The returns to human capital in D are higher than in the home country, H. A worker's output, and thus his or her gross earnings, in D are again a concave function of the worker's level of human capital.

Suppose that workers in H face a probability, $p > 0$, of obtaining the gross earnings from employment in D. With probability $1 - p$ they do not secure such employment, in which case they work in H for the home country's gross earnings. Again, the worker's decision problem is how much human capital to form. Not surprisingly, the worker's chosen level of human capital, $\tilde{\theta}^*$, depends positively on p.

Several results follow. First, $\tilde{\theta}^* > \theta^*$. In the presence of the possibility of migration, workers choose to form more human capital than in the absence of the possibility of migration. The inducement effect of migration raises the level of human capital of all workers, including the workers who stay in H. Thus the inadequacy of human capital formation arising from the externalities is mitigated, and consequently welfare can potentially be improved by the possibility of migration. (If the inducement is strong enough, the home country could even be left with more total human capital in the wake of migration. The brain gain could then exceed the brain drain for the home country's total human capital.)

Second, a complete welfare analysis is possible. Because the returns to human capital in D are higher than the returns to human capital in the home country, the net earnings of the workers who migrate to D are higher than the net returns of those who stay behind. After all, the workers who migrate incurred exactly the same costs of acquiring human capital as the workers who stay behind, yet the gross earnings of the former are higher than the gross earnings of the latter. Therefore the possibility of migration would make every home country worker better off if it makes the nonmigrants better off. To examine whether the possibility of migration made the nonmigrants better off, $W(\tilde{\theta}^*)$ and $W(\theta^*)$ are compared. Viewing the probability of migration, p, as a policy variable, the difference between $W(\tilde{\theta}^*)$ and $W(\theta^*)$ attains a unique maximum at a level of p, referred to as p^*, $0 < p^* < 1$, and the difference between $W(\tilde{\theta}^*)$ and $W(\theta^*)$ evaluated at p^* is positive.

This result reveals that a carefully designed migration policy can be welfare enhancing and that the welfare gain of the nonmigrants is maximized when the probability of migration is equal to the feasible level p^*. Furthermore, when the value of p^* is inserted into $\tilde{\theta}^*$, the level of $\tilde{\theta}^*$ is equal to θ^{**}. Therefore when the probability of migration is p^*, the level of human capital that workers choose to form is exactly the level chosen by the social planner in the absence of migration. Thus the welfare of the workers who stay behind is inadvertently maximized by the inducement effect of the possibility of migration. This is the sense in which a migration policy can correct for the human capital externality and restore the social optimum.

A skeptic could argue that the optimal probability p^* is a mere theoretical concept, and that in practice, for the government of the home country to know the exact level of p^* would be difficult, if not impossible. This may call into question the usefulness of migration as a tool to improve welfare and to correct for the disregard of the human capital externalities. To address this concern, let us examine the difference between $W(\tilde{\theta}^*)$ and $W(\theta^*)$ as a function of p. This difference is positive for any $0 < p \le p^*$. Thus as long as the probability of migration is not greater than p^*, the net earnings of a worker who stays in H under migration are higher than the net earnings per worker without migration. This suggests the practical use of migration as a welfare-enhancing policy tool even when the government of H does not know the exact level of the optimal probability.

To sum up, the analysis suggests that a controlled and restrictive migration policy can be welfare enhancing for nonmigrants. In particular, in the presence of a controlled migration policy with the probability of migration set at p^*, the level of human capital that the workers are induced to form turns out to be the socially optimal level of human capital had the workers not migrated.

Heterogeneous Workforce, Human Capital Formation, and Migration

The intersection of migration with the presence of externalities could give rise to a concern that those who leave adversely affect the productivity of those who stay behind. If the human capital of the workers who migrate is higher than the human capital of the workers who stay behind, and if a worker's output is an increasing function of the average level of human capital, the nonmigrants will end up worse off, because the workers who migrate impose a negative externality on the workers who remain. To address this concern, we examine what is likely to constitute the worst possible case from the perspective of low-skill workers: the case in which these workers cannot participate in migration at all. Even in such a harsh environment, the human capital formation response of the high-skill workers to the migration prospect can still lead to the low-skill workers being better off.

The essence of the argument is as follows. Let us relax the assumption that the workforce is homogeneous, and let us suppose that H has two types of workers: low-ability, type-1 workers and high-ability, type-2 workers. Human capital formation is costlier for type-1 workers. Let the cost of forming human capital by a type-1 worker be such that this worker cannot possibly form a level of human capital that is higher than $\underline{\theta}$. The type-2 workers do not face such a constraint and optimally choose to form human capital at the level θ_2^*. If N_1 and N_2 are the numbers of type-1 and type-2 workers, respectively, then, in the absence of migration, the average level of human capital in H is

$$\bar{\theta} = \frac{N_1\underline{\theta} + N_2\theta_2^*}{N_1 + N_2}.$$

Let the probability of being selected for employment in D for an H country worker whose human capital is θ be p if $\theta > \underline{\theta}$, and 0 otherwise. The presence of an opportunity to migrate and earn higher wages in D induces the type-2 workers to form more human capital. However, the type-1 workers are immune to this inducement effect because of their inability to form more human capital than the minimal level required for the probable employment in D. Therefore under the possibility of migration, the levels of human capital formed by type-1 and type-2 workers are, respectively, $\underline{\theta}$ and $\tilde{\theta}_2^*$, where $\tilde{\theta}_2^*$ is an increasing function of p. Hence the average level of human capital of the workers who remain in H is

$$\bar{\theta}_m = \frac{N_1\underline{\theta} + (1-p)N_2\tilde{\theta}_2^*}{N_1 + (1-p)N_2}.$$

We can, first, compare $\bar{\theta}_m$ and $\bar{\theta}$ and derive a reasonable sufficient condition under which the average level of human capital of the nonmigrants in the wake of migration, $\bar{\theta}_m$, is higher than the average level of human capital in the absence of migration, $\bar{\theta}$.

Second, and more important, we can once again perform a complete welfare analysis. When the migration prospect leads to higher average human capital, type-1 workers are obviously better off, benefiting from a greater human capital externality. Whether the remaining type-2 workers are also better off under migration is less clear. Yet when the reasonable sufficient condition yielding $\bar{\theta}_m > \bar{\theta}$ holds, the type-2 workers who remain in H are also better off when the probability of migration is small enough. This result reaffirms the main result of the previous section: a restrictive migration policy can stimulate human capital formation and improve the welfare of all workers. In addition, the possibility of a brain drain of high-ability workers from H can confer a positive externality on low-ability workers in H.

Conclusions

When the productivity of an individual in a closed economy or in a small open economy without migration is fostered not only by the individual's own human capital, but also by the average level of human capital, the individual who optimally chooses how much to invest in costly human capital formation will, from a social point of view, underinvest. Consequently, social welfare is affected adversely. Somewhat surprisingly, the facility of migration can mitigate this undesirable outcome. Indeed, a well-specified migration policy can ameliorate the tendency to underinvest in human capital and permit the formation of a socially desirable level of human capital. The favorable effect of migration and the associated welfare gain apply not only when all individuals can respond to the migration prospect, but also when only a subset of individuals can. In the latter case, even those who cannot gain from migration by participating in it stand to gain from the response of others.

The propensity to acquire skills is not invariant to the possibility that the skills will be highly rewarded. This consideration appears to have escaped the attention of scholars of migration for many years. The pioneering work of Grubel and Scott (1966) provides a careful account of why a country need not lose by the migration of highly skilled individuals. According to Grubel and Scott (1966, p. 270): "[E]migration should be welcomed whenever two conditions are met. These are, first, that the emigrant improves his own income and, second, that the migrant's departure does not reduce the income of those remaining behind." Neither Grubel and Scott nor those who followed in their footsteps have mentioned that the prospect of migration modifies the human capital formation calculus, thereby entailing a welfare gain for the nonmigrants, rather than being inconsistent with a welfare loss. This paper draws attention to this possible relationship and shows that the behavioral response to the prospect of migration nourishes both a brain drain and a brain gain, and that a skillfully executed migration policy can confine and use the response to secure a welfare gain for all workers.

Complementary Reflections

An interesting extension of the foregoing analysis would be to assess the sensitivity of the results to alternative specifications, to inquire whether the approach can be extended to incorporate welfare analysis in the destination country, and to consider the policy role that the government of the destination country can play.

In the existing model, human capital is perfectly transferable across economies: moving it does not detract from its productivity (it is perfectly "general"). The existing framework also assumes full employment. Suppose, alternatively, that there are two types of human capital: general and destination-specific (henceforth "specific"). The latter type is productive abroad but useless at home. The returns to general human capital abroad are considerably higher than the returns to general human capital at home, and the returns to specific human capital are higher still, that is, they are higher than the returns to general human capital abroad. When migration is not a possibility, no worker will acquire specific human capital. Suppose that in such a case every worker optimally acquires $\hat{\theta}$ of general human capital. When migration is possible and the probability of obtaining gainful employment abroad is $\pi > 0$, when migration into unemployment abroad is not possible, and when the two types of human capital are equally costly to acquire, it should be possible to show that while workers acquire some quantity of specific human capital because they know that $\pi < 1$, they also acquire a strictly positive quantity of general human capital. (If no general human capital is acquired then, with probability $1 - \pi$, workers will end up unemployed at home, which would confer an infinite negative utility.) It will be worthwhile to provide conditions under which the level of general human capital that a worker optimally chooses to form in such an environment, $\hat{\hat{\theta}}$, is greater than $\hat{\theta}$, and that welfare, measured by output per worker remaining at home, is also higher.

Concerning the general equilibrium analysis, suppose, for example, that the destination country's production environment is akin to the home country's production environment. If the level of human capital of the incoming skilled migrant is higher than the average level of human capital in the host country, the effect of human capital externalities in that country will bring about a welfare gain for all the workers there.

The model's insight is not contingent on migration policy formation being exclusively in the hands of the government of the home country, H. Suppose, alternatively, that the enactment of migration policy is in the hands of the government of the destination country, D. Consider a world in which D is keenly interested in raising the level of welfare of the workers of H; can exercise complete discretion as to whether to admit none, a few, or many of H's skilled workers; and searches for a migration policy that will raise the welfare of the workers of H the most. The analysis in this paper points to that policy. Moreover, if the welfare gain of the workers of D, referred to in the preceding paragraph, applies, the choice of p^* by the government of D will not be at the expense of its own workers.

Appendix

The purpose of this appendix is to derive the optimal levels of human capital in different settings and compare the measures of welfare that are associated with these levels.

Derivation of θ^*

Let the worker's cost function of forming human capital be $C(\theta) = k\theta$, where $k > 0$ is a constant, and let the worker's production function be $f(\theta) = \alpha \ln(\theta + 1) + \eta \ln(\bar{\theta} + 1)$ for $\theta > 0$, where $\alpha > k$ and $\eta > 0$ are coefficients that measure, respectively, the private returns of human capital and the social returns of human capital. The net earnings per worker function associated with human capital θ is then

$$W(\theta) = \alpha \ln(\theta + 1) + \eta \ln(\bar{\theta} + 1) - k\theta \quad \text{for } \theta > 0.$$

Because

$$\frac{\partial W(\theta)}{\partial \theta} = \frac{\alpha}{\theta + 1} - k \quad \left(\text{and} \quad \frac{\partial^2 W(\theta)}{\partial \theta^2} = -\frac{\alpha}{(\theta + 1)^2} < 0 \right),$$

the worker's chosen level of human capital is $\theta^* = \dfrac{\alpha}{k} - 1$. Thus

$$W(\theta^*) = (\alpha + \eta) \ln \frac{\alpha}{k} - \alpha + k.$$

Derivation of θ^{**}

Taking the externalities from the economy-wide average level of human capital into account, consider the function

$$W(\theta) = \alpha \ln(\theta + 1) + \eta \ln(\theta + 1) - k\theta \quad \text{for } \theta > 0.$$

Because

$$\frac{\partial W(\theta)}{\partial \theta} = \frac{\alpha + \eta}{\theta + 1} - k, \quad \theta^{**} = \frac{\alpha + \eta}{k} - 1.$$

Thus

$$W(\theta^{**}) = (\alpha + \eta) \ln \frac{\alpha + \eta}{k} - (\alpha + \eta) + k.$$

A Comparison of θ^{**} with θ^*, and of $W(\theta^{**})$ with $W(\theta^*)$

Because $\eta > 0$, $\theta^{**} > \theta^*$. Because $W(\theta^{**}) - W(\theta^*) = (\alpha + \eta) \ln \dfrac{\alpha + \eta}{\alpha} - \eta$, and because for any $x > 1$, $x \ln x > x - 1$, it follows that upon substituting $x = \dfrac{\alpha + \eta}{\alpha} > 1$, $W(\theta^{**}) - W(\theta^*) > 0$.

Derivation of $\tilde{\theta}^*$

Let the returns to human capital in D to an H country worker whose level of human capital is θ be $\beta \ln(\theta + 1) + C$, where $\beta > \alpha + \eta$ and $C \geq 0$ are constant and exogenous to the model. The expected net earnings per worker function is

$$\tilde{W}(\theta) = p[\beta \ln(\theta + 1) + C] + (1 - p)[\alpha \ln(\theta + 1) + \eta \ln(\bar{\theta} + 1)] - k\theta.$$

Because

$$\frac{\partial \tilde{W}(\theta)}{\partial \theta} = \frac{p\beta}{\theta + 1} + \frac{(1 - p)\alpha}{\theta + 1} - k$$

$$= \frac{p(\beta - \alpha) + \alpha}{\theta + 1} - k \quad \left(\text{and} \quad \frac{\partial^2 \tilde{W}(\theta)}{\partial \theta^2} = -\frac{p(\beta - \alpha) + \alpha}{(\theta + 1)^2} < 0 \right),$$

the worker's chosen level of human capital is

$$\tilde{\theta}^* = \frac{p(\beta - \alpha) + \alpha}{k} - 1.$$

Because $p > 0$ and $\beta > \alpha$, $\tilde{\theta}^* > \theta^*$.

Thus the level of social welfare, measured by the net earnings of the workers who remain in H, is

$$W(\tilde{\theta}^*) = (\alpha + \eta) \ln \frac{p(\beta - \alpha) + \alpha}{k} - [p(\beta - \alpha) + \alpha] + k.$$

A Comparison of $W(\tilde{\theta}^*)$ with $W(\theta^*)$

Let

$$G(p) \equiv W(\tilde{\theta}^*) - W(\theta^*) = (\alpha + \eta) \ln \frac{p(\beta - \alpha) + \alpha}{\alpha} - p(\beta - \alpha).$$

Claim: $G(p)$ has a unique maximum at $p^* = \dfrac{\eta}{\beta - \alpha} < 1$, and $G(p^*) > 0$.

Proof: Because $G(p)$ is concave, it has a unique maximum. Because

$$\frac{\partial G(p)}{\partial p} = \frac{\alpha + \eta}{p(\beta - \alpha) + \alpha}(\beta - \alpha) - (\beta - \alpha), \quad p^* = \frac{\eta}{\beta - \alpha}.$$

Because $\beta > \alpha + \eta$, $p^* < 1$. Inserting p^* into $G(p)$ entails

$$G(p^*) = (\alpha + \eta) \ln \frac{\eta + \alpha}{\alpha} - \eta.$$

Upon substituting $x = \dfrac{\alpha + \eta}{\alpha} > 1$, it follows that $G(p^*) > 0$. $\square$

Note that $\tilde{\theta}^* \Big|_{p \,=\, p^*} = \dfrac{\eta + \alpha}{k} - 1 = \theta^{**}$.

A Comparison of $W(\tilde{\theta}^*)$ *with* $W(\theta^*)$ *when* $0 < p \le p^*$

Claim: $G(p) > 0$ for any $0 < p \le p^*$.

Proof: Because for any $0 < p \le p^*$, $p(\beta - \alpha) \le \eta$. Thus

$$G(p) \ge [\alpha + p(\beta - \alpha)] \ln \frac{p(\beta - \alpha) + \alpha}{\alpha} - p(\beta - \alpha)$$

$$= \alpha x \ln x - (\alpha x - \alpha) = \alpha [x \ln x - (x - 1)] > 0$$

where

$$x = \frac{p(\beta - \alpha) + \alpha}{\alpha} > 1. \quad \square$$

A Comparison of $\bar{\theta}_m$ *with* $\bar{\theta}$

A sufficient condition for $\bar{\theta}_m > \bar{\theta}$ to hold is that $(1 - p)\tilde{\theta}_2^* > \theta_2^*$, which in turn is true if $(1 - p)(\tilde{\theta}_2^* + 1) > \theta_2^* + 1$. But

$$\frac{(1 - p)(\tilde{\theta}_2^* + 1)}{\theta_2^* + 1} = 1 + \frac{p\,[(1 - p)(\beta - \alpha) - \alpha]}{\alpha} > 1 \quad \text{if} \quad (1 - p)(\beta - \alpha) - \alpha > 0,$$

or if $0 < p < \dfrac{\beta - 2\alpha}{\beta - \alpha}$. To ensure that $0 < \dfrac{\beta - 2\alpha}{\beta - \alpha} < 1$, we assume that $\beta > 2\alpha$.

A Comparison of $W(\tilde{\theta}_2^*)$ *with* $W(\theta_2^*)$

Let the cost of forming human capital for a type-2 worker be $C(\theta) = k_2\theta$, $0 < k_2 < \alpha$. Then

$$\theta_2^* = \frac{\alpha}{k_2} - 1,$$

$$W(\theta_2^*) = \alpha \ln \frac{\alpha}{k_2} + \eta \ln(\bar{\theta} + 1) - \alpha + k_2$$

and

$$\tilde{\theta}_2^* = \frac{p(\beta - \alpha) + \alpha}{k_2} - 1,$$

$$W(\tilde{\theta}_2^*) = \alpha \ln \frac{p(\beta - \alpha) + \alpha}{k_2} + \eta \ln(\bar{\theta}_m + 1) - [p(\beta - \alpha) + \alpha] + k_2.$$

It follows, then, that

$$G_2(p) \equiv W(\tilde{\theta}_2^*) - W(\theta_2^*) = \alpha \ln \frac{p(\beta - \alpha) + \alpha}{\alpha} + \eta \ln \frac{\bar{\theta}_m + 1}{\bar{\theta} + 1} - p(\beta - \alpha).$$

Because

$$\frac{\partial \bar{\theta}_m}{\partial p} = \frac{-N_2 \tilde{\theta}_2^* + (1-p) N_2 (\beta - \alpha)/k_2}{N_1 + (1-p) N_2} + \frac{[N_1 \underline{\theta} + (1-p) N_2 \tilde{\theta}_2^*] N_2}{[N_1 + (1-p) N_2]^2},$$

then

$$\frac{\partial \bar{\theta}_m}{\partial p}\bigg|_{p=0} = \frac{N_2 (\beta - 2\alpha)/k_2 + N_2}{N_1 + N_2} + \frac{(N_1 \underline{\theta} + N_2 \theta_2^*) N_2}{(N_1 + N_2)^2} > 0,$$

where the inequality follows from the assumption that $\beta > 2\alpha$. Drawing on this inequality, we differentiate $G_2(p)$ with respect to p and evaluate the result at $p = 0$ to obtain that

$$\frac{\partial G_2(p)}{\partial p}\bigg|_{p=0} > 0.$$

By continuity, $G_2(p) > 0$ holds for p in a small, positive neighborhood of zero.

Note

1. In the informed press and in public debate, these two counterflows are regularly referred to as the sources of gain that could compensate for the drain. *The Economist's* (May 6, 2000) lead article states: "Yet even poor countries can benefit when émigrés send home the remittances they earn in the rich world." In an interview when he assumed the presidency of Harvard University and published in *Newsweek* (March 26, 2001), Lawrence Summers remarks: "Brain-drain questions are very difficult, but I'm inclined to think that large parts of the answer lie in countries creating economic environments that lead their most able citizens to return home."

References

Bhagwati, Jagdish, and John D. Wilson. 1989. *Income Taxation and International Mobility.* Cambridge, Mass.: MIT Press.

Carrington, William J., and Enrica Detragiache. 1999. "How Extensive Is the Brain Drain?" *Finance and Development* 36: 46–49.

Grubel, Herbert B., and Anthony D. Scott. 1966. "The International Flow of Human Capital." *American Economic Review* 56: 268–74.

Shkolnikov, Vladimir D. 1995. *Potential Energy: Emergent Emigration of Highly Qualified Manpower from the Former Soviet Union.* Santa Monica, Calif.: Rand.

World Bank. 1995. *World Development Report 1995: Workers in an Integrating World.* New York: Oxford University Press.

Appendix

Annual Bank Conference on Development Economics—Europe

Toward Pro-Poor Policies

JUNE 24–26, 2002

Oslo, Norway

Program

Web Site: www.worldbank.org/abcde-europe

THE WORLD BANK

Organized by the World Bank
Hosted by the Norwegian Government

Monday, June 24

9:00 a.m.   Registration of participants

9:45 a.m.   Welcome: Hilde F. JOHNSON, Minister of International Development, Norway

              Chair: Jean-François RISCHARD, Vice President for Europe, World Bank

10.00 a.m.   Opening Speeches: Kjell Magne BONDEVIK, Prime Minister, Norway

                               Nicholas STERN, Senior Vice President and Chief Economist, World Bank

10:45 a.m.   **Keynote Address**

              Keynote speaker: Murasoli MARAN, Minister of Commerce and Industry, India

              Chair: Balmiki Prasad SINGH, Executive Director for India, World Bank

11:20 a.m.   **Poverty, Inequality and Trade Openness**

              Speakers: Juan Luis LONDOÑO, Former Managing Director, Revista Dinero; Former Minister of Health, Colombia

                               Martin RAVALLION, Research Manager, Development Research Group, World Bank

              Chair: Kimmo KILJUNEN, Member of Parliament, Finland

              Discussants: Karl Ove MOENE, University of Oslo, Norway

                               Arvind PANAGARIYA, University of Maryland, USA; Former Chief Economist, Asian Development Bank

12:20 p.m.   **Floor discussion**

12:50 p.m.   **Keynote Address**

              Keynote speaker: Egor GAIDAR, Director, Institute for the Economy in Transition; Former Prime Minister, Russia

              Chair: Norbert MAO, Member of Parliament, Uganda

1:30 p.m.   Lunch

3:00 p.m.–   6 Parallel Workshops: First Series
4:45 p.m.

China's Increasing Openness: Threat or Opportunity to Others?

              Organizer: Ramesh ADHIKARI, Senior Capacity Building Specialist and Principle Economist, Asian Development Bank Institute, Japan

              Chair: Masaru YOSHITOMI, Dean, Asian Development Bank Institute, Japan

              Speakers: Yongzheng YANG, Senior Economist, IMF

                               Ramesh ADHIKARI, Senior Capacity Building Specialist and Principle Economist, Asian Development Bank Institute, Japan

              Discussant: Yiping HUANG, Senior Economist, Citigroup, Hong Kong

Law and Development Economics

              Organizer/Chair: Kaushik BASU, Massachusetts Institute of Technology (MIT); Cornell University, USA

              Speakers: Jaivir SINGH, Delhi University, India

                               Karla HOFF, Senior Research Economist, World Bank

                               Kenneth SOKOLOFF, University of California, Los Angeles, USA

              Discussant: Jean-Philippe PLATTEAU, University of Namur, France

Innovation and Entrepreneurship: Drivers for Sustainable Development

              Organizer/Chair: Jan-Olaf WILLUMS, Chairman, Foundation for Business and Society, Norway

Speaker:	Maria-Emilia CORREA, Vice President, Nueva Group, Costa Rica
Discussants:	Driss ALHOUARI, Founder and Managing Director, Casanet, Morocco
	David WHEELER, Director, Erivan K. Haub Program in Business and Sustainability, York University, Canada
	Ashok KHOSLA, Founder, Development Alternatives, India

Development Economics and Ethics

Organizer/Chair:	Desmond MCNEILL, Center for Development and the Environment (SUM), University of Oslo, Norway
Speakers:	Mozaffar QIZILBASH, University of East Anglia, U.K.
	Ben FINE, School of Oriental and African Studies (SOAS), U.K.
Discussants:	Des GASPER, Institute of Social Studies, the Netherlands
	Asun ST. CLAIR, Center for International Poverty Research, University of Bergen, Norway

Poverty Reduction Strategy Papers: A Pandora's Box?

Organizer:	Jean-Pierre CLING, Director, Developpement et Insertion Internationale (DIAL), France
Chair:	François ROUBAUD, Director of Research, Developpement et Insertion Internationale (DIAL/IRD), France
Speakers:	Stephan KLASEN, University of Munich, Germany
	Mireille RAZAFINDRAKOTO, Developpement et Insertion Internationale (DIAL), France; Madio, Madagascar
Discussant:	Jeni KLUGMAN, Lead Economist, Poverty Reduction Group, World Bank

Determinants of Foreign Direct Investment: Globalization-Induced Changes and the Role of FDI Policies

Organizer/Chair:	Peter NUNNENKAMP, Research Director, Kiel Institute for World Economics, Germany
Speakers:	John H. DUNNING, University of Reading, U.K.
	Ari KOKKO, Stockholm School of Economics, Sweden
Discussant:	Avik CHAKRABARTI, University of Wisconsin, Milwaukee, USA

7:00 p.m.	**Reception**

Tuesday, June 25

9:00 a.m.–1:10 p.m.	**Plenary Sessions**

9:00 a.m.	**Keynote Address**
Keynote speaker:	Jagdish BHAGWATI, Columbia University and Council on Foreign Relations, USA
Chair:	Carole L. BROOKINS, Executive Director for the USA, World Bank

9:35 a.m.	**International Human Capital Flows**
Speaker:	Oded STARK, University of Oslo, Norway; University of Vienna, Austria; University of Bonn, Germany
	Andrés SOLIMANO, Regional Advisor, Economic Development Division, United Nations Economic Commission for Latin America and the Caribbean (ECLAC), Chile
Chair:	Ndioro NDIAYE, Deputy Director General, International Organization for Migration (IOM)

	Discussants:	Alessandra VENTURINI, University of Torino, Italy
		Michel BIART, Deputy Head of Unit, DG Employment and Social Affairs, European Commission
10:35 a.m.	**Floor discussion**	
11:05 a.m.	**Keynote Address**	
	Keynote speaker:	Nicholas STERN, Senior Vice President and Chief Economist, World Bank
	Chair:	Jean-Christophe BAS, Pan-European Dialogue Manager, World Bank
11:40 a.m.	**Weak States and the Role of Institutions**	
	Speakers:	Mushtaq KHAN, School of Oriental and African Studies (SOAS), U.K.
		David DUNHAM, Institute for Social Studies, The Hague, The Netherlands
	Chair:	Robert VON LUCIUS, Correspondent, Frankfurter Allgemeine Zeitung, Germany
	Discussants:	Pranab BARDHAN, University of California at Berkeley, USA
		Paul COLLIER, Director, Development Research Group, World Bank
12:40 p.m.	**Floor Discussion**	
2:45 p.m.	6 Parallel Workshops: Second Series	

Are the Millennium Development Goals Feasible and Affordable?

	Organizer:	Jan VANDEMOORTELE, Principle Advisor and Group Leader on Socio-economic Development, BDP, United Nations Development Program (UNDP)
	Speakers:	Jeffrey SACHS, (pre-taped message) Center for International Development, Harvard University, USA
		Eric SWANSON, Program Manager, DEC Development Data Group, World Bank
	Discussants:	Giovanni Andrea CORINA, Senior Advisor to the Deputy Director of UNICEF, University of Florence, Italy
		Roberto BISSIO, Director, Third World Institute, Uruguay

International Migration as an Instrument of Development in the Middle East and North Africa

	Organizer/Chair:	Philippe FARGUES, European University Institute, Italy; Institut National d'Etudes Démographiques, France
	Speakers:	Heba NASSAR, Cairo University, Egypt
		Ahmed GHONEIM, Cairo University, Egypt
		Serdar SAYAN, Bilkent University, Turkey
	Discussant:	Hervé le BRAS, Ecole des Hautes Études en Science Sociales, France

Contested States, Contested Properties: Towards Appropriate Participatory Policy and Decision-Making in the Context of Conflicting Claims over Natural Resources

	Organizer Chair/Speaker:	Viviane WEITZNER, The North-South Institute (NSI), Canada
	Speaker:	Tony JAMES, Chief of Chiefs, Region 9, Amerindian Peoples Association, Guyana
	Discussants:	Halvor MEHLUM, University of Oslo, Norway
		Bret GUSTAFSON, Harvard University, USA

Gender-Based Discrimination and Its Contribution to Poverty

Organizer/Speaker:	Cecilia VALDIVIESO, Sector Manager, Gender and Development, Poverty Reduction and Economic Management Network, World Bank
Chair:	Unni RAMBØLL, Gender Equality Advisor, Royal Ministry of Foreign Affairs, Norway
Speaker:	Gerd JOHNSSON-LATHAM, Deputy Director, Department for Global Co-operation, Ministry of Foreign Affairs, Sweden
Discussant:	Alf Morten JERVE, Deputy Director, Chr. Michelsen Institute, Norway

Politics and Policy: New Thinking on How to Achieve Education for All

Organizer/Chair:	Robert PROUTY, Lead Education Specialist, World Bank
Speakers:	Birger FREDRIKSEN, Senior Education Advisor, World Bank
	Priscila Ole KAMBAINE, Executive Secretary, Tanzania Teacher Service Commission, Tanzania
Discussants:	Mamadou NDOYE, Executive Secretary, Association for the Development of Education in Africa (ADEA)
	Abhimanyu SINGH, Lead Manager, Dakar Follow-Up Unit, UNESCO

Aid (and Trade) Effectiveness for Poverty Reduction

Organizers:	Agence Française de Développement (AFD) and CERDI, France
Chair:	Jean-Claude FAURE, OECD Development Assistance Committee (DAC)
Speakers:	Ian GOLDIN, Director, Development Policy, Development Economics (DEC), World Bank
	Patrick GUILLAUMONT, President, Centre d'Etudes et de Recherches sur le Développement International (CERDI), France
	Pierre JACQUET, Director of Strategy, Agence Française de Développement (AFD), France
Discussant:	Allechi M'BET, Special Advisor to the Head of State, Côte d'Ivoire; Former Dean of the Faculty des Sciences Economiques, Université d'Abidjan, Côte d'Ivoire

4:45 p.m.– 6:30 p.m. **6 Parallel Workshops: Third Series**

New Public Management: Challenges for Improved Accountability and Corruption Control

Organizer/Chair:	Arve OFSTAD, Research Director, Chr. Michelsen Institute (CMI), Norway
Speaker:	Martin MINOGUE, Institute of Development Policy and Management, University of Manchester, U.K.
Discussants:	Odd-Helge FJELDSTAD, Chr. Michelsen Institute (CMI), Norway
	Mohammed SALISU, Lancaster University Management School, U.K.

How to Achieve Socially Inclusionary Development

Organizer/Chair:	Mick MOORE, Institute of Development Studies, U.K.
Speakers:	Isabel ARAUCO, Advisor to the UN Resident Coordinator for Bolivia
	Rosalind EYBEN, Senior Social Development Advisor, Department for International Development (DfID), Bolivia

| | Patrick NALERE, Acting Executive Director, National Union of Disabled People (NUDIPU), Uganda |
| Discussant: | Mick MOORE, Institute of Development Studies, U.K. |

Bridging Research and Policy

Organizer:	Carol BEST-AARON, Administrative Coordinator, Global Development Network
Chair:	Desmond MCNEILL, Center for Development and the Environment (SUM), University of Oslo, Norway
Speakers:	Cokro LEKSMONO, Bogor Agricultural University, Indonesia
	Lyn SQUIRE, Director, Global Development Network
Discussant:	Ahmed GHONEIM, Cairo University, Egypt

Development and Labor Standards

Organizer:	Liv TORRES, Research Director, Fafo Institute for Applied Social Science, Norway
Organizer/Chair:	Bjørne GRIMSRUD, Fafo Institute for Applied Social Science, Norway
Speaker:	Peter BAKVIS, Director, Washington Office, International Confederation of Free Trade Unions (ICFTU)
Discussants:	John MAWIRI, Zambian Congress of Trade Unions (ZCTU), Zambia
	Eric WATKINSON, NALEDI, South Africa

SME Support as a Means for Economic Development

Organizer/Chair:	Enrique FANJUL, Fundación Jose Ortega y Gasset, Spain
Speaker:	Juan Jose ZABALLA, Director General, Fundacion Empresa y Creciemento; Former Chairman, Cofides, Spain
Discussant:	Edward PFEIFFER, Public Policy and Economics Specialist, World Bank

The Real Opportunities and Constraints to African Development Induced by the New Round of Trade Negotiations

Organizer:	African Economic Research Consortium (AERC), Kenya
Chair:	Paul COLLIER, Director, Development Research Group, World Bank
Speakers:	Olawale OGUNKOLA, National University of Lesotho, Lesotho
	Dominique NJINKEU, African Economic Research Consortium (AERC), Kenya
	Herzon NYANGITO, Kenya Institute for Public Policy Research and Analysis (KIPPRA), Kenya
Discussant:	Zhen Kun WANG, Sussex European Institute, U.K.

| 6:30 p.m. | Closing of the workshops |
| 8:30 p.m. | Reception |

Wednesday, June 26

9:00 a.m.– 1:30 p.m.	**Plenary Sessions**	
9:00 a.m.	**Political Economy of Crisis and Reform**	
	Speakers:	Mariano TOMMASI, Director, Center of Studies for Institutional Development (CEDI), Fundación Gobierno y Sociedad, Argentina
		Jomo K.S., University of Malaya, Malaysia
	Chair:	Boris PLESKOVIC, Administrator, Research Advisory Staff, World Bank
	Discussants:	Jorge BRAGA DE MACEDO, President, OECD Development Center
		Guillermo PERRY, Chief Economist, Latin America and the Caribbean region, World Bank
10:00 a.m.	Floor discussion	
10:30 a.m.	**KEYNOTE ADDRESS**	
	Keynote speaker:	Oded GRAJEW, President, Ethos Institute, Brazil
	Chair:	David de FERRANTI, Vice President for Latin America and the Caribbean, World Bank
11:05 a.m.	**Reshaping Development Aid in Order to Reach the Millennium Development Goals**	
	Speakers:	Finn TARP, University of Copenhagen, Denmark
		Jean-Michel SEVERINO, Director General, Agence Française de Développement, France
	Chair:	Mats KARLSSON, Vice President for External Affairs, World Bank
	Discussants:	David HULME, Institute of Development Policy and Management, University of Manchester, U.K.
		Charity NGILU, Member of Parliament, Kenya National Assembly, Kenya
		Kwesi BOTCHWEY, Center for International Development, Harvard University, USA; Former Minister of Finance, Ghana
12:05 p.m.	Floor discussion	
12:35 p.m.	**Concluding Keynote Address**	
1:10 p.m.	Closing Session:	Jean-François RISCHARD, Vice President for Europe, World Bank
	Chair:	Hilde F. JOHNSON, Minister of International Development, Norway
1:50 p.m.	End of the Conference	